Photographer's Guide to the Nikon Coolpix P600

Photographer's Guide to the Nikon Coolpix P600

Getting the Most from Nikon's Superzoom Digital Camera

Alexander S. White

WHITE KNIGHT PRESS
HENRICO, VIRGINIA

Published by
White Knight Press
9704 Old Club Trace
Henrico, Virginia 23238
www.whiteknightpress.com
contact@whiteknightpress.com

ISBN: 978-1-937986-25-4 (paperback)
       978-1-937986-24-7 (e-book)

Printed in the United States of America

To my wife, Clenise.

Contents

CHAPTER 3: THE SHOOTING MODES   49

Chapter 4: The Shooting Menu   119

Chapter 5: Physical Controls   192

CHAPTER 7: THE SETUP MENU　266

CHAPTER 8: MOTION PICTURES　302

Chapter 9: Wi-Fi, Superzoom Lens, and Other Topics 333

APPENDIX A: Accessories 375

APPENDIX B: Quick Tips   388

APPENDIX C: Resources for Further Information   393

Introduction

In 2013, I published *Photographer's Guide to the Nikon Coolpix P520*, a guide to the features and operation of an earlier Coolpix "superzoom" camera. I was looking forward to doing a new book when Nikon released an upgraded version of the P520, but I was not expecting a camera like the P600, with its amazing telephoto range. The P520 certainly is a superzoom camera with its maximum optical focal length of 1000mm, but the P600 has a lens with an optical zoom range extending to an astounding 1440mm, an increase of 44%. I was eager to explore the use of this new camera's lens along with other updated and added features, particularly the camera's ability to use a Wi-Fi network for image transfer and remote control. I was not disappointed, and I was glad to be able to produce this new book.

Besides its superiority in zoom length, the P600 has a good range of sophisticated options. The camera produces excellent image quality with its 16-megapixel digital sensor and offers complete manual control of focus and exposure. It provides several modes of rapid continuous shooting and provides exposure bracketing, excellent low-light performance, and numerous special features, including a variety of ways to manipulate colors, a built-in HDR (high dynamic range) shooting mode, high-speed video shooting, and time-lapse photography. It has special settings for typical superzoom subjects such as birds and the moon. As noted above, the P600 can connect to a smartphone via a Wi-Fi connection for uploading photos and operating the camera via remote control.

Also, as is expected of a modern camera in this class, the P600 provides HD (high-definition) video shooting. In addition, it has an electronic viewfinder, which provides a clear view of your image even in bright sunlight, when the LCD screen could be washed out by the glare. The LCD display has very high resolution, with 921,000 dots, providing fine detail when viewing your images. Moreover, the screen swivels to positions that allow you to take low-level shots near ground level and to hold the camera over your head to overcome crowds of people or other obstacles.

The P600 is not the perfect camera, of course; no camera can serve as the ideal tool for all situations. One drawback is that the camera lacks an accessory shoe, which could be used to attach items such as an external flash unit. (There are other ways to use external flash units with the P600, as discussed in Appendix A.) In addition, the camera does not offer the useful Raw format for its images, though it provides a wide array of high-quality JPEG settings. Also, the camera has a limited range of aperture settings available: from f/3.3 to f/7.6 at the widest focal length, and only from f/6.5 to f/8.2 when the lens is zoomed in fully. This narrow range can limit your ability to make certain kinds of shots, such as those requiring slow shutter speeds, although you can compensate to some extent by using other techniques for such shots.

This discussion of the camera's features is not complete, but it serves to illustrate that the Coolpix P600 has capabilities that should be attractive to serious amateur photographers—those who want a camera that has many options for creative control of images without needing to change lenses, and that is compact enough to be carried around at all times, so it will be available when a good picture-taking opportunity arises.

My goal with this guide is to provide a thorough introduction to the camera's features, explaining how they work and when you might want to use them. The book is intended largely for beginning and intermediate photographers who are not satisfied with the documentation provided with the camera and who need a more user-friendly explanation of its many controls and menus. For those seeking more advanced information, I discuss some topics that go beyond the basics, and I include information in the appendices to help you uncover additional resources. This book is not a replacement for the official Nikon Coolpix P600 Reference Manual, which contains a great deal of useful information; my book should be viewed as a supplementary resource to illustrate and explain the use of the camera's features.

One note on the scope of this guide: I live in the United States, and I bought my camera in the U.S. market. I am not familiar with any variations for cameras sold in Europe, the United Kingdom, or elsewhere, such as different batteries or chargers and different video standards (NTSC in the United States and PAL in Europe). The photographic functions are not different, though, so this guide should be useful to photographers in all locations, apart from that narrow range of issues. I have stated measurements in both the Imperial and metric systems for the benefit of readers in various countries around the world.

All photographs in this book that illustrate the capabilities of the Coolpix P600 are ones that I took with that camera. The photographs of the P600 and accessories used with it are ones that I took using a Sony Alpha SLT-A99 camera with a Sony f/2.8 50mm macro lens and a Sony f/2.8 24-70mm SSM lens.

If you find any problems in this book, including typographical errors or information that appears to be confusing or incorrect, please let me know through the contact form at whiteknightpress. com or by e-mail to contact@whiteknightpress.com. Also, if the images do not look good on a particular device, such as an iPad or Kindle, let me know that as well so I can take steps to remedy the situation. Feedback from readers is the best source of information for improving books such as this one. If you have general comments or feedback to provide, you also may want to post a review of the book at Amazon.com or another site that sells the book.

CHAPTER 1: PRELIMINARY SETUP

Setting Up the Camera

If you purchase your Nikon Coolpix P600 new, the box should contain the camera itself, Nikon EN-EL23 lithium-ion battery, battery terminal cover, battery charging adapter, neck strap, USB cable, lens cap with cord for attaching it to the camera, and the brief "Quick Start Guide" instruction pamphlet. There also should be a warranty card and one or two other items, such as an advertising sheet or safety notice. Nikon does not include an audio-video cable for connecting the camera to a TV set, and it does not include the full instruction manual or software on a disc. The full Nikon reference manual is available for download as a PDF document from the following website: http://nikonimglib. com/manual/. The Nikon software for viewing and editing images, ViewNX 2, is available at http://nikonimglib.com/nvnx/.

It is a good idea to attach the neck strap to the camera right away, and in the same procedure to attach the lens cap to its cord. In this process, you loop the other end of the lens cap cord over the neck strap before it is attached to the camera.

When you're finished, the lens cap should be tethered by its cord to the strap. The lens cap cord should be attached to the neck strap where it joins the camera, on the left side as you hold the camera in position for shooting, as shown in Figure 1-1.

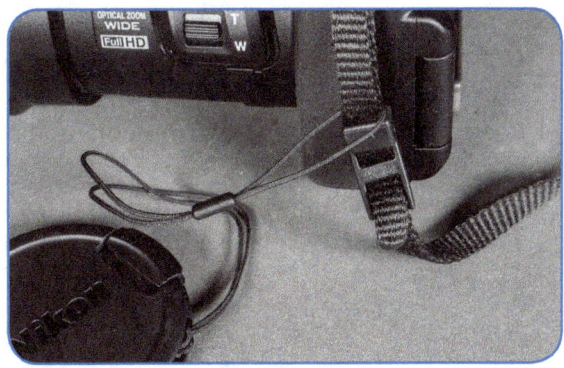

Figure 1-1. Lens Cap Attached to Neck Strap

CHARGING AND INSERTING THE BATTERY

The Nikon battery for the Coolpix P600 is the EN-EL23. With this camera, the standard procedure is to charge the battery while it's inside the camera. To do this, you use the supplied USB cable to connect the camera to an AC outlet using the supplied charger, or to a USB port on a computer or other device. There are pluses and minuses to this approach to battery-charging. On the positive side, the battery can charge automatically when the camera is connected to your computer to upload images, and you need only one cable for both charging the battery and connecting the camera to the computer. Also, you don't have to remove the battery from the camera to recharge it. You can refresh its charge by just plugging the camera into a power source.

The main drawbacks are that you cannot use the camera while the battery is charging, and you cannot charge another battery outside the camera. Therefore, once the battery dies, you cannot readily replace the battery; you have to stop and recharge the battery. The solution to this situation is to purchase extra batteries and a device that will charge those batteries outside the camera. I'll discuss batteries and other accessories in Appendix A.

For now, get the battery charged by inserting it into the camera and connecting the charger. You first need to open the battery compartment door on the bottom of the camera and put in the battery. You can only insert it fully into the camera one way; I prefer to do this is by looking for the set of three gold-colored contacts at one edge of the battery, and inserting the battery so those contacts are next to the outside edge of the camera, just under the trash-can icon on the camera's back, as it goes into the compartment. Figure 1-2 shows the battery lined up properly to go into the camera.

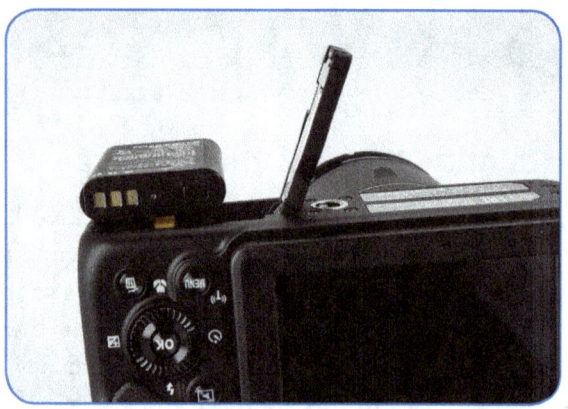

Figure 1-2. Battery Lined Up to Go Into Camera

If the battery will not go all the way down into the compartment, don't force it; check its orientation and make sure it is being inserted the correct way.

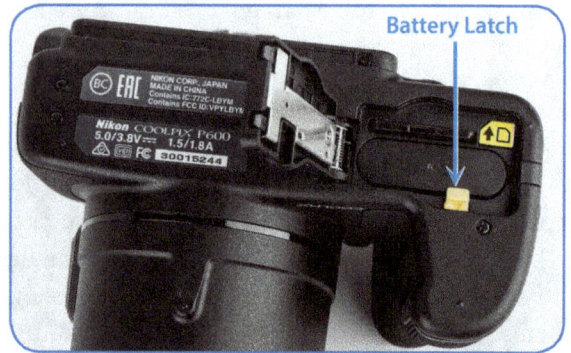

Figure 1-3. Battery Secured by Latch

You may have to push the orange plastic retaining latch to one side to allow the battery to slip all the way into its slot; the latch will then anchor the battery in place, as shown in Figure 1-3.

With the battery inserted into the camera, plug the small end of the USB cable into the USB port under the door marked HDMI and with a USB symbol on the right side of the camera, as shown in Figure 1-4, and plug the other end of the USB cable into the AC adapter that ships with the camera.

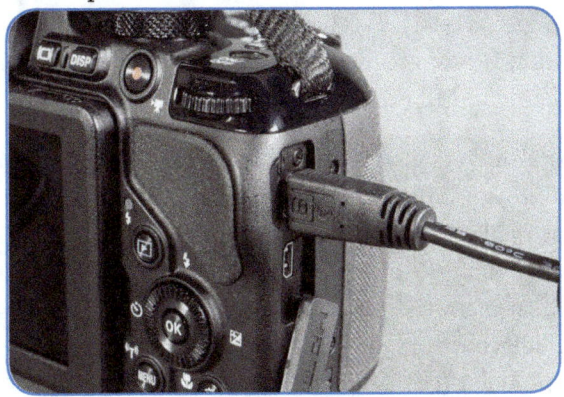

Figure 1-4. USB Cable Plugged into Camera

Then plug that AC adapter into a standard electrical outlet or surge protector. A green light on the back of the camera, next to the lightning bolt icon, will blink about twice per second to indicate that the battery is charging. When the light goes off, the battery is fully charged and ready to use. It takes about three hours to charge a fully depleted battery using this system. (This length of time is another factor that makes it a good idea to obtain other batteries and an external charger, as discussed in Appendix A.)

You also can charge the battery in the camera by connecting the USB cable to a compatible USB port on a computer, if the Charge by Computer option is turned on through the camera's menu system. I'll discuss that process in Chapter 7.

INSERTING THE MEMORY CARD

The Coolpix P600, like most cameras these days, does not ship with a memory card included. With this camera, unlike some others, this is not a fatal omission, because the P600 has a built-in memory capacity that will let you take and save a few pictures even with no memory card inserted. The amount of built-in memory is only about 56 megabytes (MB), which is minuscule compared to the capacity of modern storage cards that can hold up to 256 gigabytes (GB), about 4,600 times more. But if you're in a situation where you need to take a picture and don't have an available card, 56 MB is better than nothing.

The internal memory can hold only 7 still photos at the largest size of 4608 x 3456 pixels with Fine quality, or 515 photos at the lowest quality and the lowest size of 640 x 480 pixels, with proportional figures for intermediate levels of image size and quality. This memory can hold only about 8 seconds of the highest-quality movie footage, or about one minute 36 seconds of the lowest-quality footage.

If you have no card inserted in the camera, the letters IN will display in the lower right corner of the display, indicating that internal memory is being used, next to the number of remaining images, as shown in Figure 1-5.

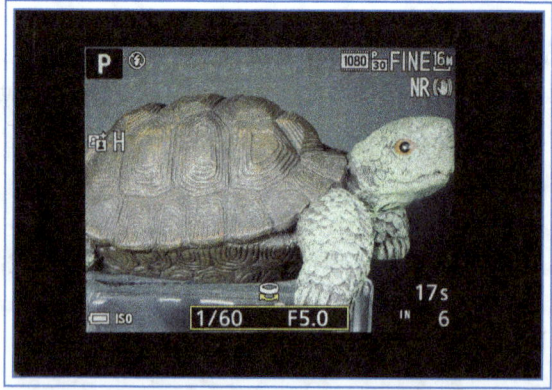

Figure 1-5. Shooting Screen when Internal Memory in Use

If a card is inserted, the letters IN are not displayed; only the number of remaining images is shown inside the brackets, as shown in Figure 1-6.

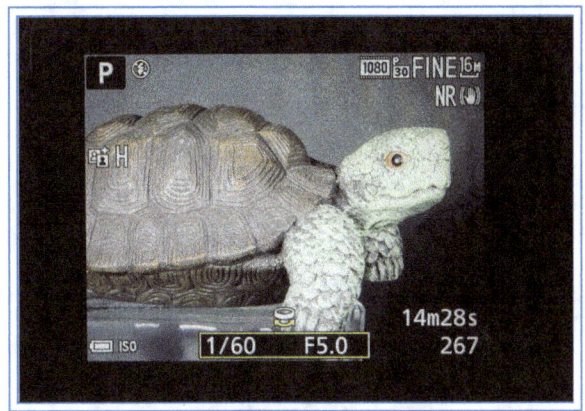

Figure 1-6. Display When SD Card in Use - No. of Images Remaining

If you fill up the internal memory, you will see the message Out of Memory on the camera's display, and your shooting will stop unless you delete some images from the internal memory or insert an SD card that has some free space on it.

Because of its limited capacity, you shouldn't rely on the built-in memory if you don't have to, so you need to insert a separate memory card. The P600 uses SD cards, which are quite small, about the size of a large postage stamp. They come in several varieties, a few of which are shown in Figure 1-7.

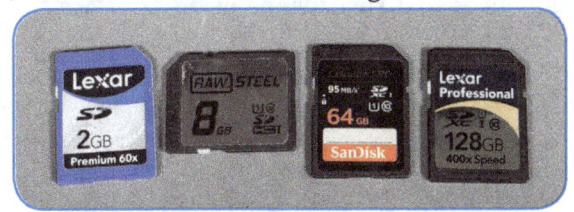

Figure 1-7. Left to Right: SD 2GB, SDHC 8GB, SDXC 64GB, SDXC 128GB

The standard card, called simply SD, comes in capacities from 8 MB to 2 GB. The next higher-capacity card, SDHC, comes in sizes from 4 GB to 32 GB. The newest, and highest-capacity card, SDXC (for extended capacity), comes in sizes of 48 GB, 64 GB, 128 GB and up to 256 GB at this writing; this version of the card can have a capacity up to 2 terabytes (TB), theoretically, and SDXC cards have faster transfer speeds than the smaller-capacity cards. Note that the P600 cannot use another type of memory card called a MultiMediaCard (MMC), even though those cards are the same size as SD cards.

The P600 also can use micro-SD cards, which are smaller cards, often used in smartphones and other small devices. These cards operate in the same way as SD cards, but you have to use an adapter that is the size of an SD card, as shown in FIGURE 1-8, to insert this tiny card into the Coolpix P600 camera.

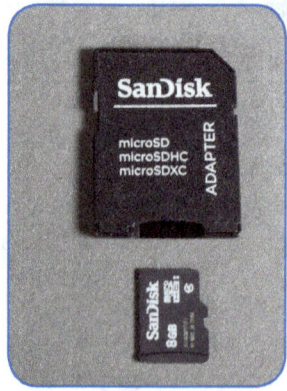

Figure 1-8. Micro SD Card with Adapter

You might want to use one of these cards so you can transfer images and videos to a smartphone or other device that accepts that size of card.

The type and size of memory card you use depends on your needs and intentions. If you're planning to record a good deal of high-definition (HD) video or large numbers of high-resolution still photos, you should get the biggest card you can afford. There are several variables to take into account in computing how many images or videos you can store on a particular size of card, such as which aspect ratio you're using (16:9, 4:3, 3:2, or 1:1), picture size, and quality. Here are a few examples of how many images (approximately) can be stored on an 8 GB SDHC card: At the largest size of 4608 x 3456 pixels and with Fine quality, an 8 GB card can hold about 950 still photos; at the next-lower size of 3264 x 2448 pixels and with Normal quality, the same card can hold about 3,300 images. At one of the smallest image sizes, 1600 x 1200 pixels, with Fine quality, the card can hold about 7,400 images. (The number of images that can be stored also varies with factors such as aspect ratio and subject matter of the image, so the numbers stated here are not exact.)

Another consideration is the speed of the card. If you plan to record high-quality video or do a lot of continuous (burst) shooting, you should get a card that is rated as Class 6 or higher for its speed.

If you have an old computer with a built-in card reader, or an old external card reader, there is some chance it will not read the newer SDHC cards. In that case, you would have to get a new reader that will accept SDHC cards or download images from the camera to your computer using the USB cable. Using the newest variety of card, SDXC, also can be problematic with older computers.

If your computer has a recent version of its operating system, it will be able to read SDXC cards if you use a compatible card reader.

As I write this, 64 GB SDXC cards cost about $30 and up. If you don't mind the risk of losing a great many images or videos if you lose the card, you might want to choose an SDXC card with a capacity of 64 GB, or even 128 GB. At this writing, 256 GB SDXC cards are selling for about $475. Those cards are extremely fast, but I question whether it is a good idea to risk $475 on your ability to keep track of a tiny item that can slip into a pocket and end up in the laundry without too much trouble.

Finally, if you will have access to a wireless (Wi-Fi) network where you use your camera, you may want to consider getting an Eye-Fi card. This special type of storage device, shown in Figure 1-9, looks very much like an ordinary SDHC card, but it includes a tiny transmitter that lets it connect to a wireless network and send your images to your computer over that network as soon as the images have been recorded by the camera.

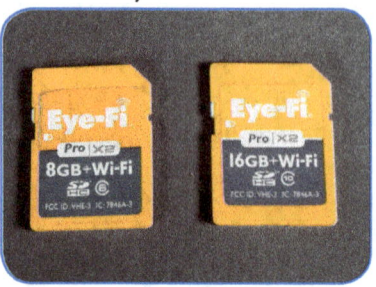

Figure 1-9. Eye-Fi Cards

I have tested the 8 GB and 16 GB Eye-Fi cards, the Pro X2 models shown here, with the P600, and they both worked well for me after some time spent configuring the cards with my wireless network. Within a few seconds after I snap a picture with either of these cards installed in the camera, a little thumbnail image appears in the upper right corner of my computer's screen showing the progress of the upload. When all images are uploaded, they are available in the Pictures/Eye-Fi folder on my computer. Also, I have installed a free Eye-Fi app for my iPad, which automatically uploads the P600's images to the iPad as they are taken with an Eye-Fi card in the camera. (You can also use this feature with the iPhone and with Android phones and tablets.)

The Pro X2 Eye-Fi cards handle Raw files as well as smaller JPEG and video files. At this writing, the Pro X2 is the only variety of Eye-Fi card that can handle Raw files. Of course, this capability does not matter with the P600, which does not use the Raw format, but you may want to use your Eye-Fi card with other cameras that do shoot in Raw, and the Pro X2 card will serve you well in both cases. An Eye-Fi card is not a necessity, but it is nice to have your images go straight to your computer or other device without having to use a card reader or a USB cable. Just be prepared for a certain amount of work to get the card configured to work properly with your camera, computer, network, and mobile device, if you use the option to send images directly to that type of device.

There also are other options available for wireless transfer of images from the camera to other devices. The Transcend SD card with Wi-Fi is advertised as having capabilities similar to those of the Eye-Fi card, and there is another option called the FlashAir Wireless SD Card from Toshiba. I have not tested either of those cards, though they sound promising.

Of course, the Coolpix P600 has built-in Wi-Fi capability that lets it transfer images to a smartphone or tablet over a wireless network and provides limited remote control functions. You therefore do not have to purchase an Eye-Fi card or the equivalent to transfer images over a network. But the camera's built-in Wi-Fi capability is limited; it cannot transfer videos and it cannot connect to a traditional computer (unless you can run an Android or iOS app on your computer using a simulation program). So, if you need those functions, or if you already have a Wi-Fi memory card or want to use one with other cameras as well as with the P600, it's good to know that the card also will work in the P600.

In summary, you have quite a few options for choosing a memory card. Personally, I like to use a high-speed 16 GB or 32 GB SDHC card, just to have extra capacity and speed in case they are needed.

Once you have selected your memory card, open the same door on the bottom of the camera that covers the battery compartment, and slide the card into the card slot until it catches, with the label facing the back of the camera. Once the card has been pushed down until it catches, close the compartment door and push the latch back to the locking position. To remove the card, push down on it until it releases and springs up so you can grab it. Figure 1-10 shows a card being inserted into the P600.

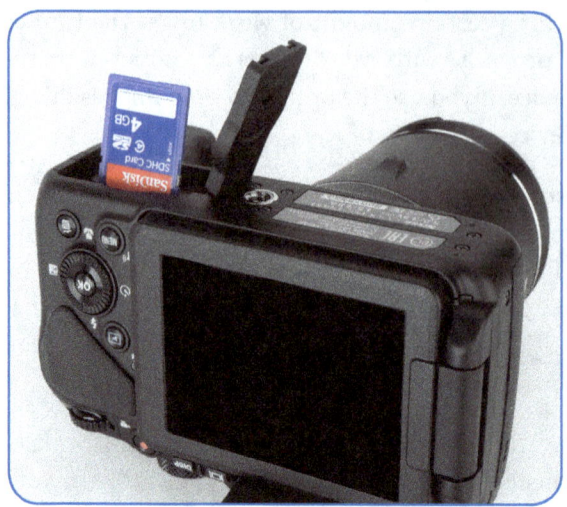

Figure 1-10. SD Card Going into Camera

One note for shooting continuous pictures with the P600: When the camera is writing its image data to the memory card, the indicator showing the number of remaining images, in the lower right of the display, blinks. When that indicator is blinking, it's important not to turn off the camera or otherwise interrupt its functioning, such as by taking out the battery or disconnecting an AC power adapter. You need to let the card complete its recording process before taking further steps.

Introduction to Main Controls

Before I discuss options for setting up the camera to take images and videos, I will introduce the main controls so you'll have a better idea of which button or dial is which as I discuss them later in this and other chapters. I will briefly mention the functions of the controls here; I will cover them in more detail in Chapter 5. The following series of images shows the major controls. As I discuss each item, I will describe its position and function; you may want to refer to these images for a reminder about each control.

TOP OF CAMERA

On top of the camera are several important controls and dials, shown in Figure 1-11.

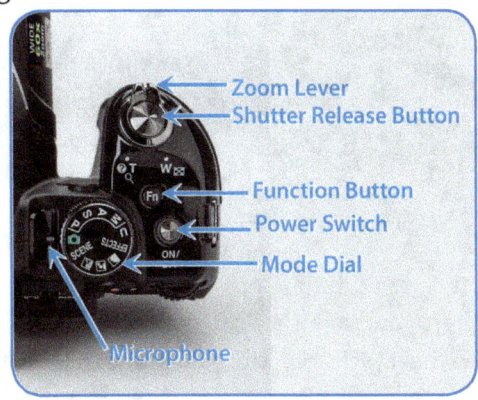

Figure 1-11. Controls on Top of Camera

The mode dial is used to select the shooting mode for still images. For basic shooting with the camera making most of the decisions, turn this dial so the green camera icon is next to the white selection marker. The shutter button is used to take pictures; press it halfway down to lock focus and exposure, and press it all the way down to record the image. The zoom lever that surrounds the shutter release button is used to zoom the lens between its wide-angle and telephoto focal lengths. The Function button is a versatile control that provides quick access to a single menu option of your choice. The power button is used to turn the camera on and off. The microphone picks up sounds when you are recording movies or voice memos.

BACK OF CAMERA

The controls on the camera's back are seen in Figure 1-12.

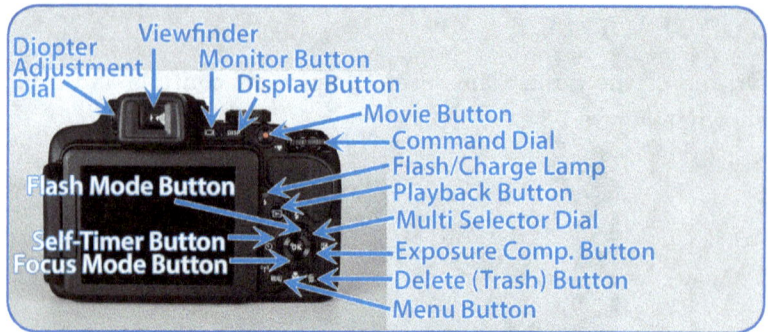

Figure 1-12. Controls on Back of Camera

The viewfinder is the window you can look through to compose your shots when you have the LCD screen folded in against the camera or you have selected the viewfinder using the Monitor button. The diopter adjustment dial directly to the left of the viewfinder is used to adjust the view according to your vision. The Monitor button switches between using the LCD screen and the viewfinder. The Display button selects screens for viewing information about shooting settings when images are being recorded and about the images themselves when they are being played back. The red Movie button starts and stops the recording of a video sequence. The Delete button (also called the Trash button) is used to delete recorded images.

The command dial lets you select various settings such as shutter speed, and helps you navigate through menu options. The Playback button places the camera into playback mode so you can view your recorded images. The Menu button calls up the camera's system of menu screens with various settings for shooting and other values, such as control button functions, audio features, and others. The multi selector dial acts as a wheel for setting values such as aperture and for navigating through menu screens. In addition, each of its four edges acts as a button when you press it in, for selecting items including flash mode, exposure compensation, focus mode, and the self-timer. (Those buttons are called the Up, Down, Left, and Right buttons in this book.) The OK button in the center of the dial is used to confirm selections and for some miscellaneous operations. The charge/flash lamp illuminates to indicate that the camera's battery is charging or that the camera's built-in flash unit is charged and will fire when the shutter button is pressed.

FRONT AND SIDES OF CAMERA

On the front and sides of the camera, there are several controls and other items, as shown in Figures 1-13 through 1-15.

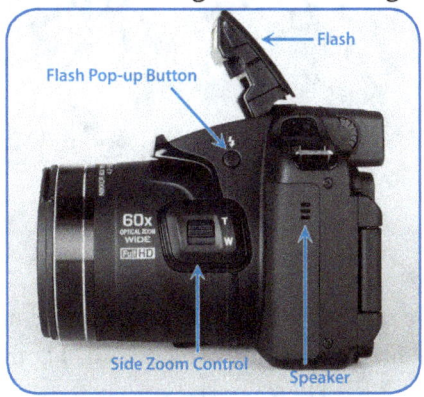

Figure 1-13. Items on Left Side of Camera

The round flash pop-up button, located on the upper part of the left side of the P600, is used to release the camera's built-in flash unit so it can fire if it is needed, as seen in Figure 1-13. The unit pops up at an angle, as shown in these images. The second microphone opening is at the left edge of the camera's top, and the single speaker, which emits audio for movies, voice memos, and operational sounds, is on the left side of the P600. The side zoom control is used to zoom the lens, or you can assign a different function to it using the Setup menu.

The AF Assist/self-timer lamp, shown in Figure 1-14, helps the camera use its autofocus technology in dimly lighted areas, and it also lights up to indicate the functioning of the self-timer. The lens is a variable focal length, or zoom lens, with an optical zoom range from 24mm to 1440mm. It has aperture settings ranging from f/3.3 to f/8.2, as discussed in Chapter 3.

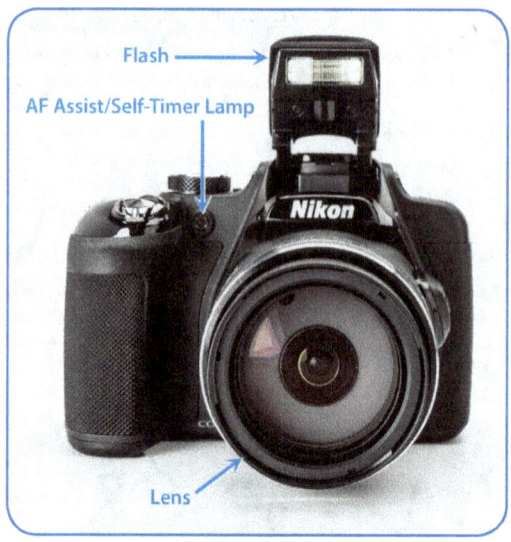

Figure 1-14. Items on Front of Camera

The ports on the right side of the camera, located under a flap that can be rotated out of the way, as shown in Figure 1-15, are the USB port, top, and the HDMI port, bottom.

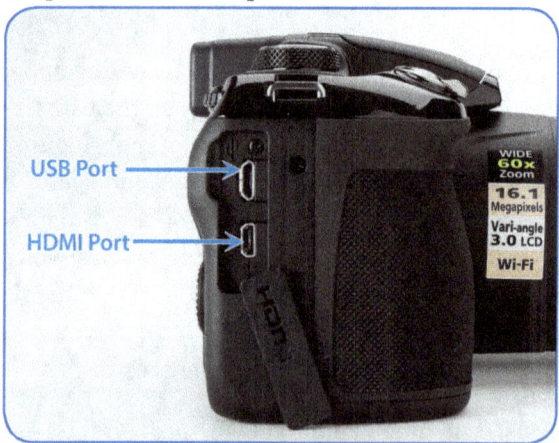

Figure 1-15. Ports on Right Side of Camera

The USB port is for connecting the camera to a computer, charger, or printer, using the cable provided with the camera. The HDMI port is for connecting the camera to an HDTV set for playback of images and videos using an optional HDMI cable. There is no audio-video port for a cable to connect the camera to a standard (non-HD) TV set.

BOTTOM OF CAMERA

Finally, as shown in Figure 1-16, there are two main items on the bottom of the camera: the tripod socket, where the camera can be attached to a tripod with a standard screw, and the latching door that covers the compartment where the memory card and battery are located.

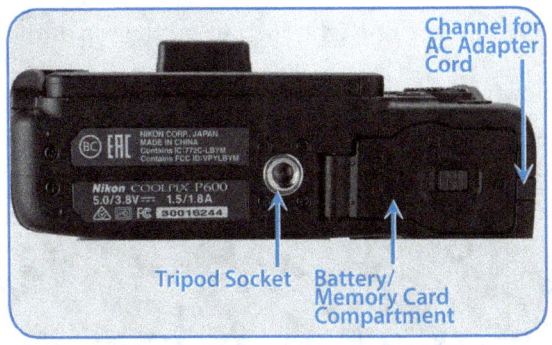

Figure 1-16. Items on Bottom of Camera

When the camera is placed on a tripod, you cannot open this door to get access to the battery or memory card. At the outer edge of the door is a flap that must be opened up when you install the optional AC adapter in the camera, so the door can close with the cord running through the channel occupied by the flap. I discuss the AC adapter in Appendix A.

Setting the Language, Date, and Time

You need to set the date and time correctly before you start taking pictures, because the camera records that information (sometimes known as "metadata," meaning data beyond the information in the picture itself) invisibly with each image, and displays it later if you want. Someday you may be very glad to have the date (and even the time of day) correctly recorded with your archives of digital images. If you purchase the camera new, it will prompt you to set the date and time when you first power it on.

If you later need to set the time and date, here is how to do so. Press down on the camera's power switch, marked On/Off, on top of the camera, to turn the camera on. Then press the Menu button to the lower left of the OK button on the camera's back. Next, press the Left button, which is marked with a timer icon. When you press the Left button, the yellow selection block will move to the far left of the screen, to the list of icons, with an icon or letter representing the current shooting mode, such as P for Program or an icon for Landscape or Night Portrait, at the top of the list.

Use the Down button, marked with a flower icon, to move the selection block down to highlight the wrench icon that represents the Setup menu, as shown in Figure 1-17.

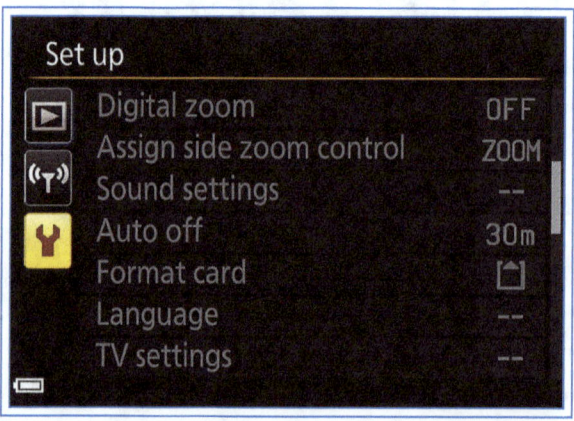

Figure 1-17. Wrench Icon for Setup Menu Highlighted

Press the Right button, marked with a plus and minus sign, to move the highlight back to the right, where it will become a yellow rectangle highlighting a menu item. Then use the Up and Down buttons to move the yellow selection bar to the Time Zone and Date line on the menu, as shown in Figure 1-18, and press the OK button to move to a screen with choices of Date and Time, Date Format, and Time Zone. Highlight Date and Time, and press the

OK button to move to the screen with a selection of settings, shown in Figure 1-19.

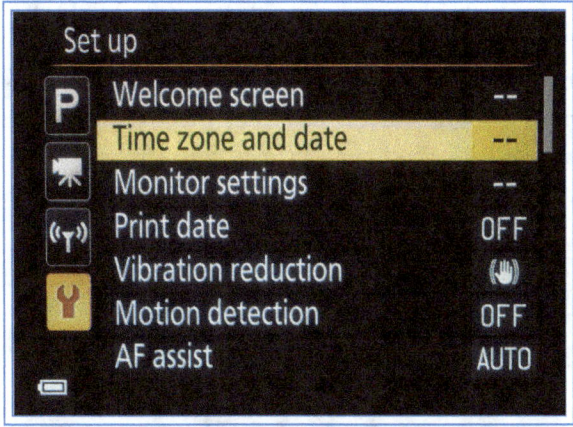

Figure 1-18. Time Zone and Date Menu Item

(You can press the Right button instead of the OK button to move to these menu screens, if you prefer.)

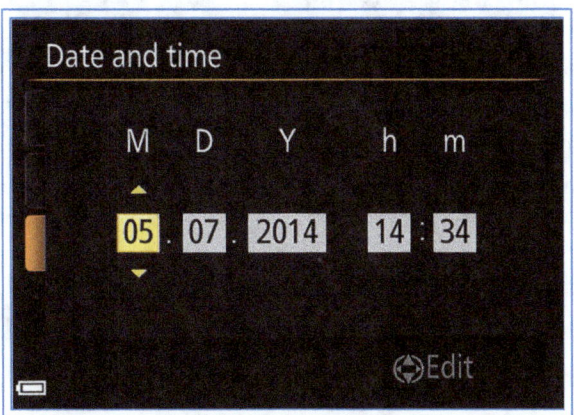

Figure 1-19. Date and Time Settings Screen

On that screen, use the Left and Right buttons to move through the date, year, and time settings, and change the settings by pressing the Up and Down buttons. (You also can turn the multi selector dial or the command dial to change the settings.) When everything is set correctly, press the OK button to confirm and press the Menu button to exit the menu system.

If you need to change the language that the camera uses for the menus and other messages, navigate on the Setup menu to the line on the second screen that says Language, and press the OK button or the Right button to select the Language menu item. Then navigate with the Up and Down buttons to the language of your choice, as shown in Figure 1-20, and press the OK button to select it.

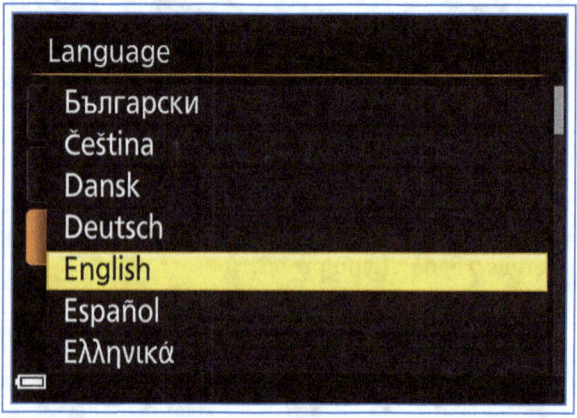

Figure 1-20. Language Selection Screen

Then press the Menu button to exit from the menu system.

Chapter 2: Basic Operations

Taking Still Pictures

N ow that the Coolpix P600 has the correct time and date set and has a fully charged battery inserted along with a memory card, I will discuss settings for basic picture-taking. For now, I won't discuss all of the available options and why you might choose one over another. I'll just outline a set of steps that will get the camera into action and will record a decent image on your memory card.

Fully Automatic—Auto Mode

Here's a procedure to use if you want to let the camera make (almost) all of the decisions for you. This is a good system to use if you need to grab a quick shot without fiddling with settings, or if you're new at this and would rather let the camera take control without having to provide much input.

1. Remove the lens cap from the lens and let it dangle by its cord. (If you forget to remove the cap before turning on the camera, that's okay; Nikon has engineered the P600 to have the lens cap attached to the moving part of the lens, so the cap will not block the motion of the lens in extending out from the camera. But you will notice that the camera's display is black, because the lens cap will be blocking the view.)

2. Press the On/Off button. The LCD screen will illuminate to show that the camera has turned on. (If the LCD screen is folded in the closed position, the viewfinder will operate instead of the screen, as discussed in Step 5, below.)

3. Find the mode dial on top of the camera and turn the dial until the green camera icon is next to the white indicator line. This selects Auto shooting mode, as shown in Figure 2-1.

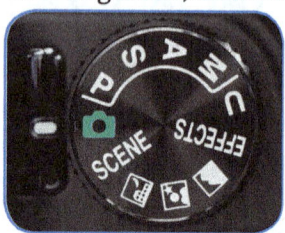

Figure 2-1. Auto Mode

4. Press the Menu button at the bottom left of the control area on the back of the camera. Use the direction buttons (four edges of the ridged multi selector dial) to navigate to the entry for Image Quality, select that line with the OK button or the Right button, highlight the Fine setting, and press OK. Then navigate down to the Image Size setting, select it, and choose 4608 x 3456 pixels, the top option, as shown in Figure 2-2. Press the Menu button to return to shooting mode.

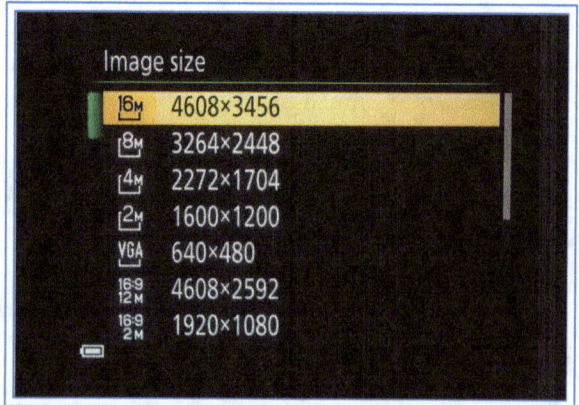

Figure 2-2. Maximum Image Size Selected

(You can choose other settings for either or both of these options if you wish, but the ones I mentioned provide the highest quality.)

5. If you want to compose your image on the LCD screen on the back of the camera, no action is needed if the LCD screen has its active surface exposed. If you want to use the electronic viewfinder instead, pull the LCD screen away from the camera, rotate it on its hinge, and then fold it back against the camera in the closed position. This action will activate the viewfinder. You can then look into the viewfinder to compose the shot and view the camera's settings. You can adjust the view for your eyesight by turning the diopter adjustment dial on the left side of the viewfinder's housing. Toggle between the LCD and the viewfinder whenever you want, by opening or closing the LCD screen. You also can toggle the viewfinder by pressing the Monitor button, directly to the left of the Display button.

6. If you are indoors or otherwise in conditions that might call for the use of flash, press the button on the left side of the camera's built-in flash unit, marked with a lightning bolt, to pop up the flash.

7. If you have popped up the flash, press the Up button on the multi selector, marked with another lightning bolt, to bring up the flash mode menu. Make sure the Auto setting, at the top of this menu, is highlighted. (Later in this chapter and in Chapter 9, I'll discuss the other flash options.)

8. Aim the camera toward the subject and look at the LCD screen (or into the viewfinder window, depending on your choice in Step 5) to compose the scene as you want it. Locate the zoom lever on the ring that surrounds the shutter button on the top right at the front of the camera. Push that lever to the left, moving its indicator toward the letter W, to get a wider-angle shot (including more of the scene in the picture), or to the right, moving the indicator toward the letter T, to get a telephoto, zoomed-in shot. Or, if you prefer, use the

equivalent zoom switch on the left side of the lens, moving it up for telephoto or down for wide-angle.

9. Once the picture is composed as you want it, press the shutter release button halfway down. You should hear a beep and see one or more green rectangles on the display, indicating that the picture will be in focus. If you see a flashing red rectangle, that means the camera is having difficulty achieving focus. In that case, try moving the camera to a different angle before pressing the shutter button halfway again.

10. Press the shutter button all the way down to take the picture.

BASIC VARIATIONS FROM FULLY AUTOMATIC

I won't discuss all of the shooting modes now, except to name them. Besides Auto, which I just discussed, there are Program, Shutter Priority, Aperture Priority, Manual, User Setting, Special Effects, Landscape, Night Portrait, Night Landscape, and Scene. I'll discuss all of those modes in Chapter 3, and movie shooting in Chapter 8. For now, I will discuss some functions and features of the Coolpix P600 you can adjust to suit whatever picture-taking situation you may be faced with. Not all of the settings can be adjusted in Auto mode, so we'll set the camera to a lower level of automation, to Program mode. In that mode, you'll be able to control most of the camera's functions for taking still pictures.

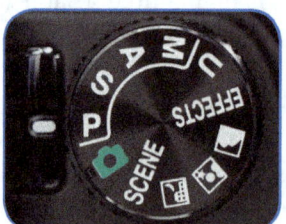

Figure 2-3. Program Mode

I'm not going to repeat the preliminary steps for taking a picture, because those are pretty basic. If you need a refresher on those items, see the list in the above discussion of Auto mode.

Start by setting the mode dial on top of the camera to P, for Program, as shown in Figure 2-3.

You will immediately see some different indications on the LCD screen, to show that some settings have changed. For example, you should see the ISO label along with a value, indicating that you now can control the ISO setting.

More importantly, if you press the Menu button you will see that many more options are now available for you to set on the Shooting menu—instead of the two menu lines available in Auto mode, you are presented with three menu screens containing 20 settings that you can adjust, including white balance, ISO, metering mode, exposure bracketing, and others. In the Program shooting mode, the camera will determine the proper exposure, both the aperture (size of opening to let in light) and the shutter speed (how long the shutter stays open to let in light). In this mode you can't make many decisions about those two settings; you can have more control over your settings in other modes, which I'll discuss in Chapter 3. That still leaves lots of decisions you can make, though, so let's talk about the various settings you can adjust in Program mode.

Focus

Now that the camera is not in Auto mode, you have more control over focus. Specifically, you can set the camera to the MF option, for manual focus, which is not available in Auto mode. You also can select which of several types of autofocus operation you want the camera to use, if you opt for autofocus.

I'll discuss focus in more detail in Chapters 4 and 5. For now, let's just select a standard focus mode. First, press the multi selector's Down button (marked by a flower icon). This action puts a small menu with four options on the display, as shown in Figure 2-4. Starting at the top, they are the letters AF, for normal autofocus; the flower icon, for macro (close-up) focus; the mountain icon, for focus on infinity; and the letters MF, for manual focus.

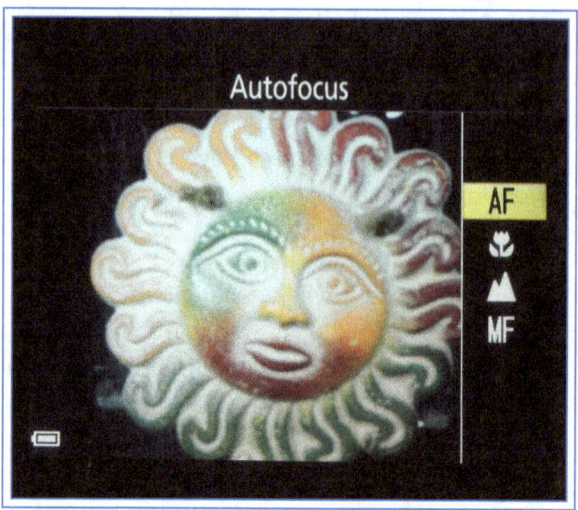

Figure 2-4. Focus Mode Menu

For now, use the direction buttons to select the top icon, for normal autofocus. (You have to be quick; the four choices disappear within a few seconds.) Press the OK button to select and confirm your choice. The letters or icon for your choice will appear at the upper left of the display, as shown in Figure 2-5, unless the choice is AF; if you select AF, those letters will appear for a few seconds and then disappear, because that is the default setting. The icon shown in Figure 2-5 represents the infinity setting.

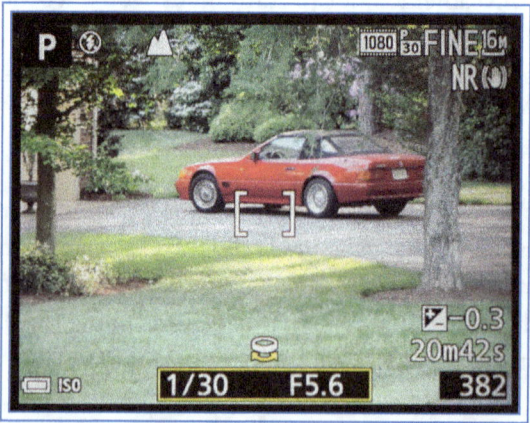

Figure 2-5. Infinity Focus Mode Icon on Display

There are several other focus-related options you can set, but for present purposes let's just use one of them. Press the Menu button at the bottom of the camera's back to enter the shooting menu. With the selection block in the list of menu items, scroll with the Up and Down buttons until the yellow selection rectangle highlights the line for AF Area Mode on the second screen of the menu, as shown in Figure 2-6.

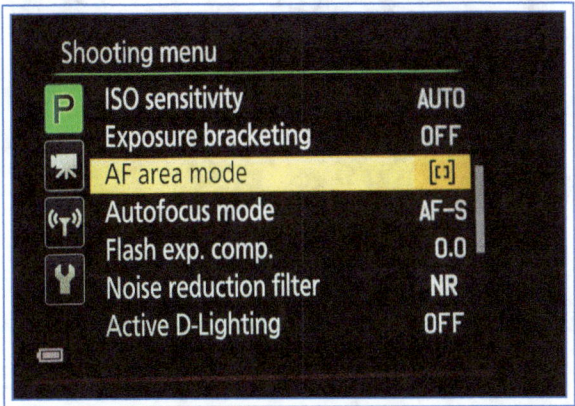

Figure 2-6. AF Area Mode Menu Item

Press OK to select that item, then use the Up and Down buttons to change the setting to Manual (normal), as shown in Figure 2-7.

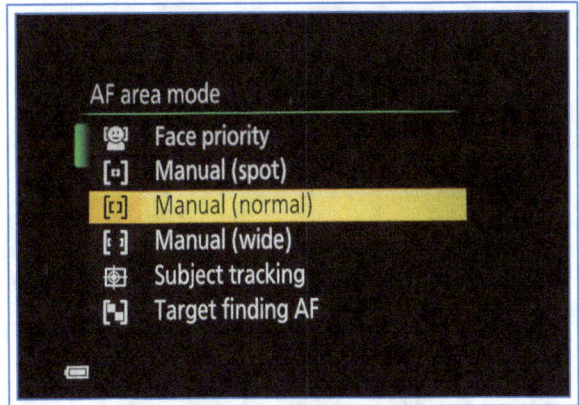

Figure 2-7. Manual (Normal) Setting for AF Area Mode

Press the OK button to confirm the selection, then press the shutter button halfway to go to the shooting screen. You should see a focus frame with 4 arrows, as in Figure 2-8. (If you don't see the arrows, press the OK button to make them appear.)

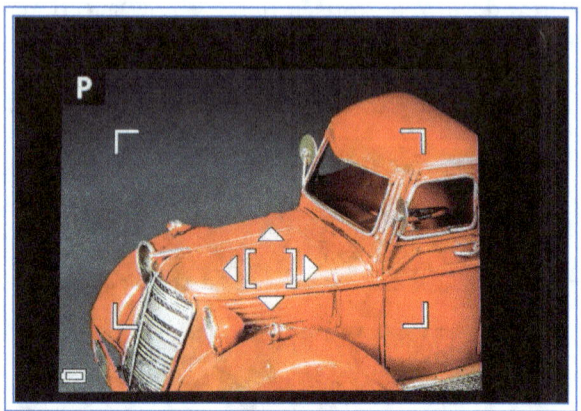

Figure 2-8. Manual Focus Frame Ready to Move

With this setting, the camera will place a focus frame in the center of the screen. You can move the frame around the screen using the direction buttons or the multi selector dial; I'll discuss that process in Chapter 4. For now, press OK to confirm, and the focus frame will be locked at its current position.

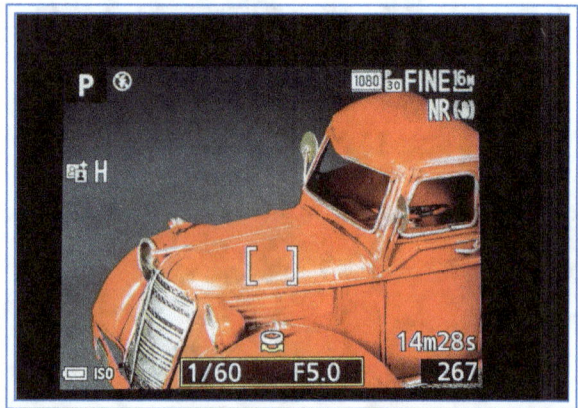

Figure 2-9. Manual Focus Frame Fixed in Place

When you aim the camera at a scene, center the subject between the white focus brackets, as shown in Figure 2-9.

Press the shutter button halfway so the camera will evaluate exposure and focus. You should hear a beep and the focus brackets should turn green to confirm the focus, as shown in Figure 2-10.

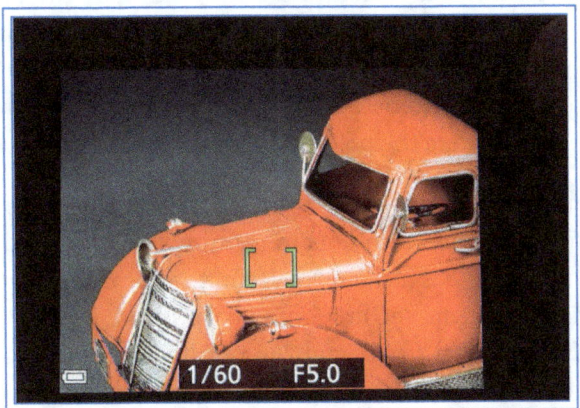

Figure 2-10. Manual Focus Frame After Focus Confirmed

If everything looks good to you, press the shutter button all the way down to take the picture.

Suppose you want to take a picture in which your main subject is not in the center of the screen. Maybe your shot is set up so that a person is standing off to the right of center, and there is some attractive scenery to the left in the scene. Place the focus frame over the part of the picture that needs to be in focus—in this example, the person to the right. Then press the shutter button halfway down until the camera focuses and beeps. Keep the button pressed halfway to lock in the focus (and exposure) while you move the camera back to create your desired composition, with the person off to the right. Then take the picture, and the area you originally focused on will be in focus.

There is another way to handle this sort of situation, by moving the focus frame so it covers the subject, as mentioned above; I'll discuss that option, as well as several other options for autofocus, in Chapter 4.

Manual Focus

Manual focus is the other major option for focusing. Many photographers like the amount of control that comes from being able to set the focus exactly how they want it. And, in some situations, such as focusing in dark areas or areas behind glass or wire fences, taking extreme close-ups, or cases where there are objects at various distances from the camera, it may be useful to control exactly where the point of sharpest focus lies.

For example, one day I went into the back yard to experiment with using the superzoom lens to capture images of birds in our small fountain. It was a cloudy day, and the autofocus mechanism was having problems settling on a sharp focus. I finally decided to switch to manual focus, and the results improved. Of course, manual focus was useful on that occasion partly because I was sitting in one place, the birds tended to stay in one place to take a bath, and the fountain wasn't going anywhere; with a moving subject, manual focus is not likely to be as useful.

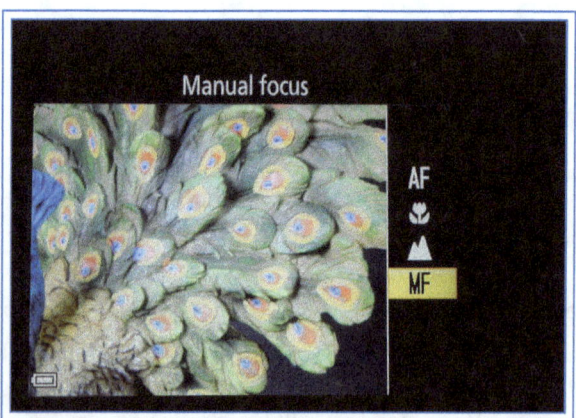

Figure 2-11. Manual Focus Icon Selected on Focus Mode Menu

To activate manual focus, with the camera in Program mode, press the Down button, with the flower icon; on the menu that appears, navigate to the MF icon and select it by pressing the OK button, as shown in Figure 2-11.

Now the camera is set for manual focusing. When the camera is first set to manual focus mode, the screen is automatically enlarged to 2 or 4 times its normal magnification, as shown in Figure 2-12. The amount of magnification is saved from the last time manual focus was used. If you see the number 4, as here, that means 2x magnification is in effect, and you can press the Left button to switch to 4x magnification. If you see the number 2, that means 4x magnification is in effect, and you can press the Left button to switch to 2x magnification.

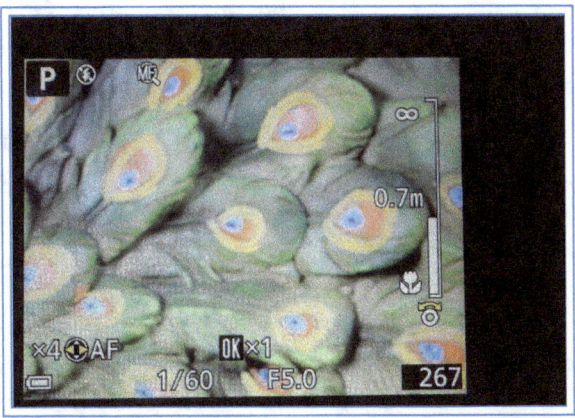

Figure 2-12. Manual Focus Screen with 2x Magnification

To adjust the focus using the manual focus setting, just start turning the multi selector dial. Look at the focusing scale on the right side of the screen and turn the dial until the focus appears as sharp as possible. As shown by the prompts in the lower left corner of the screen, you can press the Left button to switch the magnification amount or the OK button to set the screen to normal size (shown as x1 on the display) with focus locked at the current setting. If you return the screen to its normal magnification using the OK button, you can press the OK button again to go to the magnified screen to continue adjusting focus.

As you move the focus point using the multi selector dial, you will see a white bar go up and down inside the focus scale. Continue adjusting until the focus is as sharp as you can get it, and then take the picture.

If you need to use the multi selector dial for another function, such as adjusting aperture in Aperture Priority mode, press the OK button to return the screen to its normal size and lock focus. You can then use the dial for its other operations. To return to adjusting manual focus, press the OK button again.

If you want the camera to assist you with its autofocus capability, you can press the Right button, as prompted on the screen, and the camera will autofocus on the subject in the center of the screen. You can then continue adjusting focus manually using the multi selector dial.

You also can turn on the Peaking feature on screen 3 of the Setup menu to help judge when manual focus is sharp. I'll discuss that option in Chapter 7.

Exposure

Next, I'll discuss some possibilities for controlling exposure, beyond just letting the camera make the decisions. The Coolpix P600's Auto mode is very good at choosing the right exposure, and so is the Program mode. But there are some situations in which you may want to override the camera's automation.

Exposure Compensation

First, let's take a look at the control for adjusting exposure to account for an unusual, or non-optimal, lighting situation.

For example, consider Figure 2-13, which shows the P600's view of a model tractor. Because the model is in front of a white background, the camera's autoexposure system makes the exposure too dark, to account for the large expanse of white.

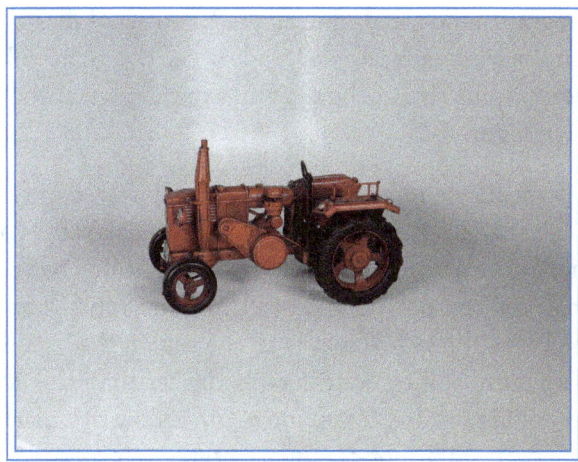

Figure 2-13. Image Needing Exposure Compensation

One solution to this problem, which is easily done with the Coolpix P600, is to use the camera's exposure compensation control. Look closely at the Right button on the multi selector. That button is labeled with little plus and minus signs, with the plus on a black background and the minus on white. This control activates the exposure compensation system, which will override the automatic exposure as much as you tell it to, within limits.

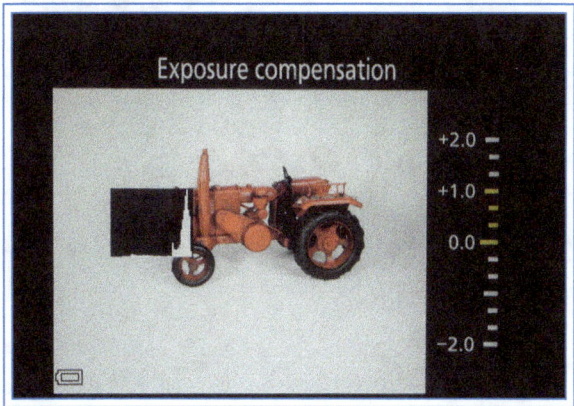

Figure 2-14. Exposure Compensation Adjustment Screen

Select Program mode and aim at your subject. Press the Right button, and a vertical scale will appear on the right side of the display, with a plus sign at the top and a minus sign at the bottom, as shown in Figure 2-14.

Once the exposure compensation scale has appeared, press the Up and Down buttons or turn the multi selector dial or the command dial to move the values higher or lower, as indicated by yellow tick marks that appears on the scale to show the value that is being set. If you move the yellow marks all the way to the bottom of the scale, the picture will be considerably darker than the automatic exposure would produce. If you move the yellow tick marks to the top, the picture will be noticeably brighter.

The camera's screen brightens and darkens to show you how the exposure is changing, before you take the picture. The camera also displays a histogram—a chart showing peaks and valleys of brightness values—on the left side of the screen. In this case, you would adjust exposure to be brighter, so the camera will expose for the tractor model properly, and let the background show up as a brighter (and more accurate) white than in the first image.

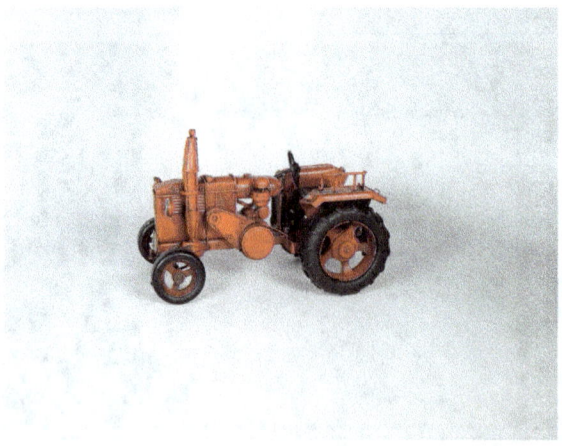

Figure 2-15. Exposure Compensation Example - After Adjustment

I'll discuss the meaning of the histogram in more detail in Chapter 6. Basically, brighter values in your image skew the peaks in the chart to the right, and darker ones skew them to the left. As you adjust exposure compensation, you should generally try to keep the peaks of the chart in the center of the histogram. In this case, I adjusted exposure upward by 1.0 EV (exposure value), resulting in a more normally exposed image, as shown in Figure 2-15.

The peaks of the histogram in Figure 2-14 are skewed to the right, because the exposure was adjusted to be brighter than normal.

After taking the picture, you should reset the exposure compensation back to zero, in the middle of the scale, so you don't unintentionally affect the pictures you take later. You need to be careful about this, because the camera will retain any exposure compensation value you set, even when it's turned off and then on again. If a positive or negative value for exposure compensation is in effect, the camera will display that value, along with the exposure compensation icon, in the lower right corner of the display, as shown in Figure 2-16.

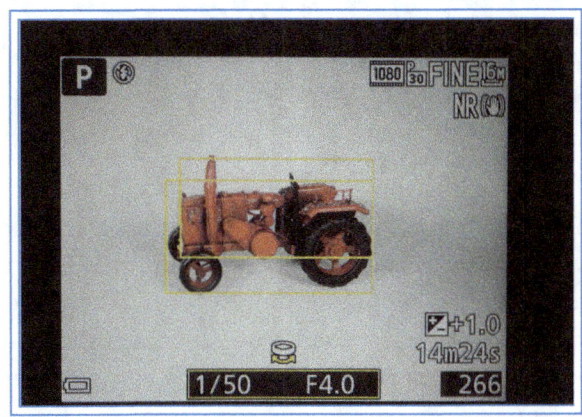

Figure 2-16. Exposure Compensation Icon on Shooting Screen

FLASH

In Chapters 3 and 4, I'll discuss several other topics dealing with exposure, such as the Manual exposure, Aperture Priority and Shutter Priority modes, exposure bracketing, Active D-Lighting, and others. Now I will discuss the basics of using the Coolpix P600's built-in flash unit. In Chapter 9, I'll discuss other options for using the flash, such as the Slow Sync mode and correcting "red-eye." In Appendix A, I'll discuss using other flash units.

The built-in flash on the P600 can provide enough illumination to let you take pictures in dark areas and to brighten up areas otherwise lost in shadows, even outdoors on a sunny day. Here is one fundamental point you need to be aware of: The built-in flash will not pop up by itself. If you are in a situation in which you think flash may be needed or desirable, you need to take the first step of popping up the flash unit. To do so, find the small, round button on the left side of the flash unit, marked by a lightning bolt. Press in on this button, and the flash springs up into place. (When you're done with the flash, just push down on the unit until it catches again.)

Even though you have popped up the flash unit, in some shooting situations it will never fire. In the situations in which you're likely to want it to, though, it will be ready to illuminate your subject as well as it can.

Let's explore a common scenario to see how the flash works. Make sure the camera is turned on and the flash unit has been released by pressing the flash pop-up button. Now turn the mode dial on top of the camera to select the Night Landscape shooting mode, represented by the icon just below the Scene mode icon, as shown in Figure 2-17.

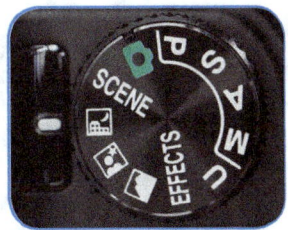

Figure 2-17. Night Landscape Mode

Next, press the Up button, with the lightning bolt icon on it. Nothing will happen. You will see the universal negative symbol—a circle with a line through it—over a lightning bolt, indicating that the flash is turned off, as shown in Figure 2-18.

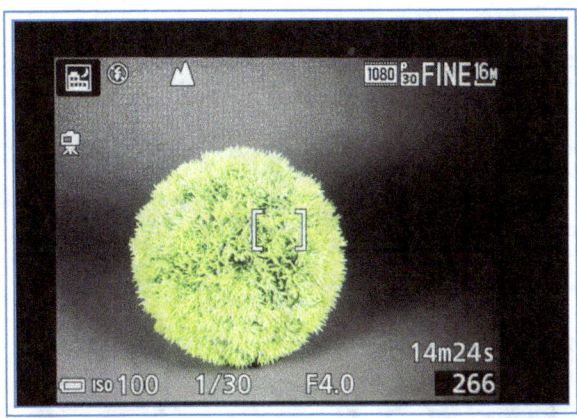

Figure 2-18. Flash Off Icon in Upper Left Corner of Screen

(If you don't see this symbol, press the Display button, to the right of the viewfinder, to switch to the more detailed shooting screen.) In this situation, because you have chosen a shooting mode (Night Landscape) that will not use flash under any circumstances, you cannot turn the flash on.

Next, with the flash still popped up, set the mode dial to the camera icon, for Auto mode, and then press the Flash button on the multi selector. You will see a menu on the screen with five options available: Auto, Auto with Red-eye Reduction, Fill Flash, Slow Sync, and Rear-curtain Sync, as shown in Figure 2-19.

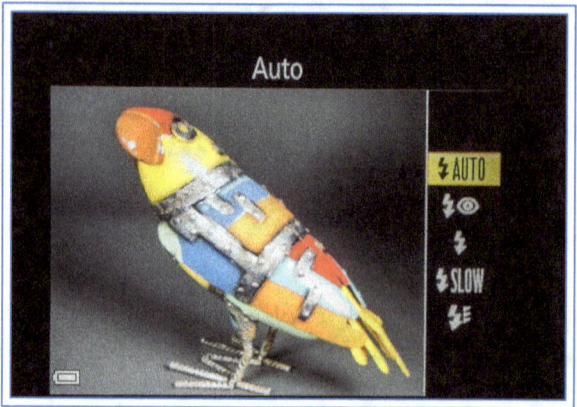

Figure 2-19. Flash Mode Menu in Auto Mode

Move through this list by pressing the Up and Down buttons or by turning the command dial or multi selector dial. Once you have selected a flash mode, you can tell if the flash will fire or not by looking at the small lamp to the left of the lightning bolt icon just above the Playback button.

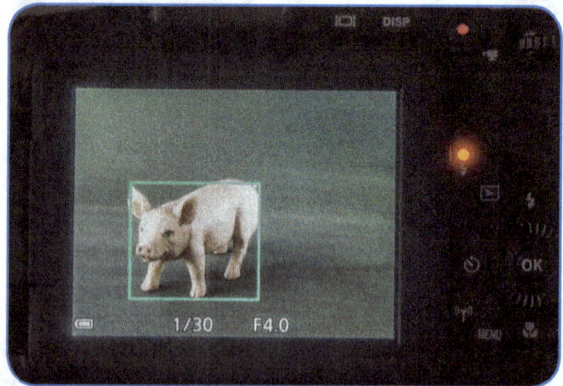

Figure 2-20. Flash Lamp on Back of Camera Lit to Show Flash Will Fire

Set up your shot in the current lighting conditions and press the shutter button halfway. If the lamp lights up in solid orange, as shown in Figure 2-20, that means the flash will fire, either because you have selected Fill Flash, Slow Sync, or Rear-curtain, or because you have selected Auto Flash and the camera senses that the flash will be needed. If the lamp does not light up, that means the flash will not fire, either because it is not available in this mode or because the lighting conditions do not require it. If the lamp is blinking orange, that means the flash unit is not available because it is charging.

Later on, in Chapter 9, I'll discuss other flash options, such as Slow Sync and Rear-curtain, and how they work. For now, you know how to choose a flash mode, and you know that they will not all be available at all times.

Motion Picture Recording

Let's take a look at recording a short video sequence with the Coolpix P600. In Chapter 8, I'll discuss other options for video recording, but for now I will stick with the basics. First, make sure the flash unit is pressed down in the off position, because it will not be needed. Once the camera is turned on, press the Menu button and then press the Left button to place the yellow selection block in the line of icons at the far left of the screen. Navigate down to the second icon, which looks like a movie camera, then press the Right button to move the selection rectangle back into the list of menu items. You will see only three items on this Movie menu screen, which provides the options for recording video footage.

Navigate to the third item on the menu screen, called Frame Rate, and press the OK or Right button to move to the screen with the two options for this setting:, as shown in Figure 2-21: 30 fps (30p/60i) and 25 fps (25p/50i). This setting determines the frames per second at which the camera will record video in the highest-quality (HD) formats. The 30 fps setting is the standard for the NTSC video system, which is used in the United States, Canada, Mexico, Japan, and some other areas. The 25 fps setting is the standard for the PAL video system, in use in Europe and other locations. If you are in the United States, select the 30 fps option unless you have a specific need to do otherwise. This

setting will affect the choices available for the Movie Options
item, discussed next.

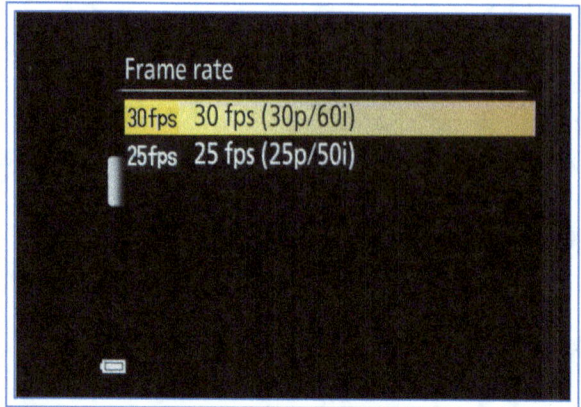

Figure 2-21. Frame Rate Options Screen

Navigate to the top option on the menu screen, which is Movie
Options, press the OK button or the Right button to move to the
next screen, and look at the list of options. If you selected 30 fps
for Frame Rate, as discussed above, the first 5 options on this
screen will include the number 30 or 60. If you selected 25 fps, the
first 5 options will include the number 25 or 50.

You should now choose the top selection for Movie Options,
which, if you chose 30 fps for Frame Rate, will be 1080/30p, as
shown in Figure 2-22. (If the top item is 1080/25p, that means
the Frame Rate menu item is set to 25 fps. Unless you have a
reason to make that choice, go back and change it to 30 fps.) This
is the highest-quality mode for shooting movies with the P600.

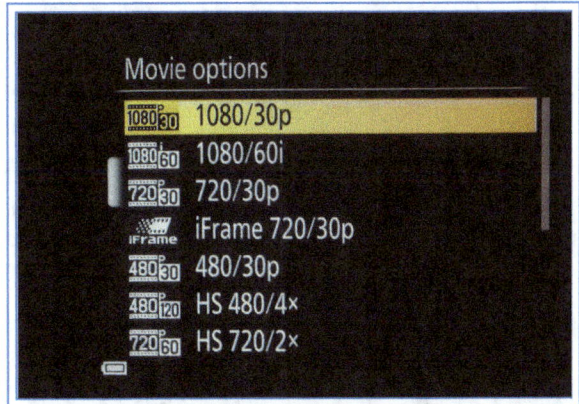

Figure 2-22. Movie Options Setting of 1080/30p Selected

Press the Left button to move back one screen, and navigate down to the second option on the screen, Autofocus Mode. Move to the next screen by pressing the OK button or the Right button, and select the second option, Full-time AF, as shown in Figure 2-23.

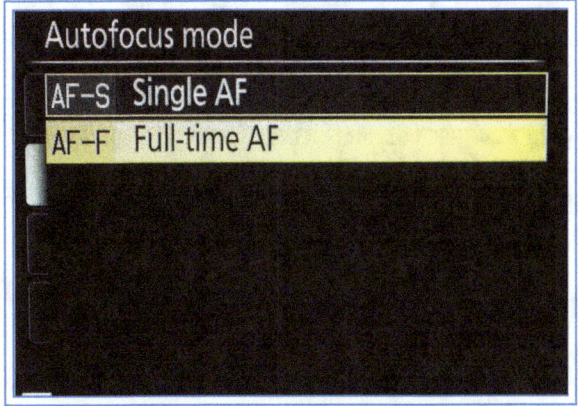

Figure 2-23. Autofocus Mode Setting of Single AF

Press the OK button to confirm this selection. This option will cause the camera to adjust its focus continuously as the distance from the camera to your main subject changes. Exit from the menu system by pressing the Menu button.

That is all the preparation you need. Now compose the shot the way you want it, and when you're ready, press the red Movie button once. (That button is at the top of the camera's back, just below the mode dial.) You don't need to hold the button down; just press and release. The camera's display will blank out briefly, then it will show a flashing red REC indicator at the upper left and the minutes and seconds remaining for your recording at the lower right, as shown in Figure 2-24.

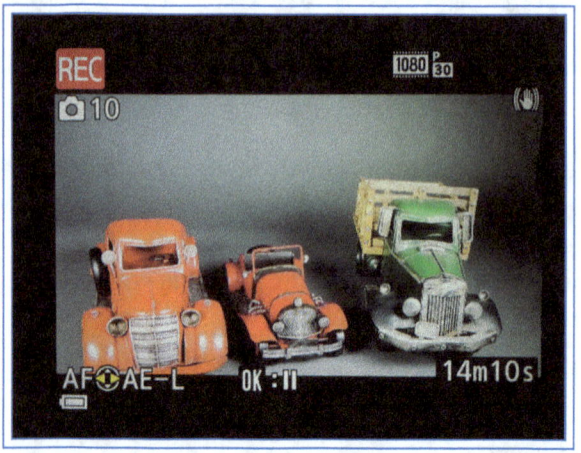

Figure 2-24. REC Indicator on Display During Movie Recording

The camera will keep recording until it reaches a recording time limit or until you press the red button again to stop the recording. Don't be concerned about the level of the sound that is being recorded, because you have no control over the audio volume while recording.

The camera will automatically adjust the exposure as lighting conditions change. As noted earlier, with the Full-time Autofocus option turned on, the camera will continue to adjust its focus as needed, when the distance to the main subject changes.

One other point that's not specific to the Coolpix P600: Unless you have a good reason to do otherwise, try to hold the camera as steady as possible (use a tripod or monopod if possible), and don't zoom unnecessarily or move the camera except in very smooth, slow motions, such as a pan (side-to-side motion) to take in a wide scene gradually. Video from a jerkily moving camera can be very disconcerting to the viewer.

Viewing Pictures and Movies

Before I delve into more advanced settings for taking still pictures and movies, as well as other matters of interest, I will discuss the basics of viewing your images in the camera.

REVIEW WHILE IN SHOOTING MODE

Every time you take a still picture, the recorded image will show up on the screen (or in the viewfinder if it's in use) for a brief amount of time, if you have the Setup menu's Monitor Settings option set to turn on the Image Review function. I'll discuss the details of that setting in Chapter 7. By default, your image will stay on the display for about one second after you take a new picture.

REVIEWING IMAGES IN PLAYBACK MODE

To review images that were taken previously, enter playback mode by pressing the Playback button, marked with a small triangle icon, to the right side of the LCD screen. You can then scroll through the recorded images using the Left and Right or Up and Down buttons on the multi selector or by turning the multi selector dial (the dial that surrounds the OK button). You can enlarge any image using the zoom lever on top of the camera, and you can scroll around in the enlarged image using the direction buttons. You can speed through the images by holding down any one of the four direction buttons.

If you have used the continuous-shooting features of the camera, you may see some images labeled with an OK followed by a colon and a triangle at the bottom center, as seen in Figure 2-25.

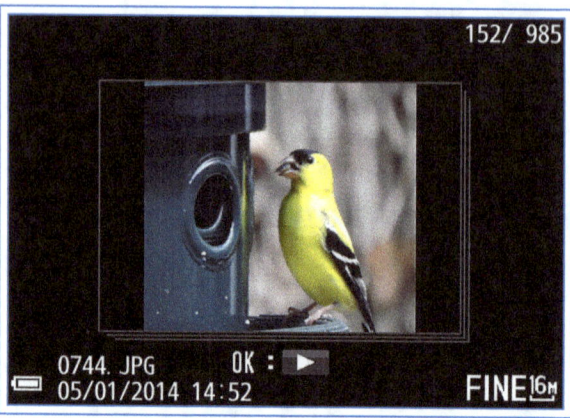

Figure 2-25. Continuous Series of Shots Ready to Play

In those cases, you can press the OK button to "open" a series of continuous shots, and then use the direction buttons to move among the various individual shots in that series. To exit to the main viewing screen so you can see other images and series of images, press the Up button. (I'll discuss playback options in more detail in Chapter 6.)

PLAYING MOVIES

To play back motion pictures, move through the recorded images by the methods described above until you find an image for which there is a movie options icon at the lower right of the screen showing a movie format such as 480p, as shown in Figure 2-26.

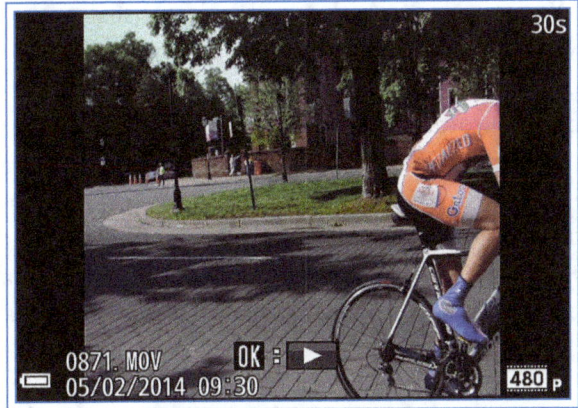

Figure 2-26. Movie Ready to Play

While the frame from the movie is displayed on the screen, press the OK button (the button in the center of the multi selector) and the movie will start playing on the LCD, or in the electronic viewfinder if that display option is active instead of the LCD.

At the bottom left of the display there will be a line of VCR-like controls, as seen in Figure 2-27.

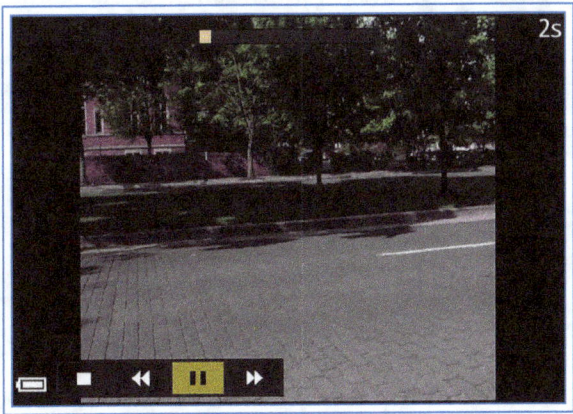

Figure 2-27. Initial Movie Playback Controls on Display

Scroll through the line of controls using the direction buttons on the multi selector and press the OK button to activate one. You have to act quickly, because the controls disappear after a few seconds. You also can turn the multi selector dial to the right to fast-forward or to the left to rewind. You can raise or lower the volume of the audio by turning the zoom lever (surrounding the shutter button) toward the T position (louder) or the W position (softer). You will see a little set of volume "waves" increase or decrease next to a speaker icon at the lower right of the screen when you adjust the sound in this way. Note, though, that you cannot adjust the sound with this control if the camera is connected to a TV set; in that case, you must use the TV's volume control to change the sound level.

If you want to play the movies on a computer or edit them with video-editing software, they will import nicely into software such as iMovie for the Macintosh or any other program for Mac or Windows that can deal with video files with the extension .mov. This is the extension for Apple Computer's QuickTime video playback software; QuickTime itself can be downloaded from Apple's web site. For some Windows-based video editing software, you may need to convert the P600's movie files to the .avi format before importing them into the software. You can do so with a program such as mp4cam2avi, which can be found on the internet at http://mp4cam2avi.sourceforge.net/.

I will discuss more options for playing movies and editing them in the camera in Chapter 8.

Chapter 3: The Shooting Modes

So far, I have discussed setting up the camera for quick shots, relying on features such as Auto mode for taking pictures with settings controlled mostly by the camera's automation. As with other sophisticated digital cameras, though, the Coolpix P600 has a wide range of settings available, particularly for shooting still images. One of the main goals of this book is to provide clear guidance about this broad range of features. To get started, I will turn my attention to the P600's several shooting modes, which provide you with many options for your photography.

Whenever you set out to record still images, you need to select one of the available shooting modes: Auto, Program, Shutter Priority, Aperture Priority, Manual exposure, User Settings, Special Effects, Landscape, Night Portrait, Night Landscape, or Scene. So far, I have discussed the use of the Auto and Program modes. Now I will describe the others, after some review of the first two.

Auto Mode

The Auto shooting mode is a good choice if you need to have the camera ready for a quick shot, maybe in an environment with fast-paced events when you won't have much time to fuss with settings. For example, in Figure 3-1, I used this mode to grab a quick shot of an impressive tree as I walked through the local botanical garden. The camera does not try to figure out what kind of scene it is photographing, though it will detect human faces and focus on them if possible.

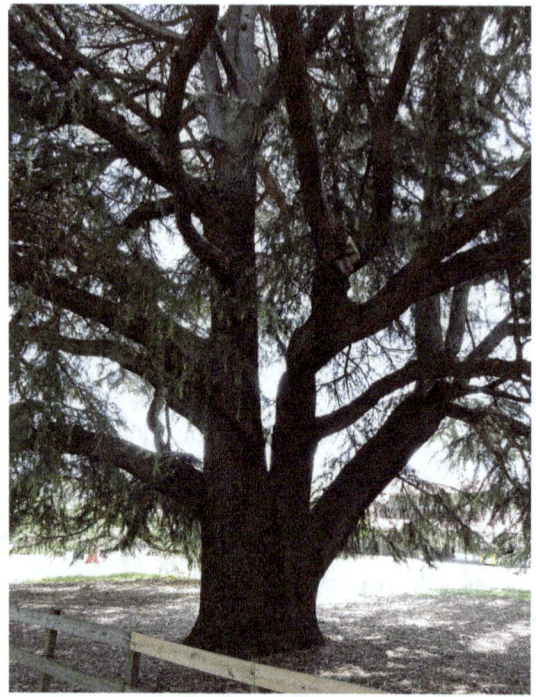

Figure 3-1. Auto Mode Example Image

To set this mode, turn the mode dial, on top of the camera to the right of the viewfinder, to the green camera icon, as shown in Figure 3-2.

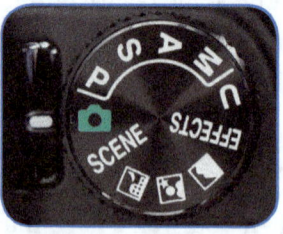

Figure 3-2. Auto Mode

When you select this mode, the camera makes several decisions for you and limits your options in some ways. For example, you can't set ISO or white balance to any value other than Auto, and you can't choose the metering method, use exposure bracketing, or use the Picture Control settings to alter the appearance of your images. In addition, you cannot select continuous shooting.

There are still a few settings you can control, however. For instance, you can choose any options for Image Size and Image Quality, you can use exposure compensation, and you can select any of five available modes for the built-in flash (if you have raised the flash unit). You also can select macro (close-up) focus or infinity focus (but not manual focus), and you can use the self-timer, including its Smile Timer option. My recommendation is that you set Image Size to the maximum value of 4608 x 3456 pixels and Image Quality to Fine, and use the other available settings (such as exposure compensation and flash mode) as needed.

Program Mode

Choose this option by turning the mode dial to the P slot, as shown in Figure 3-3.

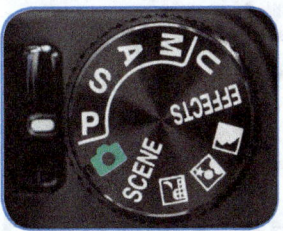

Figure 3-3. Program Mode

In this mode, the camera evaluates the light and selects both shutter speed and aperture so as to produce an exposure that the camera's programming considers to be normal. The Program shooting mode lets you control many of the settings available with the camera, but not shutter speed and aperture.

However, even though you can't directly set those two values, you can override the camera's automatic exposure to a fair extent by using exposure compensation, the Flexible Program feature, and exposure bracketing.

I discussed exposure compensation in Chapter 2, and I'll explain exposure bracketing in Chapter 4. Flexible Program is the name Nikon uses for what is often called "Program Shift" for some other cameras. This option lets you adjust the values the camera selects in Program mode for shutter speed and aperture. For example, if the camera selects, say, 1/80 second at f/3.4, the Flexible Program feature will find equivalent combinations that result in the same exposure, such as 1/60 second at f/3.5, 1/50 second at f/4.0, or 1/40 second at f/4.5. To use this feature, when the camera is in Program mode, aim at your subject and turn the command dial (the wheel at the very top right corner of the camera's back) to find an equivalent pair of shutter speed and aperture values.

When the camera is using one of these equivalent match-ups of settings rather than the originally chosen setting, it displays an asterisk at the upper right of the letter P that signifies Program mode in the upper left of the display, as seen in Figure 3-4.

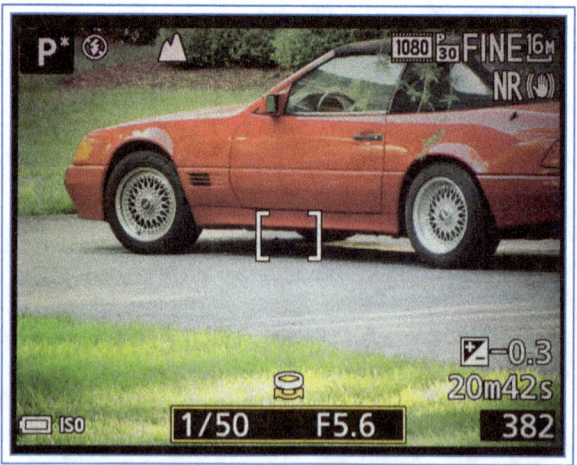

Figure 3-4. Flexible Program Indicator on Display

To cancel Flexible Program, turn the command dial back to reset the original shutter speed and aperture, select a different shooting mode, or turn off the camera.

The Flexible Program feature is useful in several situations. For example, you may want to see what the "normal" settings are and then see if you can use a wider aperture to achieve a blurred background, or a faster shutter speed to stop the action or prevent blur from camera motion. And, when you're experimenting with the camera to see what it is capable of, it can be very helpful to try various combinations of aperture and shutter speed to find out which combination gives you the best results in different situations. With a digital camera, there's no added cost for trying these different approaches, and Flexible Program is a useful way to experiment.

One way to look at Program mode is that it greatly expands the choices available through the Shooting menu. You will be able to make choices involving image size and quality, white balance, ISO sensitivity, metering method, autofocus mode, and others. I won't discuss all of those choices here; if you want to explore that topic, go to the discussion of the Shooting menu in Chapter 4 and check out all of the different selections that are available to you.

Shutter Priority Mode

Select Shutter Priority mode by setting the mode dial to the S indicator, as shown in Figure 3-5.

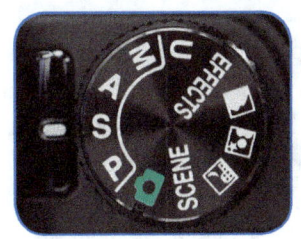

Figure 3-5. Shutter Priority Mode

In this shooting mode, you set the shutter speed and the camera will set the corresponding aperture in order to achieve a proper exposure. In Shutter Priority mode, you can set the shutter to be open for intervals ranging from 8 full seconds to 1/4000 of a second, although the camera has built-in limitations on the use of the fastest and slowest shutter speeds. For example, if the ISO is set to 800, the slowest shutter speed available is 2 seconds, and if the aperture is set to f/3.3 or f/3.8, the fastest shutter speed available is 1/2000 second. In addition, the zoom range of the lens has a limiting effect on the availability of the fastest shutter speeds. For example, the fastest shutter speed available when the lens is zoomed fully in to the telephoto position is 1/2500 second. The chart in Table 3-1 sets forth some of these limitations.

Table 3-1: Limits on Shutter Speed Settings	
Slowest Shutter Speed	**ISO Value**
8 seconds	100
4 seconds	200 or 400
2 seconds	800
1 second	1600
0.5 second	3200 or 6400
Fastest Shutter Speed	**Aperture Value**
1/4000 second	f/7.6*
1/2500 second	f/8.2**

* At wide-angle zoom setting

** At telephoto zoom setting

If you are photographing fast action, such as a baseball swing or a hurdles event at a track meet, and you want to stop the action with a minimum of blur, you will need a fast shutter speed, such as 1/1000 of a second. In other cases, for creative purposes, you may want to use a slow shutter speed of one second or more to achieve a certain effect, such as leaving the shutter open to capture a trail of automobiles' taillights at night.

Controlling shutter speed is a powerful tool for creative photography. For example, in Figure 3-6 I set the shutter speed to 1/640 second to freeze the motion of bicycle racers.

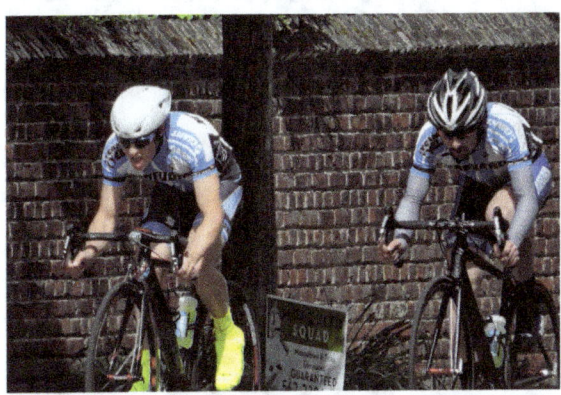

Figure 3-6. Shutter Speed 1/640 Second, f/6.5, ISO 220

In Figure 3-7 I set the speed to 1/100 second, a considerably slower speed, to produce slight blurring of other riders in the same event, to give a sense of motion from the blurring effect.

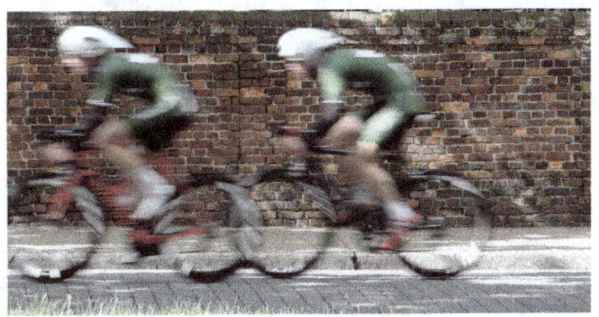

Figure 3-7. Shutter Speed 1/100 Second; f/5.5; ISO 100

To set the shutter speed on the Coolpix P600, turn the command dial—the ridged dial at the top right of the camera's back, below the power switch. (As discussed in Chapter 7, you can switch this function to the multi selector dial with the Toggle Av/Tv Selection option on the Setup menu.) The LCD (or viewfinder, if selected) will display the selected shutter speed inside a yellow rectangle at the bottom center of the screen, as shown in Figure 3-8.

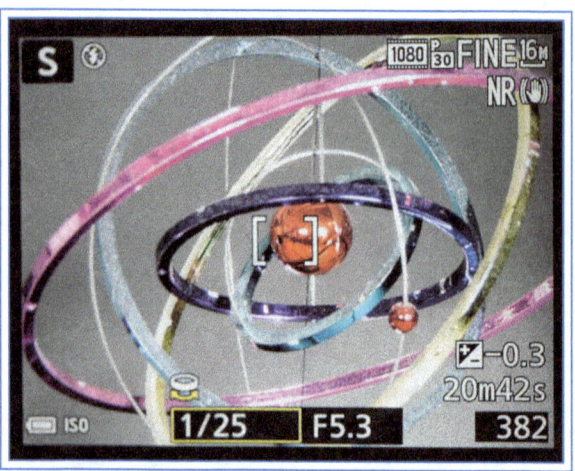

Figure 3-8. Shutter Speed Setting at Bottom of Display

As you point the camera at scenes with varying lighting, the camera will select and display the appropriate aperture (such as f/5.3 in this example) to achieve a proper exposure.

Once you've pressed the shutter button halfway, watch the shutter speed number on the screen. If that number blinks, that means proper exposure at that shutter speed is not possible at any available aperture, according to the camera's calculations. For example, with a shutter speed of 2 seconds in a well-lighted room, the shutter speed number may begin to blink, indicating that proper exposure is not possible. The camera will still let you take the picture, despite having blinked the number to warn you. The camera is saying, in effect, "Look, maybe you shouldn't do this, but that's your business. If you want an overly bright picture for some reason, help yourself." (This situation is less likely to take place when the camera is in Aperture Priority mode, because in that mode, there is a wide range of shutter speeds for the camera to choose from—a range from 8 seconds to 1/4000 second in some situations, depending on factors such as ISO, aperture, and continuous-shooting settings.)

When you are setting shutter speed, the fractions of a second are easy to read because they are displayed as standard fractions, such as 1/5 or 1/200. Some of the longer times are a bit harder to read; the camera displays them using quotation marks. So, for example, 2 seconds is displayed as 2", and 1.3 second is displayed as 1.3."

One feature of the shutter speed display on the Coolpix P600 is a bit confusing, at least to me. Some of the camera's shutter speeds are displayed as fractions whose denominators are decimal numbers, such as 1/1.3. I would have trouble understanding that number without doing some arithmetic, so Table 3-2 provides a brief chart that converts these few values into terms that may be easier to comprehend:

Table 3-2: Shutter Speed Equivalents	
1/2.5	= 0.4 = 2/5 second
1/1.6	= 0.625 = 5/8 second
1/1.3	= 0.77 = 10/13 second (0.8 sec)

Aperture Priority Mode

Aperture Priority mode, represented by the A setting on the mode dial as shown in Figure 3-9, is the inverse of Shutter Priority.

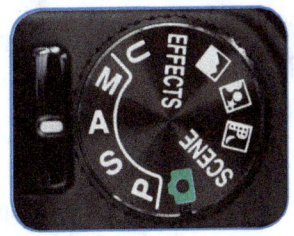

Figure 3-9. Aperture Priority Mode

In this mode, you select an aperture value and the camera selects a corresponding shutter speed to achieve a proper exposure.

Before discussing the settings for this mode, though, I will discuss aperture and why you would want to control it. The camera's aperture is a measure of the current width of its opening that lets in light to create the image. This width is measured numerically in f-stops. For the Coolpix P600, the range of f-stops is from f/3.3 (wide open) to f/8.2 (most narrow), though this range is limited in some circumstances, as discussed below. The amount of light that is let into the camera to create an image is controlled by the combination of aperture (how wide open the lens is) and shutter speed (how long the shutter remains open to let in the light).

For some purposes, you may want to control the width of the aperture, but let the camera choose the corresponding shutter speed, so you can control the depth of field. Depth of field is a measure of how well a camera is able to keep multiple objects or subjects in focus at different distances (focal lengths). For example, say you have three friends lined up so you can see all of them, but they are standing at different distances—five, seven, and nine feet (1.5, 2.1, and 2.7 meters) from the camera. If the camera's depth of field is shallow at a particular focal length, such as five feet (1.5 meters), then, if you focus on the friend at that distance, the other two will be out of focus and blurry. But if the camera's depth of field when focused at five feet is broad, then it may be possible for all three friends to be in sharp focus in your photograph, even if the focus is set for the friend at five feet.

What does all of that have to do with aperture? One of the rules of photographic optics is that the wider the camera's aperture is, the more shallow its depth of field is at a given focal length. So in the example discussed above, if you have the camera's aperture set to its widest opening, f/3.3, the depth of field will be relatively shallow, and it will be possible to keep fewer items in focus at varying distances from the camera. If the aperture is set to the narrowest, f/8.2, the depth of field will be greater, and it will be possible to have more items in focus at varying distances.

It is hard to illustrate this effect with a camera like the Coolpix P600, for a couple of reasons. First, the image sensor, where the light is gathered to form the image, is relatively small, which results in the depth of field being relatively deep at all apertures. Second, the largest aperture available is f/3.3, whereas some compact cameras have lenses that open as wide as f/2.0, or even f/1.4. With such cameras it is easier to achieve a blurred background, because the depth of field can be quite shallow at such a wide aperture. With the P600, the widest aperture you can shoot with is f/3.3, and that aperture is available only when the lens is zoomed back to its extreme wide-angle setting, where depth of field is greater. If you zoom the lens in to a telephoto setting, the maximum aperture decreases steadily. At the maximum zoom range, the widest aperture available is only f/6.5, which is not far from the narrowest aperture of f/8.2.

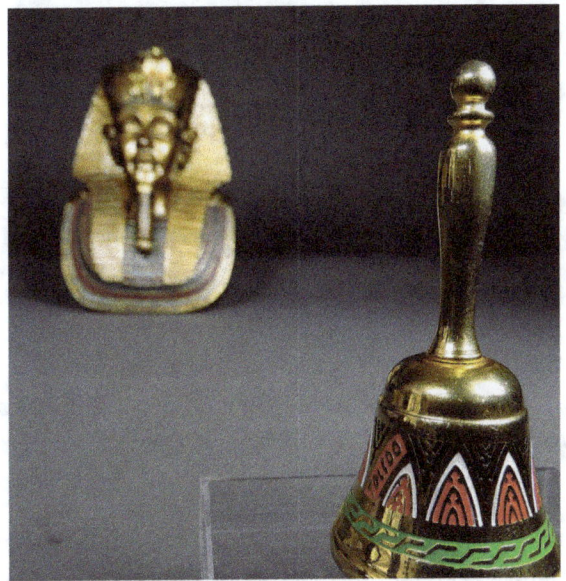

Figure 3-10. Shallow Depth of Field at Wide Aperture

Despite the difficulty of demonstrating the effects of using different apertures, the images in Figures 3-10 and 3-11 illustrate these effects to some extent. For both images, the lens was zoomed out to its wide-angle setting. I set the P600 to shoot in Aperture Priority mode. The first image was taken at f/3.3, the widest aperture available; the second one was taken at f/7.6, the narrowest aperture setting available on the camera at that focal length.

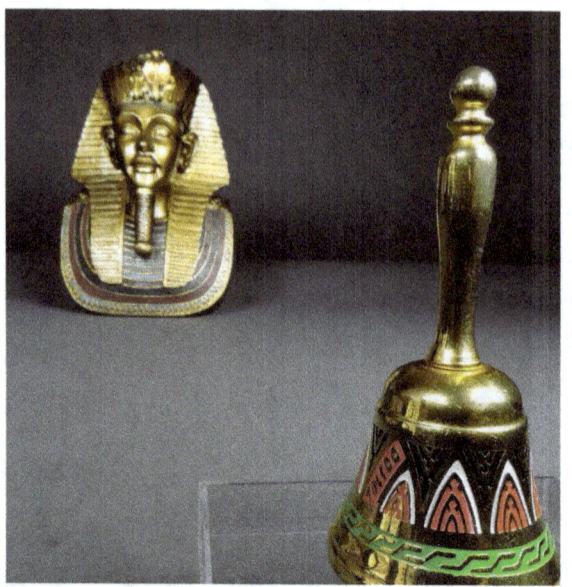

Figure 3-11. Broader Depth of Field at Narrower Aperture

As you should be able to see, in Figure 3-10, with the wider aperture, the figure in the background is noticeably blurred because the depth of field is relatively shallow at that setting. In Figure 3-11, on the other hand, the background is in somewhat sharper focus because the depth of field is greater at the narrower aperture setting.

If you want to have the sharpest picture possible, especially when you have subjects at varying distances from the lens and you want them all to be in focus, then you may want to control the aperture and make sure it is set to the highest number (narrowest opening) possible.

On the other hand, there are times when photographers prize a shallow depth of field. This situation arises often in the case of outdoor portraits. For example, you may want to take a photo of a person standing outdoors with a background of trees and bushes, and possibly some other, more distracting objects, such as a swing set or a tool shed. If you can achieve a narrow depth of field, you can have the person's face in sharp focus, but leave the background quite blurry and indistinct. This effect is sometimes called "bokeh," a Japanese term describing an aesthetically pleasing blurriness of the background.

Figure 3-12 is an example using this effect. In this situation, the blurriness of the background can be a great asset, reducing the distraction factor of unwanted objects and highlighting the sharply focused portrait of your subject.

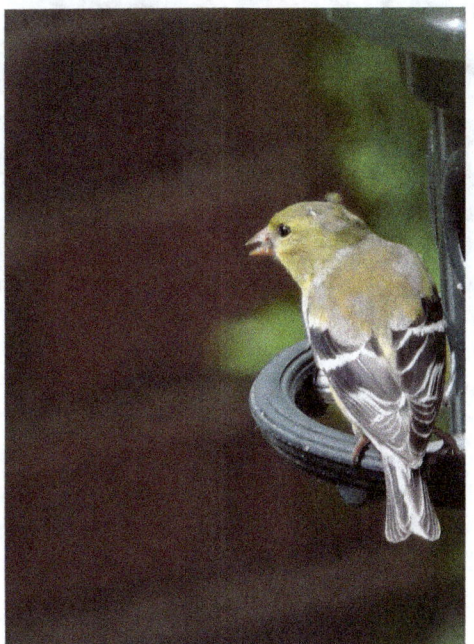

Figure 3-12. Bokeh Example Image

In this image, the bird is in fairly sharp focus, with the background heavily defocused; this image was shot with the lens zoomed in to the full optical zoom range of 1440mm with the aperture at f/6.5, resulting in a very shallow depth of field.

Here are the steps for setting the aperture. Once you have moved the mode dial to the A setting, aim the camera at your subject and turn the multi selector dial (the dial around the OK button) to change the aperture. The number of the f-stop will appear inside a yellow rectangle at the bottom right of the screen. The shutter speed chosen by the camera will show up also, to the left of the aperture, as seen in Figure 3-13.

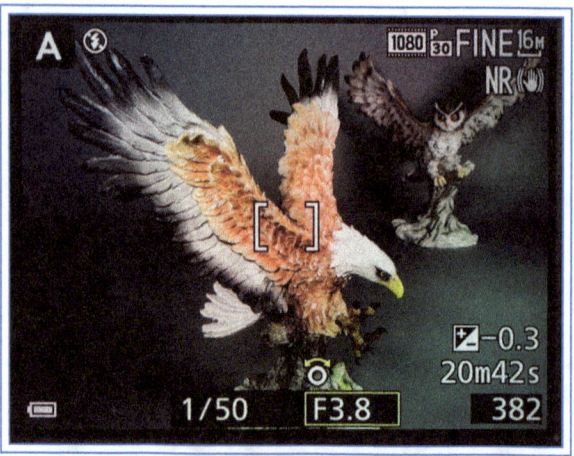

Figure 3-13. Aperture Setting at Bottom of Display

When you press the shutter button halfway, the camera will lock in the selected shutter speed.

Here is one point about Aperture Priority mode that could lead to confusion. As I noted briefly above, not all apertures are available at all times. In particular, the widest-open aperture, f/3.3, is available only when the lens is zoomed out to its wide-angle setting (zoom lever moved toward the letter W). At the highest zoom levels, the widest aperture available is f/6.5. To see an illustration of this point, here is a quick test. Zoom the lens out by moving the zoom lever all the way to the left, toward the W setting. Then select Aperture Priority mode and choose an aperture of f/3.3 by turning the multi selector dial all the way to the left. Now zoom the lens in by moving the zoom lever to the right, toward the T setting. The aperture displayed at the bottom of the screen will change to f/6.5. If you try to reset the aperture to f/3.3 after the zoom action is finished, you will see that the lowest aperture number you can set is f/6.5, because that is the widest aperture available on the P600 at the telephoto zoom level. (The aperture will change back to f/3.3 if you move the zoom back to the wide-angle setting.)

In addition, the narrowest apertures are not available in all cases. The overall aperture range for the P600 is from f/3.3 to f/7.6 when the lens is at the wide-angle setting and from f/6.5 to f/8.2 at the fully zoomed-in setting.

Manual Exposure Mode

The Coolpix P600 has a fully manual mode for control of aperture and shutter speed, which is one of the great features of this camera. Not all compact cameras have a manual exposure mode, which is a boon for photographers who want to enjoy full creative control over exposure decisions.

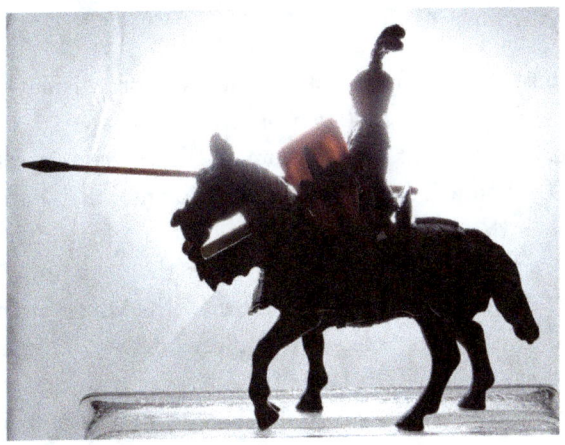

Figure 3-14. Silhouette Made Using Manual Exposure Mode

This mode is useful when you want to use settings that result in an unusual effect, such as a silhouette. For example, I used Manual exposure mode for Figure 3-14 to produce an image of a toy knight on horseback, with a large degree of underexposure to emphasize the figure's shape. I also often use Manual mode to take a series of photographs at different exposures to create HDR (high dynamic range) images using special software. I will discuss that process later in this chapter, in the discussion of the Backlighting/HDR setting.

The technique for using this mode is not far removed from what I discussed for the Aperture Priority and Shutter Priority modes. To control exposure manually, set the mode dial to the M indicator, as shown in Figure 3-15.

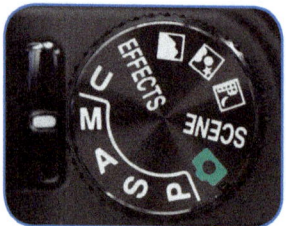

Figure 3-15. Manual Exposure Mode

You now have to control both shutter speed and aperture by setting them yourself.

To set these values, first look at the camera's display and find where the shutter speed (such as 1/13) and aperture (such as F5.3) are displayed at the bottom of the screen, as shown in Figure 3-16. You will see an icon of a horizontal dial with a yellow arrow above the shutter speed value on the left, which is inside a yellow rectangle; the dial icon means that the shutter speed value is controlled by the command dial (the wheel at the top of the camera's back, just below the power button). To the right of that value, you will see the value for the aperture, or f-stop, inside another rectangle; above that value will be an icon showing a dial that is oriented vertically; that icon represents the multi selector dial, on the back of the camera surrounding the OK button.

To adjust the settings, simply turn the command dial until you have selected the shutter speed you want, and turn the multi selector dial to set your desired aperture.

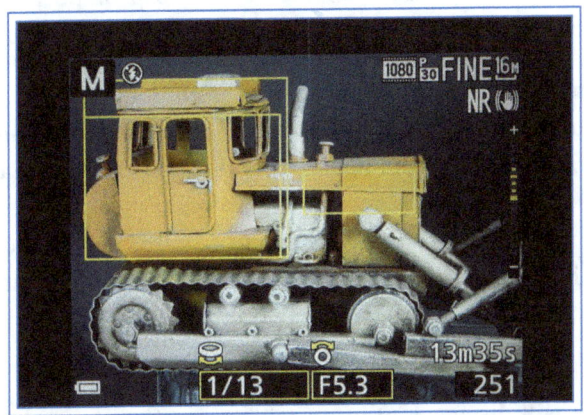

Figure 3-16. Shutter Speed and Aperture Displayed at Bottom of Screen

As you adjust these values, watch the vertical scale that appears at the right of the screen, as shown in Figure 3-16.

You will see the tick marks turn yellow, either above or below the scale's center point, as the values change. When the exposure is set as the camera judges to be normal, there will be a lone tick mark in the center of the scale, as shown in Figure 3-17.

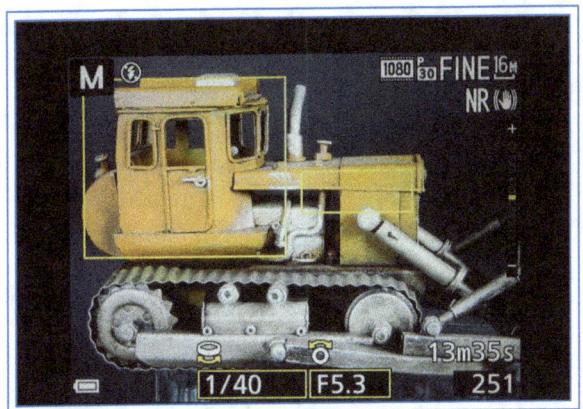

Figure 3-17. Tick Mark Centered on Exposure Scale in Manual Mode

If the marks above the center of the scale turn yellow, the exposure is too bright; if they turn yellow below the center, it is too dark. If the setting becomes more extreme than the scale can indicate, a yellow triangle appears at the top or bottom of the scale, indicating that the scale's limit has been exceeded.

If you are shooting in dim light, such as indoors or in a shadowed area, you may find it impossible to center the yellow tick mark on the exposure scale by adjusting the shutter speed and aperture unless you use a very long shutter speed, such as one second or longer. If you are handholding the camera, you won't be able to hold it steady for more than about 1/30 second, so it will be difficult to get a clear exposure.

In that situation, you can adjust exposure by changing the ISO setting. I will discuss ISO in more detail in Chapter 4, because it is an option found on the Shooting menu. Briefly, ISO is a setting that controls the sensitivity of the camera's digital sensor. The higher the ISO value, the more sensitive the sensor is to light. With higher ISO values, you can achieve a normal exposure with narrower apertures and faster shutter speeds.

With other shooting modes, the P600 can use the Auto ISO setting, which means the camera will set the ISO value as needed to reach a good exposure level. With Manual exposure mode, though, the camera will not set the ISO automatically. Even if you select Auto ISO from the ISO menu item, the camera will set ISO to 100, the lowest value possible.

If you find you need a higher ISO value in Manual exposure mode, you need to go to the ISO menu item and select a value such as ISO 400, 800, or even higher, as shown in Figure 3-18.

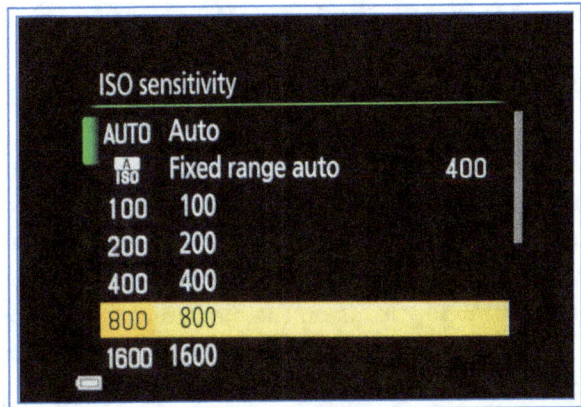

Figure 3-18. ISO 800 Setting Highlighted on Menu

Of course, you don't have to adjust the ISO or other values in an effort to center the indicator on the scale; that scale is there only to give you an idea of how the camera would meter the scene. You may want parts of the scene (or the whole image) to be darker or lighter than the metering system would indicate to be "correct." In Manual mode, the settings for aperture and shutter speed are independent of each other. When you change one, the other one stays unchanged until you change it manually. The camera is leaving the creative decision about exposure entirely up to you, even if the resulting photograph would be washed out by excessive exposure or underexposed to the point of near-blackness.

As with Aperture Priority mode, the range of available apertures in Manual exposure mode is limited as the lens is zoomed in to greater levels of magnification. Also, the range of shutter speeds has certain limits, although the camera's slowest shutter speed of 15 seconds is available only in this mode. The slowest shutter speed available at ISO 800 is 2 seconds; at ISO 3200, the slowest is 1/2 second. If ISO is set to 100, the shutter speed of 15 seconds is available. In addition, as discussed above, if ISO is set to Auto in Manual exposure mode, the camera actually uses an ISO setting of 100, so the shutter speed of 15 seconds is available when ISO is set to Auto, in this shooting mode only.

Auto Flash mode is not available with Manual exposure mode.

Scene Modes

The Coolpix P600 offers several of what I will call scene modes. The terminology can be a bit confusing, because the camera's menus and documentation use the word "scene" in several similar and overlapping contexts. First, there are three scene modes that occupy slots marked by icons on the mode dial: Landscape, Night Portrait, and Night Landscape. Next, there is another slot on the mode dial marked SCENE. When you select that setting, you can press the Menu button to the lower left of the multi selector and scroll through a list of 17 specific scene settings: Portrait, Sports, Party/Indoor, Beach, Snow, Sunset, Dusk/Dawn, Close-up, Food, Museum, Fireworks Show, Black and White Copy, Backlighting, Easy Panorama, Pet Portrait, Moon, and Bird-watching. Finally, there is an 18th entry on this list, which actually is the first entry at the top of the list: Scene Auto Selector. I will discuss all of these scene settings individually, but first I will provide some general remarks about these shooting mode options.

Scene modes are rather different from the other shooting modes I have discussed up to this point. These modes do not have a single defining feature, such as permitting control over one or more aspects of exposure. Instead, when you select a scene shooting mode, you are in effect telling the camera what sort of environment the picture is being taken in, and what type of image you are looking for, and you are letting the camera make a group of decisions as to what settings to use to produce that result.

Some photographers may not like the scene modes because these settings take some creative decisions away from you and limit your options in some ways. For example, you will find that your Shooting menu options are severely limited when the mode dial is turned to the SCENE setting or any of the scene modes with slots on the mode dial, such as Night Landscape. For example, you cannot set the white balance, but must rely on the camera's Auto

White Balance setting, which may not always properly evaluate the existing light source. In most cases, you cannot select features such as continuous shooting, and you can't choose a metering mode or an ISO setting.

Despite the limitations, though, I have found the various scene settings to be useful in certain situations. Remember that you don't have to use these settings only for their labeled purposes; you may find that some of them are well-suited for shooting scenarios you are regularly faced with. For example, you may find the Sports setting works well for shots of children at play, or that the Sunset setting, which emphasizes red hues, is great for images in a particular garden that is rich with reddish plants and flowers. The Bird-watching setting can work well for taking images of various sorts of wildlife, not just birds.

You need to know something about each of these options to decide whether it's one you would want to select. In general, a given scene setting carries with it a variety of values, including things like focus mode, flash status, range of shutter speeds, sensitivity to various colors, and others. I will discuss the complete list of scene settings so you can make informed choices. I will first discuss the settings that have their own slots on the mode dial, followed by the settings that are grouped under the SCENE setting on the dial.

LANDSCAPE

This is the setting with a mountain-range icon on the mode dial next to the EFFECTS setting, as seen in Figure 3-19. With many other cameras, including the Nikon Coolpix P500, a predecessor to the P600, this shooting mode was one of those that are selected through the Shooting menu when the dial is set to the SCENE setting. With the P600, though, the Landscape setting occupies its own slot on the mode dial, perhaps in recognition of the usefulness of this setting.

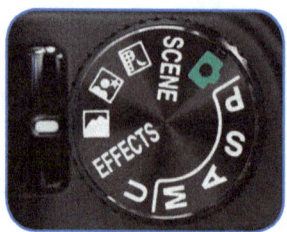

Figure 3-19. Landscape Mode

I use Landscape mode often, and I appreciate that it is easy to twist the mode dial to choose it. When you do, you can then go to the Landscape item on the Shooting menu, shown in Figure 3-20, and select one of two options from the Shooting menu: in this case, Noise Reduction Burst or Single Shot, as seen in Figure 3-21.

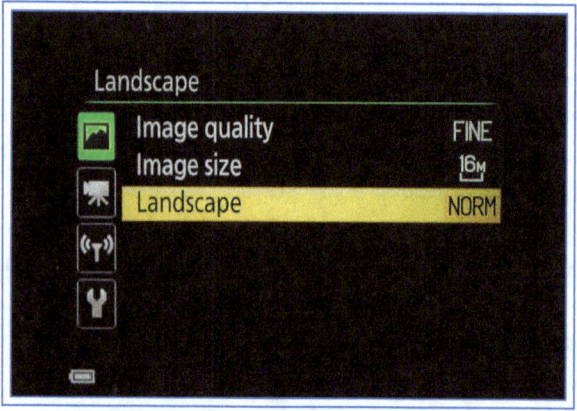

Figure 3-20. Landscape Menu Item

If you select Noise Reduction Burst, the camera will take a rapid series of shots at a relatively high ISO setting and merge them in the camera into a final image. The camera's internal processing will combine the individual shots so as to reduce the visual "noise" that results from using higher ISO settings. The final image will be cropped slightly because of this processing, so less of the scene will be included in the image. This setting is useful when you are taking photographs in subdued light, to reduce the noise effects caused by a higher ISO setting.

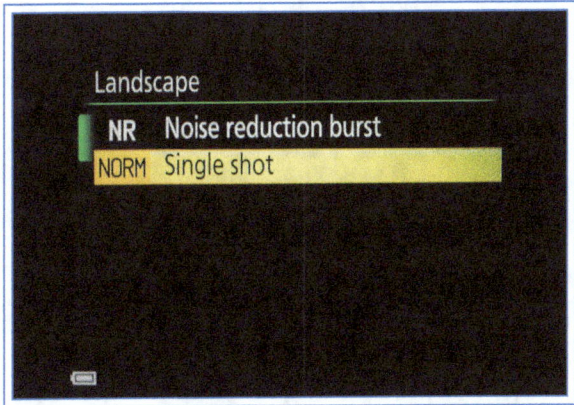

Figure 3-21. Single Shot Setting for Landscape Mode

If, instead, you select the Single Shot option, the camera will operate as you would expect for a normal Landscape setting —it will take just one shot at a lower ISO setting, which likely will result in a sharper picture than one taken with the Noise Reduction Burst setting. The example in Figure 3-22 was taken using the Single Shot setting with the camera handheld.

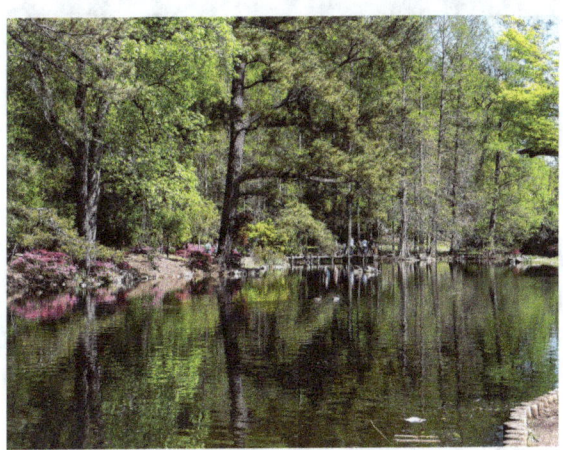

Figure 3-22. Landscape Example Image

NIGHT PORTRAIT

This mode is signified on the mode dial by an icon showing a human face under the stars, as seen in Figure 3-23.

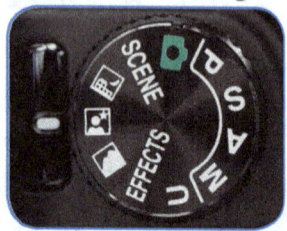

Figure 3-23. Night Portrait Mode

With this setting, the camera will use the built-in flash. The subject presumably will be close to the camera and, unlike a landscape scene, can be illuminated by the flash. The camera will select Slow Sync for the flash mode, and will not let you change it. (If you haven't popped up the flash unit, the camera will display an error message until you do.)

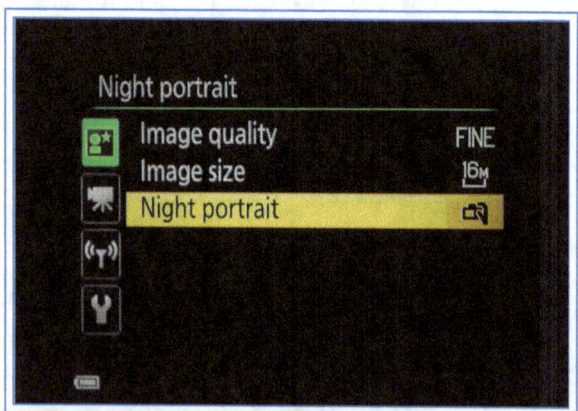

Figure 3-24. Night Portrait Menu Item

From the Night Portrait item on the Shooting menu, shown in Figure 3-24, you can select either Hand-held or Tripod, as seen in Figure 3-25. If you select Hand-held, the camera may use a faster shutter speed than with the Tripod setting, to counteract camera shake. You can use the self-timer (including the Smile Timer) or exposure compensation, but you cannot change the focus method.

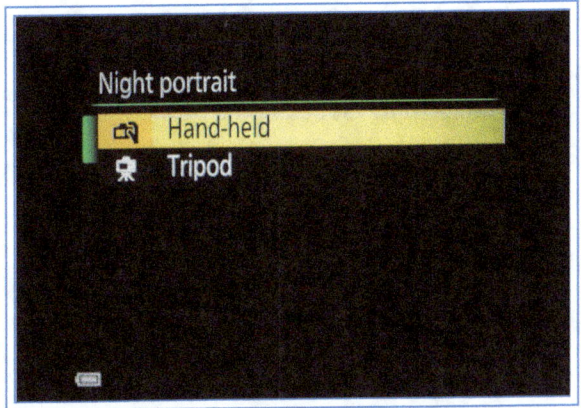

Figure 3-25. Hand-held Setting for Night Portrait Mode

The camera uses its face detection circuitry, and attempts to find a face to focus on. In Figure 3-26, I used this setting for a portrait indoors on a cloudy day.

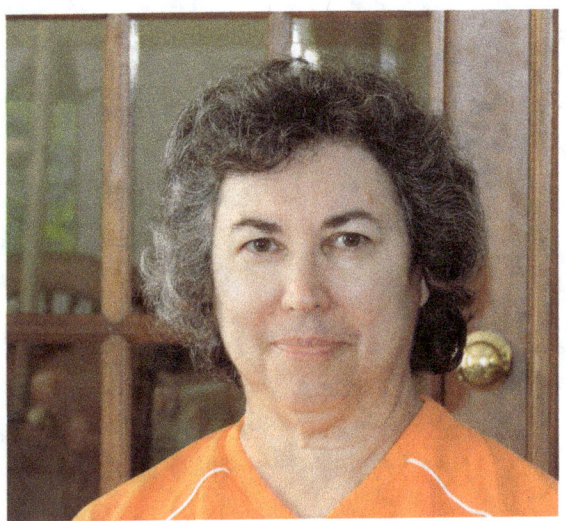

Figure 3-26. Night Portrait Example Image

If you choose Tripod from the menu, the camera will take a single shot at a slower shutter speed. It still will use the flash.

NIGHT LANDSCAPE

This mode, symbolized by a crescent moon above a building, appears on the mode dial just below the SCENE setting, as seen in Figure 3-27.

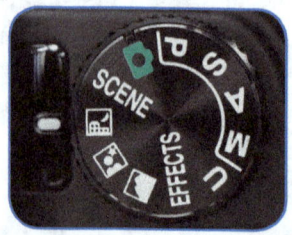

Figure 3-27. Night Landscape Mode

It is intended for use without flash at night in areas that are not brightly lighted. When you select this shooting mode with the mode dial, the Shooting menu includes an option called Night Landscape, shown in Figure 3-28.

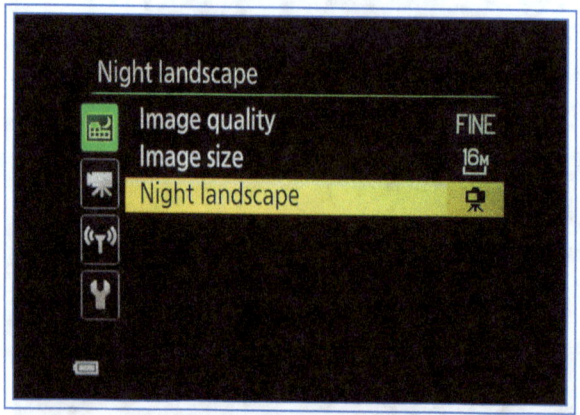

Figure 3-28. Night Landscape Menu Item

That option has two sub-options, as with Night Portrait: Hand-held and Tripod. To choose one of these options, press the Menu button, then select Night Landscape, the bottom item on the brief menu list that appears. Then press the OK button or the Right direction button, and choose either Hand-held or Tripod, as shown in Figure 3-29.

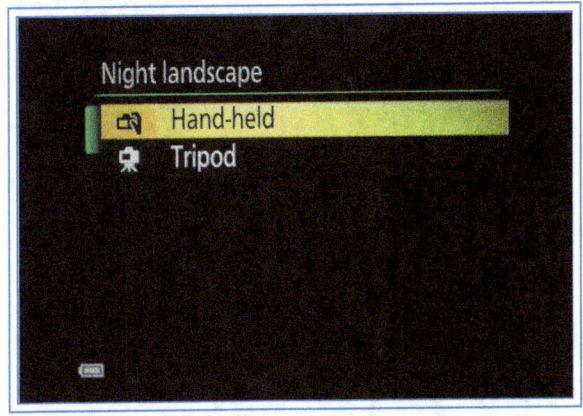

Figure 3-29. Hand-held Setting for Night Landscape Mode

With Hand-held, the camera will take a continuous group of pictures and combine them in the camera into a single image, to overcome the effects of the high ISO setting the camera uses to take a good exposure in dim light without flash. A single image could be degraded from the visual "noise" that results from the use of high ISO values; by combining several images, the camera can create a single image using the best aspects of each, and can digitally smooth away the noise. You should try to hold the camera as steady as possible when shooting, but it will use a relatively fast shutter speed if at all possible to avoid blur from camera shake.

If you choose the Tripod option from the menu, the camera will use a slower shutter speed and a lower ISO setting, to minimize noise. The use of the tripod will avoid the effects of camera shake. Of course, this setting is useful only if you actually attach the camera firmly to a tripod.

I took the image in Figure 3-30 with the P600 on a tripod after sunset on a partly cloudy evening. The camera exposed this image at f/3.3 for 1/15 second at ISO 100, to get the maximum quality.

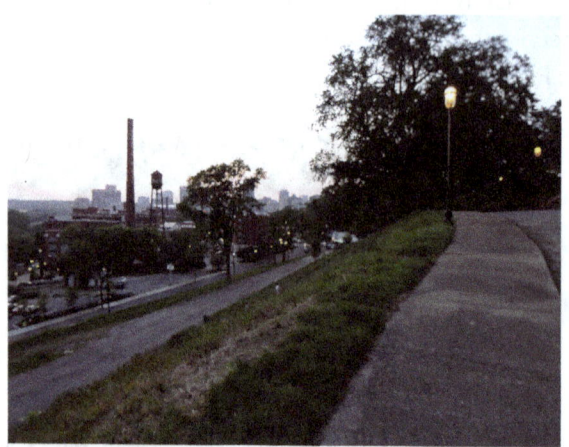

Figure 3-30. Night Landscape Image Taken Using Tripod

THE SCENE SETTING ON THE MODE DIAL

Turning the mode dial to the SCENE position, as shown in Figure 3-31, gives you access to 18 choices of settings, including Scene Auto Selector and 17 specific scene types.

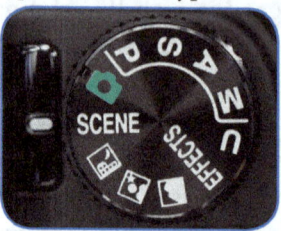

Figure 3-31. Scene Mode

You can select any one of these choices by pressing the Menu button and selecting a scene setting from the menu list, the first screen of which is shown in Figure 3-32.

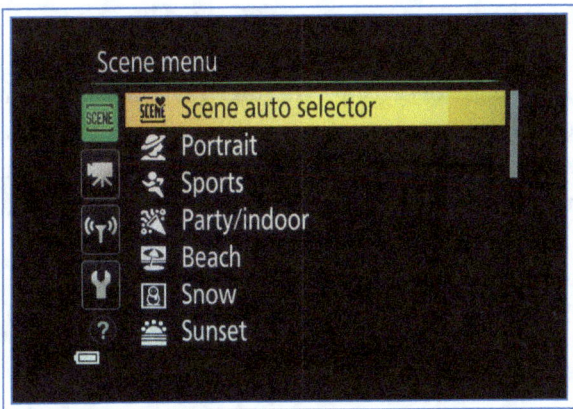

Figure 3-32. First Screen of Scene Menu

While that list is displayed, you can press the zoom lever on top of the camera toward the T position, where there also is a question mark on the camera's top. In this situation, the zoom lever activates an information screen, like the one shown in Figure 3-33, with a brief description of how the currently highlighted Scene mode setting can be used.

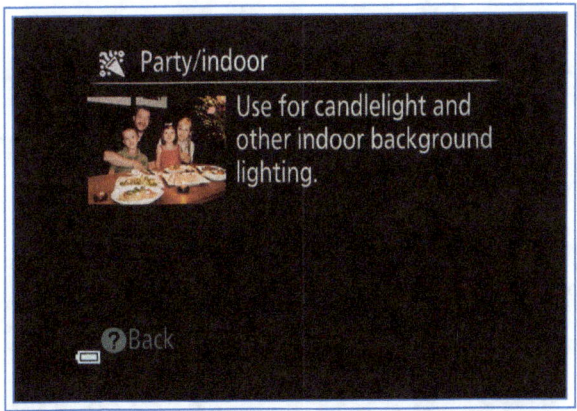

Figure 3-33. Information Screen for Party/Indoor Setting

When you select any of the 18 Scene mode settings, the Shooting menu offers few other choices; that is, when you have made a selection such as Portrait or Sunset from the Scene mode menu, you cannot make any further choices using the Shooting menu other than Image Size and Image Quality. The camera will make all other settings as it deems appropriate for the given selection. So, these Scene mode settings are convenient if you are faced with a certain type of photographic situation and you want the camera to make reasonable choices for that situation, but you have very little control over the camera's other settings. Following are details about each of the types, including what sorts of settings the camera chooses for each. I will include sample images for most of the selections.

Scene Auto Selector

If you choose this first option, the camera will analyze the live view using its digital circuitry and try to determine the most appropriate shooting mode to use from among these choices: Portrait, Landscape, Night Portrait, Night Landscape, Close-up, Backlighting, and Other Scenes.

If the camera can identify what appears to be a scene calling for one of the listed settings, it displays an icon for that setting in the upper left corner of the screen.

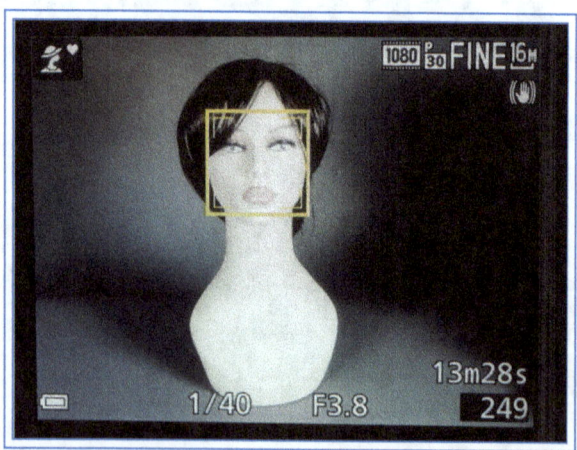

Figure 3-34. Portrait Detection with Scene Auto Selector

For example, in Figure 3-34, the camera properly identified the view of a mannequin's head as calling for Portrait mode, represented by the icon in the upper left of the screen. The heart icon next to the Portrait icon indicates the use of Scene Auto Selector. With the Portrait and Night Portrait options, the camera displays a slightly different icon with a number 1, as shown in Figure 3-35 for the Portrait setting, if it detects more than two subjects.

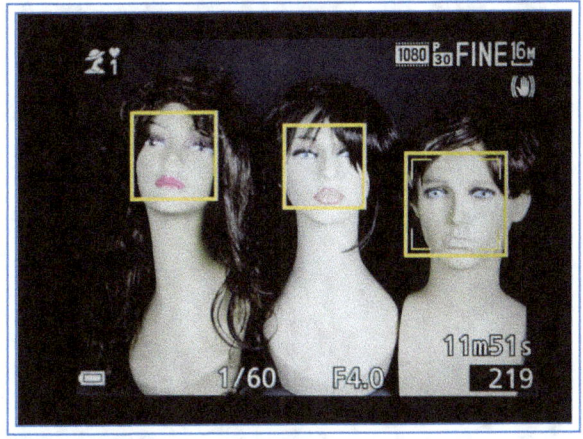

Figure 3-35. Multiple Faces Detected with Scene Auto Selector

With the Backlighting option, it will use an icon with the number 1 if it detects human subjects as opposed to non-human ones.

In Scene Auto Selector mode, you can use exposure compensation and the self-timer, but you cannot select an autofocus mode or a flash mode. The camera prompts you to raise the flash, and it uses Auto Flash mode, meaning the camera will decide whether or not to fire the flash.

If the camera chooses a scene type that you don't like, you of course have the option of using the mode dial to select another mode, such as Auto, Program, or a specific scene mode.

Portrait

With the Portrait setting, the camera automatically sets itself for face detection, which means it looks for human faces and focuses on the one closest to the camera. It automatically applies skin softening, which smooths out wrinkles and other harsh features on the skin. However, you cannot control the amount of skin softening or turn it off. There are no Shooting menu options with this Scene setting, but you can pop up the flash and select a flash mode. You cannot make any changes to the focus mode, but you can use the self-timer and exposure compensation.

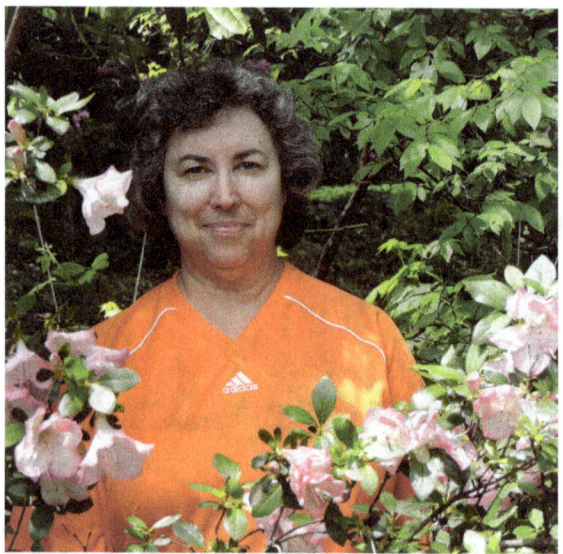

Figure 3-36. Portrait Example Image

Figure 3-36 is an example of an image I took using a tripod without the flash.

Sports

The Sports setting is intended for fast-moving subjects. The camera sets itself for continuous shooting and takes a series of as many as seven images at a rate of up to seven frames per second when you hold down the shutter button, depending on conditions. The flash is forced off, and focus and exposure are locked when the first image is taken, to increase the speed of the sequence of shots. You can use manual focus and exposure compensation, but you cannot use the self-timer, and the Shooting menu is not available. This mode is useful when you need to stop action in relatively bright lighting conditions. In Figure 3-37, I used this setting to capture an image of bicycle racers.

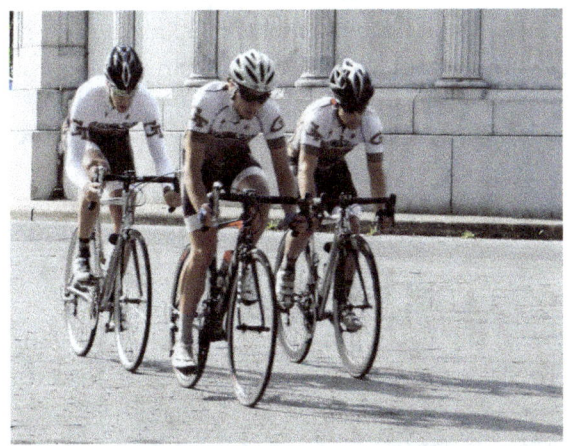

Figure 3-37. Sports Example Image

I found the Sports setting useful for stopping action and getting a fast series of shots, but I also found that this setting limited my options, because the camera takes a long time to recover after taking a rapid burst of shots. So, if another opportunity for a good image came up while the camera was still writing the burst images to the memory card, I had to wait. Be aware of this limitation and plan accordingly. If you expect to need a second burst of shots within about 30 seconds after the first burst, you should use a different setting, such as Program mode, and use single shooting or, possibly, low-speed burst shooting and take only one or two shots, so the camera will be ready for more action quickly.

Party/Indoor

This setting is meant for indoor photos of people and rooms. In most cases, you should pop up the flash; the flash mode is initially set to Auto with Red-eye Reduction, but you can change to another flash mode if you want to. If you don't want to use flash, you can leave the flash unit retracted, in which case the P600 will try to use a relatively slow shutter speed. In that case, you should hold the camera very steady or place it on a tripod. (Realistically, though, you probably are not going to be setting up a tripod for candid or impromptu pictures at a party.) The camera will focus on the subject at the center of the frame. In the example shown in Figure 3-38, which I took without a tripod, the camera boosted the ISO to 800 and shot at 1/30 second using an aperture of f/4.5.

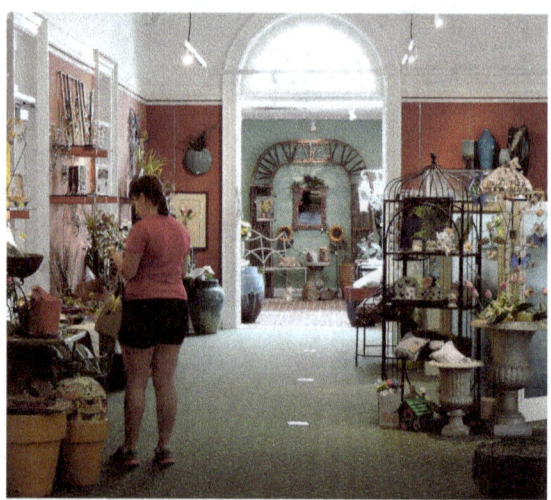

Figure 3-38. Party/Indoor Example Image

With the Party/Indoor setting, there are no Shooting menu options available. You can use exposure compensation or the self-timer, but you cannot change the focus method.

Beach

With this selection, the camera optimizes its settings for the beach, where there is likely to be bright sunlight reflected from the ground. In this environment, the camera will have a tendency to underexpose the subject because the exposure meter will be measuring the brightness of the beach. If you pop up the flash, the camera will set the flash mode to Auto in order to light the subject sufficiently, and it is quite likely the flash will fire in order to enhance the brightness of the subject so it will be clearly visible against the glare of the background. You can change the flash mode if you want to. However, you do not have to pop up the flash when using the Beach setting. You can use either macro focus or normal autofocus, but you cannot select manual focus or use infinity autofocus. You can use the self-timer or exposure compensation.

Snow

The Snow setting is similar to Beach, in that the camera may use the flash to compensate for the brightness of the snowy background, if you have chosen to pop up the flash unit. The camera appears to use a greater amount of reddish hue than with the beach setting, as a balance against the bluish color temperature of a snowy scene. Other settings are similar to those for the Beach setting.

I took a few test shots of general outdoor scenes, not shown here, using both the Beach and the Snow setting. I found that the Beach setting resulted in slightly darker images, but otherwise the results were very similar.

Sunset

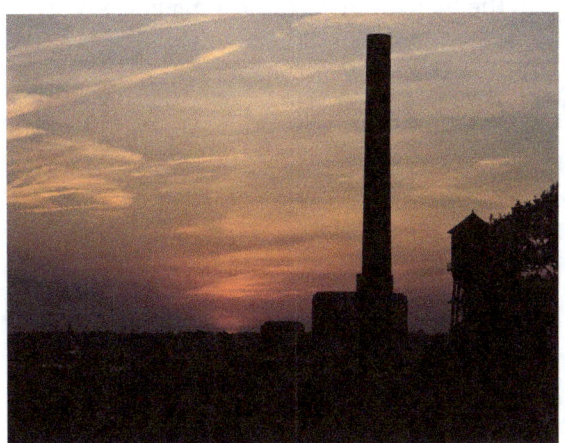

Figure 3-39. Sunset Example Image

With this setting, the P600 disables the flash, but you can use the self-timer and exposure compensation. You cannot change the focus mode from normal autofocus. The camera processes the shot to emphasize reddish tones in the rays of the late afternoon or early morning sun. Of course, you don't have to limit the use of this (or any other) scene setting by its label; if you are photographing autumn leaves, red-brick buildings, or other subjects with reds you want to emphasize, consider this setting as a tool that may be of use. For Figure 3-39, I found a good location to capture the sunset on a day when clouds enhanced the scene, so I settled for a conventional sunset shot.

Dusk/Dawn

If you are taking pictures before sunrise or after sunset, this is a setting to consider. With the Dusk/Dawn setting activated, the camera forces the flash off and intensifies the colors to add interest to images that otherwise might seem flat or washed out because of the low intensity of the available light. This scene type has the same restrictions as Sunset mode: You cannot adjust most settings on the camera, though you can use exposure compensation and the self-timer. The primary feature of this option is that it emphasizes the purplish or bluish tones that may be present in the twilight or early morning hours.

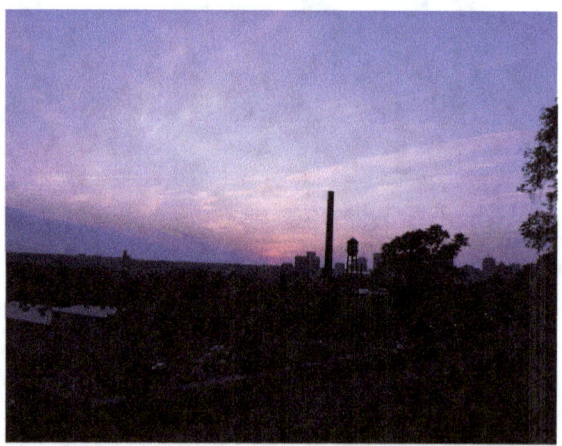

Figure 3-40. Dusk/Dawn Example Image

In Figure 3-40, I used this setting in the same general area as the sunset shot in the previous image, some time after sunset.

You can see how the camera processed these two settings with dramatically different color schemes.

Close-up

With this setting, the camera switches into macro focus mode to capture images of items close to the lens. If the lens is zoomed in to a telephoto position, when you select the Close-up setting the lens will automatically zoom back out to a position that allows the camera to focus on the subject. (You can, however, zoom the lens back in if you want to.) You can use the self-timer or exposure compensation; you cannot, naturally enough, change the focus mode, which is set on macro.

The camera also sets AF Area Mode to Manual (Spot). This means you can control exactly where the focus point is placed. To do this, press the OK button in the center of the multi selector, then press the direction buttons on the multi selector to move the focus area around the screen so it covers the point where you want the camera to focus. You also can turn the multi selector dial to move the frame around the screen; it will move up and down as it reaches the right or left edge of the display.

If you need to use one of the direction buttons for its other function (self-timer, flash if available, or exposure compensation), press the OK button again, and those functions will be available. Press the OK button once more if you need to move the focus area another time. The camera also uses continuous autofocus with this setting, so it continues to adjust the focus until you press the shutter button halfway down to lock in the focus.

As with several other scene types, with Close-up the Shooting menu gives you the option of choosing Noise Reduction Burst or Single Shot. You can choose one of these options by going to the Close-up item on the Scene menu. With Noise Reduction Burst, the camera takes a rapid set of shots to counter the effects of high ISO noise and forces the flash off. With the Single Shot setting, the camera takes just one image and lets you pop up the flash and select a flash mode. The camera also uses processing to sharpen the image's outline with added contrast.

You could, if you want, use another shooting mode, such as Program or Auto, and just select macro focusing using the focus button (Down button). But, if you want to quickly set up the camera for close-up shooting, it can be convenient to have this scene setting available. You should hold the camera very steady to avoid blurring the image. Use of a tripod or monopod is the best practice, but of course that is often impractical.

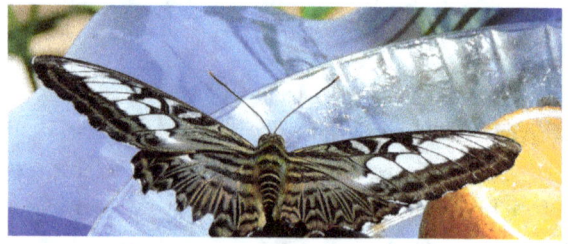

Figure 3-41. Close-up Example Image

In Figure 3-41, I handheld the camera as close as I could to capture an image of a butterfly in an indoor exhibition.

Food

This setting is similar to the Close-up setting, discussed above, though it does not offer Noise Reduction Burst mode; only single shots are available and there are no menu options. The camera switches to macro focus mode and zooms back if necessary so it can focus on a nearby subject. It turns on Manual (Spot) for the AF Area Mode, so you can move the focus point around, and it uses continuous autofocus. The flash is disabled, but you can use exposure compensation or the self-timer. The one major difference from Close-up mode (apart from the lack of the burst option) is that, in Food mode, the camera places a scale of colors at the right side of the screen, as shown in Figure 3-42, and allows you to adjust the hues of your images by moving the pointer up and down along the scale using the command dial.

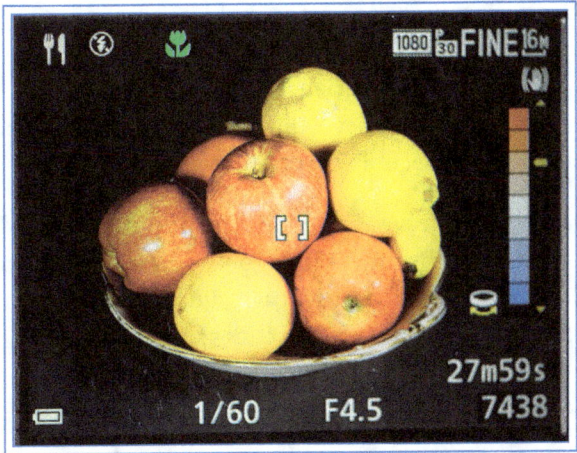

Figure 3-42. Color Scale on Display for Food Setting

Move the pointer toward the top for more reddish hues, and toward the bottom for more bluish ones.

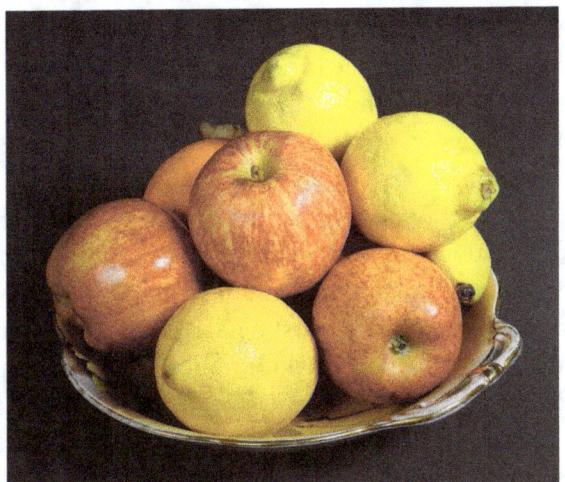

Figure 3-43. Food Example Image

In Figure 3-43, the final image resulting from setting the hue slider to the third position, I used the slider to emphasize the color of the apples in the bowl of fruit.

This setting is suited for people who are in the habit of documenting their meals through food blogs or photographic diaries of their dining experiences. With the hue slider, you can experiment until you achieve the desired effect of emphasizing the colors of meats, vegetables, or other aspects of the meal.

Unless you want to leave a hue adjustment permanently in place, be sure to return the hue slider to the neutral position when you're done shooting, because the adjustments you make will remain in place the next time you choose the Food setting, even if the camera has been turned off in the meantime.

Museum

The Museum setting is useful when you are shooting in a dimly lit place where flash is prohibited and use of a tripod is prohibited or impractical.

The camera turns the flash off and will not fire it even if the unit is popped up. The camera also disables the autofocus assist lamp, which could be distracting in a museum setting. You can use exposure compensation or the self-timer, and you can switch to macro focus if you want. Also, the P600 activates the Best Shot Selector function. With this option, which normally is controlled with the continuous-shooting option on the Shooting menu, the camera takes 10 shots in rapid succession while you hold down the shutter release button, and automatically saves the one shot that is sharpest and has the most detail. In this way, even though you are taking pictures handheld in dim light with no flash, you have a good chance of getting a usable image because the camera will take multiple shots and discard the ones that exhibit motion blur. For the image shown in Figure 3-44, taken handheld in dim lighting at an art museum, the camera set the ISO to 720 to permit the use of a reasonably fast shutter speed of 1/30 second.

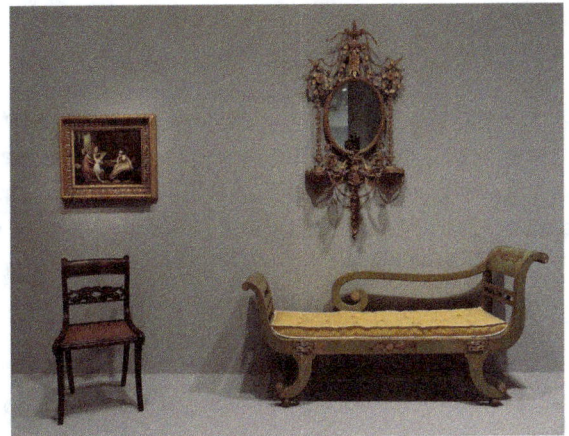

Figure 3-44. Museum Example Image

Here again, as with most of the Scene mode settings, don't let the name of this setting exclude it from consideration for other purposes. You might want to use it in any dimly lit area when you can't (or don't want to) use flash.

Fireworks Show

With this setting, the camera sets the focus to infinity and uses a shutter speed of 4 seconds so you can capture a long burst of color from a fireworks display. The camera also increases the vividness of the colors and uses a low ISO setting to maximize image quality. The flash is forced off and you cannot use exposure compensation or the self-timer, and you can't change the focus method. The camera restricts the maximum telephoto zoom range to no more than about 500mm. You should set the camera on a tripod if possible, or hold it firmly on a fence post or other solid object as an alternative.

Black and White Copy

This setting lets you copy black-and-white text, like words on a blackboard or whiteboard, or perhaps on a poster. It can be a handy way to capture a document you need to carry with you, such as a shopping list or itinerary. In effect, your P600 becomes a very portable photocopier; you can copy the item quickly and crisply, and enlarge the view on the screen.

When you choose this setting, the camera switches into a black-and-white mode and captures the image in monochrome format. The focus is initially set to normal autofocus, but you can switch into macro autofocus if you are copying something close up, such as words on a sheet of paper. You also can use the flash, exposure compensation, or the self-timer if you want.

Of course, this mode is of no use to you if you need to record any colors at all, such as colors of highlighting of the text, or of images that accompany the text. For those situations, you might want to try the Close-up scene type. Again, don't let its name limit your use of the Black and White Copy setting; you might want to try it for street photography, as discussed in Chapter 9.

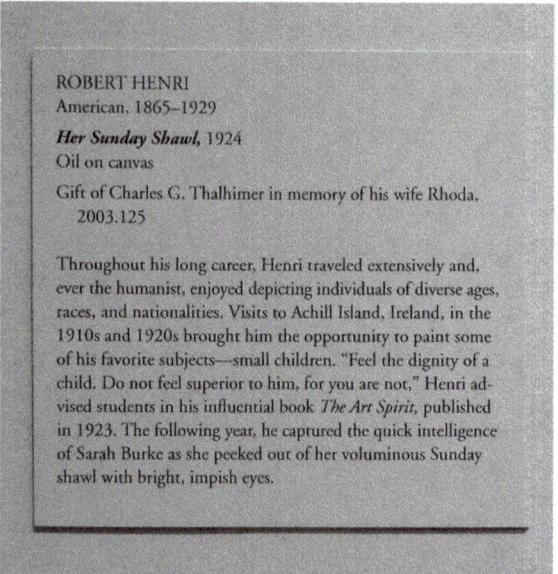

Figure 3-45. Black and White Copy Example Image

In Figure 3-45, I used this setting to record information about an interesting painting on exhibit in the local art museum.

Backlighting/HDR

This mode is designed for difficult lighting situations—in particular, when there is bright light present, but it is behind the subject. Nikon calls this mode simply "Backlighting," but its single sub-mode is HDR, which, as discussed below, is an important feature for modern cameras, so I have added HDR to the heading here for easier identification.

When this mode is selected, you have four sub-options selectable by pressing the Menu button: HDR Off, or HDR Level 1, 2 or 3, as shown in Figure 3-46.

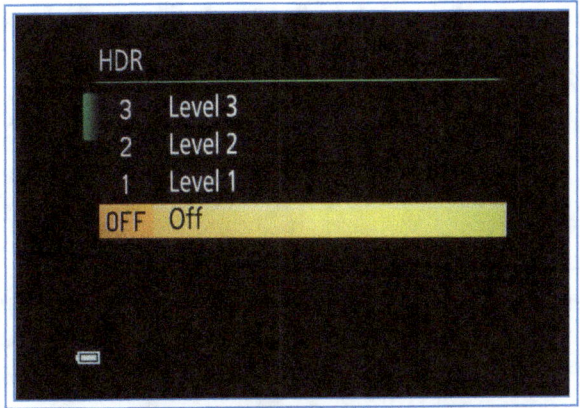

Figure 3-46. Backlighting/HDR Options Screen

If you choose the default value, HDR Off, the camera requires that you raise the flash, and it forces the flash to fire to overcome the shadows caused by your subject's being lighted from behind.

If, instead, you choose HDR at Level 1, 2, or 3, the camera uses a different approach. With this setting, the camera internally performs its own version of HDR, or high dynamic range, processing. In case you haven't encountered this phenomenon before, HDR has been a popular photographic style in recent years. Essentially, HDR photography uses special techniques to deal with subjects that include areas of extreme contrast between light and dark. For example, if a building is partly lit by bright sunshine and partly hidden in deep shadow, the contrast is likely to be so great that a photograph cannot depict both parts of the building with normal exposure. Either one area of the image will be much too bright, so highlights are blown out, or one area will be much too dark, so details are swallowed in the shadows.

In the past, HDR was carried out in post-processing, using software such as Photoshop or special programs such as PhotoAcute or Photomatix Pro. The photographer would take multiple exposures of the scene at different exposure levels, some exposing dark parts of the scene properly and some exposing bright parts properly. When combined in HDR software, the images could be blended together to result in a final composite image that shows all parts of the image nicely exposed. These HDR composite images often have an unnatural or surrealistic appearance, because it is obvious that a "normal" photograph could not include such a wide range of well-exposed areas.

With many modern cameras, including the Coolpix P600, the manufacturer includes programming that lets you take multiple photographs that are combined inside the camera to result in an HDR-like image. With the P600, I would not say the result quite matches the "true" HDR you can obtain through software, but it does make a noticeable difference. Here is how it works.

When you use the HDR setting on the P600, you first select the degree of HDR processing the camera will use: Level 1, 2, or 3, as shown earlier in Figure 3-46. The higher the level, the greater the HDR effect. With all of these levels, the camera turns the flash unit off. When you shoot using these settings, you should hold the camera very steady, or, ideally, place it on a tripod. When you press the shutter button, you will hear multiple clicks as the camera takes several exposures. It will then create and save two final images. The first of these images will be one taken with the Active D-Lighting feature turned on, to brighten shadowy areas of the image to bring out details. (Active D-Lighting is discussed in Chapter 4.) The second image will be an HDR composite that contains the best-exposed parts of multiple images, thereby expanding the dynamic range of the shot.

To illustrate the effects of this setting, I took several shots of a duck figure indoors in front of a bright window. The first shot, Figure 3-47, was taken in Program mode with no special settings, to show the contrast between the bright and shadowed areas.

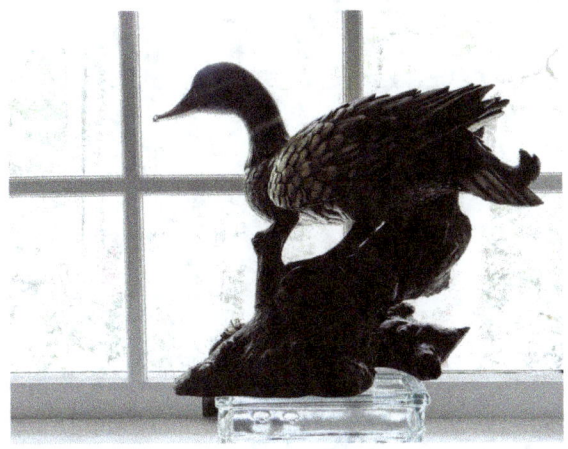

Figure 3-47. HDR Series: Program Mode, Normal Settings

Figure 3-48 was taken in Backlighting mode, with HDR turned off. In this mode, the camera always uses flash.

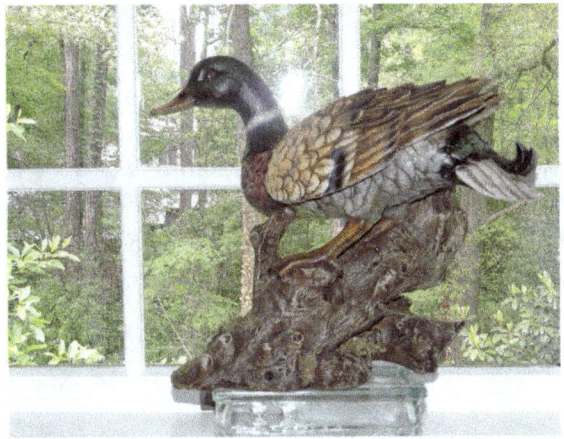

Figure 3-48. HDR Series: Backlighting Mode with Flash

The next image, Figure 3-49, was taken with the HDR setting turned on at Level 3. (This is the actual composite shot created in the camera from multiple exposures; as noted above, with this setting the camera also saves one image with HDR turned off.)

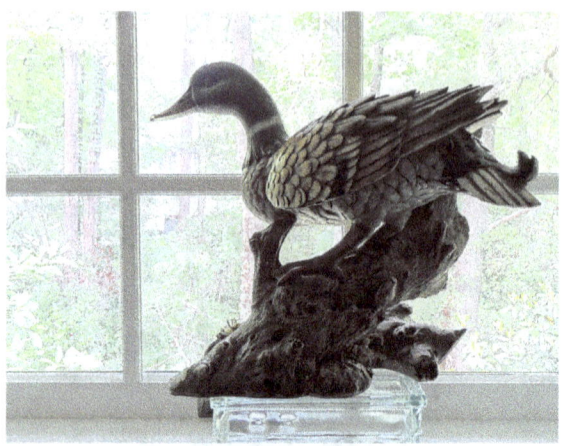

Figure 3-49. HDR Series: HDR Level 3

Finally, Figure 3-50 is a composite image created in Photomatix Pro, an HDR processing program. I took several images at different settings in Manual exposure mode to use as the basis for this composite. In my opinion, the P600's in-camera processing did a good job of reducing the contrast between the light and dark areas, but it did not quite match the performance of Photomatix Pro, especially when, as here, I took several shots in Manual exposure mode, giving the software a wide variety of exposure values to work with. Another option for taking shots to use for this purpose is the exposure bracketing feature of the P600, which I will discuss in Chapter 4. With that option, the camera takes a series of three shots at different exposure levels; you can then combine those shots using your HDR software to create the composite image.

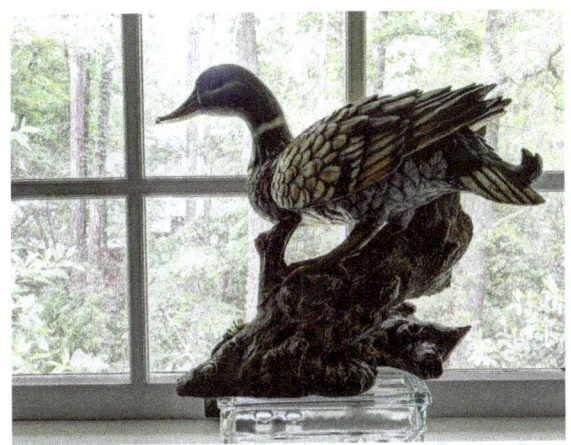

Figure 3-50. HDR Series: Composite Image from Photomatix Pro

The HDR setting in Backlighting mode is an excellent tool to have available, because it is not always practical to take multiple shots to be combined using HDR software. If you are taking photographs in an area that is partly shaded and partly sunny, or otherwise has contrasting lighting, you can take advantage of this setting to improve the overall appearance of the image.

Easy Panorama

When you select this option from the Scene menu, you are presented with a sub-menu with two options—Normal (180°) or Wide (360°), as shown in Figure 3-51. Make your selection and then aim the camera at the first part of your panoramic scene. For example, if you are shooting a panorama of a wide mountain range, you may want to aim at the far left side of the range. Press the shutter button halfway down to lock in focus and exposure; the camera will automatically zoom back to the wide-angle position, and will not let you zoom in. In addition, the flash is disabled. You can use exposure compensation, though.

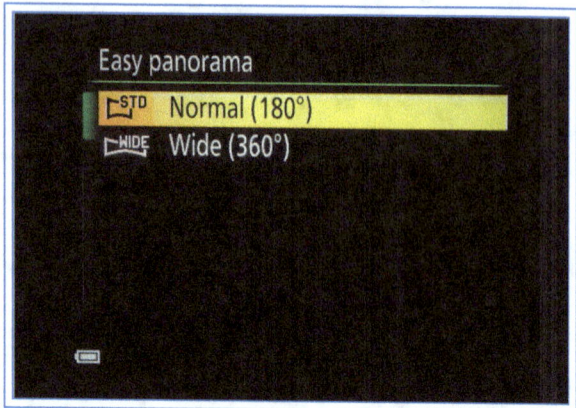

Figure 3-51. Easy Panorama Options Screen

When you are satisfied with the initial view, press the shutter button and release it; you don't need to hold it down while the panorama shooting proceeds. The camera will display the message shown in Figure 3-52, telling you to press the shutter button and start moving the camera in your chosen direction.

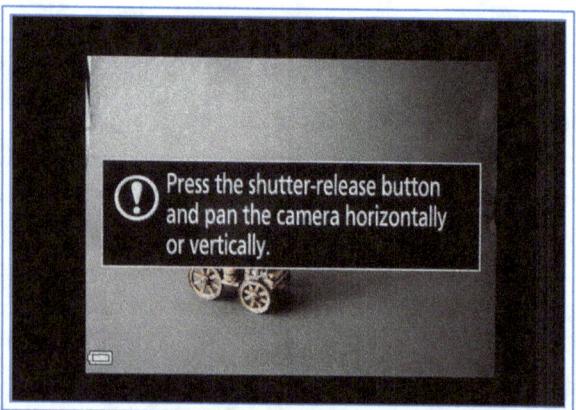

Figure 3-52. Prompt Message for Easy Panorama Setting

Hold the camera steady and level as you sweep it in the direction of your shot—in this case, from left to right—until you have covered the entire scene. The camera will detect the direction you are moving in, and it will automatically stop shooting when it detects the end point of the 180-degree shot. It will display a yellow progress bar at the bottom of the screen, as shown in Figure 3-53. You should take about 15 seconds to complete this arc.

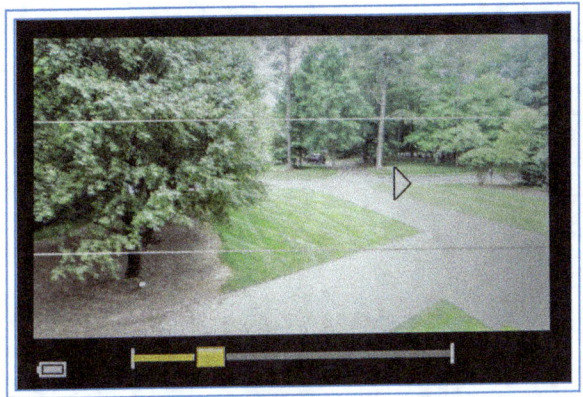

Figure 3-53. Easy Panorama Progress Bar

You can shoot the panorama moving either left to right or right to left, or you can shoot it vertically, moving from low to high or vice-versa. If you select the Wide option, you can move the camera through a complete circle to cover an entire scene. In that case, you should take about 30 seconds to complete the entire circuit.

When shooting panoramas, try to avoid including rapidly moving people, vehicles, or other objects, because they may end up appearing in multiple positions in the panorama.

When you are done, you can view the whole panorama on the screen in a small size by pressing the Playback button. To see the panorama scroll by on the screen, press the OK button, and it will scroll in the same direction in which it was taken.

The sample panorama shown in Figure 3-54 was shot using the Easy Panorama setting with the Coolpix P600 handheld, shooting from left to right. The image in Figure 3-55 was taken by moving the camera vertically.

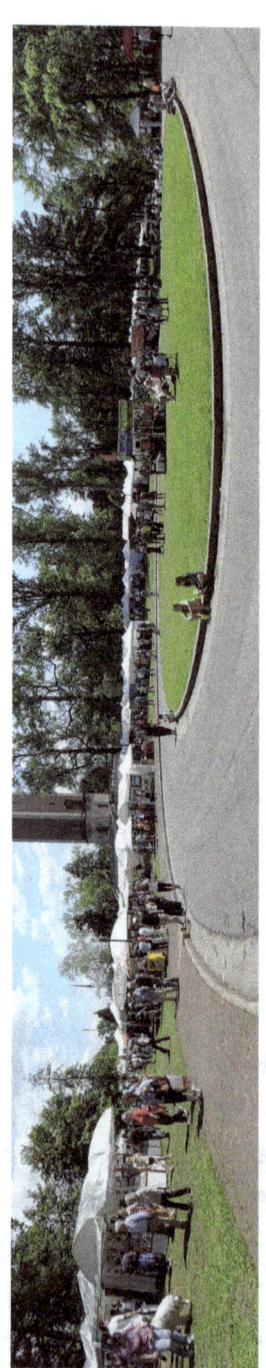

Figure 3-54. Panorama, Arts in the Park Festival, Richmond, Virginia

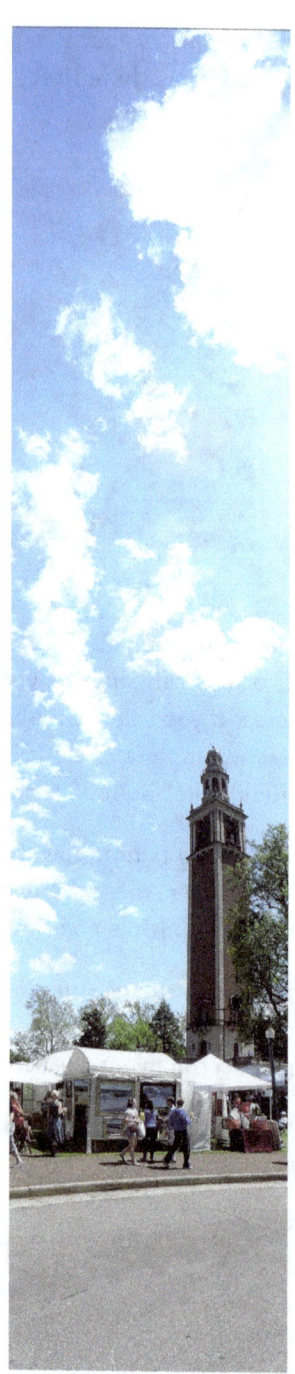

Figure 3-55. Panorama, Carillon, Byrd Park, Richmond, Virginia.

Pet Portrait

This setting is designed for shooting pictures of the family dog or cat. With this option, the camera turns on continuous shooting and activates a feature called "Pet Portrait Auto Release." With this feature, the camera looks for the face of a pet, and, if it detects one, it takes three pictures in quick succession to try to capture a good expression. If the camera does not display the double-bordered yellow frame that indicates face detection, you can press the shutter button to take the image when you're ready. For Figure 3-56, I used this setting to capture an image of an alert border collie at a sheep-herding demonstration.

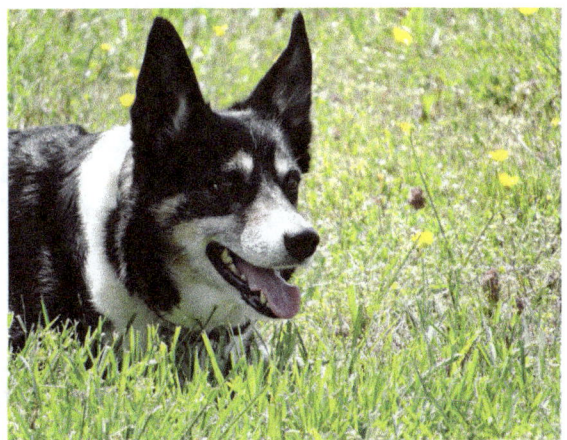

Figure 3-56. Pet Portrait Example Image

The default setting with this option is continuous shooting, but you can change that by selecting Single from the Shooting menu. You also can change the Pet Portrait Auto Release setting, which is turned on by default. To turn it off, press the self-timer button (Left button), and select the Off setting, rather than the icon of a pet's face. If you turn this setting off but leave continuous shooting turned on, the camera will take up to five shots when you press and hold the shutter button.

With the Pet Portrait setting, use of the flash is disabled, but you can use exposure compensation.

Moon

The Coolpix P600, with its great optical zoom range, is a natural for shooting images of the moon without having to attach the camera to a telescope. With the Moon setting, Nikon has provided a shortcut to using appropriate settings for these shots.

With this option, the camera does not allow you to make any settings from the Shooting menu. It disables the flash and turns on the self-timer to 2 seconds so the camera will have some time to settle down after you press the shutter button, to avoid camera shake. You can change this setting to 10 seconds or turn the self-timer off if you want. You can use exposure compensation. Focus is fixed in the center of the frame, at the infinity setting.

The camera also uses two special settings to help with this type of shot. First, as shown in Figure 3-57, when the lens is zoomed out to its wide-angle setting, the camera places a small rectangle in the center of the focus frame.

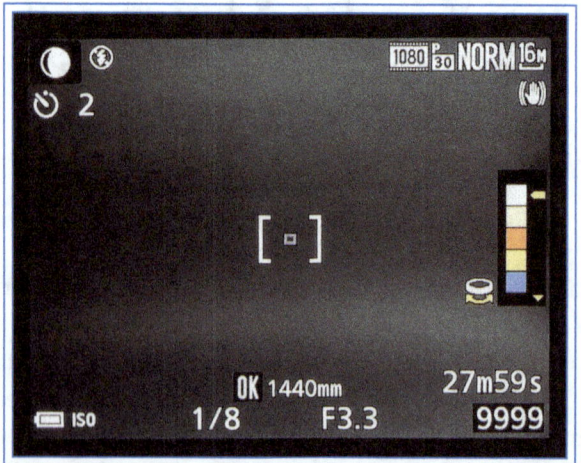

Figure 3-57. Moon Setting, Frame Indicating 1440mm Focal Length

That very small frame represents the viewing angle at the full optical zoom range of 1440mm. You can place that frame over the moon with the lens zoomed back to its wide-angle setting, then press the OK button to cause the camera to zoom immediately to its full zoom length. In that way, you can easily locate the moon in the sky and zoom in on it with confidence that you will center it in the image, as shown in Figure 3-58.

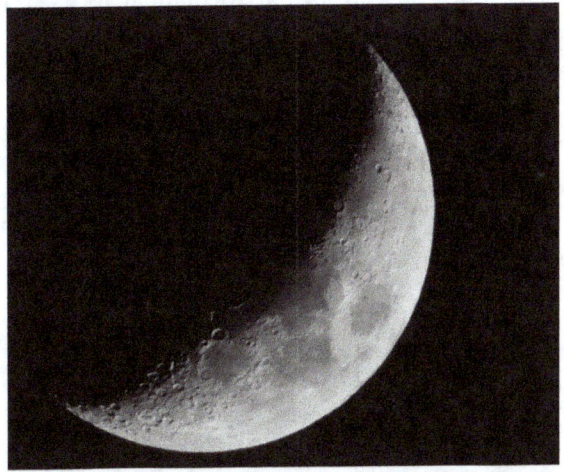

Figure 3-58. Moon Example Image

Also, the camera places on the right side of the screen a scale with a variety of hues, including white (no color change), green, red, yellow, and blue. This is not a sliding scale, but, instead, is like a set of virtual color filters. If you select the top option, you will view the moon with no color change. You can try any of the other selections to enhance your view of the moon and its craters. The yellow filter is good for enhancing the overall contrast of the image, while the blue filter can be used to reduce the glare. The green option can enhance the contrast and clarity of surface features, such as the edges of craters. My suggestion is to switch through all of the options while you are viewing the moon, to see which ones yield better results for the sort of image you are looking for. As with the Food setting, the hue setting you choose for the Moon setting will stay in place even after the camera is turned off and then on again.

Bird-watching

The last of the special Scene mode settings, Bird-watching, is, like the Moon setting, an important and natural option for the P600. With this setting, the camera disables the flash and turns on autofocus, but you can switch to manual focus if you need to adjust the focus yourself. You also can use the self-timer or exposure compensation. You can turn on continuous shooting from the Shooting menu, so you can take a burst of shots with one shutter press, increasing the chances of capturing a good image as a bird moves around. To do that, press the Menu button, and select Bird-watching from the Shooting (Scene) menu, as shown in Figure 3-59.

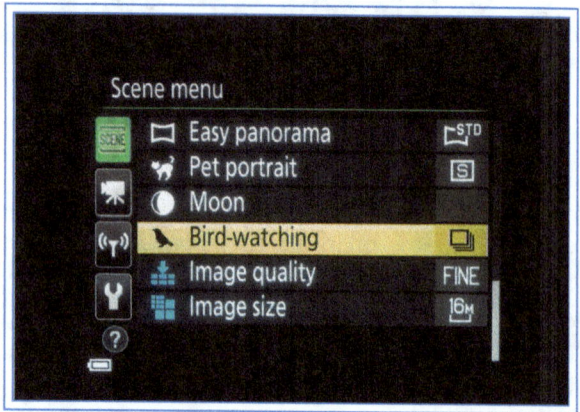

Figure 3-59. Bird-watching Setting Highlighted on Scene Menu

Press the OK or Right button to move to the next screen, shown in Figure 3-60, and select Continuous from that screen. Then, when you press the shutter button and hold it down, the camera will shoot a continuous burst of about 7 shots at a rate of about 7 frames per second.

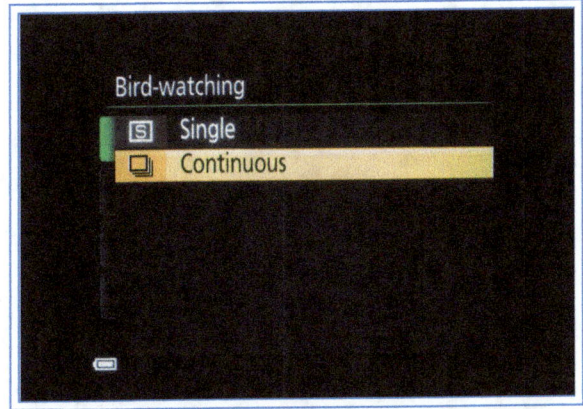

Figure 3-60. Continuous Setting for Bird-watching Mode

One important feature is that, just as with the Moon setting, when you are using a wide-angle setting, the camera places a special frame in the center of the image to indicate the angle of view at the telephoto end of the zoom scale. In this case, the frame shows the amount of the image that would be in view with the lens zoomed in to the 800mm point, rather than the full 1440mm that is used with the Moon setting. So, when you are trying to capture a close-up shot of a distant bird, you can start with a wide-angle view so it is easy to find the bird, and center the subject in the small frame. Then, just press the OK button and the camera will automatically zoom the lens to the 800mm point, with the bird centered in the image. If you then need to zoom back to a wide-angle view, just press the zoom lever to the left to zoom out. If you want to zoom in beyond the 800mm point, you can use the zoom lever to do that, also.

In Figure 3-61, I used this setting to fire off a quick burst of shots when I spotted a robin sunning itself on a fence while I was walking through a park.

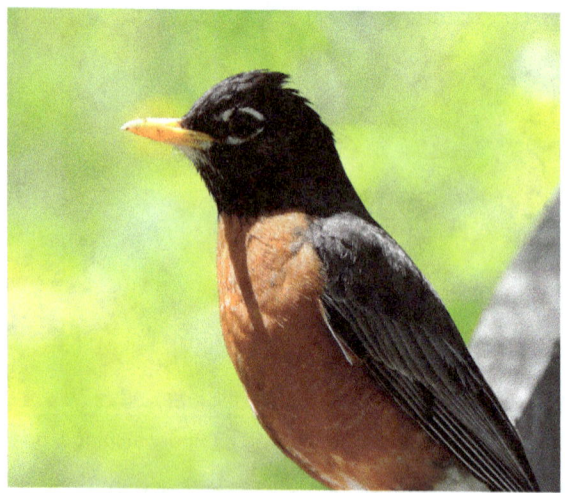

Figure 3-61. Bird-watching Example Image 1

In Figure 3-62, I set the zoom to its full optical range to catch a shot of a goldfinch perched on the bird feeder in our back yard.

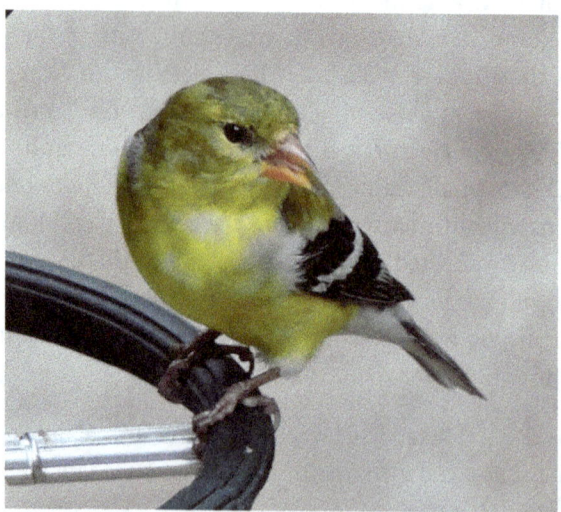

Figure 3-62. Bird-watching Setting Example Image 2

Special Effects Mode

Several notches around the mode dial from the SCENE mode is the EFFECTS slot, indicating the Special Effects shooting mode.

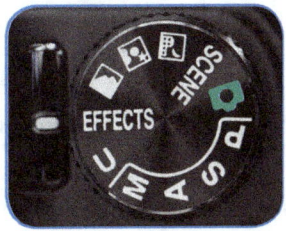

Figure 3-63. Special Effects Mode

This shooting mode provides you with interesting ways to alter the appearance of your images. These nine settings operate in a manner similar to the scene settings, but there are some differences. The Special Effects settings are not designed for particular types of subjects, such as portraits, landscapes, or fireworks, as the scene settings are. Instead, the Special Effects mode settings offer manipulations to change how an image looks, regardless of the subject.

To select one of these settings, turn the mode dial to the EFFECTS position, as shown in Figure 3-63, then press the Menu button.

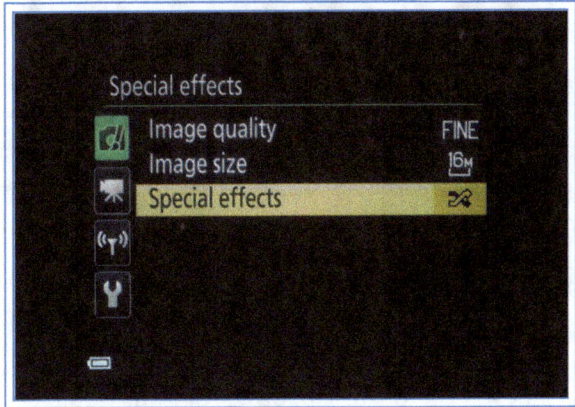

Figure 3-64. Special Effects Menu Item

There are only three choices on the Shooting menu when the camera is set to Special Effects mode: Image Quality, Image Size, and Special Effects, as shown in Figure 3-64. Once you have set the quality and size of the image as you want them (I recommend Fine and the largest size for most purposes), navigate to the Special Effects line on the menu. Then press the OK button or the Right direction button to go to the next screen, which displays the nine choices for effects: Soft, Nostalgic Sepia, High-contrast Monochrome, Painting, High Key, Low Key, Selective Color, High ISO Monochrome, and Cross Process, as shown in part in Figure 3-65. (Only the first 7 settings are shown in this image; the other 2 are on the next menu screen.)

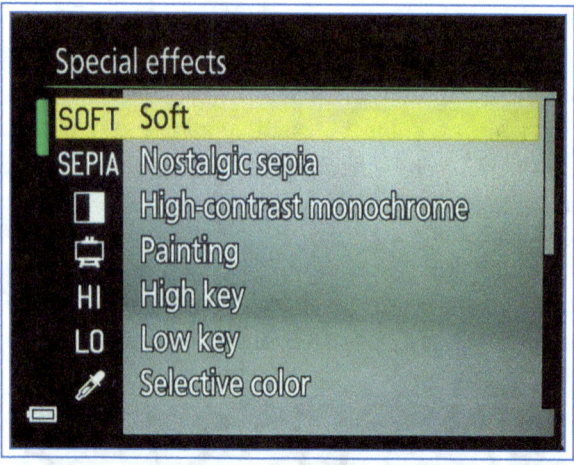

Figure 3-65. First Screen of Special Effects Menu

Highlight an option and press the OK button to confirm, then press the shutter button halfway or press the Menu button to return to the shooting Screen. The display will change according to the setting you have chosen. For example, if you choose High ISO Monochrome, the display will be in black and white and will appear grainy.

As noted above, there are no other options available on the Shooting menu when you are using Special Effects mode, apart from Image Quality and Image Size. However, you can use the buttons on the multi selector to choose exposure compensation, the self-timer, or a focus mode. You also can choose a flash mode for every setting except High ISO Monochrome. With that option, the flash is forced off. The focus area is fixed in the center of the frame for all of these settings.

I will describe each of the options along with a sample image taken with that selection to illustrate a possible use for it.

SOFT

This setting, as shown in Figure 3-66, applies a small amount of blur to the image.

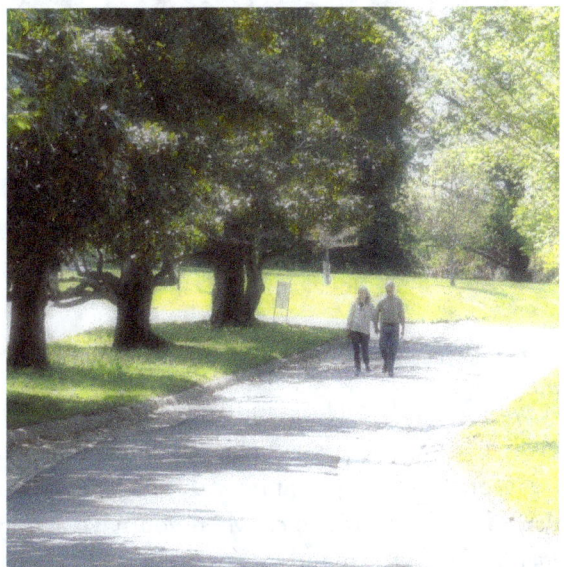

Figure 3-66. Soft Example Image

You could use this option when taking pictures of an aging movie star to soften facial wrinkles, or you might use it just to add a somewhat dreamlike or fantasy aura to the image, such as this shot of a couple walking down a tree-lined path.

Nostalgic Sepia

With the Nostalgic Sepia setting, illustrated in Figure 3-67, the camera produces a monochrome image with a sepia (brownish) tone and softens the contrast somewhat to give the look of an antique photograph. You could use this setting if you want to produce an old-looking photograph of family members. For this example, I took a shot of a structure with a somewhat old-fashioned appearance, to add to the feeling of age.

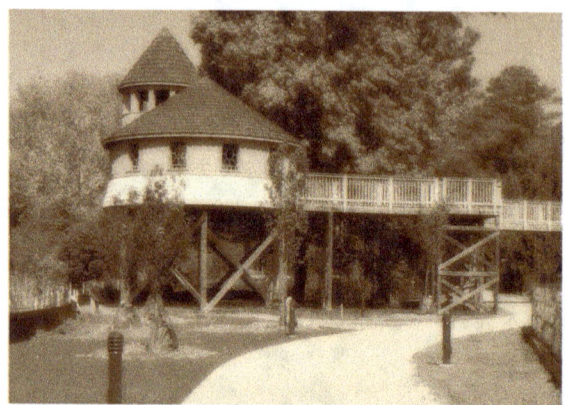

Figure 3-67. Nostalgic Sepia Example Image

High-contrast Monochrome

This effect, which yields a black-and-white image with enhanced contrast, is likely to have a stark, harsh appearance. You might want to use it for street photography with a realistic or journalistic look. It also can be a good choice when you have a subject with a regular geometric pattern and you want to emphasize its shape with the sharply contrasting areas of black and white. I felt that this setting was appropriate for an image of a Civil War-era cannon, as shown in Figure 3-68.

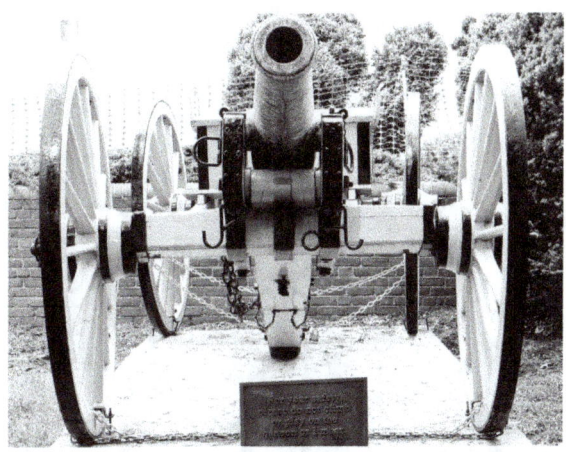

Figure 3-68. High-contrast Monochrome Example Image

PAINTING

The Painting setting is one of the more dramatic of the Special Effects settings. With this option, the camera increases the intensity of colors and uses processing to give an appearance like that of an HDR image, as discussed earlier in this chapter, with shadowed areas brightened. This setting is not appropriate if you are looking for a realistic representation of your subject; it is useful when you want a stylized, vibrant image, possibly for a poster or illustration. I have found that it tends to produce images that look overly busy and unappealing with some subjects, such as trees and foliage. I have had better results, at least for my taste, using it with subjects that have straight lines and broad spaces with solid colors. In Figure 3-69, I used this setting for a picture of a historic building. This setting gave an aura of unreality, but preserved the general character of the subject, in my opinion.

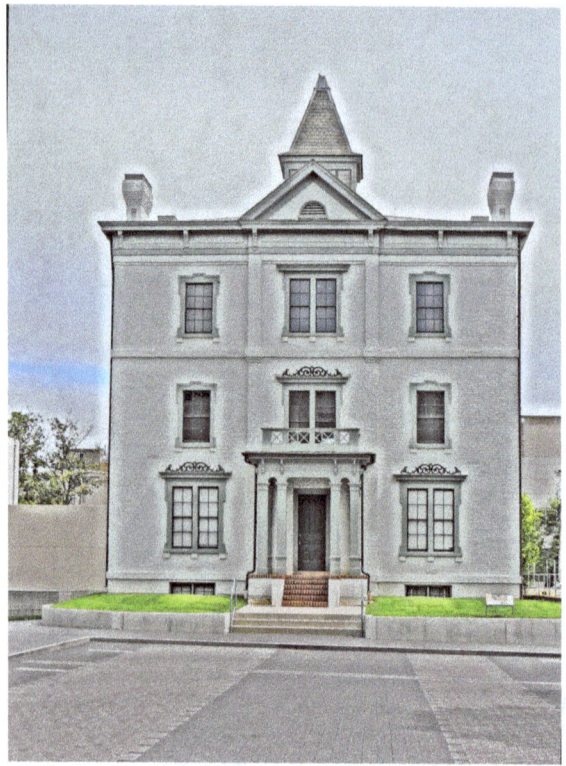

Figure 3-69. Painting Example Image

HIGH KEY

"High key" is a technique in which a photographer uses bright lighting throughout the scene, striving for a bright overall look with light colors and few shadows. This technique often is used in advertising photography. With the P600, this single setting cannot necessarily remake your image to look like a traditional high key shot, but, as seen in Figure 3-70, the camera does boost the exposure to produce a brighter-than-normal image. It works best when it is used for objects with light colors.

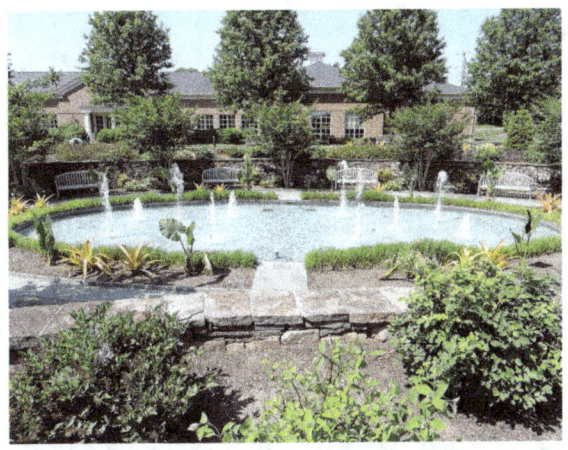

Figure 3-70. High Key Example Image

LOW KEY

The Low Key setting, of course, is the opposite of High Key. With this option, the camera emphasizes dark areas in the image. Here again, as illustrated in Figure 3-71, the P600 cannot produce a true "low key" image all by itself; what it can do is reduce the exposure and otherwise process the photograph to look darker and more shadowy than normal. It works well with dark-colored subjects and is good for producing a moody atmosphere.

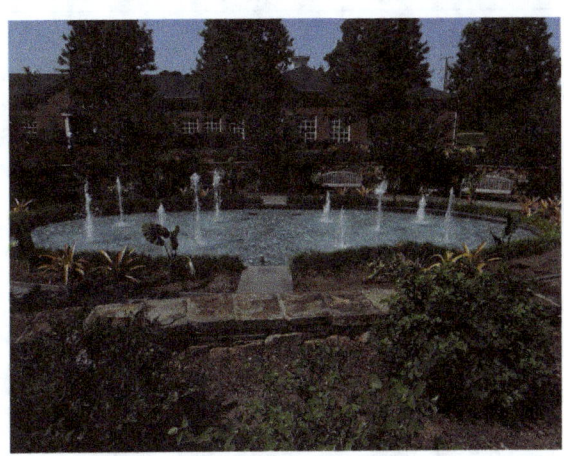

Figure 3-71. Low Key Example Image

SELECTIVE COLOR

This setting, unlike other Special Effects options, gives you the ability to control its operation. When you first choose this option from the menu screen, the camera displays a message telling you to press OK to select a color, as shown in Figure 3-72.

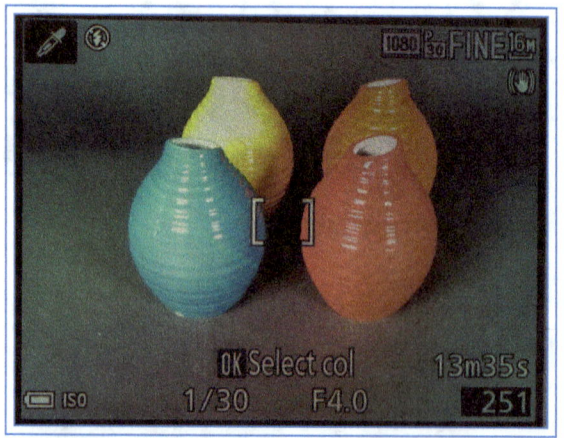

Figure 3-72. Selective Color Setting - Screen to Select Color

When you press the OK button, the camera displays a yellow indicator beside a vertical spectrum of 12 colors plus one entry for no color, as shown in Figure 3-73.

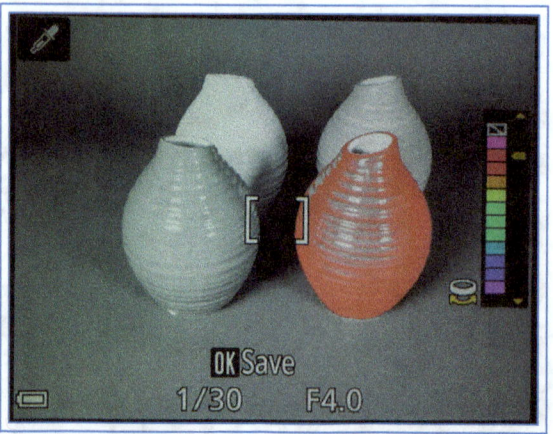

Figure 3-73. Selective Color Setting - Color Scale on Screen

Use the command dial to move the indicator to the block in the spectrum for the single color you want to retain in the image. Note that the topmost block in the spectrum has a negative symbol in it; if you select that block, the camera retains all colors and does not use the Selective Color function. The result in that case is an ordinary image with no special processing at all. It will look as if you took the image using Program or Auto mode. You might want to consider leaving the Special Effects mode setting on Selective Color with this top option selected. That way, if you accidentally turn the mode dial to the EFFECTS position, any shots (or videos) you take will not have the exotic processing of a setting such as Soft, Nostalgic Sepia, and the like.

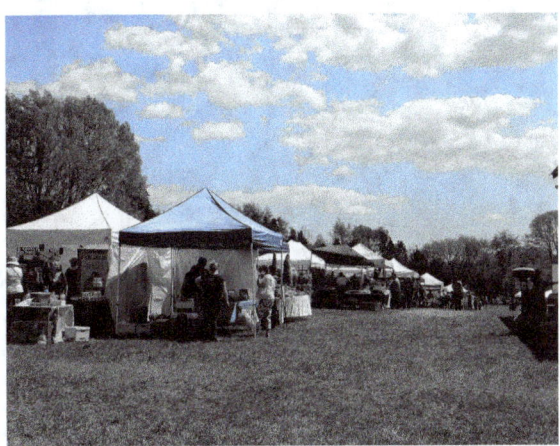

Figure 3-74. Selective Color Example Image

Figure 3-74 shows the image that resulted from setting the color to blue on a partly cloudy day at a crafts fair.

HIGH ISO MONOCHROME

With the High ISO Monochrome setting, Nikon has made it clear in the setting's name what sort of special processing is involved; the camera uses a very high ISO setting with monochrome rather than color processing. In fact, with this setting, the camera sets ISO to what Nikon calls Hi 1, which is the equivalent of ISO

12800, a setting that cannot be achieved through the ISO menu item.

Although this setting can be useful when you are shooting in very dimly lighted conditions, in my opinion its best use is for creative purposes, when you want to have the gritty, grainy effect that is produced by the visual noise from high ISO settings. I enjoy using this setting when I don't want a great deal of realism and the subject calls for an impressionistic look. In Figure 3-75, I photographed a model Ferris wheel in front of a window, which resulted in an emphasis on the geometric pattern.

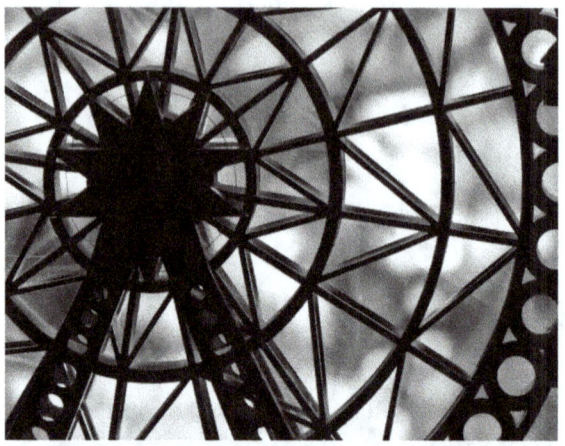

Figure 3-75. High ISO Monochrome Example Image

With this setting, the flash is forced off and cannot be used.

CROSS PROCESS

Finally, with the Cross Process effect, the P600 lets you add a color cast to an image. When you select this setting, the camera places a color scale at the right of the display with a pointer indicating one of the colors, as with the Food setting of Scene mode. Use the command dial to move the pointer to your choice of blue, red, green, or yellow, as shown in Figure 3-76.

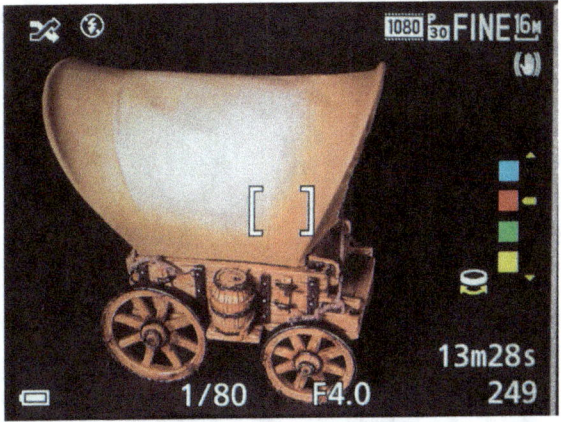

Figure 3-76. Cross Process Setting - Color Selection Screen

With the pointer in that position, take the picture; the image will be colored with the selected hue. This option can add an atmospheric aura to images. Figure 3-77 shows the use of all four settings along with an unaffected image, for comparison.

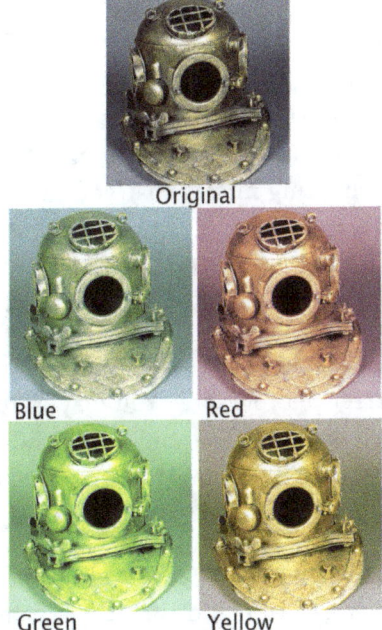

Figure 3-77. Comparison of Cross Process Settings

One final note: When the Movie Options menu item is set to the HS 480/4x option, the Soft, Nostalgic Sepia, and Painting settings of Special Effects mode are not available.

User Settings Mode

The last slot on the mode dial to be discussed is the U setting, as shown in Figure 3-78, which allows you, the user, to store a full set of your favorite or most often-needed settings for immediate recall.

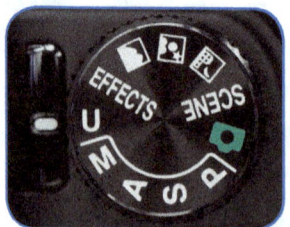

Figure 3-78. User Settings Mode

When you turn the mode dial to the U position, you take advantage of a powerful feature of the Coolpix P600. You can set up the camera exactly as you want it, with a shooting mode, zoom amount, white balance, ISO, and other settings, and then recall all of those settings instantly just by turning the mode dial to the letter U. The only shooting modes that you can save settings for are Program, Aperture Priority, Shutter Priority, and Manual; you cannot save them for the Auto, Scene, or Special Effects modes.

Here is how this works. First, set up the camera with all of the settings you want to be able to recall. For example, suppose you are going to do street photography. You may want to shoot with a fast shutter speed, say 1/250 second, at ISO 1600 in black-and-white, using continuous shooting with autofocus, at the 16:9 aspect ratio with a large image size and Fine quality.

Your first step is to make all of these settings. Turn the mode dial to S for Shutter Priority, and turn the command dial to set a shutter speed of 1/250 second. Then press the Menu button to summon the Shooting menu, go to the menu item for Image Quality, and choose Fine. For Image Size, select 4608 x 2592 pixels, which, as indicated to the left of those numbers, translates to a 16:9 aspect ratio with an image size of 12 megapixels. Then navigate in the menu system to the Picture Control selection and select the Monochrome option. Set the ISO menu option to 1600. Next, select the Continuous item on the Shooting menu and navigate to the next screen; on that screen, go down to the second option, Continuous H, marked with an H on a stack of frames, for high-speed shots. You also may want to push the zoom lever all the way to the left, for wide-angle shooting.

Once all of these settings are made, press the Menu button to call up the Shooting menu, and scroll down (or scroll up and wrap around to the bottom) to select the Save User Settings item, shown in Figure 3-79, and then press the OK button or the Right button; you will see a confirming message saying Done.

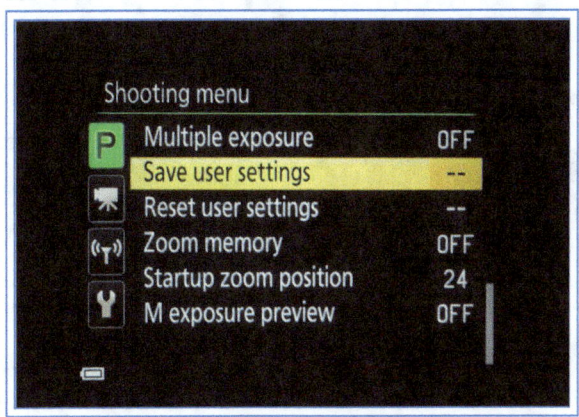

Figure 3-79. Save User Settings Menu Item

Be sure you have all the settings the way you want them before you press OK or the Right button, because the camera does not ask you to confirm your choices; it just says "Done." I was a bit taken aback the first couple of times I used this feature, because in most other cases there's a chance to back out before you make your choices final; not here.

Now, to check how this option worked, try making some very different settings, such as Manual exposure with continuous shooting turned off, a shutter speed of one second, Picture Control set to Standard, the zoom lever moved all the way to the T for telephoto, ISO set to Auto, and Image Size set to the maximum, 4608 x 3456 pixels. Then turn the mode dial to the U setting, and you will see that all of the custom settings you made earlier have come back, including the zoom position, shutter speed, black-and-white shooting at ISO 1600, and everything else. This is really a wonderful feature, and more powerful than similar features on some other cameras, which can save menu settings but not settings such as shutter speed and zoom position.

The lone flaw I find with this mode is that there is only one slot for it on the mode dial, and therefore only one group of settings that can be saved at a time. But it's much better than nothing. I suggest you experiment to find one group of custom settings that is the most useful to you, and save it to the U mode for instant recall. Of course, you can change the settings that are stored as often as you like. You may want to jot down in a notebook some of your favorite groups of settings for various situations, so you can program the most appropriate set into the U slot when you're setting out for a particular type of shooting session.

CHAPTER 4: THE SHOOTING MENU

Much of the power of the Nikon Coolpix P600 comes from the many options included in the Shooting menu, which gives you control over the appearance of images and how they are captured. Depending on your preferences, you may not have to use this menu too much. You may prefer to use the various scene settings or Special Effects mode selections, which choose many options for you, or you may prefer, at least on occasion, to use Auto mode, in which the camera makes its own choices. However, it's nice to know you have this degree of control available if you want it, and it is useful to understand what types of items you can exercise control over.

The Shooting menu is easy to use once you have played around with it a bit. As I discussed earlier, the menu options change depending on the setting of the mode dial on top of the camera. For example, if the mode dial is set to the green camera icon, for Auto mode, the Shooting menu options are very limited, because Auto mode is for a user who wants the camera to make almost all of the decisions without input from him or her. If the mode dial is set to one of the dedicated scene types with its own slot on the dial (Landscape, Night Portrait, or Night Landscape), the Shooting menu is re-named after the currently active mode.

For example, if you select the Night Landscape mode from the mode dial and then press the Menu button, the menu that appears on the display is labeled Night Landscape, rather than Shooting, as shown in Figure 4-1.

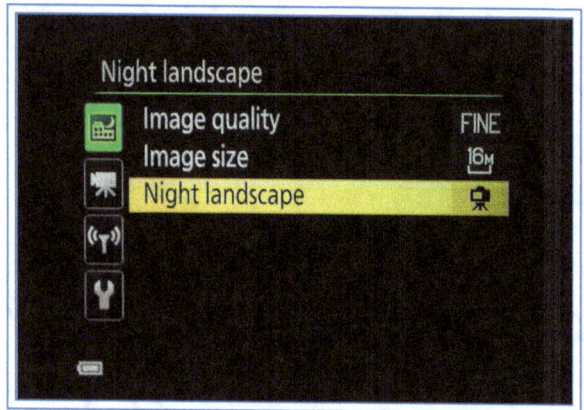

Figure 4-1. Night Landscape Menu Item

These menus, as in Auto mode, are abbreviated versions of the Shooting menu; they include only a few items from the normal Shooting menu, usually Image Quality and Image Size. In addition, they may include a specific menu item for the mode that is in effect. In this case, there is a Night Landscape menu item, which lets you select either Hand-held or Tripod for shooting.

When the mode dial is turned to the SCENE setting, pressing the Menu button brings up another version of the Shooting menu, in this case called the Scene menu. This menu provides a way to select either Scene Auto Selector or any one of the 17 specific scene types (Portrait, Easy Panorama, Sports, etc.).

In addition, at the very bottom of the Scene menu, just after the entries for Moon and Bird-watching, the camera presents you with the options for choosing Image Quality and Image Size, as shown in Figure 4-2. (The Image Quality and Image Size menu options are dimmed and unavailable for selection when Easy Panorama is selected for the scene type.)

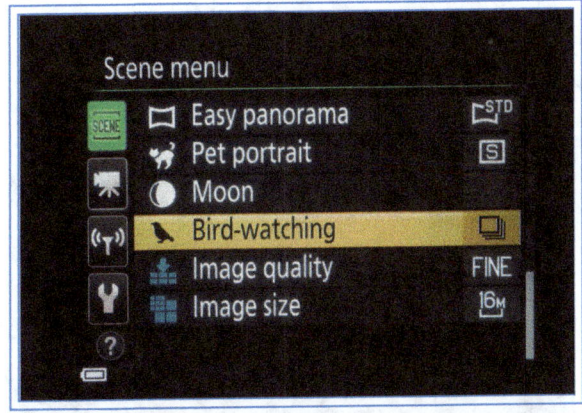

Figure 4-2. Image Quality and Image Size on Scene Menu

When the EFFECTS slot on the mode dial is selected, the menu becomes the Special Effects menu, which lets you choose only which effect to select, along with Image Quality and Image Size.

Although the Shooting menu (or its equivalent, such as the Scene menu) presents you with some choices in all shooting modes, in the more automatic modes, including Auto and the various Scene mode types, there are only a few options, apart from options specific to a given mode, such as choosing a scene type. It is only when the mode dial is set to the P, S, A, or M setting for the Program, Shutter Priority, Aperture Priority, or Manual exposure mode, that the wide variety of Shooting menu options is available.

For the following discussion, I'm assuming you have the camera set to Program mode (shooting mode dial turned to the P setting), because with that setting you potentially have access to all of the power of the Shooting menu. (Though some menu options will be unavailable in certain situations.)

So turn the mode dial to P for Program mode, then enter the menu system by pressing the Menu button. In the menu system, when the camera is in shooting mode, besides the Shooting menu (or Scene or Special Effects menu), there are the Movie menu, designated by a movie camera icon in the column at the left of the menu, the Wi-Fi Options menu, marked by a wireless network icon, and the Setup menu, marked by a wrench icon. These icons are shown in Figure 4-3.

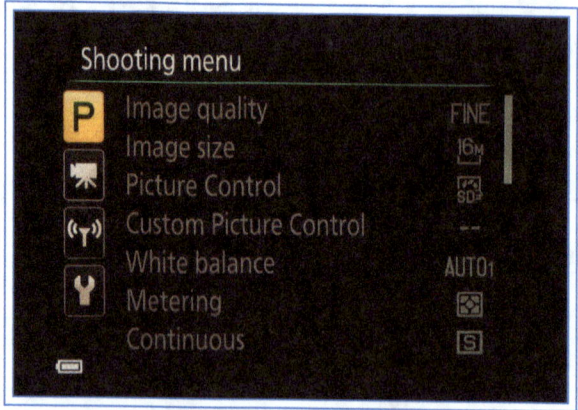

Figure 4-3. Shooting Menu Icon Highlighted

When the camera is in playback mode, the three choices are the Playback, Wi-Fi Options, and Setup menus. For now, I will discuss only the Shooting menu, which is designated by a capital letter or icon at the left standing for the current shooting mode: P, S, A, or M, or an icon for one of the more automatic modes.

On the Shooting menu (in Program mode), you'll see a fairly long list of options. Each option (such as Picture Control) occupies one line, with its name on the left and its current setting (such as the Standard icon) on the right.

You have to scroll through three screens to see all of the options. If you find it tedious to scroll using the Up and Down buttons, you can rotate the multi selector dial on the camera's back, which may help you speed through the menus a bit more quickly. Also, depending on which menu option you are trying to reach, you may be able to get there more quickly by reversing direction with the buttons or multi selector dial, and wrapping around to reach the option you want. In other words, if you're on the top line of the menu, you can scroll up to reach the bottom option. Or, if the highlight is already near the bottom option, you can scroll down to go back to the options at the top of the menu. The first menu screen is shown in Figure 4-4.

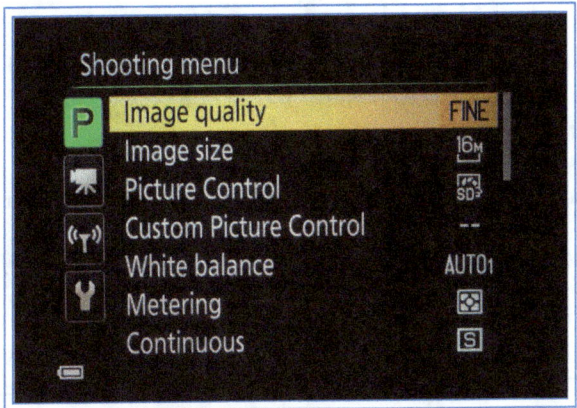

Figure 4-4. First Screen of Shooting Menu

Once you have highlighted the menu item you want, you can make any sub-selections by pressing either the OK button or the Right button, which will take you to the next screen (if one exists) for that menu item. To go back to a previous menu screen, press the Left button; to exit the menu system, press the Menu button. It is important to press the OK button to confirm your choice of a particular menu item selection; just highlighting it and then exiting from the menu screen will not activate that item.

If you like to use shortcuts, here is a way to navigate the menu system with fewer button-presses. Press the Menu button to display the menu screen, and then use the Up and Down buttons or the multi selector dial to move to the item you wish to adjust. In many cases, the menu item has a secondary screen where you make the actual setting; to get to that screen, you ordinarily press the Right button or the OK button to move to that screen. However, to shortcut that process, once the yellow highlight rectangle is on the menu item you want to adjust, just turn the command dial (the ridged wheel at the upper right of the camera's back), and the value will adjust without having to move to the secondary screen. You do not have to press the OK button to confirm the selection; just turn that wheel and the adjustment is made. This technique works for many important settings, including Image Quality, Image Size, Picture Control, White Balance, Continuous shooting, ISO, Startup Zoom Position, and others. It does not work for items such as Custom Picture Control, Save User Settings, and others that do not have a list of settings to make on the secondary screen.

On occasion you will find you are unable to select a certain menu option. That is, although an option will appear on the menu screen, you will not be able to navigate to it and select it. This situation occurs when there is an option in effect that is not compatible with the menu option you are trying to select. For example, if you have selected Multi-shot 16 by using the Continuous menu option, the Image Size setting is fixed at 5 megapixels (2560 x 1920 pixels), so that setting cannot be changed (or even selected) in the menu system, as indicated in Figure 4-5, which shows that item dimmed on the menu screen.

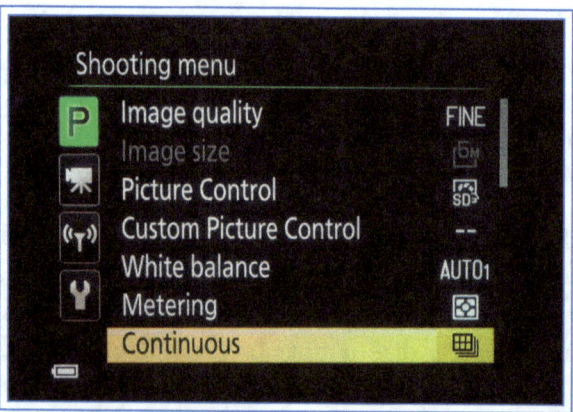

Figure 4-5. Multi-shot 16 Item Selected on Shooting Menu

Or, if you have selected the option to shoot in monochrome from the Picture Control menu setting, you will not be able to get access to the White Balance menu option.

With the mode dial set to P you should have access to just about every option on the Shooting menu. If you find you can't select certain options, check to make sure you have set other options to compatible settings. For example, use the Continuous option on the Shooting menu to select Single-shot exposures rather than a continuous setting, and set ISO to Auto. If you have trouble getting to some menu options and can't figure out what setting is causing the problem, you can go to the Setup menu (marked at the left of the screen by the wrench icon) and scroll down (or scroll up and wrap around) to the Reset All option, the next-to-last option on the menu. That action will reset all of the camera's basic shooting functions to their default values. In this way, you will undo whatever setting is causing a conflict with the setting you are trying to make. (You also will undo any custom settings you have made, so be sure you don't mind taking that step.)

Starting at the top line of the Shooting menu, I will discuss below each option on the menu's three screens.

The first screen of this menu was shown in Figures 4-4 and 4-5. Following are details about its options.

Image Quality

There are two basic settings to make when you are deciding on your overall image "quality" in the broadest sense: Image Quality, discussed here, and Image Size, discussed below. The Image Quality option lets you select how much "compression" the camera applies. That is, the camera "compresses" the data by squeezing out a certain amount of information, preserving enough to recreate the image, but trimming it down so the file does not take up too much storage space.

The two options are Fine and Normal. The Fine option uses up roughly twice as much storage space as the Normal setting. So, for example, if you choose Fine for your quality setting, the camera can store about 950 of the largest-sized images on an 8

GB memory card. If you choose Normal, it can store about 1700 of those images. Of course, there is a trade-off of quality against storage space. If you are planning to make large prints or crop the image to use a portion of it, you should choose Fine.

It is worth noting that the Coolpix P600 does not offer Raw as an option for image quality. Virtually all DSLRs and quite a few advanced compact cameras today offer the Raw format, which preserves the maximum image data and gives the photographer considerable flexibility in processing images in software. However, using Raw has its disadvantages, including very large file sizes and incompatibility with some post-processing software (at least until software updates are provided). Using a Raw format also requires that the images be processed in software; you cannot use them straight from the camera. The P600 provides a great deal of flexibility in producing excellent JPEG (that is, compressed, non-Raw) images, and you should have no problem in using this camera to make excellent prints or other photographic products.

Image Size

The next option on the Shooting menu, Image Size, works hand-in-hand with Image Quality to determine the overall quality of your images. With the Coolpix P600, Image Size actually has two components, which can be selected separately on some other cameras: resolution and aspect ratio. On the P600, these two components are not named, but their numerical values are listed on the Image Size menu. (The aspect ratio values are listed only for the settings that deviate from the normal aspect ratio of 4:3.)

The resolution of the image is the number of pixels it contains, given in a formula with the horizontal pixel count followed by the vertical pixel count. For example, the largest Image Size setting available on the P600 is 4608 x 3456, meaning the image has 4608 pixels horizontally and 3456 vertically. When you multiply these two numbers together, the result is about 16 million pixels, also written as 16 megapixels or 16M. So, as in Figure 4-6, you will see the figure 16M on the menu screen when you select this largest value for Image Size.

You can also determine the aspect ratio of the image from the Image Size setting. For example, the 4608 x 3456 setting yields an image 4 units wide for every 3 units tall, for a 4:3 aspect ratio. Most of the Image Size settings for the P600 are in that ratio, which is a standard one for digital images, being the same shape as the camera's LCD display. However, if you scroll down through the second screen on the Image Size menu, as shown in Figure 4-6, you will see a few entries that note a different aspect ratio.

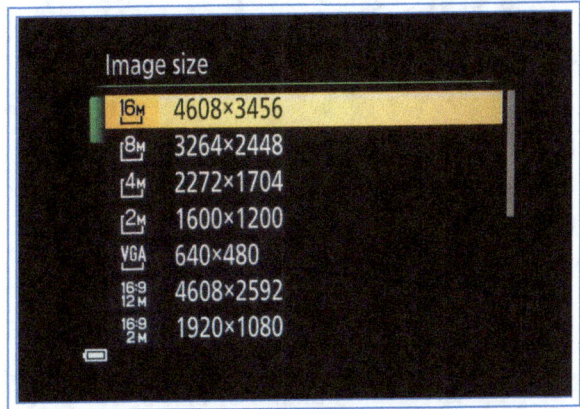

Figure 4-6. Maximum Image Size Setting Selected

Specifically, just below the setting for VGA (640 x 480), there is the entry for 4608 x 2592 pixels. At the far left on the line for this entry, above the number of megapixels, 12M, the menu shows the notation 16:9, meaning this Image Size setting is in a 16:9 aspect ratio: 16 units wide for every 9 units tall. This aspect ratio is another fairly common one, which corresponds to the shape of a widescreen HDTV set, and therefore often is called "widescreen."

Further down on the Image Size menu, another entry, 4608 x 3072, shown in Figure 4-7, is labeled as 3:2, meaning its aspect ratio has 3 horizontal units for every 2 vertical ones. This is a common aspect ratio, which corresponds to the standard print size in the United States of 6 by 4 inches (15 by 10 cm).

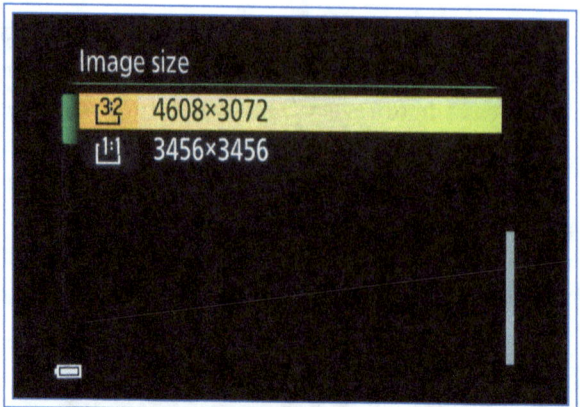

Figure 4-7. Second Screen of Image Size Menu Options

Finally, the last entry on the Image size menu, 3456 x 3456 pixels, is in an aspect ratio of 1:1, resulting in a square image. Some photographers like to use this aspect ratio because of its symmetry, or because it suits a particular composition.

With the Image Size menu setting, you have two choices to make. First, you can choose your images' resolution, or number of pixels (megapixels). The larger the number of pixels, the larger you can make high-quality prints on paper, and the more options you have for cropping the image to highlight particular details from the exposure. Second, although most of the choices on the menu are in the standard 4:3 aspect ratio, you have the option of selecting an aspect ratio of 3:2, 16:9, or 1:1 if you want.

Of course, you can always just shoot with the maximum image size of 4608 x 3456 and then crop the image down in software later; in that way, you can use any aspect ratio you want, including those listed here or any other. But, if you want to use a 1:1 aspect ratio for creative reasons, or you want your landscape photo to have the 16:9 widescreen look and you don't want to be bothered with changing the aspect ratio in software, you can select an Image Size setting that corresponds to your desired aspect ratio, so the final result will come straight out of the camera. In addition, you will have the advantage of seeing how the final image will be composed as you set it up on the camera's display screen or in the viewfinder.

Figures 4-8 through 4-11 were all taken at the same time and place; the only differences are that they were taken with different Image Size settings, resulting in different aspect ratios, as indicated in the captions.

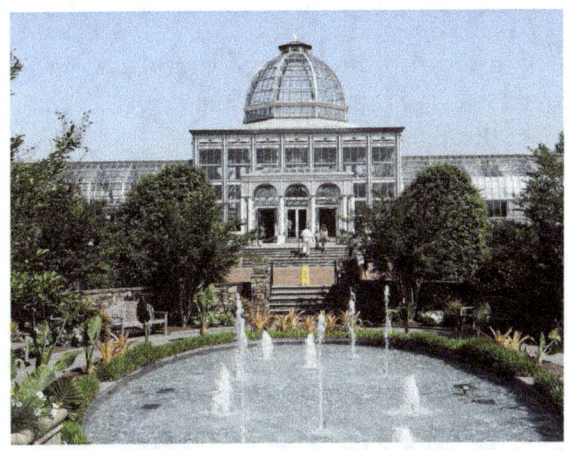

Figure 4-8. Aspect Ratio 4:3 Example Image

Figure 4-8 was taken with the largest image size, which uses the 4:3 aspect ratio. With this setting, the camera captures the maximum number of pixels, and the resulting image includes all of the pixels included with the other aspect ratios, as well as some that are cut off with other settings.

Figure 4-9, taken with the 16:9, widescreen aspect ratio, includes all of the horizontal reach of the 4:3 image, but cuts off pixels at both the top and bottom of the image, as shown here.

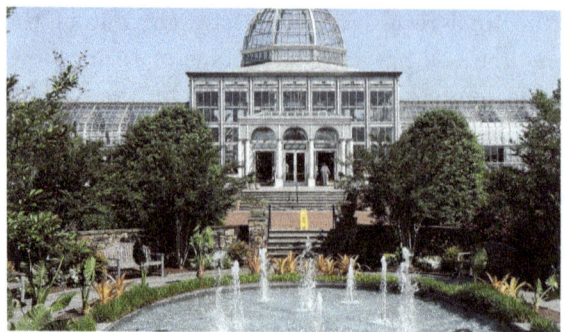

Figure 4-9. Aspect Ratio 16:9 Example Image

Figure 4-10, taken with the 3:2 aspect ratio, also includes all of the horizontal reach of the 4:3 setting, but cuts off some pixels at the bottom of the image.

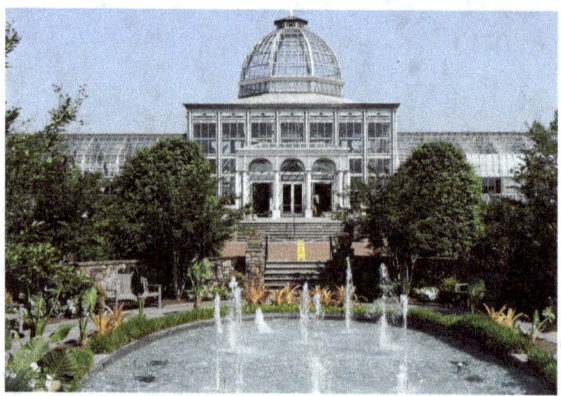

Figure 4-10. Aspect Ratio 3:2 Example Image

Finally, Figure 4-11 illustrates the use of the 1:1 aspect ratio, with which the camera cuts off pixels at the left and right sides of the image to achieve a square shape.

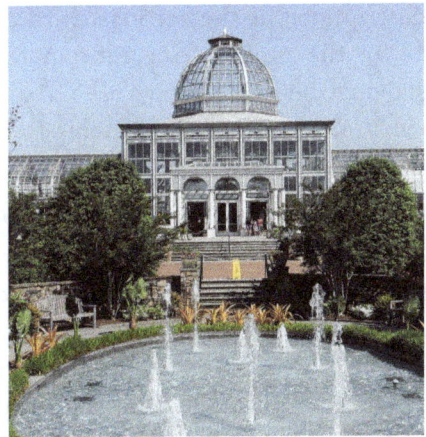

Figure 4-11. Aspect Ratio 1:1 Example Image

Picture Control

This option provides you with four choices for the appearance of your images through in-camera processing: Standard, Neutral, Vivid, and Monochrome, as shown in Figure 4-12.

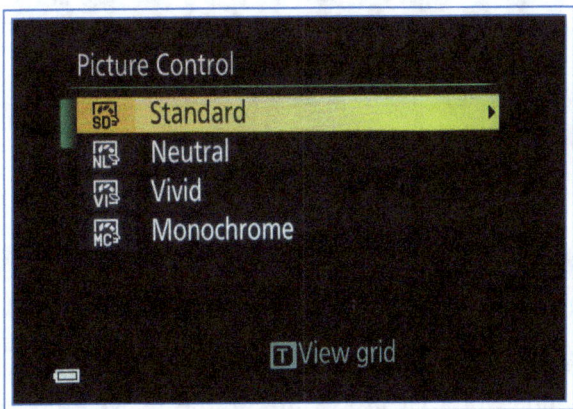

Figure 4-12. Picture Control Main Options Screen

With these options, the camera provides varying degrees of adjustment to three basic parameters: sharpening, contrast, and saturation.

Following are descriptions of the settings, with a sample photo for each one showing the same figurine, for comparison. Although the differences among the four settings are not all that dramatic (except for Monochrome), you should be able to see the general characteristics of each selection.

STANDARD

With this setting, as shown in Figure 4-13, you should see a normal rendering of the image, with no emphasis on any particular aspect. The camera does some internal processing of the captured image to make it appear suitably sharp and contrasty for ordinary purposes. This is the setting you should use for everyday shooting when you have no interest in producing a specific effect.

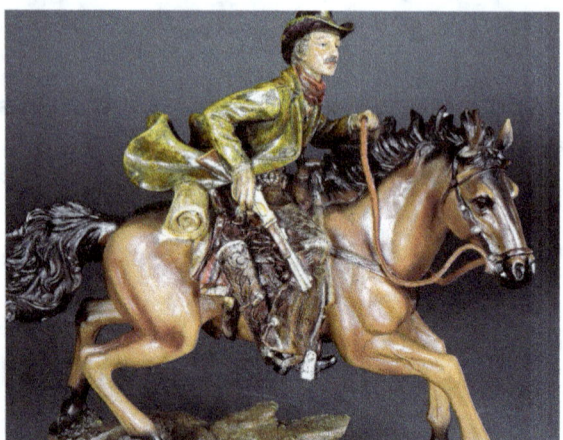

Figure 4-13. Picture Control Set to Standard

NEUTRAL

With the Neutral setting, illustrated in Figure 4-14, the camera does minimal internal processing of the image. Therefore, the image may appear less sharp and contrasty, and have less color intensity, than you would like. The intent with this setting is for you to process the image after the fact in software such as Photoshop. With minimal processing, the camera is leaving the fine-tuning of the image up to you.

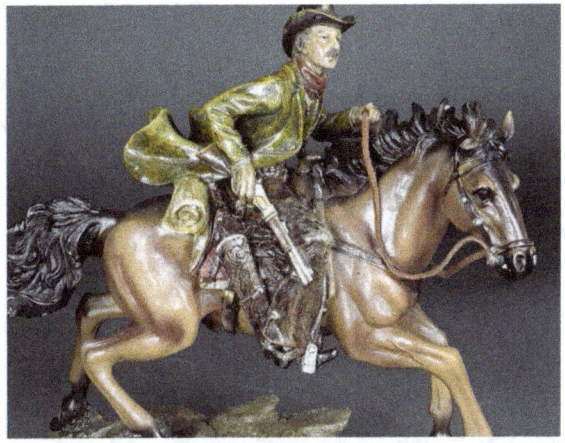

Figure 4-14. Picture Control Set to Neutral

VIVID

Use this setting to increase the saturation, or intensity, of the colors in the image, as seen in Figure 4-15.

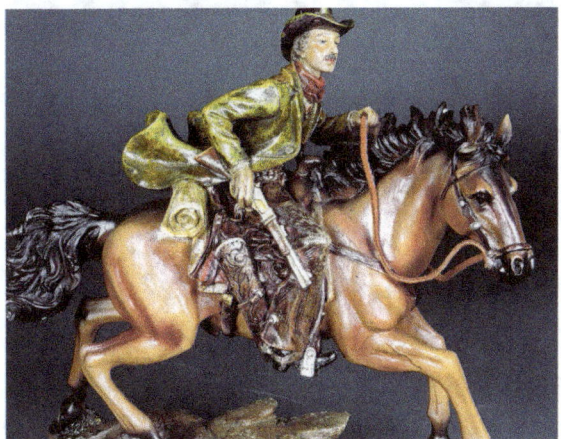

Figure 4-15. Picture Control Set to Vivid

The Vivid setting also provides some increase in sharpening and contrast, with the result that the image may "jump" off the page or the screen at the viewer with increased impact.

MONOCHROME

The Monochrome setting gives you a quick way to set the camera to take black-and-white images. Of course, as with many aspects of digital photography, you can always convert color images to monochrome using software such as Photoshop or Photoshop Elements, but it is convenient to be able to view your images in black-and-white on the camera's display before pressing the shutter button, and you may not want to devote your time and effort to converting images on the computer. The Monochrome setting is illustrated in Figure 4-16.

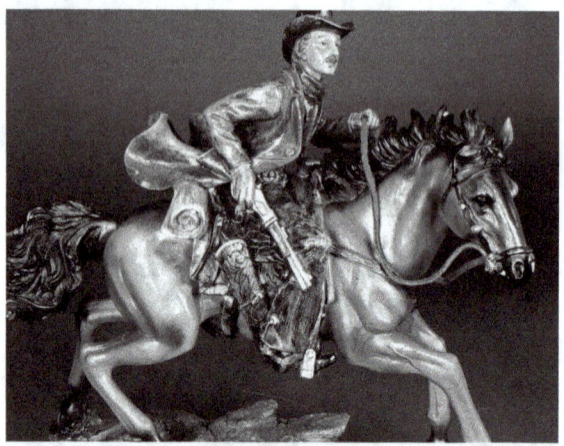

Figure 4-16. Picture Control Set to Monochrome

ADJUSTMENTS TO PICTURE CONTROL SETTINGS

Once you have selected Standard or Vivid from the Picture Control menu, the camera will display a secondary menu screen with four lines: Quick Adjust, Image sharpening, Contrast, and Saturation, as shown in Figure 4-17.

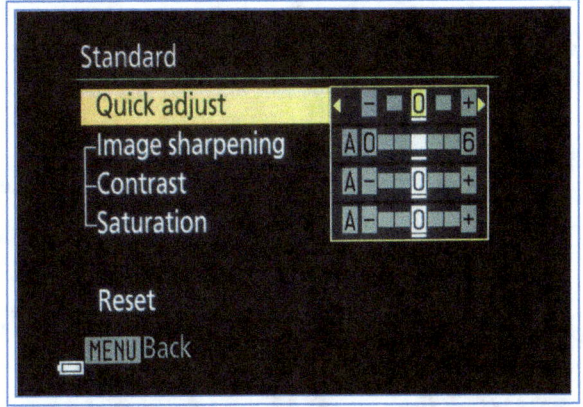

Figure 4-17. Adjustment Screen for Standard Picture Control

You can highlight any one of those four lines using the Up and Down buttons. When the line is highlighted, use the multi selector dial or the Left and Right buttons to change the settings. If you change the Quick Adjust value, you will see that the three values below it—Image sharpening, Contrast, and Saturation—also move, but not all in the same amounts. Nikon has programmed the Quick Adjust feature to move the other three values in what Nikon considers to be "balanced" amounts, so that sharpening, contrast, and saturation may be adjusted upward or downward in amounts that work well with the adjustments to the other values.

If, instead of using the Quick Adjust option, you move the highlight down to the specific line for Image sharpening, Contrast, or Saturation, you can adjust any one of those values individually. For example, suppose you especially like the punchy, aggressive look of images taken with the Vivid setting, but you don't want to have the colors quite so intense. You can set Picture Control to Vivid, and then, on the secondary screen, adjust the Saturation value to a lower level, to reduce the intensity of the colors.

Note, though, that the Contrast adjustment is unavailable if Active D-Lighting (discussed later in this chapter) is turned on in the Shooting menu.

If you select Neutral from the Picture Control menu, the secondary screen does not include the Quick Adjust option, but it does let you adjust Image sharpening, Contrast, and Saturation individually.

If you select Monochrome from the Picture Control menu, the secondary adjustment screen, seen in Figure 4-18, is even more different from the screens for the previous settings, all of which include Saturation processing that affects colors.

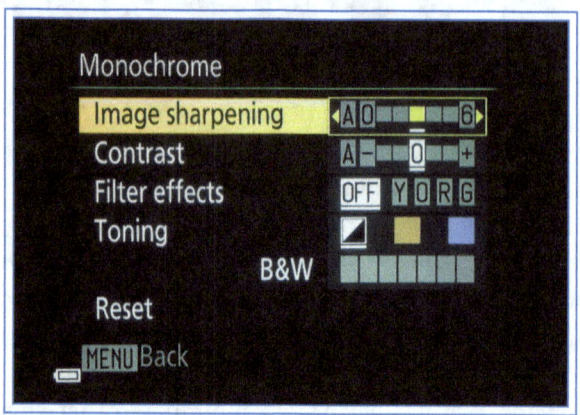

Figure 4-18. Adjustment Screen for Monochrome Picture Control

With the Monochrome setting, adjustments are available for Image sharpening and Contrast, but not for Saturation, and there is no Quick Adjustment option. However, the Monochrome setting includes two other options: Filter Effects and Toning. Contrast and sharpening work just the same as with the other Picture Control settings, as discussed above.

The third sub-option, Filter Effects, is a simulation of the use of a glass filter over the lens. If you select Filter Effects, you have four choices on the adjustment screen: Off, Y, O, R, and G, which stand for yellow, orange, red, and green. These settings are intended to mimic the effects of colored filters, which are often used with film cameras when taking photographs with monochrome films. The yellow, orange, and red filters can provide increasing levels of contrast that may, for example, darken the sky and enhance the appearance of a landscape scene. The green filter setting is intended to soften skin tones for use with portraits.

The Toning options give you the ability to add a color cast to your monochrome shots. The three Toning choices on the Monochrome menu are B&W (none), Sepia (brown), and Cyanotype (blue). Once you have selected either Sepia or Cyanotype, if you press the Down button, the cursor will move to a scale below the three options that includes gradations of intensity for the selected color tone. Using the direction buttons, the multi selector dial, or the command dial, move the cursor right for more intensity, or left for less. (The normal setting is level 4.) Then press the OK button to lock in the setting.

When you select Picture Control from the menu and have the yellow highlight rectangle on one of the main selections—Standard, Neutral, Vivid, or Monochrome—you can press the zoom lever on top of the camera toward the T (telephoto) position to display a grid, as shown in Figure 4-19, that shows the relative amounts of contrast and saturation (but not sharpening) that are currently set for each of the four options.

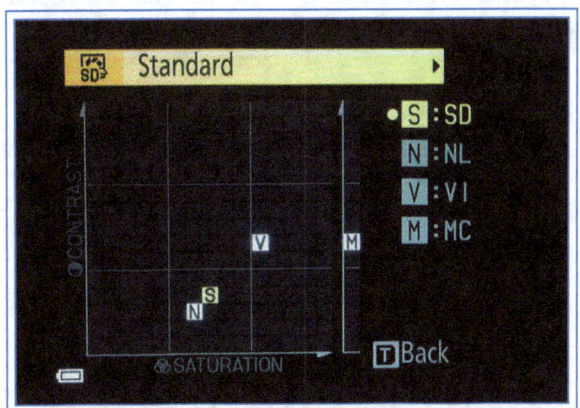

Figure 4-19. Picture Control Adjustment Grid

(Monochrome, of course, has no saturation setting, so its grid is separate from the others, in a single column at the right of the display.)

This grid may be useful if you want a graphic indication of how widely apart these parameters have been set. I have not found a need for the grid myself, but it is there if you want to use it.

Custom Picture Control

The Custom Picture Control option lets you take one of the four available Picture Control settings (Standard, Neutral, Vivid, or Monochrome) and tweak the three available parameters (sharpening, contrast, and saturation) to create a new setting that is crafted to your individual taste and that can be saved for later recall as an added selection for the Picture Control menu option.

To use this feature, select Custom Picture Control from the Shooting menu, then press the OK button or the Right button. You will first see a screen with the choices of Edit and Save or Delete. Select Edit and Save and press the OK or Right button again to bring up the menu with the four choices, as shown in Figure 4-20, and select one of them by pressing the OK button or the Right button.

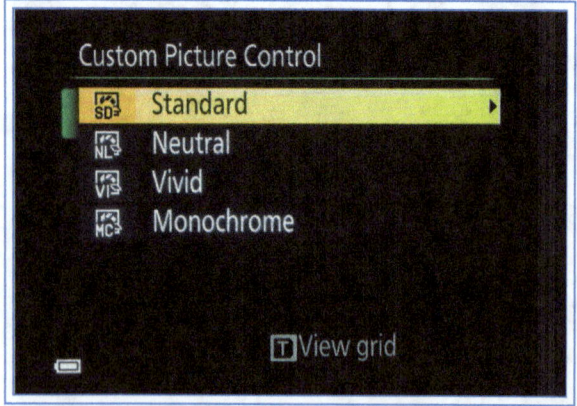

Figure 4-20. Custom Picture Control Options Screen

When the adjustment screen appears, adjust the parameters, which are the same as for the Picture Control item, discussed above. As noted before, the options are different for some of the settings: Monochrome, for example, has no Saturation adjustment, but does have Filter Effects and Toning adjustments.

For example, suppose you have found a group of adjustments to the Neutral setting that produces an appearance you want to be able to use whenever you take photographs of a certain waterfall. Go to the Custom Picture Control menu item, press OK or the Right button, and, on the next screen, select Edit and Save. You then are taken to a screen with the four basic Picture Control settings. Select Neutral, and, on the next screen, make your adjustments to sharpening, contrast, and saturation. When you are done, press OK, and you are taken to a screen that lets you save this setting to the Custom 1 or Custom 2 slot, as shown in Figure 4-21.

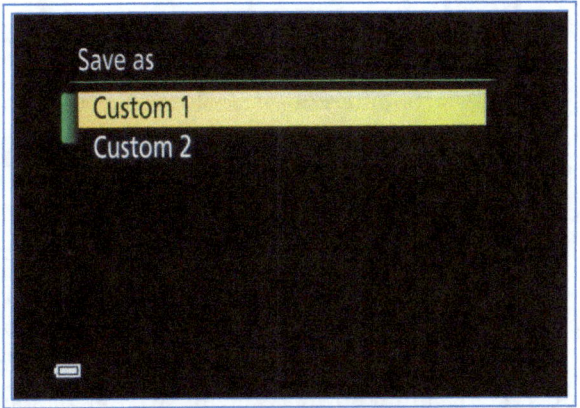

Figure 4-21. Screen to Save Custom Picture Control Setting

Highlight one of those options and press the OK button to confirm that selection. The camera will display a Done message. Then, whenever you want to recall that setting, go to the Picture Control menu item, where Custom 1 (or Custom 2) will now appear as an option below Monochrome, as shown in Figure 4-22.

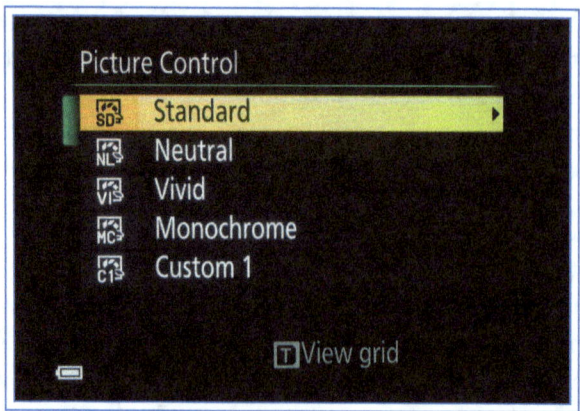

Figure 4-22. Picture Control Menu with Custom 1 Setting Added

If you later want to delete the Custom 1 or 2 option, use the Custom Picture Control item and select Delete instead of Edit and Save.

White Balance

One issue that arises in photography is that film, or a digital camera's sensor, reacts differently to colors than the human eye does. When you or I see a scene in daylight or indoors under various types of artificial lighting, we generally do not notice a difference in the hues of the things we see depending on the light source. However, the camera does not have this auto-correcting ability. The camera "sees" colors differently depending on the "color temperature" of the light that illuminates the object or scene in question. The color temperature of light is a numerical value expressed in a unit known as kelvins (K). A light source with a lower kelvin rating produces a "warmer" or more reddish light. A light source with a higher kelvin rating produces a "cooler" or more bluish light. For example, candlelight is rated at about 1,800 K; indoor tungsten light (ordinary light bulb) is rated at about 3,000 K; outdoor sunlight and electronic flash are rated at about 5,500 K; and outdoor shade is rated at about 7,000 K.

What does this mean in practice? If you are using a film camera, you may need a colored filter in front of the lens or light source to "correct" for the color temperature of the light source. Any given color film is rated to reproduce colors accurately at a particular color temperature (or, to put it another way, with a particular light source). So if you are using color film rated for daylight use, you can use it outdoors without a filter. But if you happen to be using that film indoors, you will need a color filter to correct the color temperature; otherwise, the resulting picture will look excessively reddish because of the imbalance between the film and the color temperature of the light source.

With a modern digital camera you do not need to worry about filters, because the camera can adjust its electronic circuitry to correct the "white balance," which is the term used in the context of digital photography for balancing color temperature. The Coolpix P600, like most digital cameras, has a setting for White Balance, which lets you choose the proper color correction to account for any given light source. Here is how to make this setting through the Shooting menu.

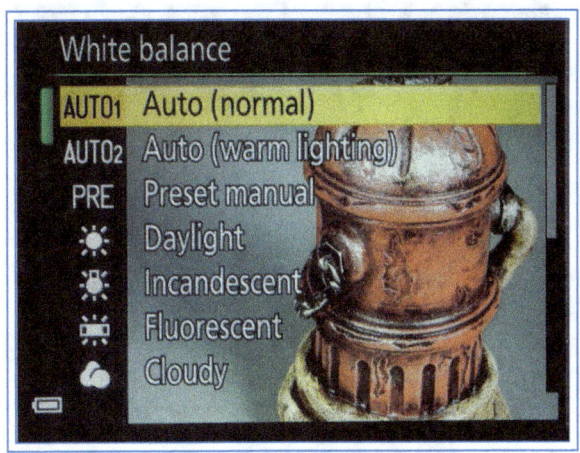

Figure 4-23. First Screen of White Balance Menu

Once you have highlighted the White Balance setting, which is the fifth item down on the first screen of the Shooting menu, press the OK button or the Right button to bring up the list of the following choices for the White Balance setting, each of them represented by an icon or a word or abbreviation: Auto (normal) [AUTO1]; Auto (warm lighting) [AUTO2]; Preset Manual [PRE]; Daylight [sun]; Incandescent [round light bulb]; Fluorescent [rectangular light bulb]; Cloudy [cloud]; Flash [lightning bolt]; and Choose Color Temperature [K]. The first 7 of these are shown in Figure 4-23.

The labels for these settings are self-explanatory, although you need to know a few details about how each one works. To select a setting, highlight it and press the OK button to confirm. If you select either Auto setting, you are done; there are no further adjustments available. With each of the other selections, though, you can fine-tune the setting, as described below.

If you highlight Daylight, Incandescent, Cloudy, or Flash, you can then press the Right button to bring up a screen with a scale at the left going from -3 at the bottom to +3 at the top, as shown in Figure 4-24.

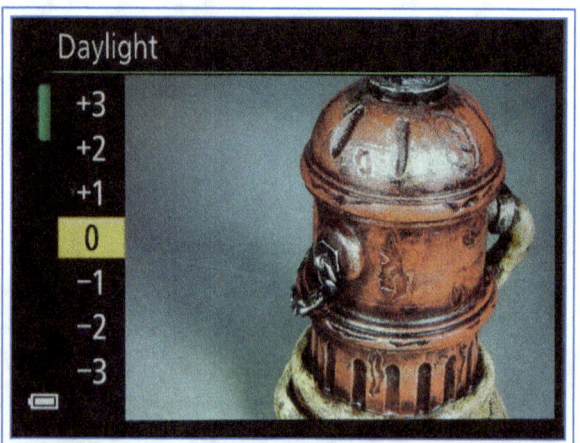

Figure 4-24. Daylight Setting Adjustment Screen

You can use the Up and Down buttons or the multi selector dial to move the yellow selection block up and down this scale to select a value. If the value is positive, the white balance is biased toward a bluish tint, and if it is negative, it is biased toward a reddish tint. If you want to save a step, you can just turn the command dial to adjust these values when the main setting (such as Daylight) is highlighted on the menu screen.

If you highlight the Fluorescent option, pressing the Right button brings up the further choices of 1, 2, or 3. These three sub-varieties of Fluorescent range from white to neutral to daylight. There are no other adjustments available with this setting.

Finally, if you select Preset Manual, you can set the white balance manually. Use this option when you are faced with mixed light sources, or a reddish or otherwise unusual light source. To make this setting, highlight Preset Manual, then press the OK button or the Right button. The next screen will present the options to Cancel or Measure, as shown in Figure 4-25.

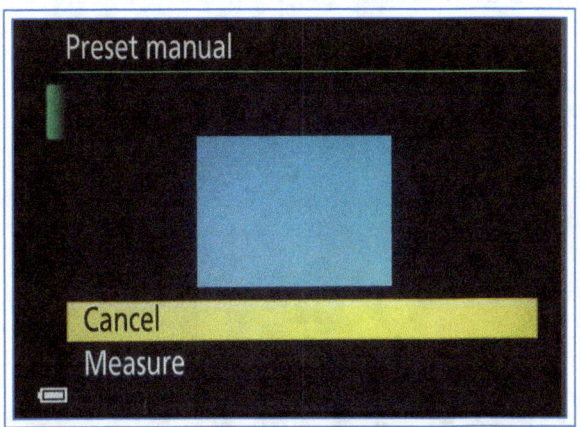

Figure 4-25. Preset Manual Measurement Screen

Highlight Measure, and then aim the square in the middle of the screen so it will be filled by a white or gray surface that is illuminated by the light source you will be using. Then press the OK button, and the camera will measure the white balance and store the setting. To use this setting now or in the future, turn back to the Preset Manual option at any time, even after the camera has been turned off and back on.

You can take advantage of the Preset Manual setting as a way to add a color tint to a scene for creative effect if you want. For example, you can set the white balance manually using a red or orange surface for the measurement, which will result in a pronounced blue tint for any pictures taken under the same light source that you used when setting that white balance value. Just be careful to turn the white balance setting back to Auto or another more normal setting when you don't want that special effect for your images.

The other choice for the White Balance menu option is Choose Color Temperature, the last item on the second screen of this menu item. Highlight this option, then press the OK button or the Right button to bring up the screen shown in Figure 4-26, with a scale of values at the left ranging from 2500 K to 10,000 K.

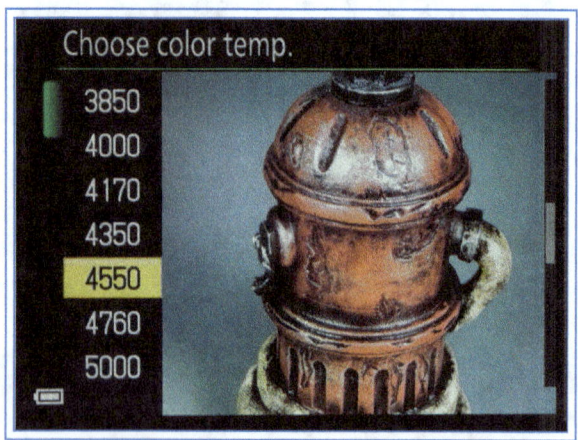

Figure 4-26. Choose Color Temperature Selection Screen

You can use this scale to set the numerical kelvin reading of your light source if you know it. You can determine this number using a color temperature meter, such as the one shown in Figure 4-27.

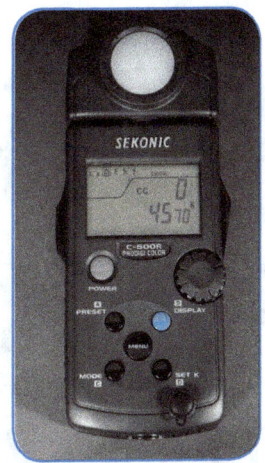

Figure 4-27. Sekonic Prodigi Color Meter

That meter works well when I need extra accuracy. It is expensive, though, and you may not want to use that option. In that case, you can still use the Choose Color Temperature option, but you will have to use guesswork or your sense of color. For example, if you have lighting from incandescent bulbs, you can use 3,000 K as a starting point, then change the value and watch the camera's display to see how natural the colors look. As you lower the color temperature setting on the menu, the image will become more "cool," or bluish; as you raise it, the image will appear more "warm," or reddish. Once you find the best setting, leave it in place and take your shots.

If you want to change the setting without moving to the screen with the scale at the left, just turn the command dial to change the value when the Choose Color Temperature option is highlighted on the White Balance menu screen.

Before I leave this topic, I'm going to include a chart of images showing how the various White Balance settings on the P600 affect the colors of your shots. All of these images, shown in Figure 4-28, were taken under the same indoor lighting, which was balanced for daylight; the only thing that changed from shot to shot was the camera's White Balance setting, as indicated.

White Balance Chart for Coolpix P600

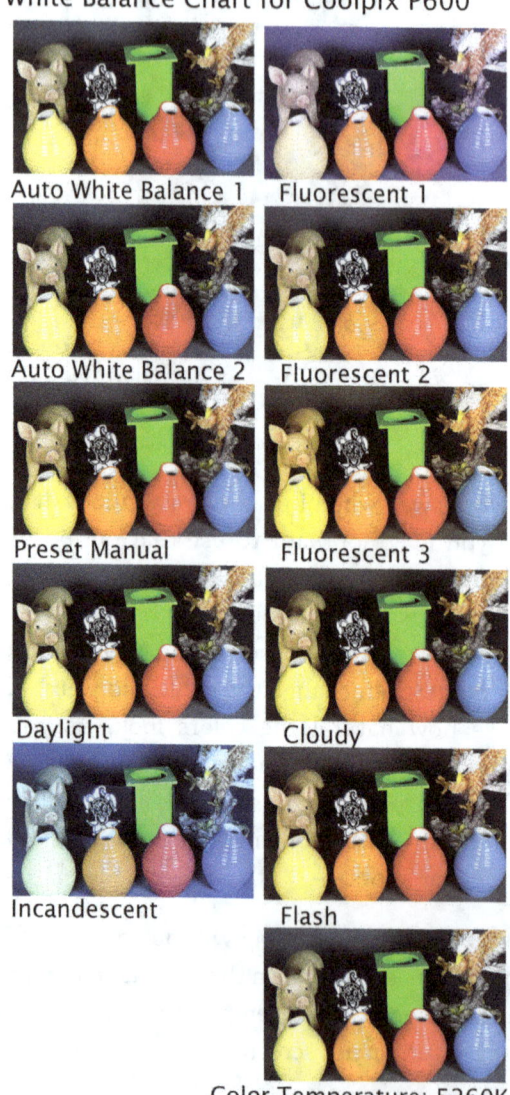

Color Temperature: 5260K

Figure 4-28. White Balance Settings Comparison Chart

The background for these shots was a sheet of neutral gray paper. When the white balance is set properly, the background should appear gray, as it does in several of the images. In my opinion,

Auto 1, Preset Manual, Daylight, Fluorescent 2, Flash, and Choose Color Temperature (using a value of 5260) all resulted in good color balance. Auto 2, Fluorescent 3, and Cloudy would be acceptable. However, even the results of those settings could be improved if you were to make further adjustments to tweak them for more or less bluish and reddish tints. The only settings that probably would not be usable in this situation were Incandescent and Fluorescent 1. In practice, I usually leave White Balance set to Auto 1, but it is good to know that you have the option to make more individually crafted settings when the occasion calls for it.

Metering

This next option on the Shooting menu lets you choose one of the three patterns of exposure metering offered by the Coolpix P600: Matrix, Center-weighted, and Spot. The menu selection screen is shown in Figure 4-29.

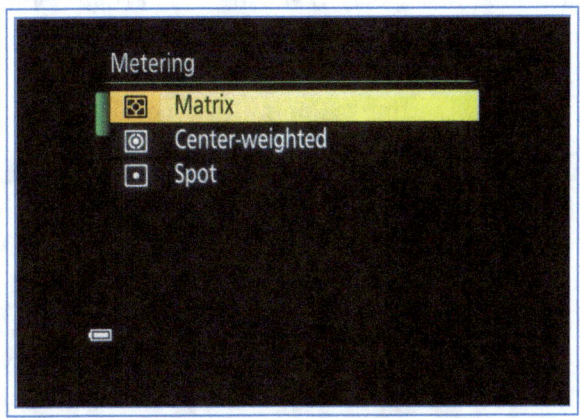

Figure 4-29. Metering Options Screen

This setting tells the camera's automatic exposure system what part of the scene it should evaluate when deciding how to set the exposure. If you choose Matrix, the default option, the camera uses the entire scene that is visible on the LCD and bases its exposure setting on the overall average brightness of the scene.

So, for example, if the camera is aimed at a landscape scene with trees, grass, buildings, sky, and people, the camera will measure the light being reflected from all of those parts of the scene and set the exposure accordingly. The resulting image is likely to look properly exposed.

If, instead of a standard landscape scene, the camera is aimed at a small, dark object in front of a large, white wall, the camera will take into account the large expanse of white and likely will set the exposure to be too dark to show the dark object properly. In that case, the Matrix metering mode probably will not work well. You can use exposure compensation or Spot metering to achieve a better exposure measurement.

Note, though, that there is one major exception to the way Matrix metering works. If you set the AF Area Mode menu item, discussed later in this chapter, to any of the three Manual settings (Spot, Normal, or Wide), the camera uses a focus frame that can be moved around the display. If you move that frame while Matrix metering is in effect, the camera will measure the exposure within that focus frame. In effect, the AF Area Mode setting of Manual changes the Matrix setting to Spot, with a movable spot.

If you choose Center-weighted for metering, as shown in Figure 4-30, the camera still considers all of the light from the scene, but it gives additional weight to the center portion of the image, on the theory that your main subject is in or near the center. The camera displays two large arcs to mark the area that is being emphasized. This is a good metering method to use when you have a subject in the center of the scene that is the most important item in your composition—for example, the subject of a portrait, or an antique that you are photographing for an auction.

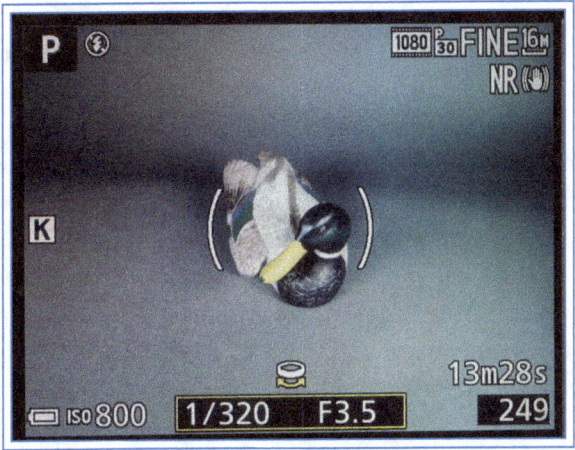

Figure 4-30. On-screen Arcs for Center-weighted Metering

With the Center-weighted setting, the autofocus mode has no effect on metering. Even if you set AF Area Mode to Manual and move the focus frame away from the center of the screen, the camera will meter the area outlined by the Center-weighted arcs.

With Spot, as illustrated in Figure 4-31, the camera considers only the light in the part of the scene covered by the small circle that appears in the center of the screen.

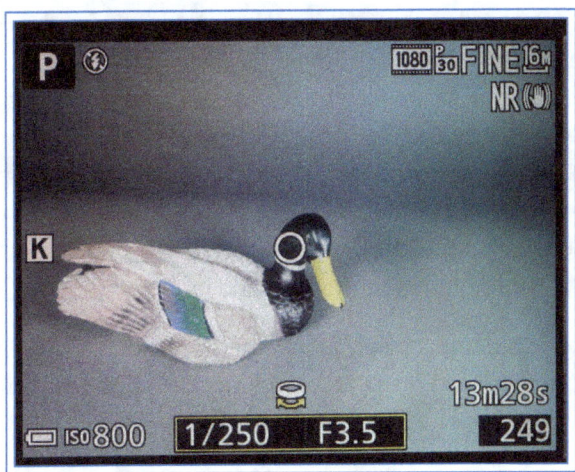

Figure 4-31. On-screen Circle for Spot Metering

When you set the metering method to Spot, you can see the effects of the exposure system quite dramatically by setting the camera to the Program exposure mode and aiming the small circle at various points, some bright and some dark, and seeing how dramatically the brightness of the scene in the LCD changes. If you try a similar experiment by moving the camera around to aim at differently lit areas in Matrix mode, you will still see changes, but more subtle and gradual ones. (However, as discussed above, if you have AF Area Mode set to Manual, Matrix metering acts more like Spot metering, and you may see dramatic changes when you move the camera around.)

The Spot setting is appropriate when you have a small subject for which proper exposure is particularly important, such as a small collectible item that you are photographing for a catalog or online auction. With this setting, as with Center-weighted, the AF Area Mode setting has no effect on the metering. The camera will meter the area inside the small circle in the center of the screen, even if you have the focus frame moved to one side.

My preference is to use Matrix metering for outdoor shots with even lighting, such as landscapes, groups of people, and views of buildings, monuments, and the like. I use Spot metering on occasion, primarily when I am photographing an object whose brightness level contrasts sharply with the background. For example, if I am photographing a black camera against a white background, I may use Spot metering on the camera in order to avoid confusing the metering system because of the expanse of bright white in the scene. The Center-weighted method is useful when taking portraits and other images with one central subject that is of primary importance to the scene.

The Metering menu option is dimmed and unavailable if Active D-Lighting is turned on at any level; in that case, the camera sets the metering mode to Matrix.

Continuous shooting

With some cameras, there is a button you can use to turn on continuous (or "burst") shooting. With the P600, the numerous options for continuous shooting are located on the Shooting menu, under the item called "Continuous." However, as discussed in Chapter 5, the Function button on top of the camera can be assigned to call up the Continuous option, so you can use a physical control for this purpose if you want to.

Regardless of whether you reach the Continuous shooting options through the menu system or by pressing the Function button, when the camera is set to a shooting mode in which burst shooting is available, the Continuous options give you an impressive array of features. Before describing them, I will provide a brief introduction to continuous shooting.

With film cameras, continuous shooting requires a motor to advance film rapidly, and often a high-capacity cassette to hold a large quantity of film. This equipment is bulky and expensive, and, of course, shooting and developing large numbers of exposures is expensive. With digital cameras like the Coolpix P600, expense is not a factor. Continuous shooting is available at your fingertips whenever you want to take advantage of it.

The usefulness of rapid bursts of exposures is clearer in some contexts than in others. For example, when you're shooting sports, you can fire off a swift sequence of shots to catch the instant when a baseball player tags a runner, or to catch a soccer ball as it bounces off a player's head. But continuous shooting also can be helpful in more ordinary shooting, such as pictures of children at play. You have a better chance of capturing a fleeting smile or gesture if you keep the exposures rolling. Even if your subject is not moving, it can be useful to take multiple shots. When you're taking a portrait there may be subtle changes in the subject's expression, or in the way sunlight falls on a cheek.

Taking a series of shots gives you some insurance against coming away from the photo session with no winning images.

In Figure 4-32, I used the continuous high-speed option to capture a series of images of bike riders in a national race.

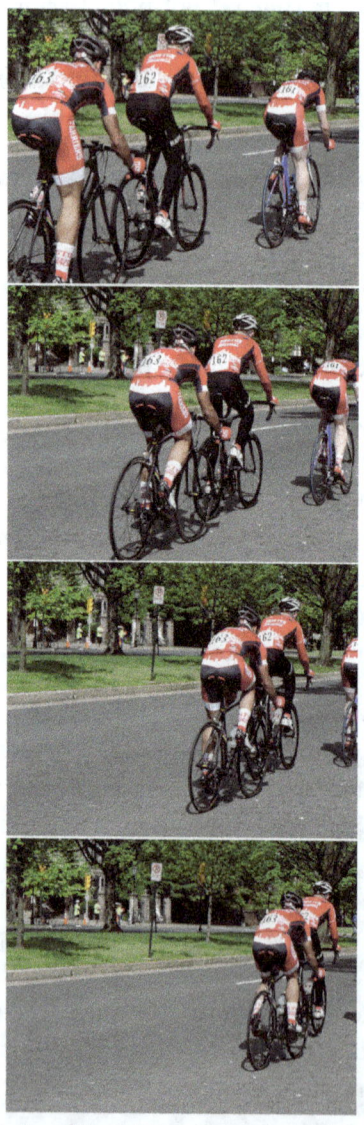

Figure 4-32. Series of Shots Using Continuous High-Speed Setting

The P600 provides an excellent set of continuous-shooting options. To get access to these options, the camera has to be in the Program, Aperture Priority, Shutter Priority, or Manual exposure mode. Select the Continuous menu item, press the Right button or the OK button, and the next screen will display the first 7 of the 9 available settings, as shown in Figure 4-33. (Or, as noted above, press the Function button if it is assigned to call up the Continuous menu option.)

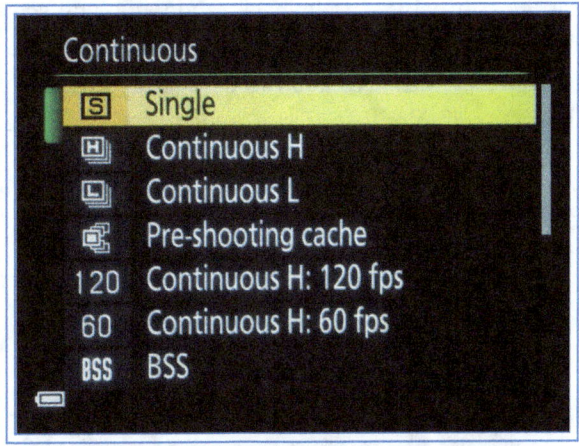

Figure 4-33. First Screen of Continuous Menu

These settings (except the first, for single shots, and the last, for intervals) offer various ways to take multiple shots while you hold down the shutter button. In each case, the exposure, focus, and white balance settings are fixed when the first image is taken, and they will not vary for later shots, even if conditions would require different settings. You cannot use flash for any of the multiple-shot settings except for the last one, the Interval Timer option.

You can activate the self-timer and it will work, but, with several continuous settings (Continuous H, Continuous L, Pre-shooting Cache, and Best Shot Selector), when the timer triggers the shutter only one image will be taken, even if you continue to hold down the shutter button. So there is no point in turning on continuous shooting and the self-timer at the same time, with those settings. However, with the Continuous H: 120 fps and Continuous H: 60 fps settings, the camera will take the full 60 shots when the self-timer triggers the shutter, and, with the Multi Shot 16 setting, although 16 images are recorded, they are all recorded in one shot, so the operation will succeed even when the self-timer is used. Also, the self-timer can be used to start a sequence using the interval timer setting.

As I discuss in Chapter 6, playing back continuous shots in this camera can be confusing. In playback mode, you will see the first image of a continuous series displayed on what looks like a stack of frames, indicating that this is the first of a continuous set, or, using Nikon's terminology, the "key" image of a "sequence."

There also will be a message at the bottom of the screen indicating that you have to press the OK button to display the full set of images, as shown in Figure 4-34.

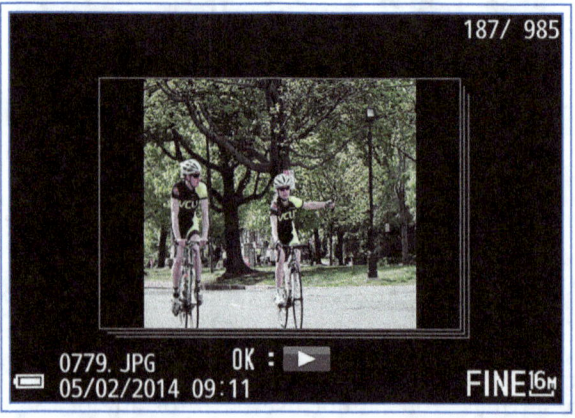

Figure 4-34. Prompt to Press OK to Play Continuous Images

After you press the OK button, you can move through this group of continuous shots using the normal navigation tools—the Left and Right buttons and the multi selector dial. To return to the main playback screen, press the Up button. You can then keep navigating through the other individual shots and sequences on the memory card.

Following are details about the choices for continuous shooting with the Coolpix P600, as shown in Figure 4-33. The first option at the top of the Continuous menu screen is an icon with an S, for single shots. This is the default option. In effect, choosing this first option turns off continuous shooting.

The second option on the menu is the first selection for multiple shots. It is marked by an icon that looks like a stack of rectangular frames with the letter H inside, representing high-speed continuous shooting. With this option, the camera shoots up to 7 shots at a speed of up to 7 frames per second, depending on factors such as image size, image quality, lighting conditions, and the like. You can use any settings for the image quality and size, including the maximum Fine at 4608 x 3456 pixels.

The next icon, marked by an L for low-speed shooting, provides a capability similar to that for high-speed shooting, except that there is a trade-off of increased capacity versus slower speed. That is, you can take up to 200 images, but at a speed of no more than about one frame per second.

The next icon on the list looks like a stack of frames branching out into two directions. Selecting this icon activates an interesting feature called Pre-shooting Cache. With this option, the camera actually captures several images before you press the shutter button to take pictures.

In practice, this option has its limitations, though it is still a welcome innovation. When you press the shutter button halfway to evaluate exposure and focus, the camera will capture up to 5 images before you press the button the rest of the way down, and up to 15 more as you hold the button down to take the images. The Pre-shooting Cache icon on the display turns green while images are being recorded to the cache; once you press the shutter button all the way down, the last 5 of those cached images are saved to the memory card, along with up to 15 shots taken while the shutter is pressed all the way down. The maximum rate is a speedy 15 frames per second, but the catch is that the images are fixed at a small size of 3 megapixels, or 2048 x 1536 pixels, and at Normal quality.

Pre-shooting Cache is a tool to use when you are monitoring a scene and waiting for just the right moment to catch a particular action or expression that may come up very quickly, and possibly will fade away quickly as well. When it looks as if the action is about to happen, you can press the shutter button halfway down to get ready, and, if the action comes up faster than expected, you won't miss it because of slow reactions. You can then press the shutter button all the way down to capture the rest of the sequence. If you don't mind a reduction in the resolution of your images, this is an interesting option to have available.

Be sure to note one possible pitfall here: If you press the shutter button down halfway but never press it all the way to take any pictures, the contents of the pre-shooting cache will be discarded and no pictures at all will be recorded. You have to press the shutter button down all the way at some point in order to "lock in" the pre-shooting images. Note also that, when you have finished shooting, you may see an hour-glass icon on the screen, indicating that the camera needs time to process the contents of the cache as well as the contents of the other images you have taken.

The next choice on the menu, Continuous H: 120 fps, is indicated by the number 120, representing the extremely rapid rate of 120 frames per second. With this setting, the camera emphasizes both speed and volume, giving you 60 images at this super pace, but at a drastic reduction in quality down to 640 x 480 pixels (VGA), which is the resolution of an old-fashioned computer monitor. Images shot using this option may look fine on your computer, but they will be quite grainy and will not be suitable for any degree of enlargement. Still, if you need to analyze a golf swing or otherwise shoot a sequence of many pictures over a period of about one-half second, this is the choice for you. Here again, you will almost certainly see the hour-glass icon after shooting, as the camera processes the large quantity of image information that it sucked in like a vacuum cleaner.

The next option, Continuous H: 60 fps, is similar to the previous one,except that the camera takes 60 shots at a somewhat larger resolution of 2 megapixels, or 1920 x 1080 pixels. Use this option if you need a super-speedy sequence of shots, but need a bit better quality or prefer the 16:9 widescreen aspect ratio of this setting.

The last option on the first screen of the Continuous menu is Best Shot Selector, marked by the BSS icon. This is a very useful setting, though it is quite different from those discussed above. With the BSS feature, the camera does not emphasize speed. Rather, it takes up to 10 shots at a rather leisurely pace. When it has finished shooting, it "examines" them internally to determine which one is the sharpest, with the most details. The camera then discards all but that "best" shot, and displays it as if it were the only shot taken.

The BSS feature is intended for use with non-moving subjects, such as taking a portrait inside a dimly-lit room without flash. (In fact, you cannot use flash when you're using BSS, just as you cannot with most other continuous-shooting options.) The idea is to give you several chances to capture an image that is not marred by blur from camera motion. You can set the image quality and size to their highest levels if you like, and you can control all other settings. (Though, as with all of the continuous-shooting options, the focus, exposure, and white balance will be fixed with the first shot.) Also, you may recall that the Museum setting in the Scene shooting mode uses the BSS feature, though you cannot make many other settings if you choose the Museum option, because of the limited menu options available in Scene mode.

The first item on the second screen of the Continuous menu is a feature called Multi-shot 16, marked by an icon that looks like a frame subdivided into smaller squares. When you press the shutter button with this setting activated, the camera takes a series of 16 images at a speed of about 30 frames per second, and places them all into a single image, arranged in 4 rows of 4 pictures each. The result looks like a proof sheet, as shown in Figure 4-35.

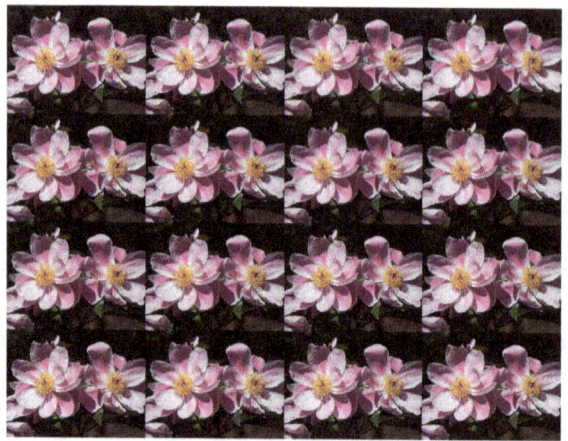

Figure 4-35. Multi-shot 16 Example Image

Of course, there may be some variations among the images if the subject moved at all during the half-second it took to capture all the images. This feature seems like a novelty, but you may find a good practical application for it, such as studying the motion of a subject over a short period of time, and it might be useful for analyzing some sports actions. The image quality is fixed at Normal, and the image size is limited to 2560 x 1920 pixels, or about 5 megapixels. (That is the image size for the whole, composite image; the 16 individual images are very small and would not be useful in themselves.)

The last entry on the continuous-shooting menu is Interval Timer shooting, which gives the Coolpix P600 a capability for time-lapse shooting. When you select this option and move to the next screen, the camera displays two blocks, as shown in Figure 4-36—one for minutes and one for seconds.

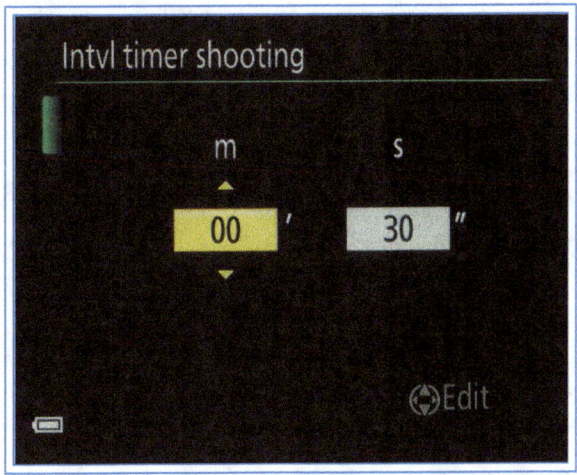

Figure 4-36. Interval Timer Options Screen

You can select a value from 0 to 60 for minutes, and either 0 or 30 for seconds, up to a maximum time of 60 minutes overall. So, the shortest interval available is 30 seconds; the next is 1 minute; then 1 minute 30 seconds, and so on.

There is no setting for the number of shots; the camera will keep taking shots at the specified interval until the memory card (or internal memory, if in use) is filled up, or you stop the process.

When you press the shutter button all the way, the camera takes the first image, then blanks out the display. The green light around the power button will blink slowly while interval shooting is active. Shortly before each interval elapses, the display will turn back on, and at the specified time the camera will take the next shot. To interrupt the sequence of shots before it is complete, you can press the shutter button and the sequence will end.

The resulting images are stored on your memory card in specially designated folders with the letters INTVL in their names. For example, a folder with shots from one shooting session might be labeled as 102INTVL, and the images inside it might be labeled DSCN001.jpg, DSCN002.jpg, and so on.

The Interval Timer option gives you excellent opportunities for creative photography. For example, you can aim the camera at a construction site and record all work that is done over a period of time, then play back the images as a time-lapse movie using software such as Adobe Premiere Elements or iMovie. If you set the camera to shoot one image every minute for 24 hours, you would end up with 1440 images. If you play them back at the standard video rate (in the United States) of 30 frames per second, the video showing 24 hours of action would play back in just 48 seconds. You may have seen sequences of this sort on television showing weather patterns unfolding at rapid speeds or speeded-up views of crowds gathering for events.

Also, interval shooting can be used to operate the camera remotely, such as when you place it on a pole or other location that is out of your reach, to record images from a high or otherwise inaccessible vantage point. If you are able to attach the P600 to a remote-controlled aerial drone like the DJI Phantom, you could turn on interval shooting to capture images from the air.

When you use interval shooting on the ground, you need to set the camera on a sturdy, steady tripod; the slightest motion of the camera will be obvious when the sequence is played back. Also, you need to be able to keep the camera powered on continuously. The camera does turn off its display between shots, so its battery power is conserved to some extent. However, if you are shooting a sequence that lasts several hours or more, you should use the Nikon AC adapter designated for this camera, model number EH-67A, which is discussed in Appendix A. Finally, it's generally a good idea, if it is practical under the circumstances, to use Manual exposure mode and to set the white balance and ISO to definite settings rather than to Auto settings, so that there is no distracting flickering among the images when the camera adjusts these settings automatically.

Next, I will discuss the items on screen 2 of the Shooting menu, shown in Figure 4-37, starting with ISO Sensitivity.

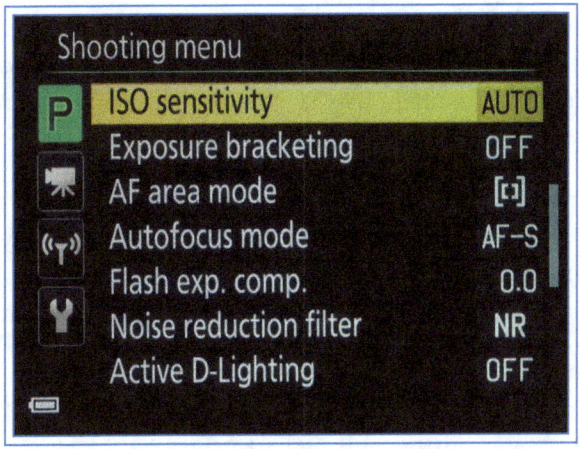

Figure 4-37. Second Screen of Shooting Menu

ISO Sensitivity

ISO is a standard for gauging the light sensitivity of photographic film or digital sensors. The higher the ISO rating, the more sensitive the film or sensor is to light. Therefore, if you shoot an image or video using a high ISO value, you will not need as much light to achieve a normal exposure as you would with a lower value. One result is that you can use a faster shutter speed, narrower aperture, or possibly both, than with a lower ISO.

The trade-off is that, with higher ISO values, the sensor is likely to produce visual "noise" that affects the image with an appearance of graininess. Camera makers have made considerable strides in creating sensors that can use high ISO values without too much noise, but there still is some drop-off in quality, especially at the highest ISO values.

Generally speaking, you should shoot your images with the camera set to the lowest ISO possible that will allow the image to be exposed properly. (One exception to this rule is if you want, for creative purposes, the grainy look that comes from shooting at a high ISO value.) For example, if you are shooting indoors in low light, you may need to set the ISO to a high value (say, ISO 800) so you can expose the image with a reasonably fast shutter speed. Otherwise, if the camera uses a slow shutter speed, the resulting image would likely be blurry and possibly unusable.

To summarize: Shoot with low ISO settings (usually 100 with the P600) when possible; shoot with high ISO settings (say 400 or higher, up to 1600 or even 3200) when necessary to allow a fast shutter speed to stop action and avoid blurriness, or when desired to achieve a creative effect with graininess.

With that background, here is how to set ISO on this camera. Press the Menu button and move to the ISO Sensitivity line at the top of the second screen of the Shooting menu, then press the Right button to get to the screen that lets you select either ISO Sensitivity or Minimum Shutter Speed, as shown in Figure 4-38.

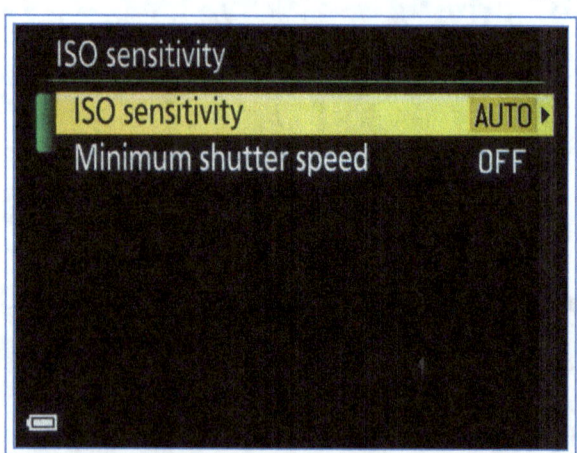

Figure 4-38. ISO Main Options Screen

For now, select ISO Sensitivity and press the Right button again to get to the ISO Sensitivity options. This first of the two ISO menu screens is shown in Figure 4-39. (As an alternative, you can assign the Function button to call up a menu with the ISO settings, as discussed in Chapter 5.)

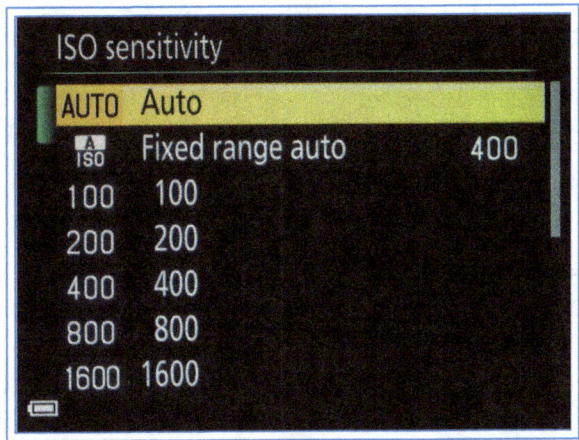

Figure 4-39. First Screen of ISO Values

With the first option at the top of this list, Auto, the camera sets the ISO to 100 in relatively bright light, and it will raise the level as high as 1600 as the light grows dimmer. The second option, Fixed Range Auto, has two choices, reached by pressing the OK button or the Right button. You can choose from two ranges, 100-400 or 100-800, if you want to limit the camera's ISO choices to a fairly narrow range of possibilities. You can use this approach if you want the camera to use some flexibility, but you want to make sure the ISO value does not go high enough to cause noticeable noise in your images.

Finally, instead of choosing Auto or Fixed Range Auto, you can choose any one of the individual ISO values, to specify exactly what ISO setting the camera uses. The choices are 100, 200, 400, 800, 1600, 3200, and 6400. (There is one higher level, called Hi 1 by Nikon, which is equivalent to ISO 12800; it cannot be selected from the ISO menu; it is activated only when the camera is set to High ISO Monochrome in the Special Effects shooting mode, described in Chapter 3.)

I usually leave the ISO setting at Auto for everyday shooting. However, in some cases, I will choose a specific numerical value. When I am using a tripod and want to have the best possible quality, I will set the ISO to 100. Because of the tripod, I am not concerned about image blur from camera motion if a slow shutter speed is needed. However, if I am shooting fast action such as sports or shooting in dim light, I often will set the ISO to a high value, such as 800 or 1600, so the camera can use a fast shutter speed to stop the action or to make a bright enough exposure.

I rarely set ISO as high as 3200 or 6400, because of the negative effect of such a setting on image quality. Figure 4-40 is a composite image containing two shots I took of a duck decoy's head, the top one at ISO 100, and the bottom one at ISO 6400, to illustrate the difference in quality that often results from using such a high ISO value.

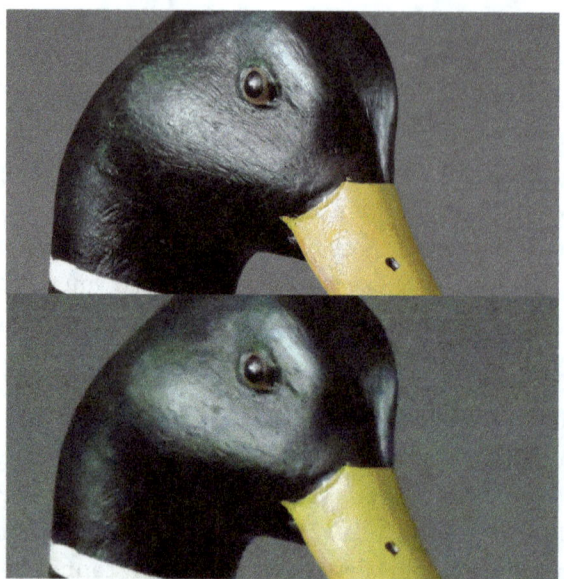

Figure 4-40. Top: ISO 100, Bottom: ISO 6400

As you can see, the bottom image, taken with the high ISO setting, shows considerable graininess and distortion of the colors of the decoy. That image would not be usable for many purposes. The top image, taken at ISO 100, is a high-quality image that depicts the subject clearly.

MINIMUM SHUTTER SPEED

Going back to the first branch on the ISO menu screens, you can use the Minimum Shutter Speed setting to specify the slowest shutter speed the camera will use when it is set to the Program or Aperture Priority mode and either of the Auto ISO settings (Auto or Fixed Range Auto) is in effect, before it starts to increase the ISO sensitivity.

To understand this setting, it's helpful to consider an example. Set the camera to Program mode and the ISO Sensitivity setting to Auto. Press the Menu button, use the multi selector dial or the Up and Down buttons to highlight ISO sensitivity on the display, and press the Right button to get to the next screen. Then highlight Minimum Shutter Speed, press the Right button, and select 1/30 second from the list of values on the screen shown in Figure 4-41.

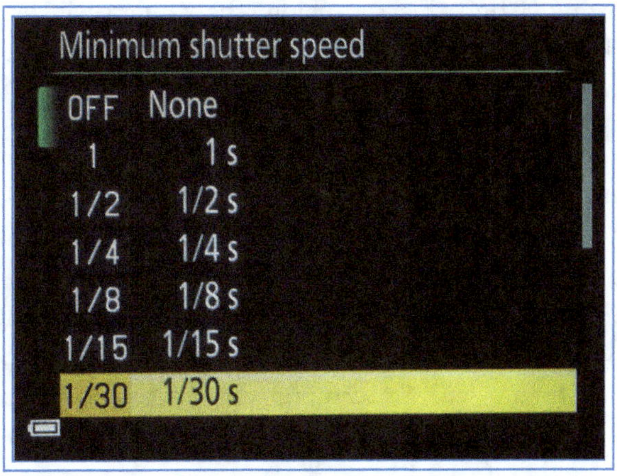

Figure 4-41. Minimum Shutter Speed Selection Screen

With those settings, the camera will attempt to expose the image properly using a shutter speed no slower than 1/30 second, your Minimum Shutter Speed setting. If the Auto ISO setting increases to its maximum limit and the image is still too dark, then the camera will drop to a slower shutter speed in order to achieve a good exposure. So, in effect, this setting forces the camera to try to keep the shutter speed at 1/30 second or faster, but if that's not possible, the camera will then change to a slower shutter speed. You may want to use this setting to avoid using slow shutter speeds that are likely to result in blurred photos because of camera motion, or to capture images of moving subjects, such as children playing. If you use a setting such as 1/125 second (the fastest setting possible) for Minimum Shutter Speed, along with an ISO setting such as Auto, which allows the ISO to go as high as 1600, you are likely to be able to take all of your exposures using the 1/125 second shutter speed (if the light is bright enough), preserving your ability to avoid camera shake and to capture ordinary action.

Here are some more notes on the Auto ISO options. If you select either of the two Auto ISO settings in Manual exposure mode, the camera will set the ISO to 100. You can select any other numerical ISO value if you want, and the camera will use that setting. However, and I find this confusing, the camera will let you set Auto or Fixed Ranged Auto for ISO, but it will actually set the ISO to 100, regardless of that menu setting.

In Auto shooting mode and with all of the scene settings, Auto ISO is automatically set and you cannot adjust the ISO setting. The same is true of the Special Effects shooting mode, although, as noted earlier, if you choose the High ISO Monochrome setting, the camera sets the ISO to Hi 1, which is the equivalent of ISO 12800. With several continuous-shooting options (Pre-Shooting Cache, Multi-shot 16, Continuous H:120 fps, and Continuous H:60 fps), ISO is automatically set to Auto.

Exposure Bracketing

Exposure bracketing is a feature that lets you take three pictures with one press of the shutter button, with different exposure settings, thereby giving you an added chance of getting one good, usable image. In addition, exposure bracketing is an excellent way to take three pictures that can be combined later in software to produce an HDR (high dynamic range) composite, which shows clear details in both the highlights and the shadows throughout the image by combining the best-exposed parts of each shot.

To use exposure bracketing, the camera must be set to the Program, Aperture Priority, or Shutter Priority mode. Navigate to the second line on the second screen of the Shooting menu. Then press the OK button or the Right button to get access to the next screen, which will present you with four choices: ±0.3, ±0.7, ±1.0, and Off, as shown in Figure 4-42.

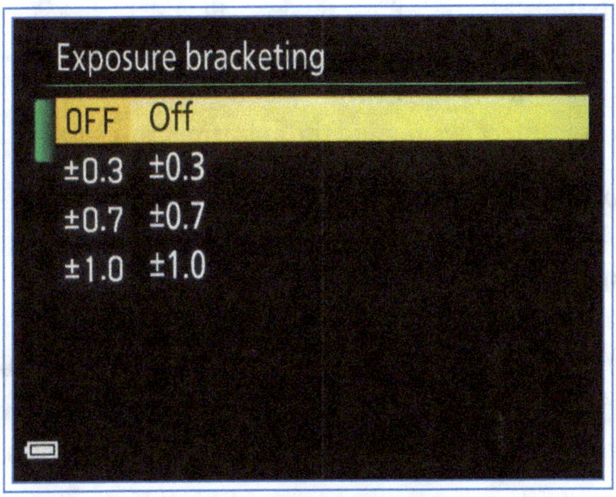

Exposure bracketing

OFF	Off
±0.3	±0.3
±0.7	±0.7
±1.0	±1.0

Figure 4-42. Exposure Bracketing Options Screen

Use the multi selector dial or direction buttons to highlight your choice, then make the selection by pressing the OK button. When you exit to shooting mode, the camera's display will include a notation such as BKT±0.7, as shown in Figure 4-43, unless you left bracketing turned off. (Press the Display button if necessary to show this detail on the screen.)

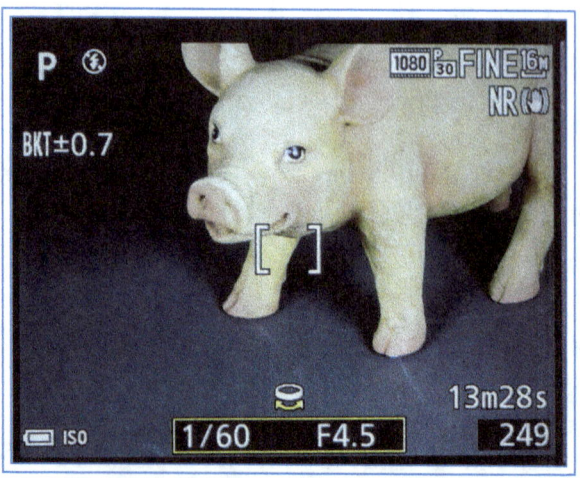

Figure 4-43. Exposure Bracketing Icon on Shooting Screen

This notation means the camera will take three exposures separated by the indicated amount of exposure value (EV, a standard measure of brightness). Adding a single unit of EV, +1.0, has the same effect as opening the aperture by one full f-stop.

When you are ready to shoot, press and release the shutter button and hold the camera steady (or use a tripod) while it takes the three exposures. The first picture taken is always at the metered level, or 0 change in exposure value (EV); the second is at the lower EV (darker), and the third is at the higher EV (brighter). If you have added exposure compensation, the bracketed exposures are taken at three levels relative to the adjusted exposure.

Note that the flash cannot be used when bracketing is in effect. If you press the Flash button (Up button) when bracketing is turned on, nothing will happen. If the flash was previously set to forced on (Fill Flash) or any other mode in which the flash might fire, the camera will turn the flash off when bracketing is selected.

Be sure to cancel exposure bracketing when you are done using this feature; otherwise, it will stay in effect even after you turn the camera off and back on again.

AF Area Mode

This next option on the second screen of the Shooting menu gives you several options for controlling how the autofocus frame is set up when the camera is in autofocus mode.

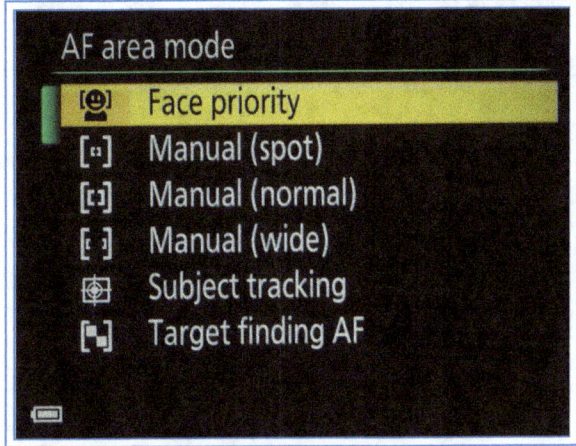

Figure 4-44. AF Area Mode Options Screen

Once this menu option is highlighted, press the OK button or the Right button to display the next menu screen, and then use the multi selector dial or the Up and Down buttons to select from the six possible options shown in Figure 4-44, as follows:

FACE PRIORITY

With this option, the camera looks for human faces. If it detects what it believes are faces, it puts a yellow, double-bordered frame on the closest face, and single-bordered frames on other faces, as shown in Figure 4-45. When you press the shutter button halfway, the camera will focus on the main face, place a double-bordered green frame on it, and set the exposure and white balance for that face.

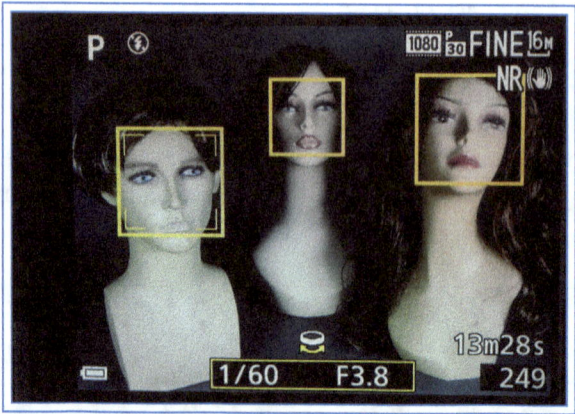

Figure 4-45. Face Priority Detection Screen

This is a good option to choose when you're at a picnic or other group function and you need to take a quick snapshot with focus fixed on people's faces rather than on trees, buildings, or other objects. In other situations, you may want to take more time and select the focus point and other options yourself.

MANUAL (SPOT, NORMAL OR WIDE)

The next three options for AF Area Mode are variations of the Manual setting. The only differences among these three settings are the sizes of the focus frames used—Spot, Normal, or Wide. The illustrations here all use the Normal size.

If you select one of the three Manual settings for AF Area Mode, the camera displays a focus frame of the chosen size in the center of the screen, with arrows pointing in each direction outside the frame. You can now use the four direction buttons or the multi selector dial to move the focus frame to any of 99 possible locations around the screen, as shown in Figure 4-46. (There are only 81 locations available if you are using the 1:1 aspect ratio, with Image Size set to 3456 x 3456.)

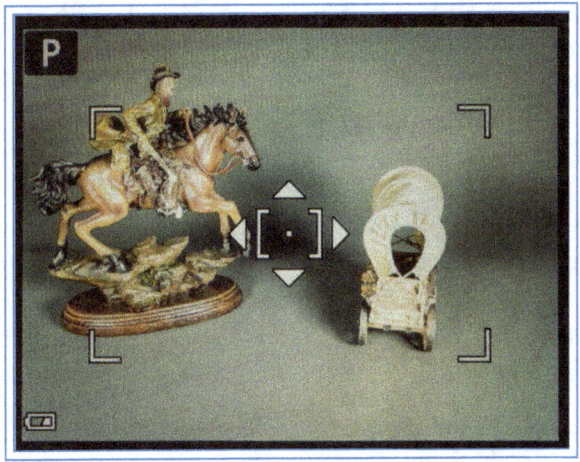

Figure 4-46. Movable Focus Frame Ready to Move

This is a good option to use if you are shooting a scene with items at varying distances from the camera and you want to focus on an item that is not in the center of the scene. Of course, this type of focusing is useful only if you have time to select this option and move your focus frame to the location where you want it. If you don't have time, it may be easier simply to place the center of the frame over the item you want to focus on, press the shutter button halfway to lock the focus, and then move the camera back to compose the image as you want it. That method is also the best way to proceed when you are using Center-weighted or Spot for the Metering option and you want to lock both focus and exposure for a subject that is not in the center of the scene. If you use the Manual setting for AF Area Mode in that situation, the focus will be set on the off-center subject, but the exposure will be based on the subject in the center of the screen.

If you do have the time to use the Manual option for AF Area Mode, here is how to use it. Once you have located the focus frame where you want it using the buttons or dial, press the shutter button to lock focus and then take the picture. The focus frame will stay in this location even after the camera is powered off and back on, so be sure to reset it to the center when you no longer need it in an off-center position. You can tell when the frame is in the center of the screen because a dot will appear in the center of the frame while it is movable.

If you need to use one of the four direction buttons on the multi selector for another purpose while using Manual AF Area Mode, press the OK button to return the direction buttons to their other functions (flash mode, focus mode, self-timer, and exposure compensation); then, after using a button for another function, press OK again to return the buttons to controlling the location of the focus frame.

SUBJECT TRACKING

This next AF Area Mode option is designed for situations in which you need to track a moving subject, such as a sports competitor or a child at play. Once you have selected this mode, you will see a small, white, square-shaped bracket in the center of the screen, with the words OK Start below it, as shown in Figure 4-47.

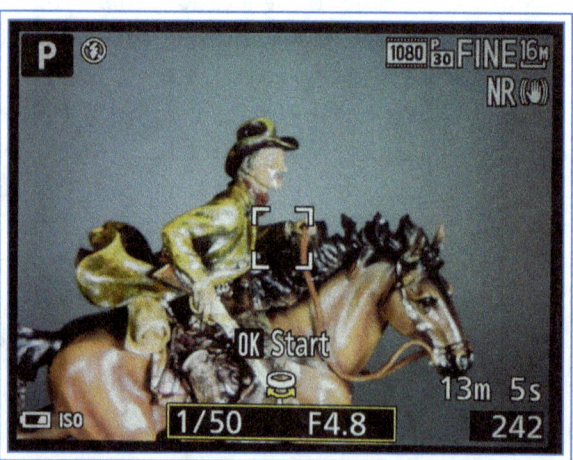

Figure 4-47. Subject Tracking Ready to Start

Aim this square bracket at the subject you want to track and press the OK button. The frame will change to a double set of yellow brackets, as shown in Figure 4-48, which the camera will try to keep centered over the subject, even as the subject (or the camera) moves.

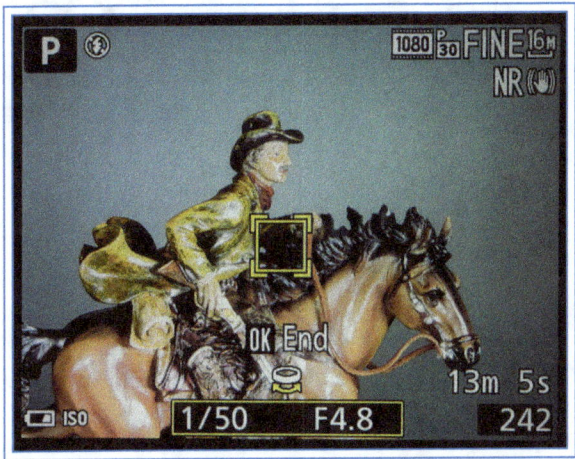

Figure 4-48. Subject Tracking Frame Activated

When you press the shutter button down halfway to check exposure, the frame will turn green to confirm exposure, and the tracking will stop. Press the shutter button all the way down when you are ready to take the picture.

TARGET FINDING AF

The final option for AF Area Mode, Target Finding AF, is the default setting and the one the camera uses when it is set to the Auto shooting mode. With this option, the P600 uses its programming to try to select the main focus point(s). The camera does not have any focus frame on its display screen at first. As you aim the camera at a scene, though, the camera may display yellow frames of varying sizes and shapes on the screen, as shown in Figure 4-49, as it tries to detect the subject to focus on.

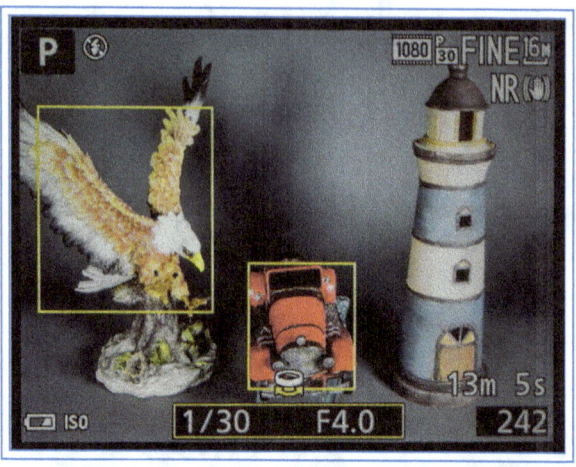

Figure 4-49. Yellow Focus Frames for Target Finding Setting

When you press the shutter button halfway to lock in the focus, the camera will try to select the "main" subject. It will first look for a human face, then for a subject that matches its programmed factors, such as size, position, and color. If it has not determined a main subject, it will focus on the item or items closest to the camera within 9 focus blocks in the central part of the display. It will display one or more green rectangles on the screen to show the point(s) it chose for focusing, as shown in Figure 4-50.

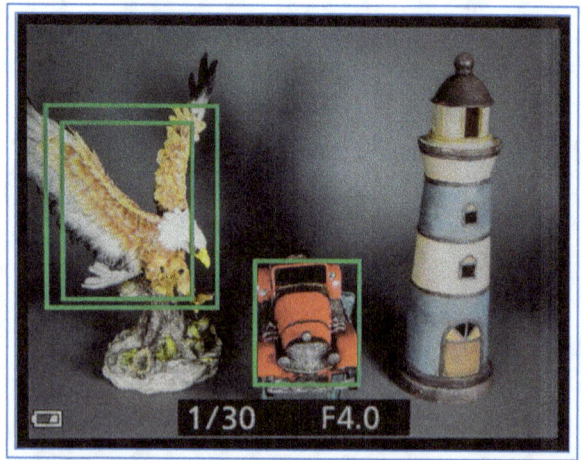

Figure 4-50. Green Focus Frames for Target Finding Setting

This focusing mode is good for shots of general scenes when you don't have time to choose a focus point yourself or when there is not much doubt about where the camera will set its focus. For example, if you are taking a snapshot of a person in front of a scenic view, you can safely assume that the camera will focus on the person. If the scene includes multiple objects fairly close to the camera, you might be better off using one of the Manual settings to make sure the subject you want to focus on is inside the focus frame.

Autofocus Mode

This feature, whose menu screen is shown in Figure 4-51, lets you decide whether the camera will focus just once, when you press the shutter button halfway, or will focus continuously before you press the button halfway.

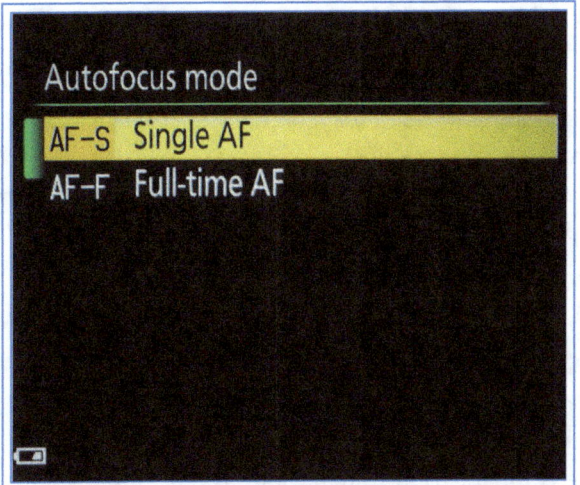

Figure 4-51. Autofocus Mode Options Screen

Choose Single AF if you want to conserve the battery and wait until you are ready to take the picture before the camera uses its autofocus mechanism; choose Full-time AF if you want the camera to focus continuously. Although the Full-time option will use up your battery more quickly, it has the advantage of keeping the image in focus as you move the camera or your subject moves around; in that way, when you are ready to capture the image, the camera can make the final focusing adjustments quickly when you press the shutter button.

This option does not apply for shooting movies; you need to select an autofocus mode from the Movie menu for that situation. Also, you cannot use this setting when AF Area Mode is set to Face Priority, Subject Tracking, or Target Finding AF. In those cases, Single AF is automatically selected. When manual focus is in effect, you can select this menu option, but it will not have any effect until you switch the camera to autofocus or macro focus. With the infinity focus mode, the camera uses Single AF for Autofocus Mode, regardless of the setting for this option. When the Smile Timer is active, the camera uses Single AF in all cases.

Flash Exposure Compensation

This option works in similar fashion to standard exposure compensation, discussed in Chapter 2. It is available only in Program, Aperture Priority, Shutter Priority, and Manual exposure modes. You can dial in an amount of positive or negative flash exposure compensation up to 2 EV units in either direction, in increments of 1/3 EV. When you do that, the camera will increase or decrease the output of the flash, unless it was already using its maximum or minimum power.

I find this setting to be of most use when I'm taking a portrait using the flash. I like to dial in a small amount of negative flash exposure compensation to make sure the flash does not wash out the image with excessive brightness.

To use this setting, go to its entry on the second screen of the Shooting menu and press the OK button or the Right button to get to the adjustment screen. At that screen, turn the multi selector dial or use the Up and Down buttons to dial in up to +2.0

EV or -2.0 EV, to make your flash exposures that much brighter or darker, as shown in Figure 4-52.

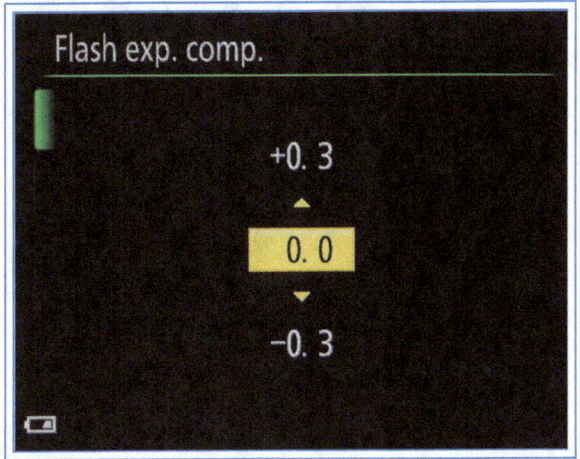

Figure 4-52. Flash Exposure Compensation Adjustment Screen

Press the OK button to confirm your selection when the value you want to choose is highlighted in the yellow bar in the middle of the screen. When you have activated a positive or negative amount of flash exposure compensation, that value will appear on the camera's display in the lower right-hand corner, but only when the flash is popped up. That value will remain in effect even after the camera has been powered off and back on, so be sure to cancel it when you no longer need the compensation.

Noise Reduction Filter

Noise reduction is an electronic feature built into the P600's programming to compensate for visual noise in your images, which can be caused by long exposures or by the use of high ISO settings. By default, this option is set to Normal, which causes the camera to use a moderate amount of noise reduction. If you want to have larger or smaller amounts of noise reduction applied in every case, you can switch the setting to High or Low, as shown in Figure 4-53. You cannot turn noise reduction completely off.

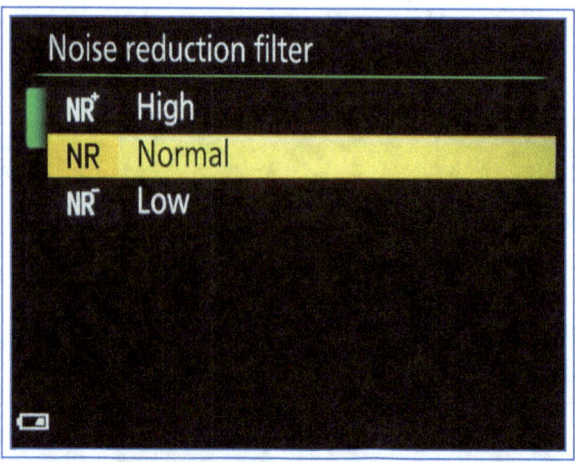

Figure 4-53. Noise Reduction Filter Options Screen

What you do with this setting is a matter of personal preference. If you are going to be using Photoshop, Photoshop Elements, or similar software to process the images on your computer, you may want to leave Noise Reduction Filter set to Low, so you can minimize the amount of processing done in the camera. Excessive noise reduction can reduce the detail and other positive features of an image. However, if you will be using the shots straight from the camera and you are shooting with long shutter speeds or high ISO settings, you may well want to turn this setting up to High to avoid the graininess that comes from visual noise.

Active D-Lighting

This final entry on screen 2 of the Shooting menu can help you avoid problems with excessive contrast in your images. Such problems arise because digital cameras cannot easily process a wide range of dark and light areas in the same image—that is, their "dynamic range" is limited. So, if you are taking a picture in an area partly lit by bright sunlight and partly in deep shade, the resulting image is likely to have dark areas in which details are lost in the shadows, or areas in which highlights, or bright areas, are excessively light, or "blown out," so, again, the details of the image are lost. One approach to this problem is to use HDR techniques, with which multiple photographs of the same scene with different exposures are combined into a composite image that is properly exposed throughout the entire scene. I discussed that technique in Chapter 3, in connection with the Backlighting/HDR setting of Scene mode.

The Active D-Lighting menu option gives you another way to approach the problem of uneven lighting. This feature uses processing in the camera to boost details in dark areas and reduce overexposure in bright areas, resulting in a single image with better exposure than would be possible otherwise. If you turn this option on, the camera reduces the overall exposure and performs digital processing as it records the image, resulting in some restoration of details in the shadows and in the highlights, to even out the lighting. The Shooting menu, as shown in Figure 4-54, provides three levels of this processing: High, Normal, and Low, as well as Off, the default setting.

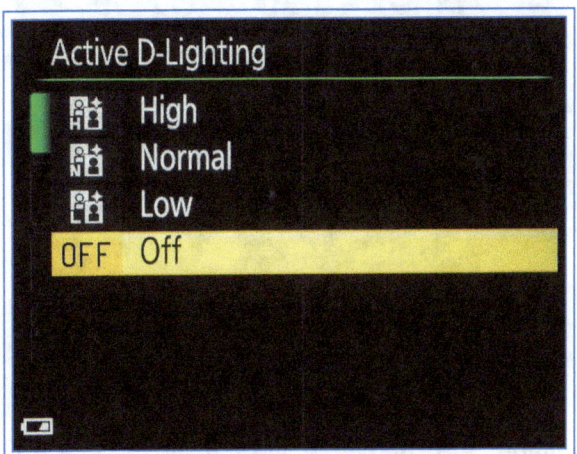

Figure 4-54. Active D-Lighting Options Screen

To illustrate the effects of this setting, I took a pair of photographs of a shaded passageway on a sunny day at the local botanical garden. For the first sample image, Figure 4-55, Active

D-Lighting was turned off; for Figure 4-56, it was turned on to the High setting.

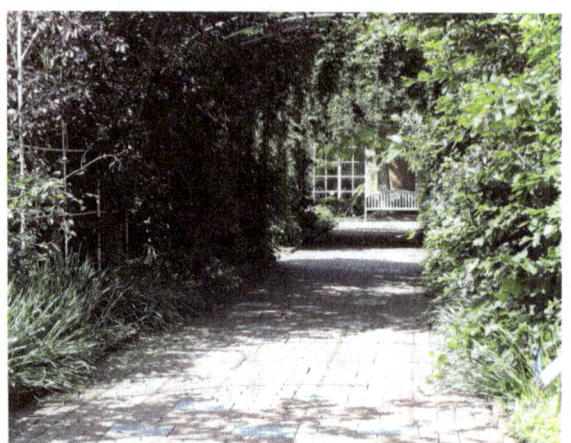

Figure 4-55. Active D-Lighting Off

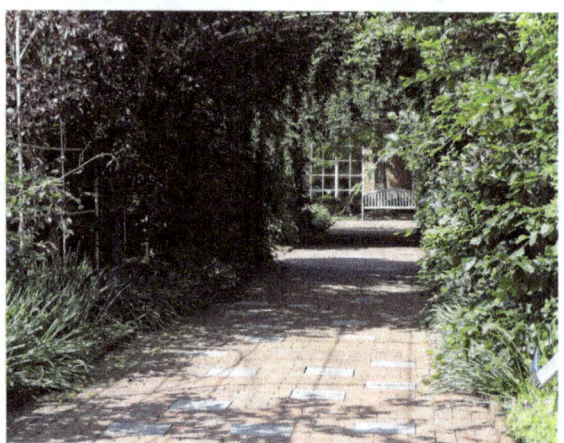

Figure 4-56. Active D-Lighting High

In my opinion, with Active D-Lighting set to High, the camera noticeably reduced the overexposure in the brighter part of the image, especially on the tiles on the ground. I did not notice much improvement, if any, in the level of details in the shadowed areas. My recommendation is to turn on Active D-Lighting when you are shooting a scene like this one, that is partly in the sun and partly in the shade. In those cases, if you have time, I would try setting this menu option to its various levels to see how the results compare. You also might want to use exposure bracketing, discussed earlier in this chapter, and merge those three exposures using HDR software, as discussed in Chapter 3. Or, you can use the Backlighting/HDR setting of Scene mode, also discussed in Chapter 3.

The Metering option is not available on the Shooting menu when Active D-Lighting is turned on to any level; in that case, the camera uses the Matrix setting for metering.

Note that the Coolpix P600 has a related feature called simply D-Lighting, which is used in playback mode for images that have already been taken. I'll discuss that feature in Chapter 6.

The third and final screen of the Shooting menu is shown in Figure 4-57.

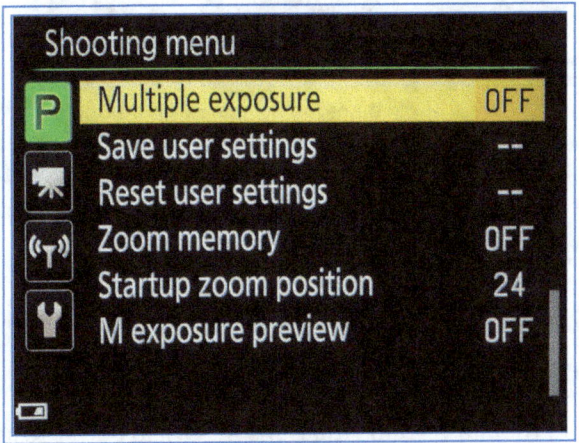

Figure 4-57. Multiple Exposure Menu Option

Multiple Exposure

This first item on screen 3 of the Shooting menu lets you shoot multiple exposures in the camera. You can shoot either two or three images on the same digital frame. When you highlight this option and press the OK button or the Right button, the camera displays the options screen, shown in Figure 4-58.

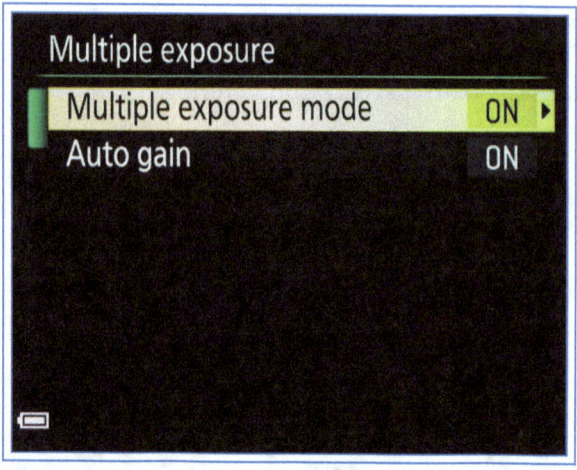

Figure 4-58. Settings for Multiple Exposure Option

To shoot multiple exposures, set the Multiple Exposure Mode option to On. You can set the Auto Gain option to On, which is the default setting, or turn it off. If it is turned on, then the camera will use its programming to adjust the relative brightness of the multiple images as it sees fit. If you turn this option off, then the images will be recorded without adjustment. In my experience, this feature produces better results with Auto Gain turned on, though certain situations may yield better results with it turned off.

After you turn Multiple Exposure mode on, aim at your first subject. If you will be shooting the second subject to appear beside the first one, then be sure to plan ahead, leaving space where the second subject will appear. Plan for a third subject also, if you will be shooting three items. If the positioning of the subjects will be critical, you should use a tripod to keep the composition precise.

Press the shutter button to take the first picture. After some processing time, the camera will display the first image on the screen in a translucent mode, so you can continue to view the first image while you compose the next one. Now, line up the second image while viewing the first one, as illustrated in Figure 4-59.

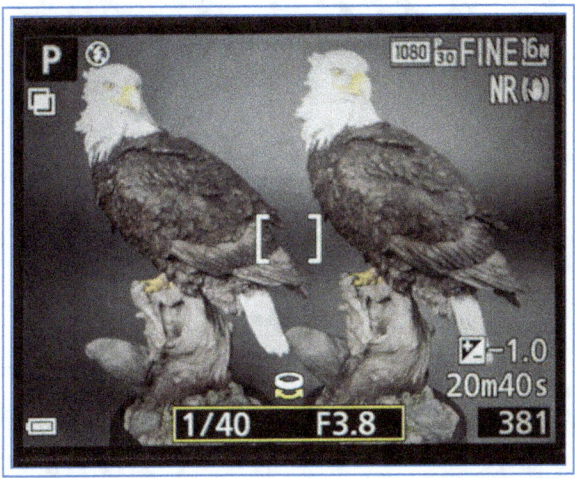

Figure 4-59. Multiple Exposure Screen After First Shot

When this composition looks right, press the shutter button to take the second image. The camera will take even longer to process this exposure. When it has finished processing, the double exposure will be displayed on the screen. It will still appear translucent, because you now have the option of taking one more picture to add to the composition. If you want to do that, go ahead and line up the third shot and press the shutter button. After the camera finishes processing the third image, it will return to the shooting screen. To view the final composition with three exposures, press the Playback button and you will see the finished product.

If you want to use only two exposures, then, after you take the second one, go to the Menu system and turn off the Multiple Mode Exposure option, or just turn the mode dial to a shooting mode that does not provide access to this menu item, such as Auto, Scene, or Special Effects.

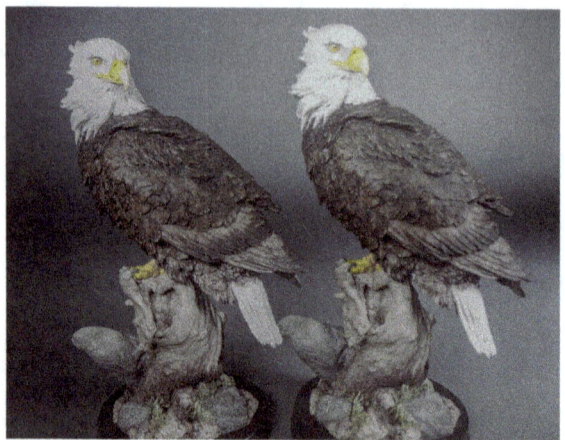

Figure 4-60. Multiple Exposure Final Image

Figure 4-60 shows the finished image from two shots of a single eagle figurine. I added some contrast and sharpening to the final image in Photoshop, because it looked a bit faded as it came out of the camera. The camera also saves each individual image you take for the multiple exposure composite.

Save User Settings

I discussed this feature in Chapter 3 in connection with the User Settings shooting mode, marked by the letter U on the mode dial. To save your current shooting settings for instant recall with the U slot on the dial, navigate to the Save User Settings option on the Shooting menu, as shown in Figure 4-61, and press the Right button or the OK button to save the settings.

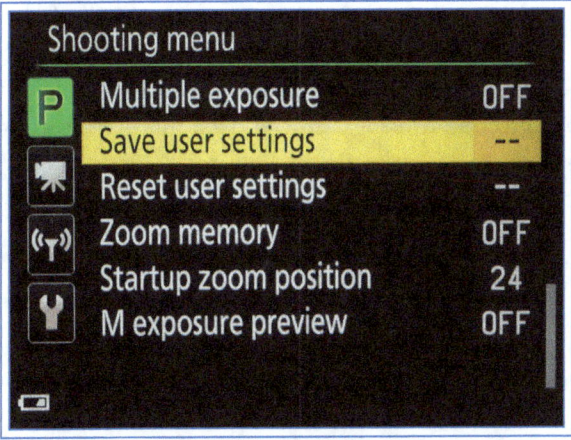

Figure 4-61. Save User Settings Menu Option

Be sure the settings are as you want before you press the button, because the camera does not ask you to confirm your choice; it just displays a "Done" message once you press the button.

Reset User Settings

This option on the Shooting menu, shown in Figure 4-62, lets you reset the settings that have been saved to the User Settings mode (U slot on the mode dial).

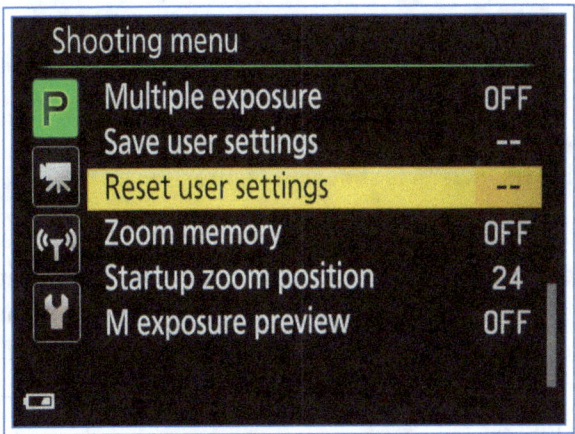

Figure 4-62. Reset User Settings Menu Option

When you select this option, the camera resets all of those items to their default values without your having to go through the menus to adjust each one. For example, choosing this option sets the shooting mode to Program, the flash mode to Auto, exposure compensation to 0.0, the zoom lens to its wide-angle position, and all items on the Shooting menu to their default settings.

Note that this option affects only the settings saved for the User Settings shooting mode; if you want to reset all settings for the camera for all modes, you have to use the Reset All menu option, which is found on the Setup menu, as discussed in Chapter 7.

Zoom Memory and Startup Zoom Position

The next two items on the Shooting menu are closely related, so I will discuss them together. The first option is Zoom Memory. This feature lets you control whether the zoom lever zooms the lens in continuous increments or in distinct, separate steps. By default this option is turned off, so you can zoom continuously in any amounts, zooming either in or out.

If you turn the Zoom Memory setting on using this menu option, the camera displays a list of focal lengths, from full wide-angle to full telephoto: 24mm, 28mm, 35mm, 50mm, 85mm, 105mm, 135mm, 200mm, 300mm, 400mm, 500mm, 600mm, 800mm, 1000mm, 1200mm, and 1440mm, the maximum range of the optical zoom. It takes three menu screens to include all of these values; the first screen is shown in Figure 4-63.

Each focal length has a check box to its left. Move the selection rectangle through this list using the Up and Down buttons or the multi selector dial. As each focal length is highlighted, you can press the OK button to check or un-check its box. If the box is checked, then the camera will include that focal length in the zoom memory.

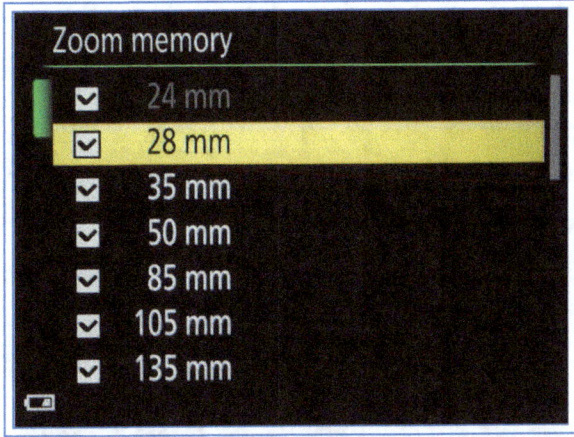

Figure 4-63. First Screen of Zoom Memory Settings

When you have finished checking the boxes for the focal lengths that you want to have included in the zoom memory, exit from the menu screen by pressing the Menu button or by half-pressing the shutter button. Now, when you press the zoom lever, each press will take the lens to the next focal length that was checked on the Zoom Memory menu screen.

For example, suppose you turned on the Zoom Memory option and checked the boxes for 50mm, 200mm, and 1000mm. Then, if you are starting from the full wide-angle position of 24mm, when you press the zoom lever to the right, the lens will zoom in to 50mm. If you press it again, the lens will zoom to 200mm, and one more press will take it all the way to 1000mm. You will not be able to zoom the lens to any other positions. The same will be true when you zoom back out by pressing the zoom lever in the other direction. It does not matter if you use a very quick press of the lever or hold the lever in position; it will zoom only to the next level that has its box checked on the Zoom Memory menu screen.

As I noted above, the Zoom Memory option is closely related to the Startup Zoom Position option, which is directly below it on the menu screen.

With that option, whose screen is seen in Figure 4-64, you select a focal length where the zoom lens will start when you turn the camera on.

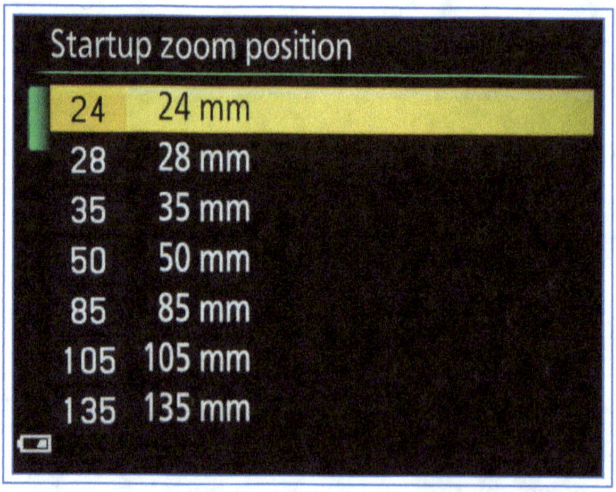

Figure 4-64. Startup Zoom Position Options Screen

In this case, the choices of focal lengths are more limited: 24mm, 28mm, 35mm, 50mm, 85mm, 105mm, or 135mm. You select this menu option, then move to the next screen and position the yellow selection bar on the focal length you want to choose. Press the OK button to confirm. Then, when you turn the camera on the next time, the lens will automatically zoom to that focal length.

Here is how these two settings are related. When you select a focal length for Startup Zoom Position, you will see that that value is automatically checked on the screen for Zoom Memory, and its menu item is dimmed, meaning you cannot alter it. In other words, you cannot un-check the box for that focal length, because the camera is going to start up at that focal length. For example, suppose you select 50mm for Startup Zoom Position, and 35mm, 200mm, and 1000mm for Zoom Memory. The next time you turn on the camera, the lens will zoom automatically to the 50mm position. If you press the zoom lever to zoom out, the lens will move to 35 mm. If you then press the lever to zoom in, the lens will zoom back to 50mm, the startup position. From there, it will zoom to 200mm, then 1000mm.

These two menu options, working together, give you a great deal of control over how your lens zooms. Of course, you don't necessarily need to have that degree of control; you may be quite content to use the default settings, having the startup position of 24mm and allowing the lens to zoom to any setting, without using the Zoom Memory option. However, it can be quite convenient to know what focal length you are using for a given shot. If you turn Zoom Memory off, the camera's display will not show you what focal length it is using; if you turn it on, you will see the focal length displayed at the top of the display.

Note that the Zoom Memory option does not control the operation of the side zoom control, the switch on the left side of the camera that can be used for zoom or for another purpose assigned through the Setup menu. So, even if you have turned on the Zoom Memory menu option, thereby restricting the zoom lever to certain focal lengths, you can still use the side zoom control to zoom the lens continuously, as long as that control is assigned to the zoom function.

Manual Exposure Preview

This last item on the Shooting menu has a narrow, specific purpose—to control whether the camera's display reflects the brightness of the image that will result from current settings when the camera is in Manual exposure mode. When you select this item and press the OK button or the Right button to move to the next screen, you will see a screen with options to turn this feature on or off, as shown in Figure 4-65.

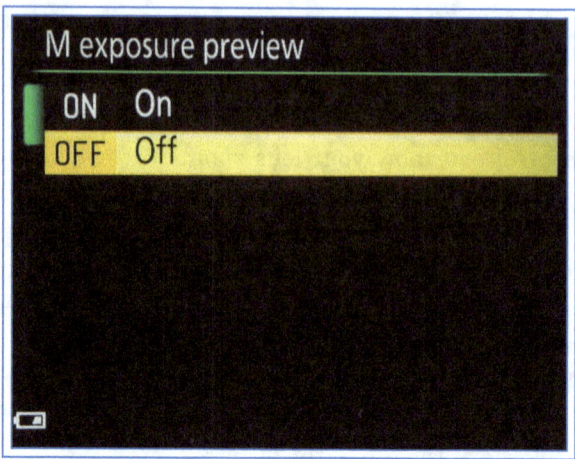

Figure 4-65. Manual Exposure Preview Options Screen

If you leave it at its default setting of Off, then, when the camera is in Manual exposure mode, the camera's display will show a normally exposed view of the scene, even if the current settings of aperture, shutter speed, and ISO would result in a heavily underexposed or overexposed image.

If you turn this feature on, then, when you adjust the shooting settings in a way that would result in an unusually dark or bright image, the camera's display will become darker or brighter also, so you will have notice that the image may be improperly exposed.

There are limits to the operation of this feature. First, it works only in Manual exposure mode, although the menu option is available for selection in Program, Aperture Priority, and Shutter Priority mode. Second, even when this option is turned on, it does not show the full effect of a severe underexposure or overexposure. For example, for an experiment I turned this option on and set the camera to 1/4000 second at f/7.6, with ISO set to 100. With these settings in my normally lighted office, the screen grew somewhat dark, as shown in Figure 4-66.

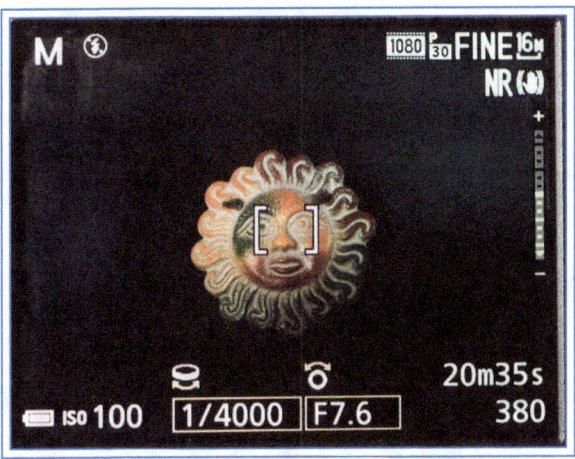

Figure 4-66. Manual Exposure Preview Feature in Use

When I took a picture with these settings, though, the resulting image was completely black. And, when I used settings causing strong overexposure, the display showed only mild overexposure.

There is one more aspect of this option that I need to point out. As discussed in Chapter 7, you can turn on a shooting-mode histogram using the View/Hide Histograms option of the Monitor Settings item on the Setup menu. If you do that, the camera will display a histogram to help you gauge the exposure level of your shot. However, in Manual exposure mode, this histogram will not be accurate unless you turn on the Manual Exposure Preview menu option. If you leave this option turned off, the histogram will reflect the exposure level seen on the camera's display, which, in most cases, will look normal, even if the exposure settings would result in a heavily underexposed or overexposed image. If you turn this menu option on, the histogram will reflect the actual shooting conditions more accurately, though it does not fully reflect the effects of extreme exposure settings, in my experience.

Because this feature does not give you a fully accurate representation of underexposure or overexposure, even with the histogram, I prefer to leave it off and rely on my own judgment, or just take a test shot to see how the final image will look.

Chapter 5: Physical Controls

The Coolpix P600, like many compact cameras, does not have very many physical controls, relying heavily on its menus for changing settings. But the P600 is an advanced camera, and it has more controls than many cameras, because experienced photographers generally prefer to make settings with a button or a dial whenever possible, for speed of access. In this chapter, I'll discuss each of these controls and how they can be used to best advantage. I'll start with the controls on the top of the camera, as shown in Figure 5-1.

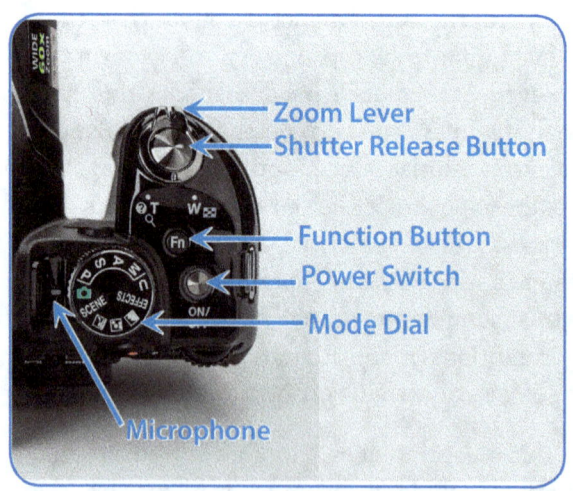

Figure 5-1. Controls on Top of Camera

Power Switch

The power switch, at the right side of the camera's top, has only one function—to turn the camera on and off. When the camera is turned on, the green light around this button illuminates. When the camera enters standby mode to save power, the green light starts to blink, and does so for about three minutes. During that time, you can press the power button, the Playback button, the shutter release button, or the Movie button, or you can turn the mode dial, to cancel standby mode and restore the camera to full power. After the three minutes, the camera turns itself off and you have to use the power button to turn it back on again.

Shutter Release Button

The shutter release button (often called simply the shutter button) is the single most important control on the camera. When you press it halfway down in most shooting modes, the camera evaluates exposure and focus (unless you're using manual focus). Once you are satisfied with the settings, you press the button all the way down to record the image.

When you press the button halfway, it locks exposure and focus. If you need to set the camera's automatic exposure and focus for a subject that is not in the center of the scene, you can aim the center of the display at that subject, half-press the shutter button to lock exposure and focus, and then move the camera back to the position for taking the picture, with that subject at one side. This procedure works when you are using Center-weighted or Spot for the metering mode, and Manual for the Autofocus Area mode, with the focus frame set in the center of the screen.

When the camera is set for continuous shooting, you hold this button down while the camera fires repeatedly.

You can press this button halfway to switch from playback mode to shooting mode, so you can take more pictures. You also can press it to exit from a menu screen. Note, though, that you have to press the OK button to confirm your selection on the menu screen before pressing the shutter button; otherwise, your setting on the menu screen will not be saved. You can press the shutter button to re-awaken the camera from standby mode, which it enters after a period of inactivity. You have to press this button (or the Playback, power, or Movie button) or turn the mode dial while the green light around the power button is flashing.

The shutter button also can be used while recording a movie, to take a limited number of still images. You can take up to ten still pictures, at a small image size of 1920 x 1080 pixels. There are more details about this option and its limitations in Chapter 8.

Mode Dial

The mode dial, located at the right side of the camera's top, is central to the operation of the camera. Its main function is to change from one shooting mode to another. In addition, as noted above, when the camera has gone into standby mode and the power light starts blinking, you can cancel standby mode and return the camera to full power-on mode by turning the mode dial (or by pressing one of the major buttons on the camera).

Zoom Lever

The zoom lever is a small ring with a handle, surrounding the shutter release button. The lever's main function is to change the focal length of the lens to various settings between its wide-angle setting of 24mm and its telephoto setting of 1440mm. If you have the camera set for digital zoom, the lever will boost the focal length to a maximum of 5760mm. (That impressive-sounding zoom amount is illusory, though, because the quality will be degraded by the electronic enlargement of the image.) If you move the lever sharply to either side, the zoom range will adjust quickly; if you move it more gradually, the range will change more slowly.

When you turn the camera on, the lens moves to whatever position has been selected with the Startup Zoom Position option on the Shooting menu, as discussed in Chapter 4. And, the behavior of the zoom lever will change depending on the settings for the Zoom Memory menu option, also discussed in that chapter. As a brief reminder, if Zoom Memory is turned on, pressing the zoom lever will move the lens to the next zoom level that was selected through the Zoom Memory menu option. If that feature is turned off, pressing the lever will zoom the lens continuously through its full range of focal lengths.

In playback mode, moving the zoom lever to the left (pointing to the W setting) produces index screens with increasing numbers of images, and moving the lever to the right enlarges the current image. These functions are discussed in Chapter 6.

When the mode dial is on the SCENE setting and a scene type is highlighted on the menu, you can move the zoom lever to the right, so it points at the question mark, to produce a screen giving some tips about the scene type. Move the lever to the right again to make the tips vanish. This help function also is available when you have highlighted one of the Picture Control menu options on the Shooting menu. In that case, it displays a grid showing the adjustments currently in effect for the highlighted option.

Function Button

Nikon has provided the user with a useful control in the form of the Function button—the small, recessed button marked with the Fn designation, just behind the shutter release button.

As discussed in Chapter 4, many of the most important settings on the Coolpix P600 are buried in the Shooting menu, including Image Size, ISO, White Balance, Continuous, and others. It can be inconvenient to change these settings when you have to press the Menu button, navigate to the Shooting menu, and move to the proper line on the menu before you can make a change.

With this small button, you can program any one of nine of the most useful settings of the camera into a physical control. The options available for choice are Image Quality, Image Size, Picture Control, White Balance, Metering, Continuous, ISO, AF Area Mode, and Vibration Reduction. When you press the Function button, a menu for the item that is assigned to the button pops up on the screen, as shown in Figure 5-2, letting you quickly change the setting.

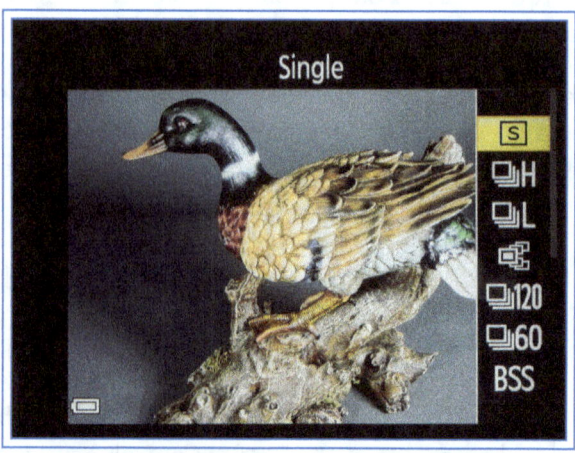

Figure 5-2. Continuous Menu Produced by Pressing Function Button

You can move through that menu using the Up and Down buttons or by turning either the command dial or the multi selector dial; you have to press the OK button to confirm your selection once it is highlighted.

The default choice, as shown here, is Continuous, for continuous shooting, which I tend to prefer as the item assigned to this button. If I want to fire off a burst of shots, it is convenient to press the Function button and switch to one of the burst modes for a short time. When that situation has passed, I can just as quickly press the button again and reset the camera to single-shot mode. However, it also can be very useful to be able to adjust ISO quickly. Of course, the value you choose to assign to this button will depend on your own particular circumstances. If you like to experiment with various different image-processing settings, you might want to program Picture Control as the setting. In any event, it is great to have this option available.

To change the feature assigned to the Function button, use the same menu that pops up when you press the button. The last item, on the second screen of the menu, is the Fn item, shown in Figure 5-3.

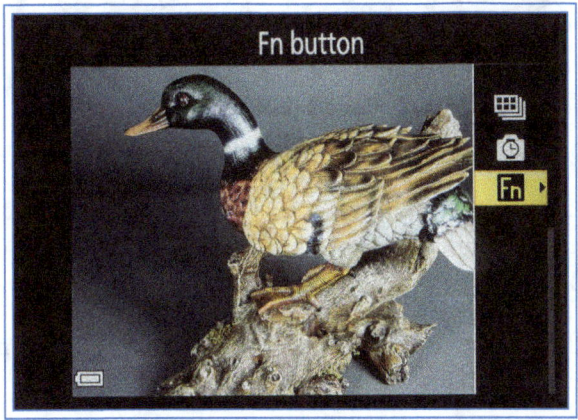

Figure 5-3. Menu Item for Assigning New Option to Function Button

After you press the Function button, the easiest way to reach this entry on the menu is to press the Up button, which will wrap around to the bottom of the menu, to the Fn item.

Then, press the Right button or the OK button, and the camera will display a menu of the options available for assignment to the Function button, with a yellow highlight block marking the one that is currently assigned, as shown in Figure 5-4.

Using the Up and Down buttons, the multi selector dial, or the command dial, scroll through the choices until the one you want to select is highlighted, and then press the OK button. The next time you press the Function button, the menu for the newly selected item will appear on the display.

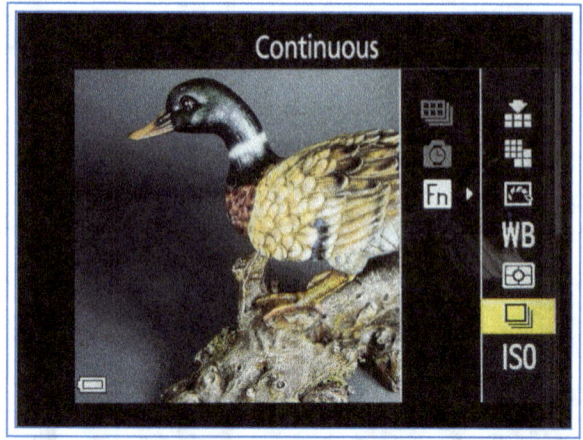

Figure 5-4. Current Assignment for Function Button Highlighted

The Function button operates only when the camera is in shooting mode and the mode dial is set to the Program, Aperture Priority, Shutter Priority, Manual exposure, or User Settings mode.

Next, I'll discuss the controls on the left side of the camera, as shown in Figure 5-5.

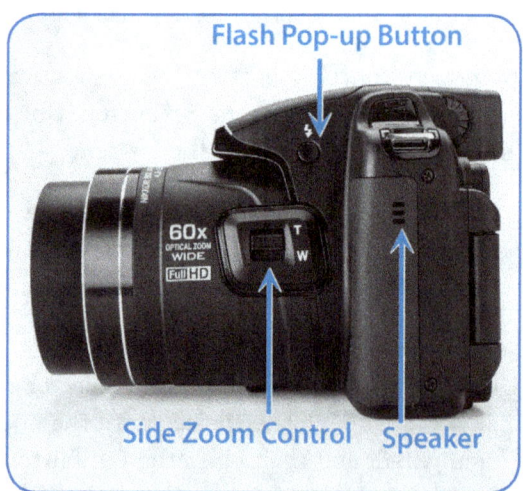

Figure 5-5. Items on Left Side of Camera

Flash Pop-up Button

This small round button on the left side of the flash housing has one simple purpose—to release the built-in flash unit so it will pop up and be available for use. If you expect you will be using the flash, you need to press this button to make the unit available; if you don't press the button, the flash will not pop up and cannot fire. If you select a shooting mode that requires use of the flash, such as Night Portrait, the camera will display a message prompting you to raise the flash. When you have finished with the flash unit, press it gently back down until it clicks into place.

The requirement that you press this button to pop up the flash has one clear advantage: When you are in a museum or other location where photography is permitted but the use of flash is prohibited, you can just leave the flash unit stowed away and you can be sure it will never pop up by itself and send out a flash that proves to be embarrassing. (With some compact cameras, the flash is always available to fire, and you have to remember to set the flash mode properly to avoid having it go off unexpectedly.)

Side Zoom Control

One of the welcome features of the P600 is the existence of a second zoom switch, located on the left side of the lens barrel as you hold the camera in shooting position. One reason for having this alternative control available is to free up your right hand to hold the camera firmly, rather than having to reach up to the standard zoom lever on top of the camera. With the super-powerful zoom range of the P600, you need to hold the camera as steady as possible when zooming in to the longer ranges.

The functioning of the side zoom control is not governed by the Zoom Memory setting on the Shooting menu. That is, when Zoom Memory is turned on, restricting the operation of the zoom lever to certain focal lengths, the side zoom control can still be used to zoom the lens continuously to any focal length.

Another helpful aspect of the side zoom control is that its function is assignable. That is, you can use this switch to control one of two other functions besides ordinary zooming, depending on your preference. To do this, you use the Setup menu, as discussed in Chapter 7. The first possibility other than standard zooming is to assign the side zoom control to adjust manual focus. If you do so, you still can use the multi selector dial to control manual focus, but you then have the option of using the side switch as an alternative. You may like the feel of pressing this control for fine-tuning the focus rather than turning the dial.

The other option that can be assigned to this switch is a function that Nikon calls "snap-back zoom." Here is how this function works. When you have zoomed the lens in to a powerful telephoto setting, you can "snap" the focal length back to a wider view in a preset amount by a quick press of the side switch down towards the wide-angle (W) position. Another quick press will snap the lens back another definite step towards wide-angle. Then, at any time, as long as you have not used any other controls on the camera in the meantime, you can give a quick press upward on the side zoom control, which will snap the lens all the way back to the original telephoto position.

In essence, with the snap-back setting, when you have the camera zoomed in for a magnified, telephoto view, you can experiment with different telephoto settings. You can "snap" the lens back out to a wider view once or twice (or more, depending on how far in the lens was zoomed), and then, once you've checked out those views, which can help you get a sense of your ultimate subject by seeing a wider view, you can snap the camera back to its original telephoto setting without having to use trial and error; that setting has been preserved precisely for you in the camera's "snap-back" memory.

I did not see much need for the snap-back function at first. However, when I was trying to photograph a bird at a long distance using the superzoom lens, I found this feature very useful. When the lens was zoomed all the way in, I found it hard to locate the bird. I eventually realized that I could quickly snap the lens back to a wider view until I found the bird in my field of view. Once I had the bird centered again, I could press the side zoom control upward to snap the zoom back to the full-power telephoto view. To help you stay oriented when using the very long focal lengths available with the P600, the snap-back control can be quite useful. This function is available for shooting still images only, not for movies.

The next controls to be discussed are those located on the camera's back, most of them to the right side of the LCD screen, as shown in Figure 5-6.

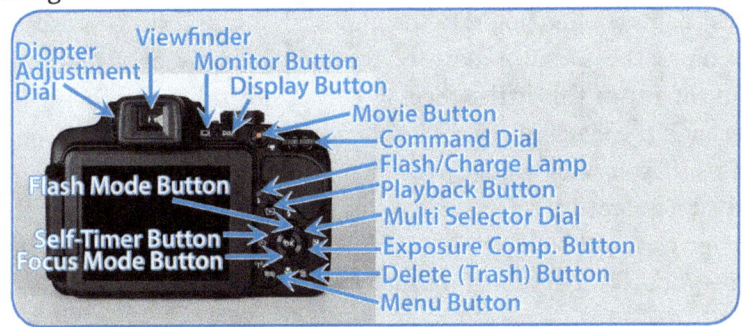

Figure 5-6. Controls on Back of Camera

Playback Button

This button, marked with a small triangle, is used to put the camera into playback mode, which allows you to view your images on the LCD (or in the viewfinder) and lets you get access to the Playback menu by pressing the Menu button. You also can use the Playback button instead of the power button to turn the camera on, placing it immediately into playback mode. You might want to do this if you know you're only going to view your recorded images, and won't be using shooting mode.

If you turn the camera on using the Playback button, pressing it again will not turn the camera off; it will just switch the camera into shooting mode. When the camera is in playback mode, you can always press the shutter button down halfway to change into shooting mode.

When the camera enters power saving mode and the light around the power button starts to blink, you can press the Playback button, among others, to stop the camera from powering off.

Diopter Adjustment Dial

The small wheel on the left side of the viewfinder is used to dial in optical correction to the viewfinder, so you can see a sharply focused image in the viewfinder window. As discussed later in this chapter, when you fold the LCD screen in the closed position or press the Monitor button, the viewfinder is activated. You can then turn this little wheel in either direction until the image through the viewfinder is at its clearest for your eyesight. In some cases, if you wear glasses, you may be able to dial in enough of an adjustment that you can take your glasses off and still see the image clearly through the viewfinder. (I am a glasses wearer, and this works for me, though I usually just keep my glasses on.)

Monitor Button

The button with a monitor icon, directly to the right of the viewfinder, is used to switch the view of shooting screens and playback screens between the LCD screen and the viewfinder. Press the button to toggle those views. This button can switch the views only when the LCD screen is unfolded and visible; when it is folded in against the camera in its protective position, the viewfinder is activated and the Monitor button will not change the view.

Display Button

The button marked DISP, to the right of the Monitor button, switches among the various displays of information on the camera's LCD or viewfinder, in both shooting and playback modes. In shooting mode, there are three displays available that are called up by successive presses of the Display button.

The display screen that I use the most, seen in Figure 5-7, shows the live view overlaid with icons for shooting mode, flash mode, shutter speed, aperture, image size and quality, images remaining, and a few other items.

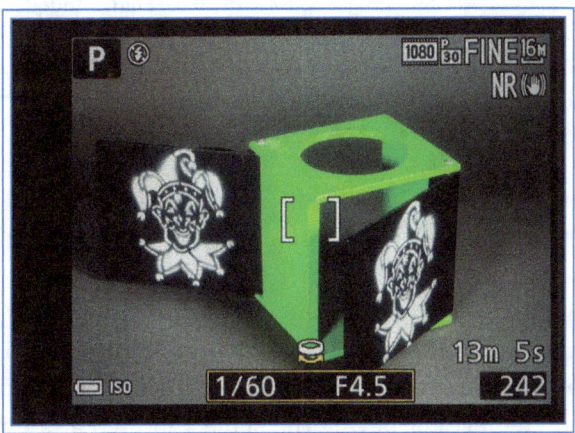

Figure 5-7. Shooting Display: General Information

Another press of the Display button produces a similar screen, illustrated in Figure 5-8, which includes the same shooting information with a frame overlaid that shows the area of the image that would be used for shooting a movie.

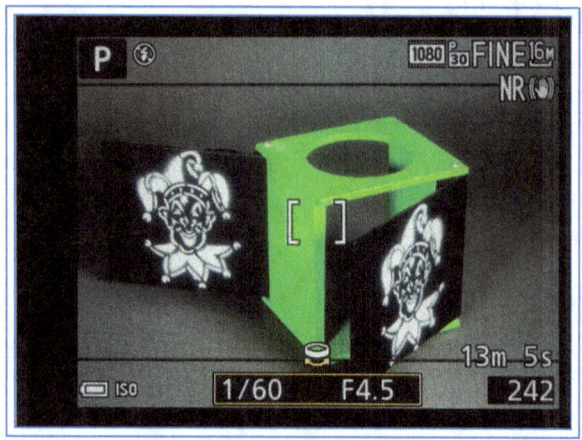

Figure 5-8. Shooting Display With Movie Frame Added

One more press of the button produces a view of the image alone, with no information.

Through the Monitor Settings item on the Setup menu, as discussed in Chapter 7, you can add a histogram and a framing grid to the shooting information display if you want to. The framing grid, if activated, will appear on all shooting screens, including the screen with no shooting information. This grid can be useful in framing your composition with a level horizon and for arranging a composition according to the Rule of Thirds, which states a preference for having the subject located at a point one-third of the way from an edge of the frame.

The histogram will appear only on the screens that contain shooting information. The histogram is discussed in Chapter 6, in connection with the histogram that displays in playback mode. Figure 5-9 shows the shooting screen with both the framing grid and the histogram in use.

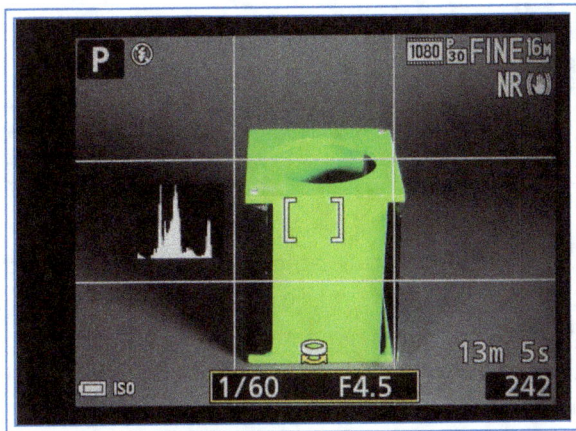

Figure 5-9. Shooting Display With Histogram and Grid

In playback mode, there also are three screens available through presses of the Display button. The first option provides photo information, which shows the recorded image overlaid with icons and figures showing the date and time the picture was taken, its identification number, image quality and size, and which image is being shown out of how many total images. The battery status icon also is shown. The second view is a detailed display of shooting information, including a thumbnail image and a histogram that shows the brightness values in the image along with details about shutter speed, aperture, exposure compensation, ISO value, and image number. The third and final view is of the image only, with no information added. I will provide information about the playback displays in Chapter 6.

Movie Button

The red Movie button, at the top of the camera's back just below the mode dial, has one major purpose: to start and stop recording of your videos. Press it once and release it to start recording; press it again to stop recording. I will discuss movie recording options in Chapter 8. You also can press this button to cancel standby mode when the monitor turns off in connection with the camera's power-saving function.

Flash/Charge Lamp

This small lamp sits to the left of the Playback button, above a lightning bolt icon. It provides information about the status of the charging of the camera's battery, as well as the status of the built-in flash unit.

When you are charging the camera's battery by connecting the camera to a power outlet, this lamp blinks slowly with a green light throughout the charging process. When charging of the battery is complete, the lamp turns off. If the lamp blinks green quickly, that indicates a problem with the battery, the USB cable, or the ambient temperature.

This lamp also indicates the status of the built-in flash unit when that unit is popped up. When you press the shutter button halfway, the lamp will light up in solid orange if the flash will fire for the next shutter press. If the lamp flashes orange, that means the flash will not fire because it is still charging. If the lamp does not light up at all, that means the flash will not fire because the situation does not call for it to fire (because it is in Auto Flash mode and the light is not dim enough to need flash, for example).

Command Dial

This wheel, sticking out near where your right thumb is likely to grip the camera at the top of the right side of the camera, has several functions. It is used to adjust shutter speed in the Shutter Priority and Manual exposure modes. In the Program exposure mode, this dial is used to activate the Flexible Program function, which causes the camera to choose an alternative pair of shutter speed and aperture values. If you use the Toggle Av/Tv Selection option on the Setup menu, these functions of the command dial are switched with those of the multi selector dial, so the command dial controls aperture rather than shutter speed, and the command dial no longer controls the Flexible Program feature.

In playback mode, you can turn the command dial to magnify and shrink an image once you have pressed the zoom lever to begin enlarging it.

In addition, when you are navigating in the menu system, the command dial can help you speed your menu adjustments considerably. When you have navigated to a menu option that has a list of possible settings, such as ISO, White Balance, Image Size, and others, instead of having to press the OK button or the Right button to move to the next screen to make those settings, you can just turn the command dial and the various settings will appear at the right side of the selection bar on the menu screen. You can spin through the values until you find the one you want, and the setting will be made with no further button-presses needed.

Also, the command dial can be used to adjust values in the on-screen menus after you have pressed one of the direction buttons to bring up a menu on the display. That is, the command dial can be used to adjust exposure compensation after the Right button has been pressed to put that scale on the display; it can be used to select a focus mode after the Down button has been pressed to put the focus mode menu on the display; it can be used to set the mode for the self-timer after the Left button is pressed; and it can be used to select a flash mode after the Up button is pressed. This dial also can be used to select an item from the menu that appears on the screen when the Function button is pressed.

One nice feature of the Coolpix P600 is that it puts an icon on the screen representing the command dial when there is a value that can be adjusted by turning the dial. For example, as shown in Figure 5-10, in Shutter Priority mode, the icon, which looks like a white disk with a yellow arrow underneath it, is positioned above the value for shutter speed. This means you can turn the command dial to adjust that setting.

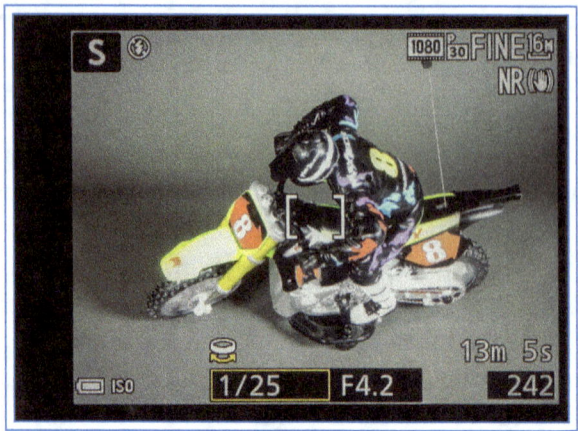

Figure 5-10. Icon for Command Dial Controlling Shutter Speed

Menu Button

The Menu button, to the lower left of the multi selector, is straightforward in its basic function. Press it to enter the menu system, and press it once more to return to whatever mode the camera was in previously (shooting mode or playback mode). There are several different menus available, depending on what mode the camera is in. The main menu systems are for Shooting, Playback, Wi-Fi Options, and Setup, but there also are more specific menus for various shooting modes, including Scene, Special Effects, Night Landscape, Night Portrait, and others, as well as a separate menu for Movie mode. I discuss the menu systems in Chapters 4, 6, 7, and 8.

Trash Button

To the right of the Menu button is a round button marked with a trash can icon. This is the Delete button, which can also be called the Trash button. Its operation is simple; this control has no function other than to delete images and videos. When the camera is in playback mode, press the Trash button and the camera will display a short menu of choices: Current Image, Erase Selected Images, or All Images, as shown in Figure 5-11.

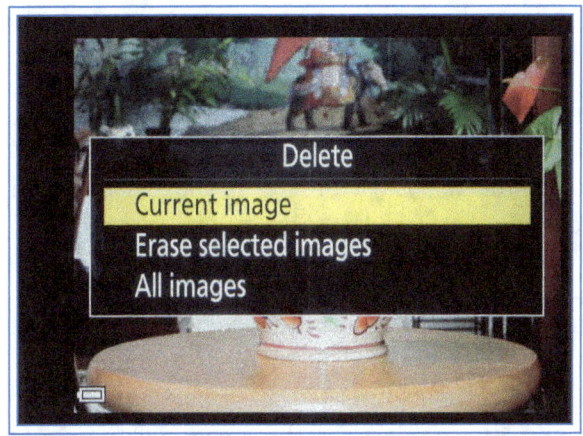

Figure 5-11. Trash Button Delete Confirmation Screen

Use the multi selector dial or the Up and Down buttons to highlight your choice. If you select Current Image and press the OK button, the camera will display a message asking you to confirm. You can cancel out of this (or any) deletion message by pressing the Menu button. When you are using the Trash button to delete images in this way, if the image displayed is the key image for a sequence of continuous shots (see discussion of continuous shooting in Chapter 4), choosing Current Image will delete all images in the sequence. (If the images in the sequence are displayed individually, only one image at a time will be deleted.)

If you choose Erase Selected Images and press OK, the camera displays an index screen showing thumbnail versions of all recorded images. Navigate through them with the Left and Right buttons or the multi selector dial, and press the Up button to mark (or Down button to unmark) any image you want to delete. Check marks will appear on images marked for deletion. You can enlarge any of the thumbnails to get a better view of an image by turning the zoom lever toward the telephoto position; turn it back the other way to reduce the image back to the thumbnail size. When all selected images have been marked, press the OK button and the camera will ask you for one final confirmation before deleting the selected images.

If you choose All Images, the camera will delete all images that are not protected using the Protect function, as discussed in Chapter 6.

The Trash button also is used to delete voice memos from images with voice memos attached, as discussed in Chapter 6. In addition, this button can delete movies.

When the camera is in shooting mode, if you press this button, the camera will ask if you want to delete one image. The camera will then display the last image that was recorded, and present a Yes/No choice. If you select Yes, that image will be deleted and the camera will return to shooting mode.

Multi Selector and its Buttons and Dial

The most prominent set of controls on the back of the camera is contained within the perimeter of the multi selector, the circular area with raised edges, also known as buttons, that function as the four direction buttons. Each of these four buttons also has another purpose designated by an icon on the button. In the center of the multi selector is the OK button, and the round, ridged wheel functions as a rotating dial. I will discuss each of these controls in turn.

MULTI SELECTOR DIAL

The ridged wheel that surrounds the OK button, known as the multi selector dial, is a very important control. It is easy to operate, because you can easily catch it on your thumbnail or just engage it with the flesh of your thumb or finger and spin it freely. One of its most significant duties is to control the aperture setting when you are shooting in Aperture Priority mode or Manual exposure mode. If you turn on the Toggle Av/

Tv Selection option on the Setup menu, then the functions of this dial and the command dial are reversed, and the multi selector dial controls shutter speed for Shutter Priority mode and Manual exposure mode. In addition, if that menu option is activated, the multi selector dial controls the Flexible Program feature, which ordinarily is controlled by the command dial.

When you are navigating in the menu systems, this dial moves up and down the lists of menu options, and it can be used to highlight an item from the pop-up menu that appears on the screen when the Function button is pressed. When the camera is in playback mode, the dial navigates through your individual images, and it also moves through the screens of images when index screens are displayed. As with the command dial, the camera displays an icon representing the multi selector dial when the dial controls a given function, such as aperture.

OK Button

This button in the center of the multi selector is one of the P600's most-used controls. It serves as a selection, confirmation, or "set" button when you choose certain options. For example, whenever you highlight a desired menu option, you press the OK button to confirm and set your selection. Similarly, when you press the focus mode button (Down button) and then highlight a focus mode on the pop-up menu (autofocus, macro focus, infinity focus, or manual focus), you press the OK button to confirm that choice. You also can use this button to get access to sub-menus. For example, after you highlight Image Quality on the Shooting menu, you can press the OK button to bring up the sub-menu with the list of choices: Fine and Normal. Then, you can press the OK button again to confirm the actual selection after you highlight it.

In manual focus mode, pressing this button toggles the shooting screen between an enlarged view and the normal-sized display.

In playback mode, when the first frame of a movie is displayed on the screen, the OK button is used to start the movie playing.

The button also is used to select any one of the playback controls that appear at the bottom of the screen during movie playback. (You use the direction buttons to highlight one of these controls, such as play, stop, or rewind, and then press OK to choose that function.) The button is also used to "open up" a sequence of continuous shots so you can view them individually. The button can be used to pause and resume video recording, and to start a panorama scrolling across the display screen at a larger size.

DIRECTION BUTTONS

Each edge—Up, Down, Left, and Right—of the multi selector dial is a "button" you can press to get access to a setting or operation. This may not be immediately obvious, and sometimes it can be tricky to press the dial in exactly the right spot, but these four direction buttons are important to your control of the camera. You use them to navigate through menus and screens for settings, whether moving left and right or up and down.

You also use them in playback mode to move through your images and, when you have enlarged an image using the zoom lever, to scroll around within the magnified image.

Besides these navigational duties, the direction buttons have miscellaneous functions in connection with various settings. When you are navigating in the menu system, you can use the Left button to move back one screen in the system. When you are on the main screen of a given menu system (Shooting, Playback, Scene, etc.), pressing the Left button moves the yellow selection block to the left column of the screen, which contains the icons that identify the currently available menus. For example, when you are on the main screen of the Shooting menu, pressing the Left button takes the selection block to the column that contains a letter or icon for the Shooting menu, a movie camera icon for the Movie menu, a network icon for the Wi-Fi Options menu, and a wrench icon for the Setup menu. You can navigate up and down through these icons to select the symbol for the menu you want to use. You can then press the OK button to select that menu.

The Right button also can be used to move to the sub-menu screens within the menu system. In most cases, you can press either the OK button or the Right button to move to the sub-menu screen that contains further options for a given menu item.

The Up button also has a non-obvious extra function. When you are viewing a "sequence" of continuous shots, as discussed in Chapters 4 and 6, pressing the Up button returns the camera to normal playback mode, in which you view only the "key" image from the continuous set (assuming the Sequence Display Options setting on the Playback menu is set to show key images rather than individual images from sequences).

Finally, each of the four direction buttons has its own separate identity, as indicated by the icon that appears next to each of the buttons, as discussed below.

Up Button: Flash Settings

When the camera is in shooting mode, pressing the Up button displays a small menu showing the options for setting the behavior of the flash unit, as shown in Figure 5-12.

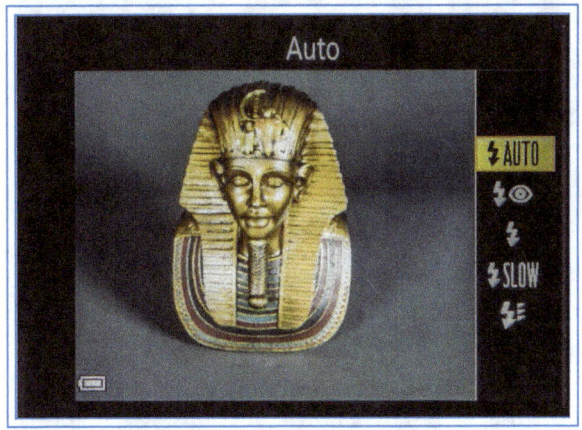

Figure 5-12. Flash Mode Menu

(If the flash unit is not popped up, the camera will display a message telling you to raise the flash.) Depending on the shooting mode, these options may include Auto, Auto with Red-eye Reduction, Fill Flash/Standard Flash, Slow Sync, and Rear-curtain Sync, or in some cases only three or four of those options. In other cases, such as when you have selected Night Landscape, Landscape, or Night Portrait on the mode dial, pressing the Up button will not bring up any menu, even if the flash unit is popped up. The camera makes all flash decisions for you in those modes. Once the menu with options has appeared, you need to press the Up and Down buttons or turn the command dial or multi selector dial to highlight your choice, and press the OK button to select it. With this menu, as with all four of the menus that are summoned by the direction buttons, you have to make your selection quickly, because the menu disappears in about 5 seconds if you don't take some action with a control button or dial.

Right Button: Exposure Compensation

When not acting as the Right button, this control serves as the exposure compensation button.

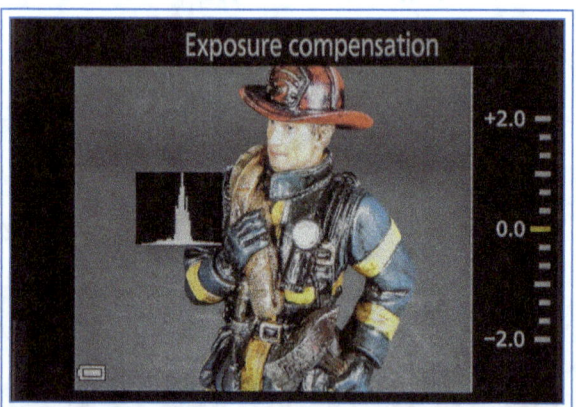

Figure 5-13. Exposure Compensation Adjustment Screen

As I discussed in Chapter 2, you press this button to bring up an EV scale on the screen, as shown in Figure 5-13, and then press the Up and Down buttons on the multi selector or turn the command dial or multi selector dial to adjust the value. You do not need to press the OK button to select the value; just let the pop-up menu disappear and the setting will take effect. This adjustment is available in all shooting modes except for Manual exposure mode and the Fireworks setting of Scene mode.

When you are using manual focus, you can press the Right button to force the camera to use its autofocus mechanism on the subject in the center of the screen. You can then adjust the focus further manually by turning the multi selector dial.

When you are recording a video, the Right button can be used to lock exposure, as discussed in Chapter 8.

Down Button: Focus Mode

In shooting mode, press this button to bring up the menu of options for the camera's focus mode: autofocus, macro focus, infinity focus, and manual focus, as shown in Figure 5-14.

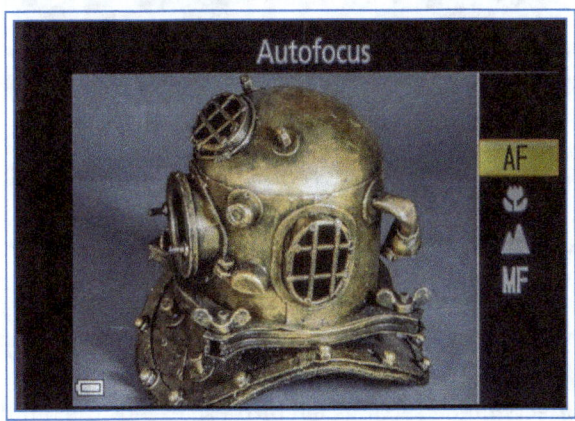

Figure 5-14. Focus Mode Menu

You have limited choices for focus mode in the Auto shooting mode and some of the scene modes. You can make the full range of choices in the Program, Aperture Priority, Shutter Priority, Manual, and Special Effects modes. After you press the Down button, use the Up and Down buttons or the multi selector dial or command dial to navigate to the icon for your desired mode, then press the OK button to confirm. I discussed manual focus in Chapter 2; I'll discuss macro focus (for close-up shots) in Chapter 9. For most purposes, the normal autofocus setting works well. Use the infinity setting when you want to force the camera to focus in the distance. Note that the flash is disabled when infinity is selected for the focus mode.

Left Button: Self-timer; Smile Timer; Pet Portrait Release

Press this button in shooting mode and the camera displays the menu of available choices for setting the self-timer, as shown in Figure 5-15.

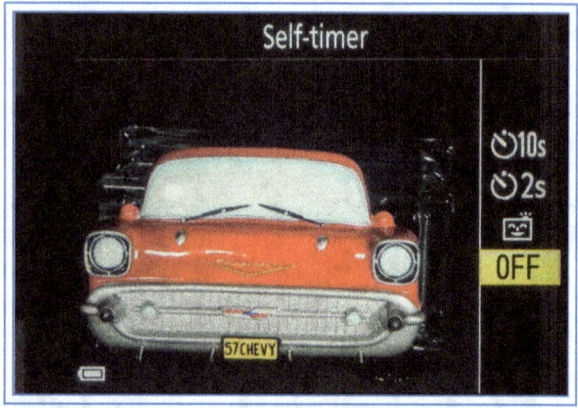

Figure 5-15. Self-timer Options Screen

Those choices may include 10 seconds, 2 seconds, Smile Timer, and Off, or, in some cases, such as with most scene modes and all Special Effects mode settings, all of these except the Smile Timer. (The Smile Timer is available with the Portrait and Night Portrait settings of Scene mode, but not with the other Scene mode settings.)

If you set a self-timer delay of either 10 seconds or 2 seconds, the camera will delay the specified amount of time before taking the picture, after you press the shutter button. Choose 10 seconds if you need a substantial delay so you can get into a group picture after pressing the shutter button; choose 2 seconds if you just need to avoid touching the camera during the exposure, to minimize the camera shake that can accompany a shutter press. You might need to use the 2-second delay when you're taking extreme close-ups, because any camera motion could be magnified by the closeness to the subject. Also, the 2-second delay can help when you're shooting in dim light and a slow shutter speed is needed, because any camera motion during the long exposure could blur the image.

When you turn on continuous shooting through the Shooting menu, the self-timer is available to a certain extent, though it is not useful with the higher-quality continuous settings. When you select the higher-quality settings of Continuous H, Continuous L, Pre-shooting Cache, or Best Shot Selector, you can turn on the self-timer and it will operate. However, when it triggers the shutter, only one shot will be taken, despite the continuous-shooting setting. So, in effect, the self-timer cannot be used for this sort of continuous shooting.

However, the self-timer will trigger a full series of continuous shots when used with the super-fast settings of Continuous H: 120 fps and Continuous H: 60 fps. With either of these settings, the camera will take the full set of 60 shots when the shutter is triggered by the self-timer. Of course, as was discussed in Chapter 4, the quality of these images is quite low, particularly for the 120 fps option, whose images are recorded at the very low quality image size of 640 x 480 pixels. The images taken at the 60 fps speed are larger in size, at about 2 megapixels. So, if you are trying to capture a series of images of your own golf swing, for example, you can set the self-timer and then stand in front of the camera as it captures a rapid series of shots at this reasonable level of quality. You also can use the self-timer effectively along with the Multi-shot 16 setting on the Continuous menu, because with that setting the camera records only one shot, even though that shot contains 16 sub-images. The self-timer functions properly with the Interval Timer setting as well.

You also can use the self-timer normally with movie recording, so you can turn on a delay with the self-timer and then press the red Movie button to start a movie recording after the specified delay.

When the camera is set to the Auto, Program, Aperture Priority, Shutter Priority, or Manual exposure mode, or to the Portrait or Night Portrait Scene mode setting, the Smile Timer is added to the options on the self-timer menu.

The Smile Timer is a special feature that fires the shutter automatically when the camera detects a smile. This function works together with the camera's face detection system, which is automatically turned on when the Smile Timer is selected.

When this option is turned on, whenever the camera detects faces, it focuses on the face closest to the center of the image and places a yellow double border around that face, as shown in Figure 5-16; the self-timer lamp starts blinking slowly to indicate that a face has been detected.

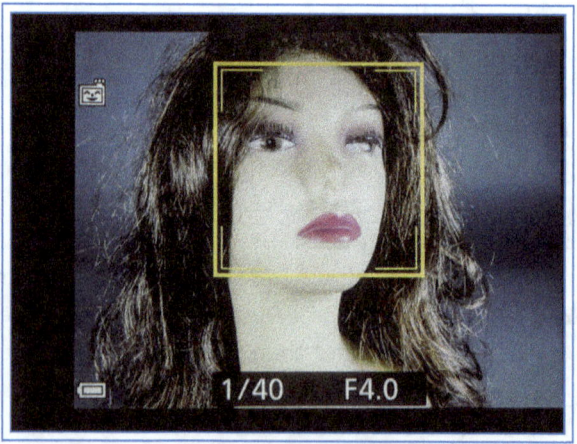

Figure 5-16. Smile Timer Face Detection Screen

The shutter is triggered automatically if the face inside the double border smiles. Once that happens, the lamp will blink rapidly to indicate that a picture of a smile has been taken.

This feature is more of a novelty than a particularly useful function in my opinion, though it may be of use in some situations, such as when you need to encourage a child to smile by telling him or her that a smile will automatically trigger the camera. Also, the Smile Timer acts as a sort of remote control for the camera; each time the subject smiles, the camera is triggered again. So, if you are taking self-portraits, you can stand in front of your P600 on its tripod, and control the camera's operation with your smile as it takes repeated portraits.

In the Pet Portrait setting in Scene mode, the Left button has a special function of turning on or off the Pet Portrait Auto Release function. As was discussed in Chapter 3, when that feature is turned on, the shutter is automatically triggered when the camera detects the face of a cat or dog. In that situation, neither the self-timer nor the Smile Timer is available.

When the camera is using manual focus, pressing the Left button toggles between views that are enlarged two times or four times. Press the OK button to exit the manual focusing screen; press it again to recall the focusing screen to continue focusing manually.

When you are recording a video with the Autofocus Mode option on the Movie menu set to AF-S, you can press the Left button to cause the camera to refocus on the subject.

Finally, there are a few other controls that are located in their own particular areas, described below.

AF Assist/Self-timer Lamp

The small lamp on the front of the camera, shown in Figure 5-17, has multiple functions. Its reddish light blinks to signal the operation of the self-timer and smile detection when the Smile

Timer is used, and it also turns on in dark environments to assist with autofocusing.

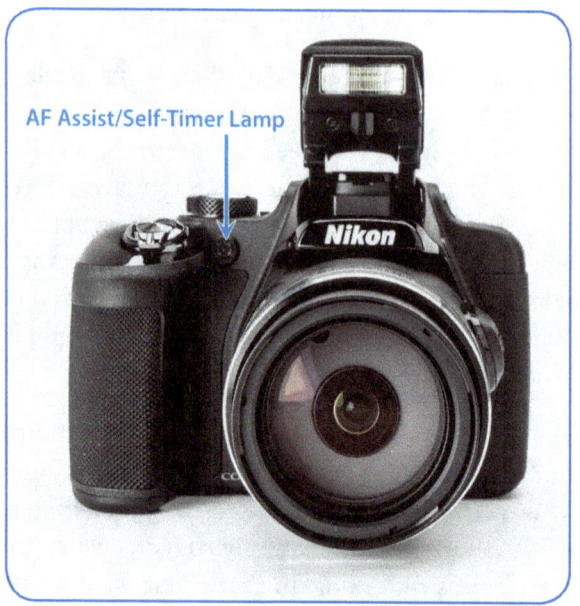

Figure 5-17. AF Assist/Self-timer Lamp

You can control the use of the lamp for autofocusing with the AF Assist item on the Setup menu, as discussed in Chapter 7. You might want to disable it when taking pictures during a religious ceremony or in another environment where this rather bright light could be distracting. Even if you disable it for purposes of autofocus, though, the lamp will still light up to indicate the functioning of the self-timer and Smile Timer.

USB and HDMI Ports

These small openings under a little door on the right side of the camera, shown in Figure 5-18, have several functions.

The smaller one at the top, the USB port, is where you plug in the charging cable when you charge the battery inside the camera. It also is where you connect the camera to a computer to transfer your photos and movies using the supplied USB cable.

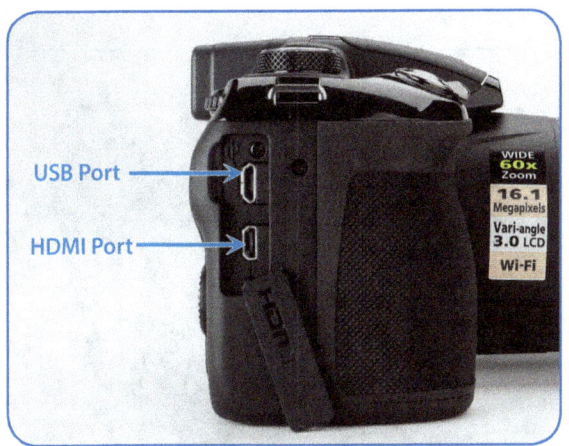

Figure 5-18. Ports on Right Side of Camera

The larger port is where you plug in an HDMI cable (which you need to purchase as a separate option) to view photos or videos on an HDTV set. The end going into this port is a micro-HDMI connector; the end going to the HDTV should be a standard HDMI connector. These cables are available through Amazon.com, Radio Shack, eBay, and elsewhere. I discuss connecting the P600 to TV sets in Chapter 9.

Tilting and Swiveling LCD Screen

The last item to be discussed in this chapter is not really a "control," but it does allow physical adjustment, so I will discuss it here. This is the articulated LCD display on the back of the camera. This screen, even without its tilting and swiveling ability, is a notable feature of the camera. It has a diagonal span of 3 inches (7.5 cm) and provides a resolution of 921,000 dots, giving a very clear view of your images before and after you capture them.

With its ability to pivot both horizontally and vertically, the monitor gives you a considerable amount of added flexibility for your shooting.

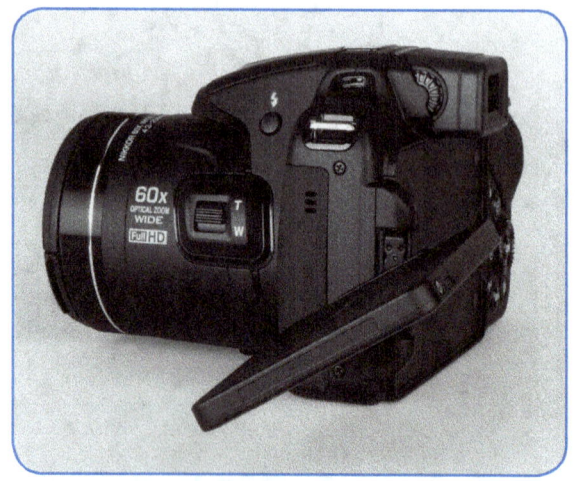

Figure 5-19. LCD Positioned for High-Angle Shots

If, as shown in Figure 5-19, you pull it out to the left and then rotate the screen so it aims downward, you can hold the camera high above your head and view the scene as if you were an arm's-length taller, or were standing on a small ladder.

If you attach the camera to a monopod or other support and hold it up in the air, you can extend the camera's vertical height even farther and still view the LCD screen quite well. You can activate the self-timer before raising the camera up in the air to take the photo, or you can turn on interval timer shooting with the Continuous option on the shooting menu, and set the camera to take a series of shots at 30-second intervals while it is raised up in the air. You also can use the camera's Wi-Fi capability, discussed in Chapter 9, to trigger the camera by remote control from a smartphone or tablet while the camera is raised overhead.

On the other hand, if you need to take images from a very low vantage point near ground level, you can rotate the screen so it tilts upward toward your eye, as shown in Figure 5-20, and hold the camera down as far as you need to get a mole's-eye view of the world.

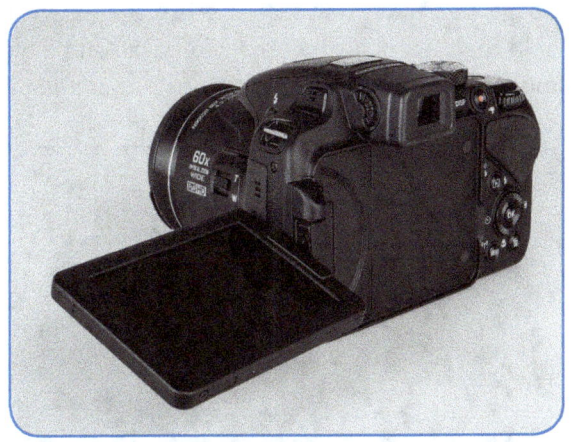

Figure 5-20. LCD Positioned for Low-Angle Shots

If you fold the screen out so that its viewing area faces in the same direction as the lens, as shown in Figure 5-21, you can take a self-portrait while observing your image on the display.

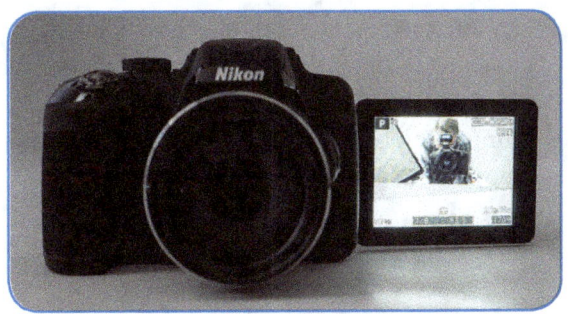

Figure 5-21. LCD Positioned for Self-Portrait

Also, as I discuss further in Chapter 9, the tilting display is useful for street photography, because you can fold the screen upward and look down at the camera while taking long-zoom photos of people on the streets without drawing attention to yourself.

Finally, the screen can be folded in so its viewing surface is hidden. In this configuration, shown in Figure 5-22, the LCD display is protected against damage, and the camera automatically switches to using the viewfinder. This is a good option to have if you're taking photos in bright sunlight, when it can be hard to view the image clearly on this screen. Also, some photographers prefer to hold the camera against their forehead and look through the viewfinder, at least in some situations. So, it's good to have this option.

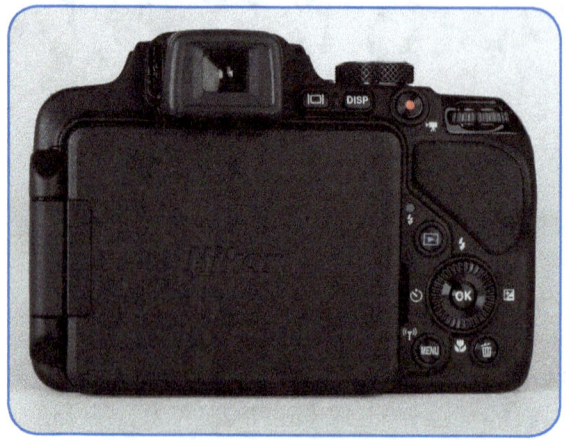

Figure 5-22. LCD in Closed Position

Note that the Coolpix P600 does not provide any automatic switching between the viewfinder and the LCD screen when your head approaches the viewfinder. The only ways to switch views are by folding or unfolding the LCD display screen, or by pressing the Monitor button, discussed earlier in this chapter.

CHAPTER 6: PLAYBACK

You may not spend a lot of time viewing your images and videos in the camera, but even if you don't, it's useful to know how the various in-camera playback functions work. You may need to examine an image closely in the camera to check focus, composition, and other aspects, or you may want to share images with friends and family. So it's worth taking a look at the various playback functions of the Nikon Coolpix P600. I'll also discuss options for printing images in this chapter.

Normal Playback

Here is a summary of basic playback techniques. First, when you take a new photo, the recorded image stays on the screen for about one second for review. If your major concern with viewing images in the camera is to check them right after they are taken, this feature is helpful, but the review time is very brief and there is no way to adjust its duration. You can turn this feature off using the Monitor Settings/Image Review item on the Setup menu, as discussed in Chapter 7.

If you want to view your images in more detail, you need to use the features that are available in playback mode.

For ordinary image review in playback mode, the process is simple. Press the Playback button, marked by a right-facing triangle, to the right of the LCD screen on the camera's back. Once you press that button, the camera is in playback mode and you will see the most recent image saved to the memory card that is in the camera (or, if no card is inserted, to the internal memory). To move back through older images, press either the Left button or the Up button or turn the multi selector dial (the dial that surrounds the OK button on the camera's back) to the left. To move through the increasingly recent images, use the Right button or the Down button, or turn the multi selector dial to the right. To scroll through your images rapidly, hold down the Left or Right (or Up or Down) button. To delete images, press the Trash button and follow the prompts on the screen, as discussed in Chapter 5.

INDEX VIEWS, CALENDAR VIEW, AND ENLARGING IMAGES

In playback mode, you can press the zoom lever on top of the camera to view an index screen of your images or to enlarge a single image. When you are viewing an image, press the zoom lever once to the left (toward the W setting), and you will see a screen showing 4 images, one of which is outlined by a yellow frame, as shown in Figure 6-1.

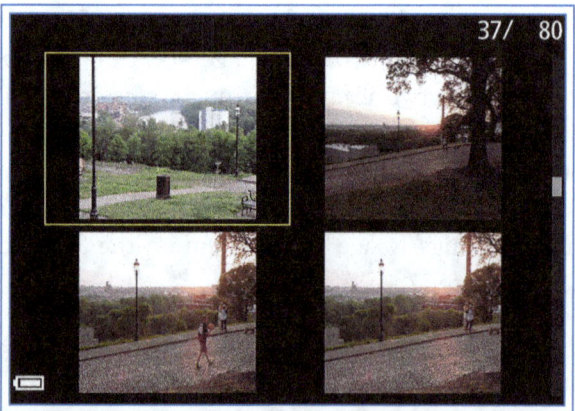

Figure 6-1. Index Screen with 4 Images

You can then press the OK button to bring up the outlined image as the single image on the screen, or you can move through your images with the 4-image index screen by pressing the 4 direction buttons or by turning the multi selector dial.

If you move the zoom lever to the W mark once more, the camera will show an index screen of 9 images; another press brings 16 images; and another press brings a 72-image screen, as seen in Figure 6-2 (assuming in each case that you have that many images; if not, there will be blank spaces on the screen).

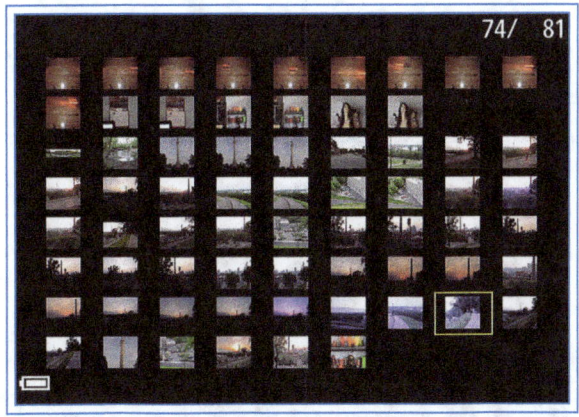

Figure 6-2. Index Screen with 72 Images

If you press the lever in the same direction one more time, the camera displays a calendar screen with a yellow line indicating each date for which images exist, as shown in Figure 6-3.

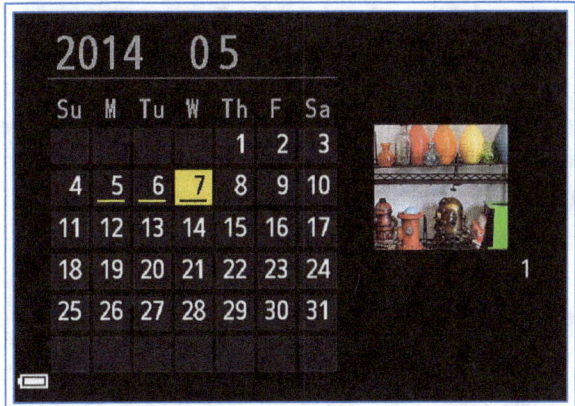

Figure 6-3. Calendar Screen

You can maneuver through any of the index screens to select a single image for viewing. If you want to reduce the number of images per screen, press the zoom lever to the right (toward the T position) repeatedly to reverse the progression of index screens. On the calendar screen, highlight a date and press the OK button to display images from that date.

When you are viewing a single image, a press of the zoom lever to the right enlarges that image, as seen in Figure 6-4.

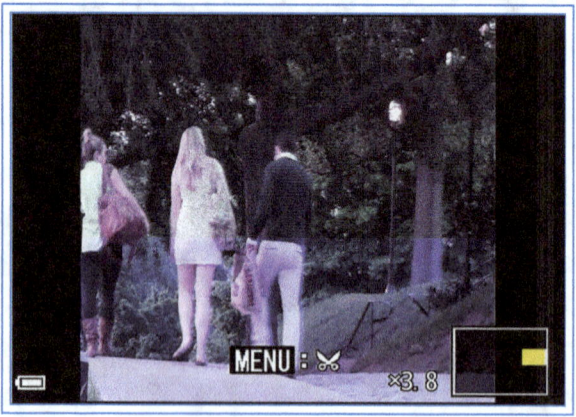

Figure 6-4. Enlarged Image with Inset Block

You will see a display in the lower right corner with an inset yellow block that represents the portion of the image that is now filling the screen in enlarged view. The display with the inset block appears only if you are viewing the display with basic information. With the display that includes no information and the display with detailed information with a histogram, the image will be enlarged, but without the inset block.

If you press the zoom lever to the right repeatedly, the image will be enlarged up to a maximum of about 10 times normal. While the image is magnified, you can scroll around within it using the 4 direction buttons; you will see the inset yellow block move around within the white rectangle that represents the whole image. To reduce the image size again, just press the zoom lever to the left as many times as necessary. You can also increase or decrease the zoom level by turning the command dial right or left. Press the OK button to restore the image to its original size immediately.

While the image is enlarged, the word MENU appears on the screen with a scissors icon, as shown in Figure 6-4. When you see that display, you can press the Menu button to save the enlarged area as a separate file. This feature gives you a rough-and-ready way to edit your images in the camera. So, if you want to crop a group photo to save just the face of one person, you can enlarge the image and scroll it around until just that face is visible, and then press the Menu button to save a separate file with that face as the only subject. This process is no match for editing with a computer, but it could come in handy when no computer is available and you need a particular part of an image for a special purpose, such as a business presentation.

DIFFERENT PLAYBACK SCREENS

When you are viewing an image in playback mode, pressing the Display button repeatedly cycles through three screens.

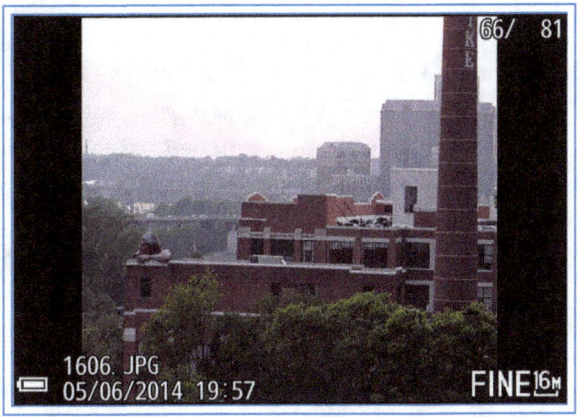

Figure 6-5. Playback Display: Basic Information

These are the full image with no added information except movie format for movies (not shown here); full image with basic information, including date and time it was taken, file name, image number, image size and quality (Figure 6-5); and reduced-size image with detailed recording information, including aperture, shutter speed, ISO, recording mode, exposure compensation, and other data, plus a histogram (Figure 6-6).

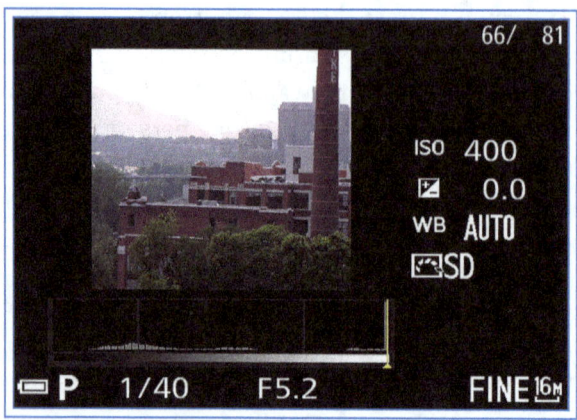

Figure 6-6. Playback Display: Detailed Information

These three screens are available for still images. For movies there are only two screens; the screen with the histogram is not available.

The recording mode information included on the detailed screen is basic; it will display the P icon for Program mode even if you have used a Scene or Special Effects mode setting. If you want to see accurate information about what recording mode was used, you can use the ViewNX 2 software that is available for free from Nikon.

The detailed display screen, as noted above, includes a histogram. The histogram is a graph, or chart, representing the distribution of dark and bright areas in the image that is being displayed on the screen. The darkest blacks are represented by vertical bars on the left, and the brightest whites by vertical bars on the right, with continuous gradations in between.

If you have a histogram in which the pattern looks like a tall ski slope coming from the left of the screen down to ground level in the middle of the screen, that means there is an excessive amount of black and dark areas (high points on the left side of the histogram), and very few bright and white areas (no high points on the right), as shown in Figure 6-7.

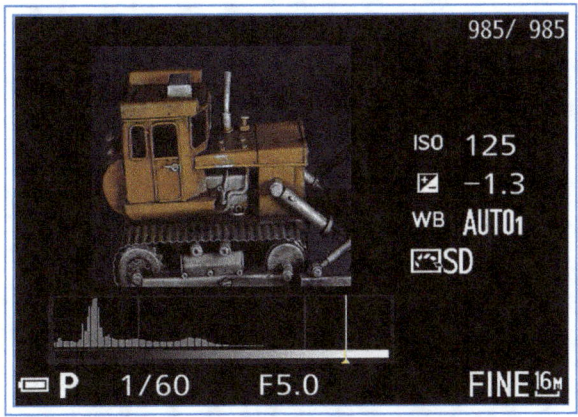

Figure 6-7. Playback Histogram: Underexposed

A ski slope moving from the middle of the screen up to the top of the right side of the screen would mean just the opposite—too many bright and white areas, as illustrated in Figure 6-8.

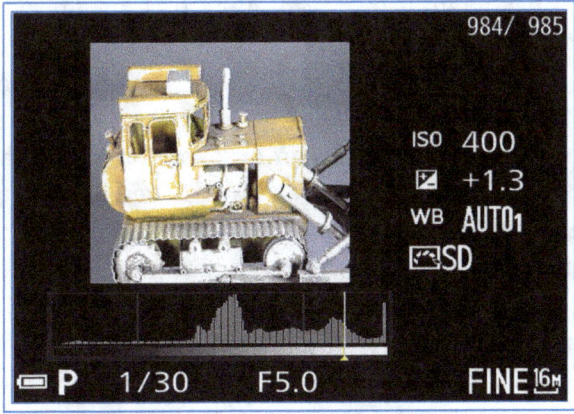

Figure 6-8. Playback Histogram: Overexposed

A histogram that is "just right" would be one that starts low on the left, gradually rises to a medium peak in the middle of the screen, then moves gradually back down to ground level at the right. That pattern indicates a good balance of whites, blacks, and medium tones. Figure 6-9 shows an image with a histogram of that sort.

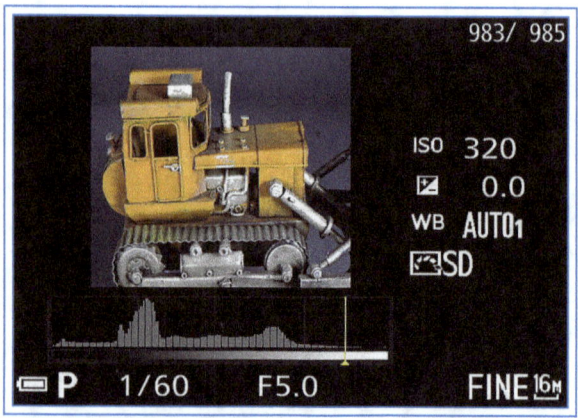

Figure 6-9. Playback Histogram: Normally Exposed

The histogram is an approximation, and should not be relied on too heavily. It may be useful to give you some feedback as to how evenly exposed your image is likely to be.

When the histogram is displayed in playback mode, you can see information about the tone levels in the image. To do this, look closely at the histogram, just below the thumbnail image, and you will see a vertical yellow line. If you press the Left and Right buttons or turn the multi selector dial, you can move that yellow line across the histogram. As you do this, you will see different parts of the image flash. What happens with this screen is that the camera gives you a way to select which parts of the tone map to check. As you move the line over the chart, corresponding parts of the image will flash to show where in the image there are tones at that level. For example, as you start out with the line at the extreme right of the gray data area of the histogram, the whitest areas of the image will flash, and, as you move the line to the left, progressively darker areas of the image will flash. Using this tool, you may be able to gather some information about what parts of the image may be too dark or too bright, so you can take another image that avoids having details swallowed up by blown highlights or excessively dark shadows.

When the histogram screen is displayed, you cannot use the Right and Left buttons to move through your images, because those buttons move through the tone level information. You can use the Up and Down buttons to navigate through the images in that situation.

VIEWING SHOTS TAKEN IN A SEQUENCE

When you take photos with the Coolpix P600 in certain shooting modes or with certain functions, the images become part of what Nikon calls a "sequence." When you enter playback mode to view those images, you ordinarily will see only the "key" image of the sequence, usually the first one of the group that was taken. To see the rest of the images in the sequence, you have to take other steps. I'll discuss this process in some detail, because it can be a bit confusing at first.

Let's start with an example, which will make it easier to illustrate the way the P600 handles sequences of still photos. Suppose you have placed the camera in Program mode by turning the mode dial to P, and then selected continuous high-speed shooting by selecting Continuous H from the Continuous item on the Shooting menu. We'll say you have selected Fine for the image quality and the maximum image size, 4608 x 3456 pixels, from the Shooting menu. Now, when you aim the camera at your subject and hold down the shutter button for a second or two, you will hear the sounds of the camera operating. The LCD screen (or viewfinder) will display the captured images for several seconds and then return to the view of the live image.

When the camera settles back to the live view, you can press the Playback button to start viewing your images. If everything worked as expected, there will be as many as seven new images to view, because that is the longest burst the camera can take using the Continuous H setting. However, when you press the Playback button, you will see only one image from this sequence. If you press any of the direction buttons or turn the multi selector dial, you will move to an entirely different image, assuming one exists; you will not see the other images from this sequence.

Where did those other images go? Look at the display on the screen, as shown in Figure 6-10, which has a few unusual aspects. (If you see a display with no information, press the Display button to show the screen with basic information.)

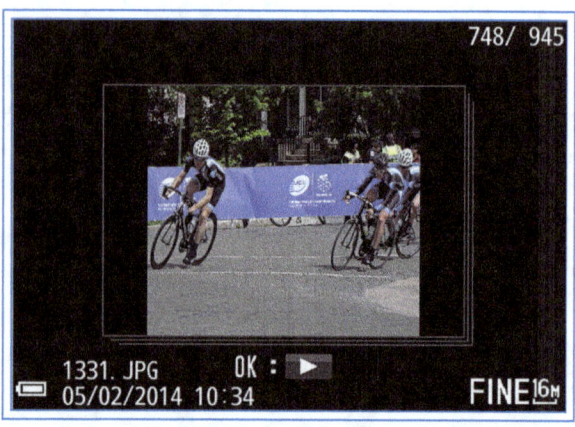

Figure 6-10. Continuous Series Ready to Play

For one thing, if you press the Display button, the basic image information will appear or disappear, but you cannot produce the detailed display with the histogram, because you are viewing the "key" image of a sequence rather than an individual picture. For another thing, you will see the notation OK at the bottom of the screen with a triangle, indicating the Play function, to its right. What this means is that, to view the other images in this sequence, you need to press the OK button.

If you now press the OK button, you will see the same image as before, but with a different appearance, as shown in Figure 6-11.

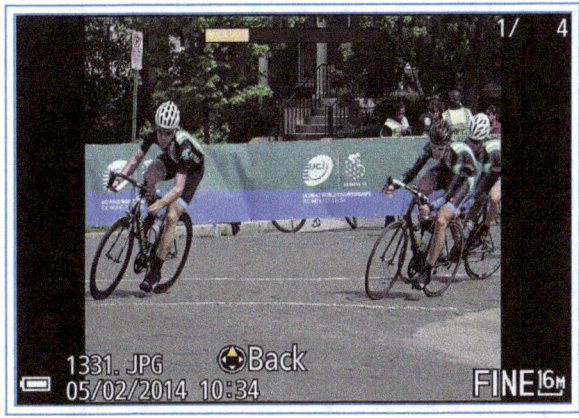

Figure 6-11. Continuous Series Opened Up as Individual Shots

Now, pressing the Display button will cycle through the 3 possible views of each image, including the histogram view, because you are viewing this photo as an individual image, not as a key image.

You will no longer see the OK notation; instead, you will see a short yellow bar at the top center of the display, and the number 1 with a slash over the total number of images at the upper right. In Figure 6-11, the numbers are 1/4, because the sequence includes only 4 images. The yellow bar will progress across the top of the screen as you navigate through the images in the sequence using the Left and Right (but not Up and Down) buttons or the multi selector dial, and the numbers will increase up to 4/4 as you move to the most recent images in the sequence.

You can magnify each individual image by moving the zoom lever toward the T position, but (naturally enough) you cannot call up an index screen by pressing the zoom lever in the other direction, because only the images in the single sequence are available for viewing at this point.

Once you have "entered" the sequence by pressing OK, you will be "stuck" inside it—you can keep navigating through these images, but you will continue to navigate through the same set of images, over and over, until you exit from the sequence and go back to viewing the key image. There is a prompt on the screen that tells you how to do this: an icon highlighting the Up button with the notation Back, meaning you have to press the Up button to go back to the key-image view. That is, when you want to stop viewing these individual images and return to the key image so you can navigate through the rest of the images on your memory card, you have to press the Up button—the one marked with a lightning bolt, which controls flash functions when the camera is in shooting mode rather than playback mode.

If you would rather not have the camera display your continuous-mode shots in sequences, but would prefer to have them displayed as individual shots at all times, you can select that option using the Sequence Display Options item on the Playback menu, as discussed later in this chapter. However, if you take many sequences using a feature such as Continuous H: 120 fps, which takes 60 shots at a time, you may appreciate the ability to display just the key frame from the sequence when you browse through your images in playback mode.

The Playback Menu

Now it's time to discuss the numerous options that are available through the Playback menu. As you recall, to get access to this menu, you must put the camera into playback mode by pressing the Playback button (right-facing triangle). Then press the Menu button and, if necessary, move the yellow block on the screen to the left column and navigate to the triangle icon to select the Playback menu, as shown in Figure 6-12.

Then move the yellow block back to the right to highlight the various entries in the menu, whose first screen is shown in Figure 6-13. I'll discuss the options on the Playback menu one by one.

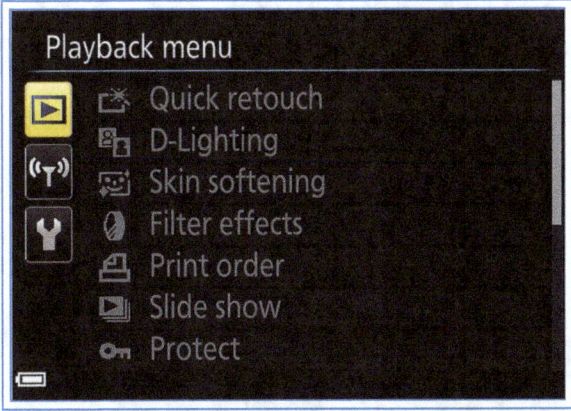

Figure 6-12. Playback Menu Icon Highlighted

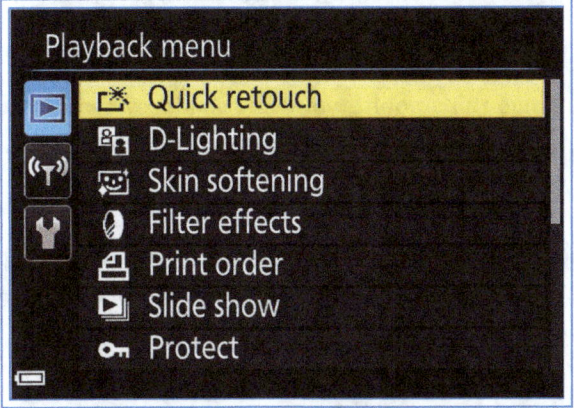

Figure 6-13. First Screen of Playback Menu

QUICK RETOUCH

The Quick Retouch option gives you a way to add "punch" to your recorded images with in-camera processing. You can apply this enhancement to any individual image. If the image you want to enhance is displayed as part of a sequence, you have to use the technique described earlier (pressing the OK button) to display the individual images from the sequence. When the image you have selected is displayed, press the Menu button and choose Quick Retouch from the menu. You can then use the Up and Down buttons or the multi selector dial to choose the desired amount of alteration—Low, Normal, or High, as shown in Figure 6-14.

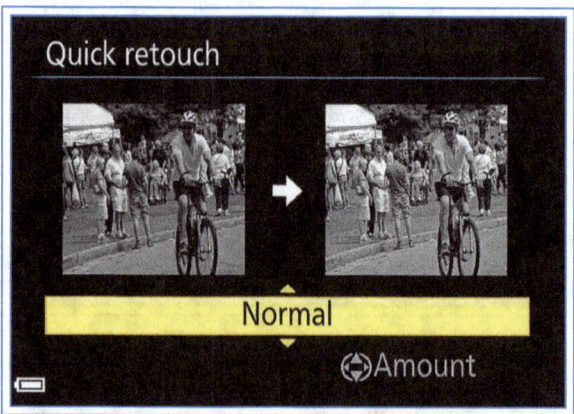

Figure 6-14. Quick Retouch Adjustment Screen

As you change the amount, you will see a preview of the finished product in a thumbnail on the right side of the screen, with the unchanged original on the left, for comparison. When you have selected the amount of change, press the OK button to confirm, and a new image will be saved with the retouched appearance and a new file number. It will have the Quick Retouch icon in the upper middle area of the image, as shown in Figure 6-15.

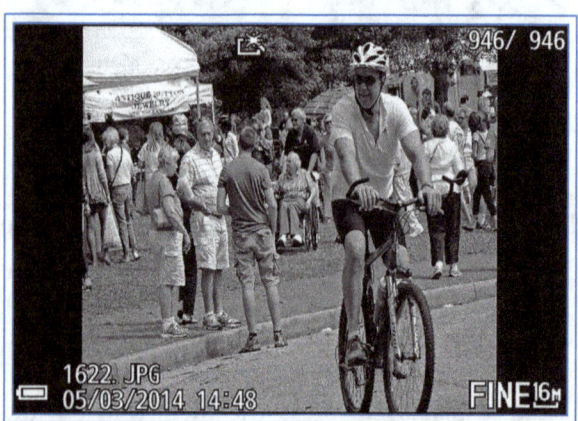

Figure 6-15. Retouched Image with Quick Retouch Icon

You cannot make any choices other than the level of the retouching. When it applies this processing, the camera increases the image's contrast (amount of difference between light and dark areas) and saturation (intensity of the colors). Some images, such as panoramas, cannot be modified.

This is a feature I don't use often, because I prefer to do my processing with software such as Photoshop. But there could be times when you take images at a party to display on a TV set during the party. You could use this function to brighten up some muddy images and make them livelier for the audience.

D-Lighting

The D-Lighting option works in the same way as the Quick Retouch feature. Select a still image that is being displayed individually (not as the key frame of a sequence), press the Menu button, select D-Lighting, press the OK button or the Right button to move to the next screen, and then choose Low, Normal, or High for the degree of enhancement, as shown in Figure 6-16.

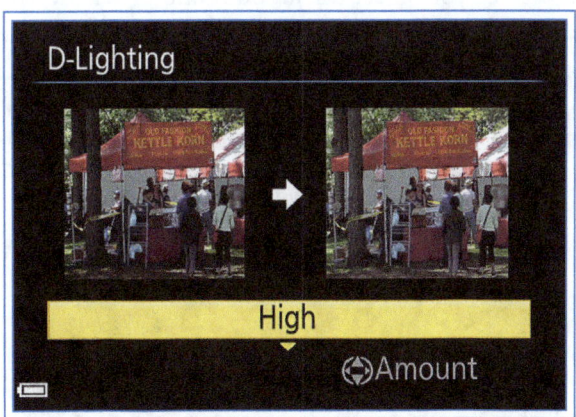

Figure 6-16. D-Lighting Adjustment Screen

In this case, the camera will attempt to add details in both the shadow and highlight areas, as it does when you use the Active D-Lighting option in shooting mode. (I discussed that option in

Chapter 4.) This feature can be quite useful, because you can use it to recover details from an image that was taken in conditions with excessive contrast, or even one that was taken with inadequate lighting, at least to some extent.

SKIN SOFTENING

This next entry on the Playback menu gives you another way to modify your already-recorded images. In this case, you can add a softening effect to the areas in an image that the camera considers to be showing human faces. As with the previous two menu options, you select the image, press the Menu button, and then select how strong the effect should be. One difference with this feature from the other ones is that the camera will decide whether or not there are any faces in the image you have selected.

If the P600 does not detect any faces, it will display an error message saying the image cannot be modified and return you to the menu without doing any processing. If it does detect a face, it will take you to a screen where you select the amount of processing. Once you select the amount and press OK, the camera will show you a larger view of the image with a preview of the effect, as shown in Figure 6-17; you can then press OK to save the processed image, or press Menu to go back and revise your setting.

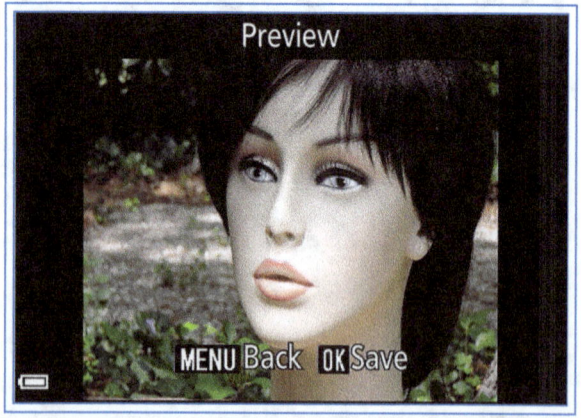

Figure 6-17. Skin Softening Preview Screen

FILTER EFFECTS

The Filter Effects menu selection has 9 sub-options, the first 7 of which are shown in Figure 6-18, which the camera can use to make copies of your images with altered aspects. Some of these are similar to settings in the Special Effects shooting mode.

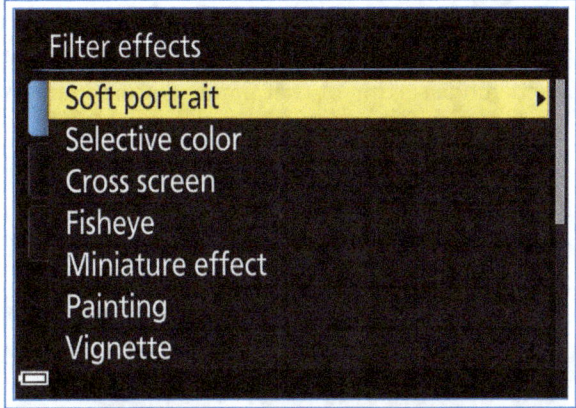

Figure 6-18. Filter Effects Menu Screen

The first entry on the list of effects is called Soft Portrait, which was used for Figure 6-19.

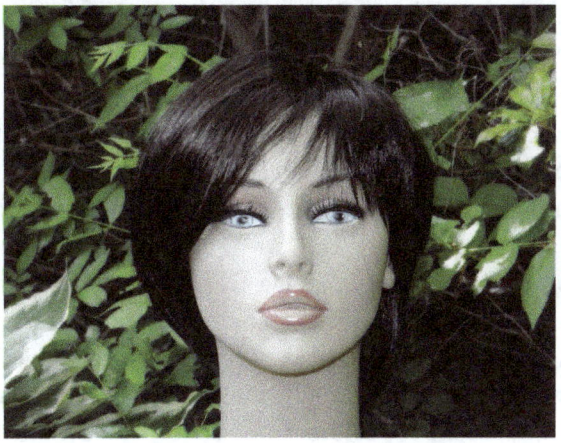

Figure 6-19. Filter Effects Soft Portrait Example Image

With this option, the camera softens the focus of the image, leaving the center of the image, or a human face if one was detected, in sharp focus, and blurring the focus toward the edges of the image. As with the Skin Softening effect, after you have selected the effect, the camera displays a screen with a preview of the image with the effect applied; you then can press the OK button to apply the effect.

Second on the list is the Selective Color effect, similar to the Special Effects mode setting of that name, discussed in Chapter 3.

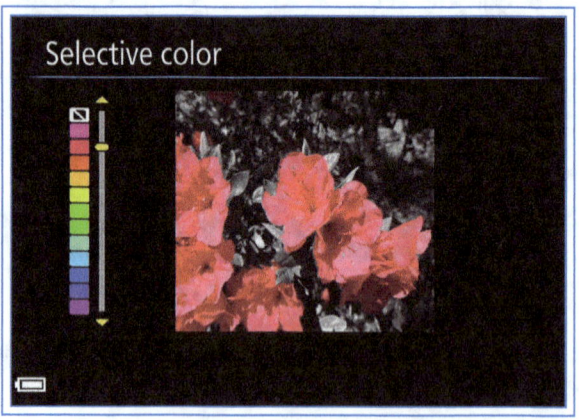

Figure 6-20. Filter Effects Selective Color Adjustment Screen

As you can see in Figure 6-20, when you display an image on the screen, the camera places a vertical spectrum of colors to the left of the image, with a pointer that you can move up and down the scale using the multi selector dial or the Up and Down buttons. As you move the pointer next to a color on the scale, the image changes to preserve only the portions that are approximately that color. If no parts of the image are that color, the image turns completely black-and-white. If you use this effect carefully, you can take an image with one area of bright color, remove all other colors using this effect, and end up with a photo that dramatically highlights the single colored object or area that remains, surrounded by a monochrome environment, as shown in Figure

6-21. As with earlier effects, the camera presents you with a large preview screen before you decide whether to apply the effect.

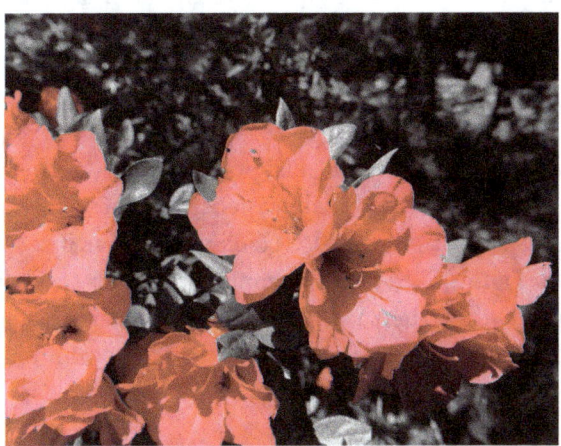

Figure 6-21. Filter Effects Selective Color Final Image

The third choice on this menu is Cross Screen, illustrated in Figure 6-22.

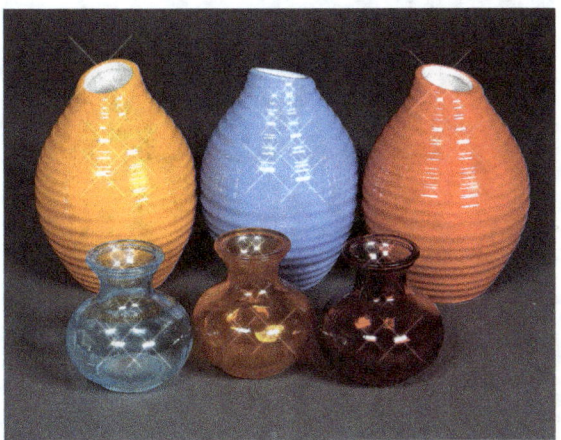

Figure 6-22. Filter Effects Cross Screen Example Image

With this option, as with Soft Portrait, there are no adjustments to make; you either save a copy of the image using this processing feature, or you cancel out of the selection. If you choose to go ahead, the camera makes a copy of your selected image with streaks radiating outward from bright objects such as lights. If there are no objects of that nature in the image, this option will not produce any changes at all, though the camera will still produce the new image. Figure 6-22 shows the final product, after the camera saved a new copy.

Next on the list is the Fisheye Effect, which simulates photographs taken with a fisheye lens, a super wide-angle lens that distorts the image, making it look spherical as if seen through a fishbowl. Figure 6-23 is an example of this effect, showing the final product after the camera produced its new image. In this case, the effect warped a sundial, making it look fluid like one of the works of Salvador Dalí.

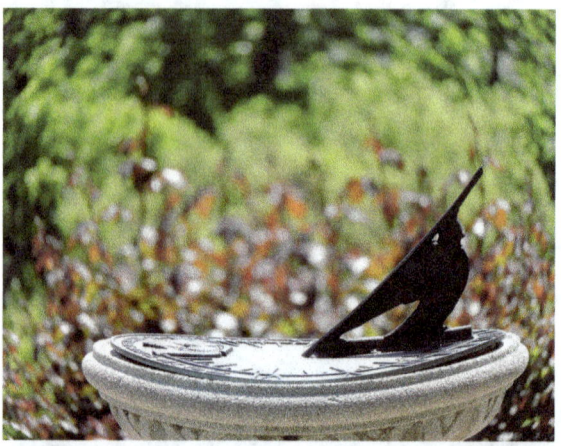

Figure 6-23. Filter Effects Fisheye Example Image

The result of using this effect will not look good unless you choose your subject carefully. It may be fun to distort a person's face or a building. I find this effect works best with a single, clearly identifiable subject. If you use the Fisheye effect on a busy or cluttered scene, it may be difficult to make out the subject at all, because of the distortion.

The next option is called Miniature Effect. With this feature, the camera adds blurring at the sides of the image to simulate a photograph of a tabletop model or miniature. Such images often appear blurred at the edges, either because of the shallow depth of field of these close-up photos, or because of the use of a tilt-and-shift lens, which causes blurring at the edges. Here, again, you need to choose an appropriate subject. I have found that it works well with something like a street scene or a house, which might actually be reproduced in a tabletop model. For example, if you are able to get a photo from a vantage point above a parking lot, you can use this processing to make it look as if you had photographed a tabletop display with model cars. This was the approach I took for Figure 6-24.

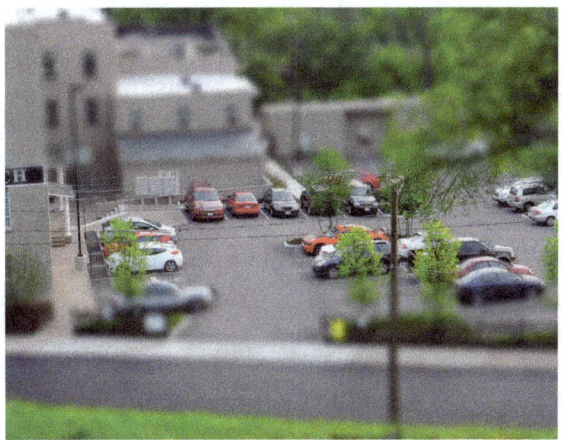

Figure 6-24. Filter Effects Miniature Effect Example Image

With the next option on the Filter Effects menu, Painting, the camera applies a distinctive form of processing that results in heightened emphasis on colors and imbues the image with a pastel-like look, as shown in Figure 6-25. It is somewhat like one of the more exotic types of HDR processing, and also is similar to posterization, in which the number of colors used in the image is decreased to make it seem as if the image was created from just a few poster paints; the result has an unrealistic but dramatic effect.

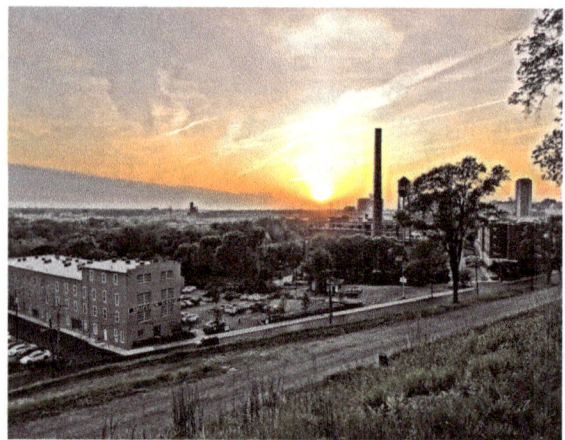

Figure 6-25. Filter Effects Painting Example Image

This setting is useful to achieve an artistic effect, perhaps for a poster or greeting card. It seems to work best when you start with an image that is underexposed, possibly using negative exposure compensation. For Figure 6-25, I started with an image taken with the Low Key setting in Special Effects mode.

The next option, Vignette, darkens the image toward its edges to create the appearance of an old-fashioned vignette, with the center highlighted but fading out on the edges. An example is shown in Figure 6-26.

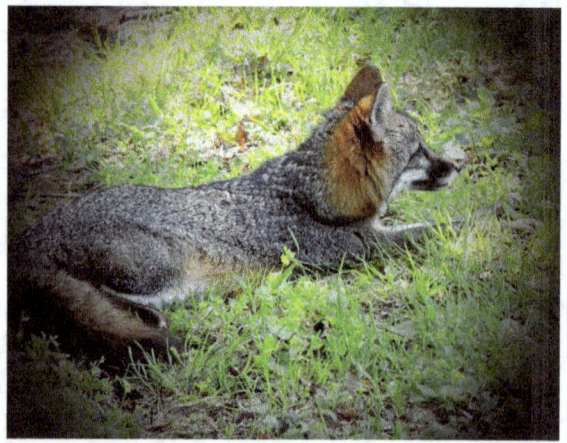

Figure 6-26. Filter Effects Vignette Example Image

In this case, I felt the Vignette setting would be an appropriate way to highlight a gray fox I saw in a nature park to give it a somewhat exotic or antique aura.

There are two more selections for Filter Effects on the second screen of the menu item. The first of these, Photo Illustration, alters the image by darkening the outlines of objects and reducing the number of colors, to make the image appear like a pen-and-ink illustration that has been colored in with poster paints. This option can create a very pleasant effect if used with an appropriate subject. I have enjoyed the results of using it with fairly large, colorful subjects like the food stand sign in Figure 6-27. It also can work well when used with images including people, to give an impressionistic look for the scene.

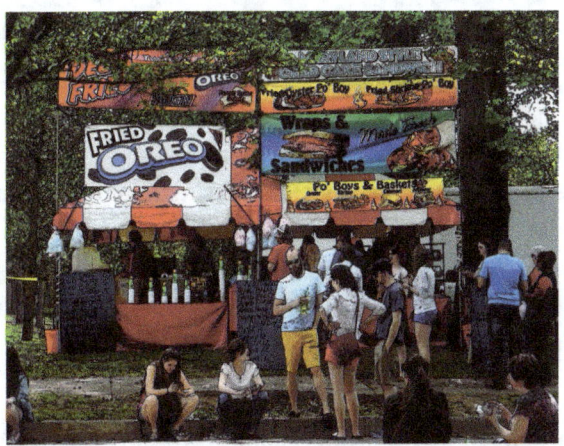

Figure 6-27. Filter Effects Photo Illustration Example Image

The final choice for the Filter Effects option, Portrait (Color + B&W), is somewhat like the Selective Color option, discussed above, but it is specially designed for images of people. If the camera detects a human face, it will leave the face in color and convert the background to black-and-white, as in Figure 6-28. If the camera does not detect a human subject, it will leave the central part of the image in color and convert the rest of the image to black-and-white. This can be an effective way to highlight a portrait subject and isolate him or her from the background.

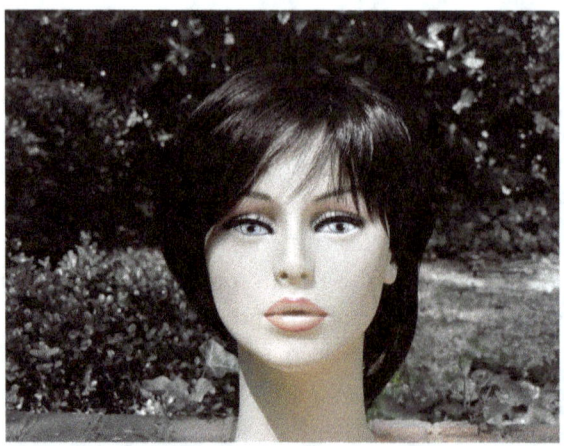

Figure 6-28. Filter Effects Portrait - Color & Black and White Example Image

PRINT ORDER

The Print Order menu option lets you print your images directly from the camera without first processing them on a computer. You can do this either by connecting the Coolpix P600 directly to a printer with the USB cable or by saving the images to a memory card and taking the card to a shop that prints images.

If you want to select multiple photographs before sending them to the printer or to the print shop, use the DPOF (Digital Print Order Format) function, which is built into the camera. The DPOF system lets you mark various images on your memory card to be added to a print list, which can then be sent to your own inkjet or laser printer or to the shop.

To add images to the DPOF print list, select the Print Order option from the Playback menu, then choose the Select Images option from the next screen, shown in Figure 6-29.

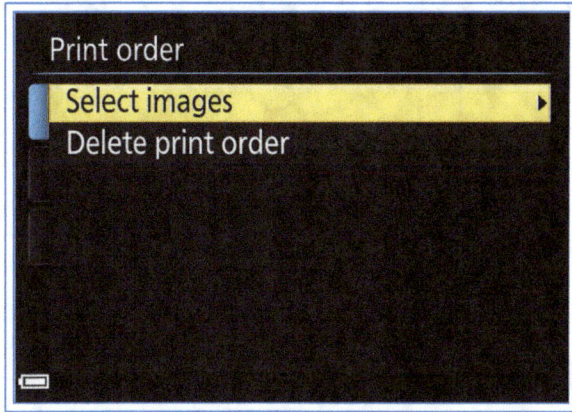

Figure 6-29. Print Order Options Screen

The camera will display thumbnail versions of your images in groups of 12 per screen, as shown in Figure 6-30.

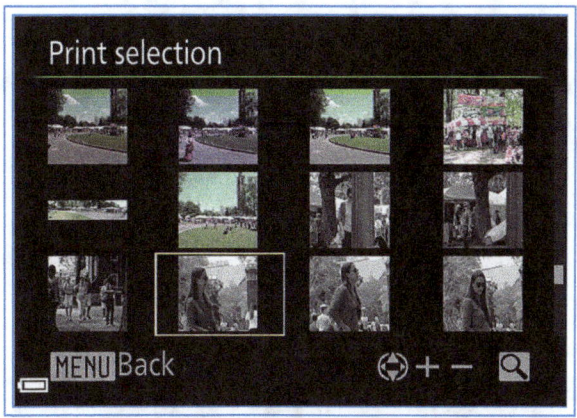

Figure 6-30. Print Order Print Selection Screen

Use the multi selector dial or the Left and Right buttons to move through the images. When an image you want to have printed is highlighted with a yellow frame, press the Up button to mark it for printing; press repeatedly to increase the number of copies to as many as nine. Press the Down button to decrease the copies or unmark the image. You will see a yellow check mark and a number of copies on any marked image, as shown in Figure 6-31.

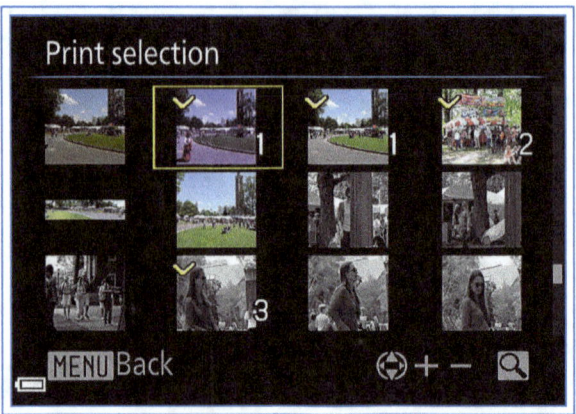

Figure 6-31. Print Selection Screen with Some Selections Made

You can then keep browsing through your images and adding (or subtracting) them from the print list. To see a larger thumbnail, press the zoom lever toward the T position for any given image.

When you have finished selecting images to be printed, press the OK button to confirm your choices and exit from the selection screen. On the next screen, shown in Figure 6-32, you can navigate to boxes for Date and Info to specify whether the printed images will include the date and shooting information.

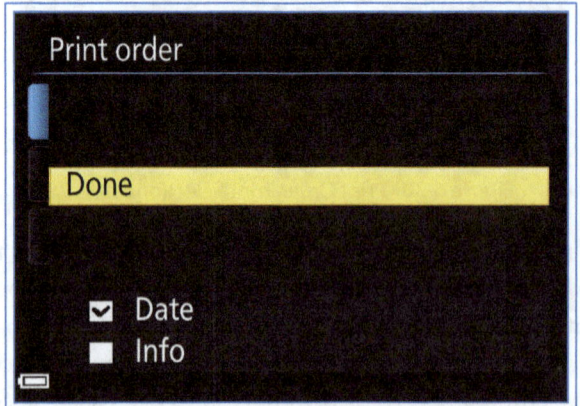

Figure 6-32. Print Order Confirmation Screen

Then highlight the Done message and press the OK button. You can take the memory card to a service that prints photos using the DPOF system, or you can connect the camera to a PictBridge compatible printer to print the selected images.

If you need to delete a print selection you have made, go to the Print Order menu and choose the Delete Print Order option.

SLIDE SHOW

Like most modern digital cameras, the Coolpix P600 can display the images on your memory card (or in the camera's internal memory) in a slide show that plays back on the camera's display or on a connected HDTV. The P600 does not offer elaborate options such as music or a variety of transitions; your pictures are played back with straight cuts between them and in silence.

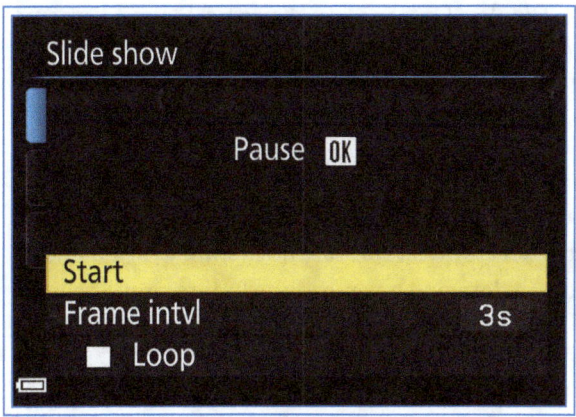

Figure 6-33. Slide Show Options Screen

The only choices you can make from the Slide Show menu option, shown in Figure 6-33, are the length of time between images and whether or not the show should repeat in a loop. (The loop is not endless; the show will repeat for a maximum of 30 minutes.)

To start a slide show, go to the Playback menu and choose Slide Show. You can then navigate to the option for Frame Interval and select 2, 3, 5, or 10 seconds for the time between images. Next, press the Left button to go to the previous screen and press the OK button while the Loop option is highlighted, if you want the show to repeat. After selecting these options, highlight the Start option and press OK to start the show. To pause the show, press OK again. To restart it, highlight the playback triangle that appears on the screen and press the OK button. To stop the show, highlight the square "stop" icon and press the OK button. You also can stop the show at any time by pressing the Playback button. To skip forward or backward to the next image, you can press the Left or Right button at any time; hold either of those buttons down to move more rapidly through the images.

There is no way to select the images that will be played; all images on the memory card (or in the internal memory) will be played. For movies, only the first frame will be played. For sequences of continuous shots, only the key images will be displayed, if the Sequence Display Options item on the Playback menu is set to Key Picture Only.

PROTECT

With the Protect feature, you can "lock" selected images so they cannot be erased with the normal erase functions using the Trash button. However, if you format the memory card using the Format command, all data will be erased, including protected images.

To protect images, after selecting this menu option, navigate through your images using the Left and Right buttons or the multi selector dial, and use the Up and Down buttons to mark or unmark any image you want to protect.

Press the Up button to mark an image or the Down button to unmark it. A yellow check mark will appear on the thumbnail of each marked image, as shown in Figure 6-34. As with the Print Order function, you can use the zoom lever to enlarge an image before deciding whether to apply protection to it.

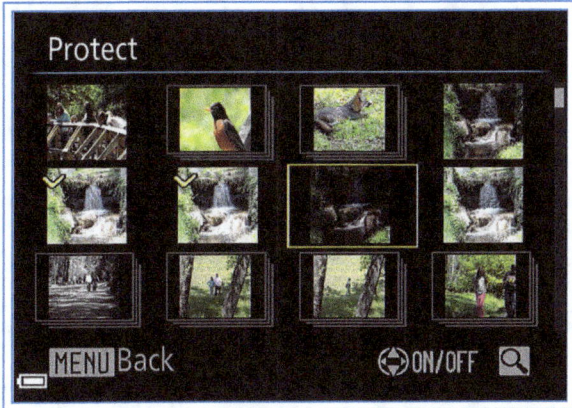

Figure 6-34. Images Marked to be Protected

When you have marked all images as you want them, press the OK button to apply the protection. An image that is protected will have a key icon in the upper left corner, as shown in Figure 6-35.

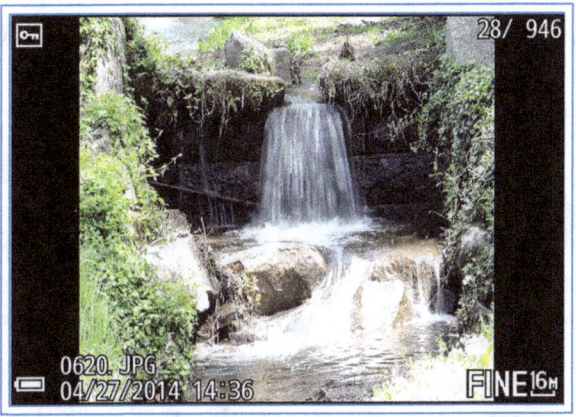

Figure 6-35. Protected Image with Key Icon

That icon will be visible when the image is viewed with the basic information screen; the icon will not appear in the image-only view or in the detailed view with the histogram.

The other Playback menu items are found on the second screen of the menu, which is shown in Figure 6-36.

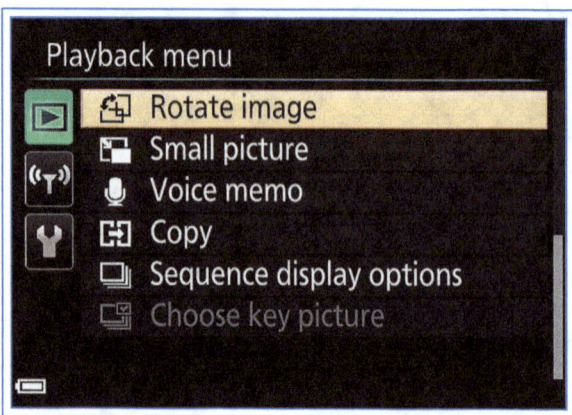

Figure 6-36. Second Screen of Playback Menu

ROTATE IMAGE

Using this first option on the Playback menu's second screen, you can rotate still photos 90 degrees clockwise or counter-clockwise.

You cannot rotate the key image of a sequence when it is displayed in sequence mode; you have to display the pictures from the sequence individually in order to rotate them.

After you select the Rotate Image option from the Playback menu, the camera displays the Select Image screen. Navigate with the multi selector dial or the Left and Right buttons until you have highlighted with a yellow frame the image you want to rotate, then press the OK button to select it.

On the next screen, as shown in Figure 6-37, use the Left or Right button to rotate the image counter-clockwise or clockwise. (You can also do the rotation by turning the multi selector dial.) Press OK when the image is rotated to the orientation you wish, then press the Menu button to exit from the Rotate screen.

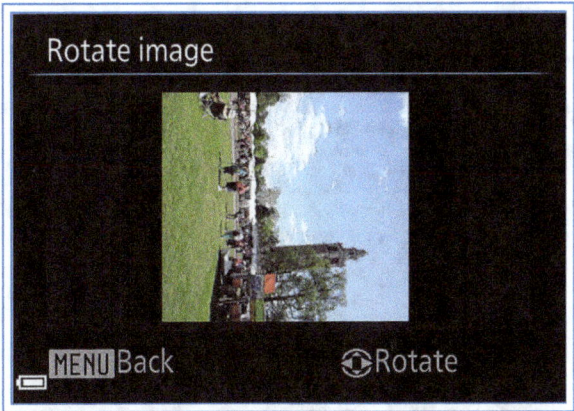

Figure 6-37. Rotate Image Screen

If an image was taken with the camera turned sideways, so the camera ordinarily has to be turned in order to view the image right-side-up, the camera will let you rotate it as much as 180 degrees; other images can be rotated only 90 degrees.

SMALL PICTURE

This option lets you do a simple form of in-camera editing. This feature allows you to take any saved image and create a new version in a file small enough to send by e-mail or post on the internet. This function could come in handy if you need to take a quick photo and e-mail it to a friend or colleague. If you don't have software available on your computer to edit the image down to a smaller size, you can let the camera take over this task. Of course, you could take the image in the small size to begin with, but you might want to have a higher-resolution version available for later editing or printing, and be able to create a small version for e-mailing after you have already recorded the original version.

To use this feature, navigate to the image you want to alter. Once it is displayed, in either full-frame or thumbnail view, press the Menu button, then select the Small Picture option. On the next screen, as shown in Figure 6-38, you can choose from 3 options: 640 x 480 pixels, 320 x 240 pixels, or 160 x 120 pixels. Each of these choices produces a low-resolution image, well under 1 megapixel in size.

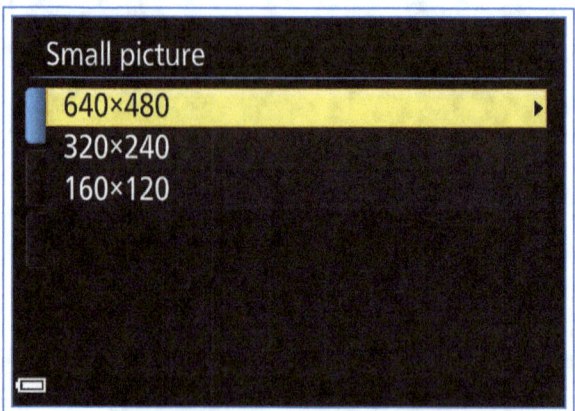

Figure 6-38. Small Picture Options Screen

If you confirm the operation on the next screen, the camera will copy the selected image at your chosen size and save it at the end of the images on the memory card (or in internal memory).

The image will be displayed in the camera with a large, black border area around the image itself, as shown in Figure 6-39, to show that this is a "Small Picture" copy. This border does not become part of the actual image; it displays only in the camera.

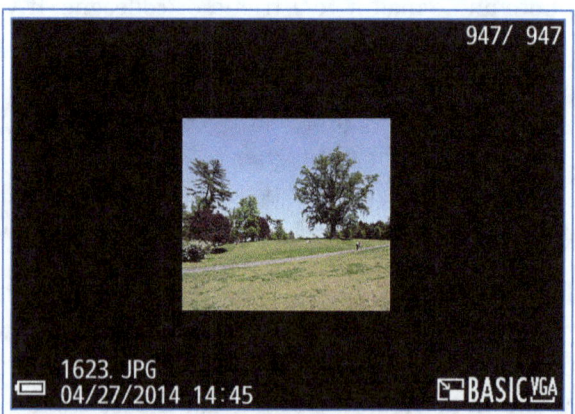

Figure 6-39. Small Picture with Black Border

Voice Memo

This option lets you record an audio memo of up to 20 seconds with any picture that is stored on your memory card; the image must have been taken with the Coolpix P600, not with another camera. When the image is displayed on the screen, press the Menu button, select the Voice Memo option, and press the OK button or the Right button to get to the voice memo recording screen, shown in Figure 6-40.

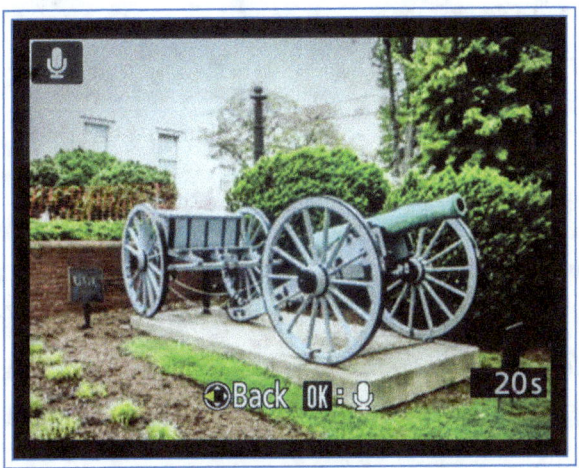

Figure 6-40. Voice Memo Recording Screen

You will see a microphone icon in the upper left corner and another one in the bottom center of the screen, with the word OK next to it. When you're ready to record, press and hold the OK button and talk into the microphone, which is on top of the viewfinder housing. The recording will stop when you release the button, or after 20 seconds, whichever comes first. Make sure you actually hold the button down; if you just press and release it, nothing will be recorded.

To play back a voice memo, display an image that has a voice file attached; the image will have a musical note icon in the upper left, as shown in Figure 6-41, when it is displayed with the basic information screen.

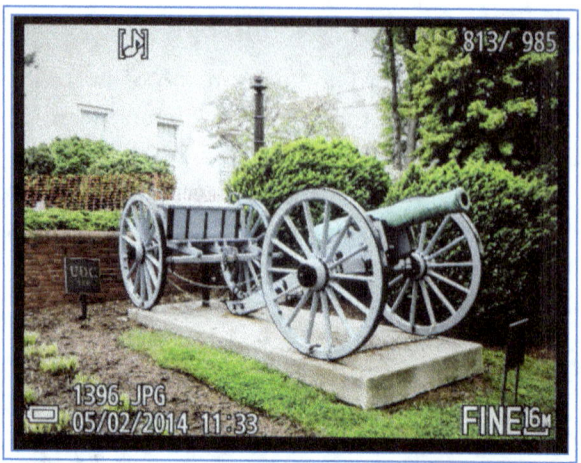

Figure 6-41. Musical Note Icon Indicating Voice Memo

When an image with the musical note is displayed, press the Menu button and select the Voice Memo option. Press OK or the Right button, and then press OK on the next screen to play the audio file. You can adjust the volume using the zoom lever.

To delete a voice memo, from the Voice Memo playback screen, press the Trash button, then press OK to confirm when prompted by the camera. You also can delete the voice memo by deleting the image that has the memo attached.

COPY

The Copy option lets you copy your images from the camera's internal memory to the currently installed memory card, or from the memory card to the internal memory. When you choose this menu option and then press OK or the Right button, the camera displays a screen with the two choices, Camera to Card and Card to Camera, as shown in Figure 6-42.

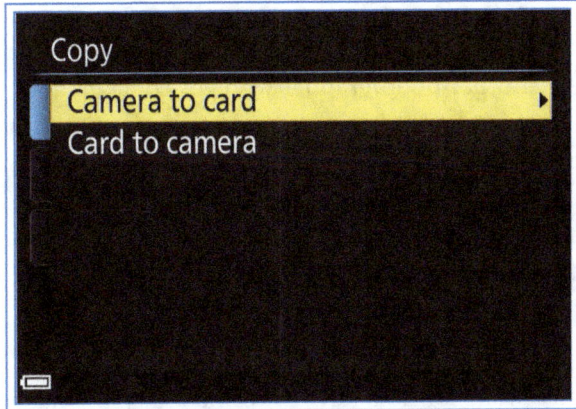

Figure 6-42. Copy Menu Option

If there are no images available to be copied in one or the other of these locations, that option will be dimmed and unavailable for selection. For example, if no images are currently stored in the internal memory, the Camera to Card option will be dimmed.

Highlight one of the two options and press OK or the Right button to move to the next screen. The camera will give you the choice of copying all your images or just selected ones. If you choose the latter, the camera will take you to the familiar image selection screen. There, you can mark (or unmark) each image to be copied using the Up (or Down) button. Then press OK, and the camera will ask you once more to confirm the operation. If you choose to copy all images or a large volume of images from a memory card to the internal memory, they will not all fit, and the operation will terminate with an error message.

If you regularly copy your images to a computer, you probably won't have much need for this option, but, like many of the options on the Playback menu, it can serve as a backup procedure when a computer is not available. Also, if you have taken a few images with the internal memory, it can be quite convenient to copy them to a memory card so you can save them, and then format the internal memory for further use.

Copying from an SD card to the internal memory is not likely to be a function you need often, but it could be useful if you're at an event with another photographer who got some great shots with another camera that you need copies of. You could copy several shots from his or her SD card to your internal memory to take home with you. You also could use this procedure if you made a one-time shot of great importance and want to make sure the copy on the card is backed up immediately.

SEQUENCE DISPLAY OPTIONS

This menu option controls how the camera displays images taken in one of the continuous-shooting modes such as Continuous H, Continuous L, Pre-shooting Cache, and others, which normally are displayed as "sequences." This option is straightforward: You have just two choices—Individual Pictures or Key Picture Only, as shown in Figure 6-43.

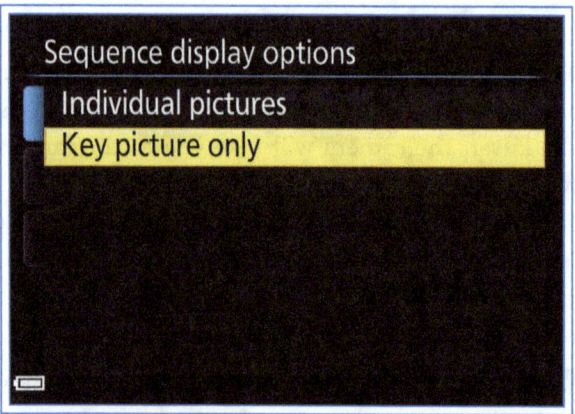

Figure 6-43. Sequence Display Options Menu Options

If you choose Key Picture Only, then, as you navigate through your images, when you come to a sequence, only the key image will display; it will be displayed in a frame that appears like a stack of images, indicating that it is the key frame of a sequence, and there will be a prompt to press the OK button to view the individual images from the sequence.

You cannot call up the detailed information for the key image with the Display button or use the Playback menu options to manipulate the image; you first have to press the OK button to "enter" the sequence and display the individual images. If you choose the Individual Pictures option, all sequences will automatically be opened up, so the images from the sequences all display as you scroll through your saved images; you will not see any key images or have to "enter" into the sequences.

CHOOSE KEY PICTURE

This final option on the Playback menu lets you change the key picture that displays for a sequence. Ordinarily, the first image in a sequence is used as the key picture. If you would prefer to display one of the other images when the shots are displayed in sequence mode, you can use this feature. First, you have to set the previous menu option, Sequence Display Options, to Key Picture Only. Then display the sequence whose key picture you want to change. Select this menu option and press the OK button or the Right button to activate it.

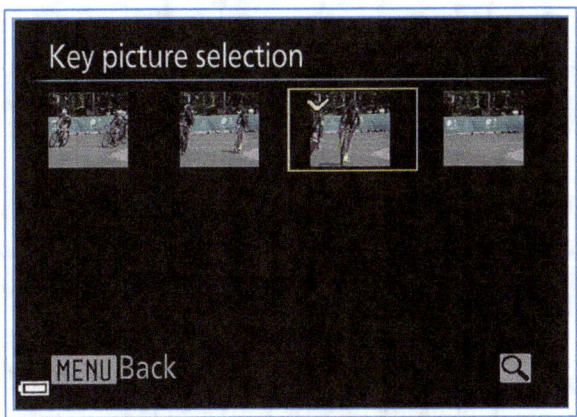

Figure 6-44. Key Picture Selection Menu Option

The camera will display all of the images from the sequence, as shown in Figure 6-44.

Navigate through those images using the multi selector dial or the Left and Right buttons. Press the OK button when the picture you want to use is highlighted.

Because of the nature of continuous shooting, which captures a stream of images rapidly, in most cases the images will be quite similar. However, there may be occasions when one image stands out above the others in quality and you will want to have it display as the representative of its sequence, so it will show up in slide shows, for example.

Printing Images

There are various ways to produce copies of digital photographs on paper. You can import the photographs into a program such as Adobe Photoshop or Photoshop Elements, or use the ViewNX2 software supplied by Nikon with the Coolpix P600, or any of many other programs that are available for photo editing. Once you have edited the images to your satisfaction, you can print the finished products from that software.

However, in some cases you may not be willing or able to spend the time to manipulate the pictures in software before printing them out. You may have access to a printer that will connect directly to the camera, and you may need or want to print out copies on photo paper without going through the time-consuming process of transferring the images to a computer first. The following discussion covers the high points of this procedure.

PRINTING DIRECTLY FROM THE CAMERA

The Coolpix P600 uses the PictBridge printing protocol, which lets the camera communicate directly with a wide variety of printers. The basic procedure is quite simple: First, make sure the Charge by Computer option on the Setup menu is set to Off. Then, plug the black USB cable that came with the camera into the mini-USB port inside the door on the right side of the camera. (This is the upper of the two ports in that location.)

Then plug the other end of the cable into the USB port of a PictBridge-compatible printer. (This USB port is different from the one for the cable that connects the printer to a computer; this one is rectangular; the port for the cable to the computer has more of a square shape.) The printer does not have to be made by any particular company; I plugged the camera directly into my HP Photosmart C6180 printer, and the two devices communicated with no problems.

Once the connection is made and the printer is turned on, the camera should turn on automatically and display the PictBridge logo, shown in Figure 6-45.

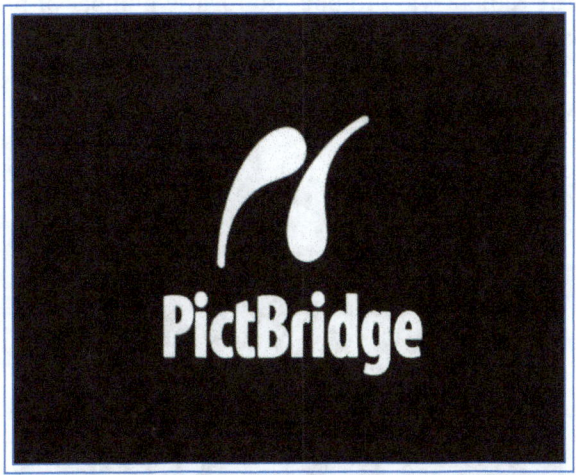

Figure 6-45. PictBridge Screen

The PictBridge logo is followed quickly by a special screen that appears only when the P600 is connected to a PictBridge printer, as shown in Figure 6-46.

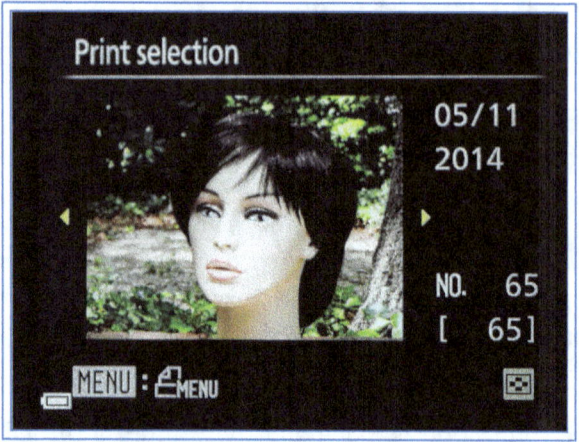

Figure 6-46. Print Selection Screen

To print an individual image, navigate to it and press the OK button; the camera will prompt you for the number of prints and the paper size. To print multiple images, when the print display screen initially displays, press the Menu button to bring up the Print menu, shown in Figure 6-47.

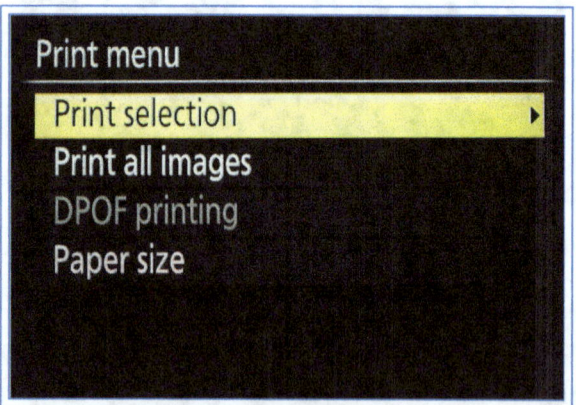

Figure 6-47. Print Menu

From that screen, you can select images to print, print all images, or use the DPOF selection of images, as discussed earlier in this chapter.

Once you have all of the settings as you want them, press the OK button on the camera to print out the photograph or photographs. For further details about these procedures, see the reference section of the Nikon P600 Reference Manual at pages 14-18.

Chapter 7: The Setup Menu

Now I have discussed the options available to you in the Shooting menu and Playback menu systems. The next menu system to discuss is the Setup menu. (I'll discuss the Movie menu along with the various options for video recording in Chapter 8 and the Wi-Fi Options menu in Chapter 9.)

The Setup menu gives you various choices for housekeeping matters such as screen brightness and operational sounds, but it also includes some settings that affect how you take your images, including Vibration Reduction, Motion Detection, and Digital Zoom. In addition, this menu is where you perform the crucial operation of formatting a memory card or the internal memory.

As a reminder, you enter the menu system by pressing the Menu button. The available menus change depending on whether the camera is set to shooting mode or playback mode, and, in shooting mode, which exposure mode is selected (Program, Shutter Priority, or Scene, for example). However, no matter what mode the camera is set to, you can always enter into the Setup menu. After you press the Menu button, use the Left button to move the yellow selection block to the far left column and highlight the wrench icon that indicates the Setup menu, as shown in Figure 7-1.

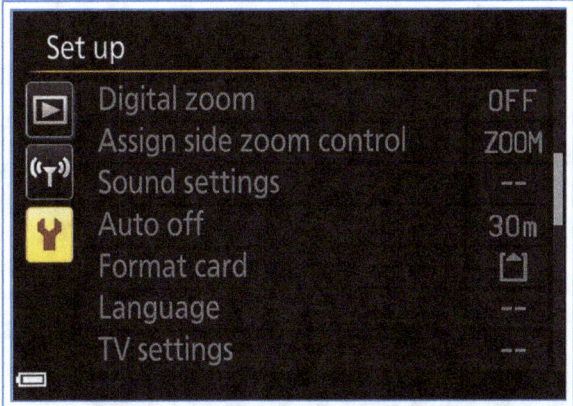

Figure 7-1. Setup Menu Icon Highlighted

Once that icon is highlighted, use the Right button to move the selection block back into the list of menu items, and then use the multi selector dial or the Up and Down buttons to navigate through the various options on the menu. The first screen of the Setup menu is shown in Figure 7-2.

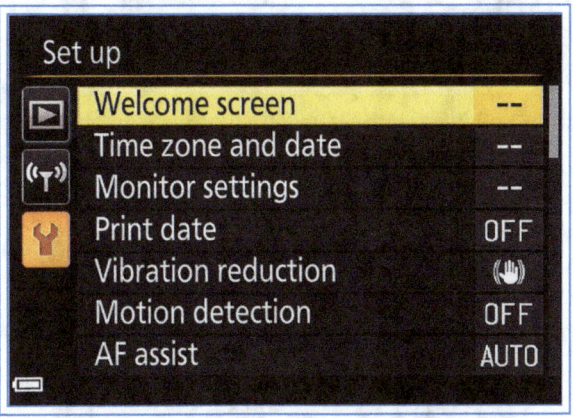

Figure 7-2. First Screen of Setup Menu

I'll discuss all of the choices on the menu in the order in which they appear.

Welcome Screen

When the camera comes from the factory, it does not display a start-up image when you turn it on. This option lets you have it display a Nikon logo or one of your own images. Choose this item on the Setup menu, then use the Right button or the OK button to move to the next screen, where you can select from None, Coolpix, or Select an Image, as shown in Figure 7-3.

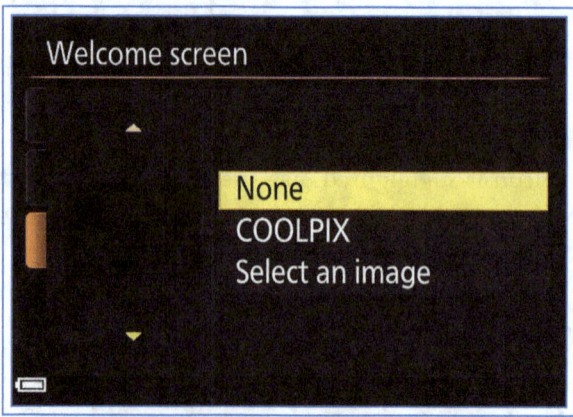

Figure 7-3. Welcome Screen Options Screen

If you want the Nikon image, select Coolpix, and the next time the camera powers on it will display the Coolpix logo in a nice-looking graphic on the screen for a few seconds, as shown in Figure 7-4.

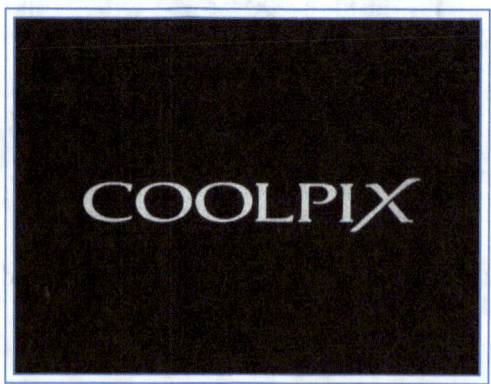

Figure 7-4. Coolpix Logo for Welcome Screen

You also have the option of selecting an image that is stored in the camera's internal memory or on the memory card in the camera. Choose the Select an Image option from the Welcome Screen menu item and then navigate through your images. When you find the image you want, press the OK button to select it. That image will then appear for a couple of seconds every time you start up the camera, until you change it again using the same process. The image you select must be in the 4:3 aspect ratio and must not have been reduced in size to 320 x 240 pixels or smaller.

Time Zone and Date

Chances are you set the date, time, and time zone when you first set up the camera. If you haven't done so or need to change them, use this menu option. First, select Time Zone and Date, and press the Right button or the OK button to move to the Time Zone and Date options screen, shown in Figure 7-5.

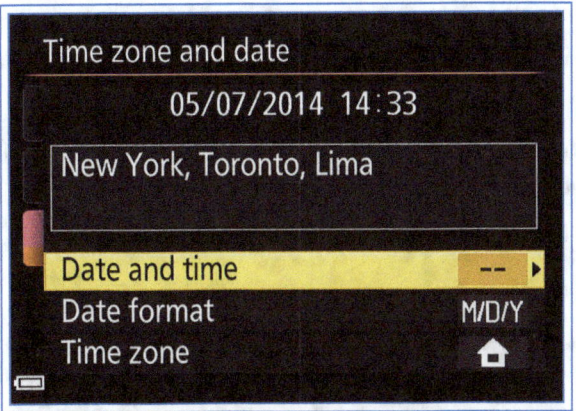

Figure 7-5. Time Zone and Date Options Screen

Select Date and Time and press the Right or OK button to get to the Date and Time Settings screen, shown in Figure 7-6. Navigate through the selections for month, day, years, hour, and minute using the Left and Right buttons; change the values using the multi selector dial, the command dial, or the Up and Down buttons.

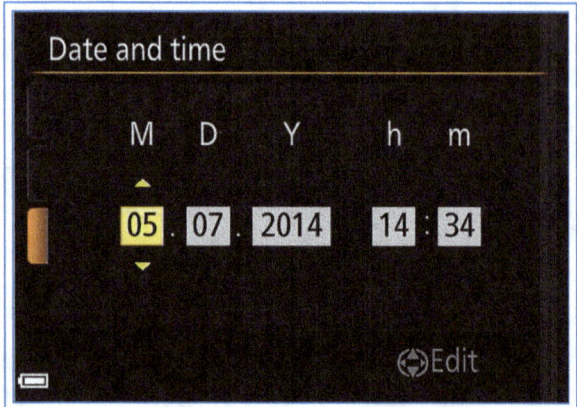

Figure 7-6. Date and Time Settings Screen

When you have finished with the minutes setting, press the OK button to confirm all of the settings. You can then return to the Time Zone and Date screen, select Date Format, and choose your preferred order for displaying the month, day, and year.

Finally, return to the Time Zone and Date page and select Time Zone. For this option, you have two choices—the home time zone and the travel destination, as shown in Figure 7-7.

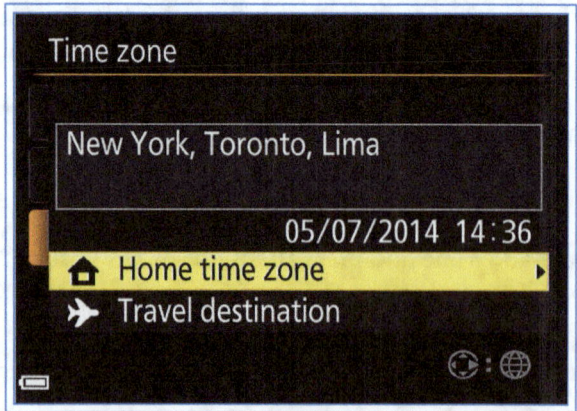

Figure 7-7. Time Zone Options Screen

Set the home zone to the location where you spend most of your time, and, if you want, set the travel zone for an area you are most likely to travel to. Or, you can wait until you travel to set this zone.

When you take a trip, select the travel time zone from this menu option and the camera's time and date will change as required, so your images will have the correct dates and times when you take pictures in your destination time zone.

Monitor Settings

With this menu item, you can control several aspects of the way your camera's monitor (LCD screen or viewfinder) displays images, as shown in Figure 7-8.

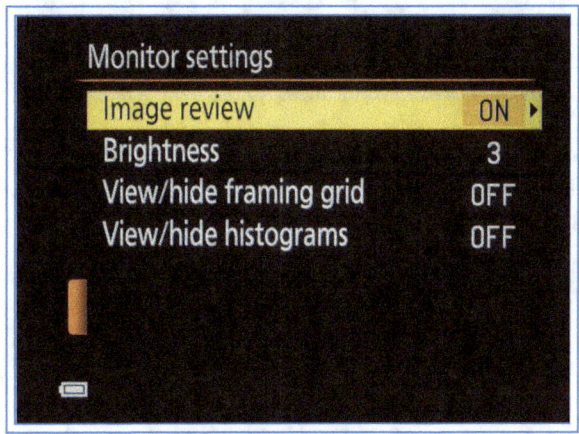

Figure 7-8. Monitor Settings Options Screen

First, you can turn the Image Review feature on or off. If it is turned on, a new image shows up on the screen for about a second when you first take the picture. If it is turned off, the display immediately goes back to the shooting screen when you take a picture. There is no way to control the length of time the image displays; this feature is either on or off. If you want to view a new image for a longer period of time, press the Playback button and use the normal playback procedures.

The next option, Brightness, lets you select from 6 levels of brightness for the LCD screen, as shown in Figure 7-9, including levels 1-5 and a final level called Hi.

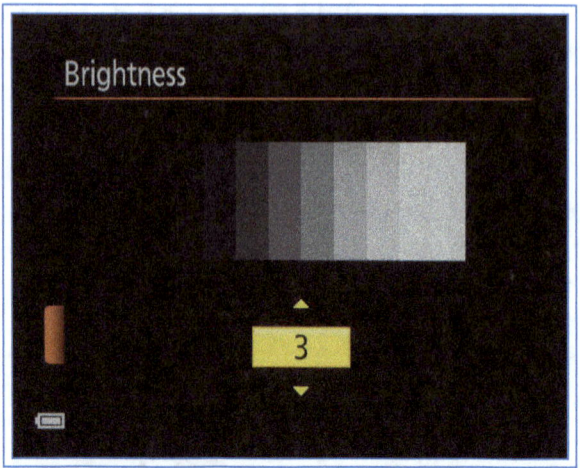

Figure 7-9. Brightness Adjustment Screen

Select the level you want using the Up and Down buttons or the multi selector dial. The default value is level 3. The Hi setting is extremely bright, and can be used when you are shooting in bright conditions but still want to use the LCD screen rather than the viewfinder. If you use the higher settings, the camera's battery will run down faster than usual, so take that factor into account when increasing the brightness.

This setting has no effect on the brightness of the display in the viewfinder window or on a TV set; if you have activated the viewfinder by folding in the LCD screen or pressing the Monitor button, or if you have the camera connected to a TV set, the Brightness option will be unavailable for selection.

Next, the View/Hide Framing Grid option, shown in Figure 7-10, lets you turn on or off a grid of vertical and horizontal lines that divide the screen into nine blocks. The grid itself is shown in Figure 7-11.

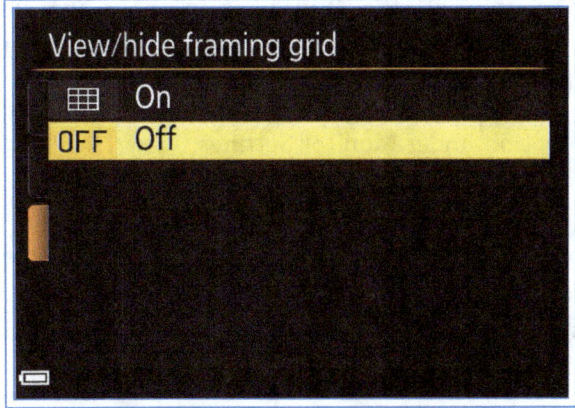

Figure 7-10. View/Hide Framing Grid Options Screen

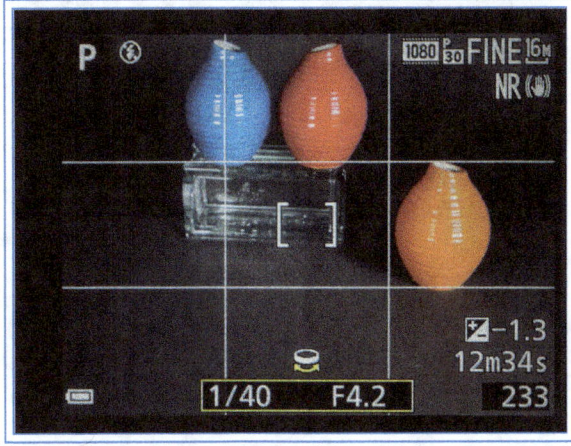

Figure 7-11. Grid in Use on Shooting Screen

You may appreciate having this grid available to help you compose your images according to the Rule of Thirds, which calls for placing the most important subject close to the intersections of these lines, to increase visual interest in the photo.

The grid also may help you keep the horizon or your subject, such as a building, properly horizontal or vertical by lining it up against one of the lines on the screen. The grid displays whenever the camera is in shooting mode, regardless of what display mode has been selected with the Display button. It also appears when a video is being recorded. If you don't find the grid useful, just leave it turned off.

The final option under Monitor Settings, View/Hide Histograms, controls whether or not the histogram is displayed when the camera is in shooting mode. If you turn this option on, the histogram appears in the left half of the screen when the camera is set to shooting mode, as shown in Figure 7-12. However, unlike the framing grid, the histogram displays only when the more detailed information display is selected with the Display button.

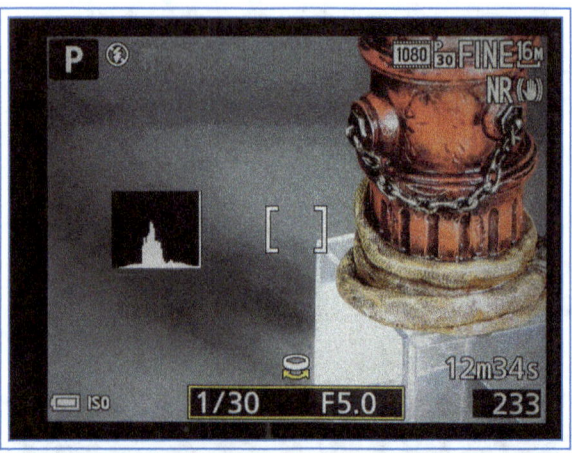

Figure 7-12. Histogram in Use on Shooting Screen

Even when this option is turned on and the detailed information screen is activated, the histogram does not display under certain conditions, including when you are recording a movie, using the enlarged view for manual focus, or using the pop-up menu to select focus mode, the self-timer, or flash mode.

If this option is turned off, you can still display the histogram in shooting mode by pressing the exposure compensation button (Right button) to adjust the exposure. The histogram will turn on in that situation to help you gauge how much exposure compensation to apply, as shown in Figure 7-13.

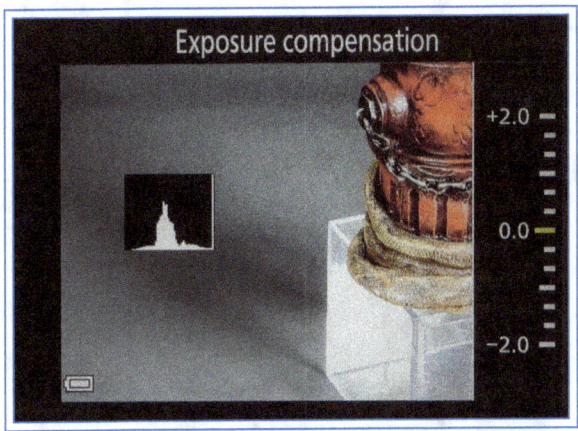

Figure 7-13. Exposure Compensation Adjustment Screen

I prefer to display histograms in shooting mode using the exposure compensation control, because I can call up the histogram when I want it and it will disappear quickly after I am finished using it. However, exposure compensation is not available with Manual exposure mode, so this menu option is the only way to display a histogram when shooting in that mode. If you want to display a reasonably accurate histogram in Manual mode, you need to turn on the Manual Exposure Preview option on the last screen of the Shooting menu; otherwise, the histogram will not reflect the settings you have made for your manual exposure.

You should also note that the histogram will always display for still images in playback mode when you have selected the histogram display screen by pressing the Display button, as discussed in Chapter 6.

As also discussed in Chapter 6, the histogram is useful for indicating whether your image will be underexposed or overexposed. In most cases, it's a good idea to adjust exposure settings so the histogram looks roughly like a mountain with gradual slopes from left and right to a moderate peak in the center.

Print Date

With this option, you can control whether the camera places the current date, or date and time, on the image when the image is recorded, as shown in Figure 7-14.

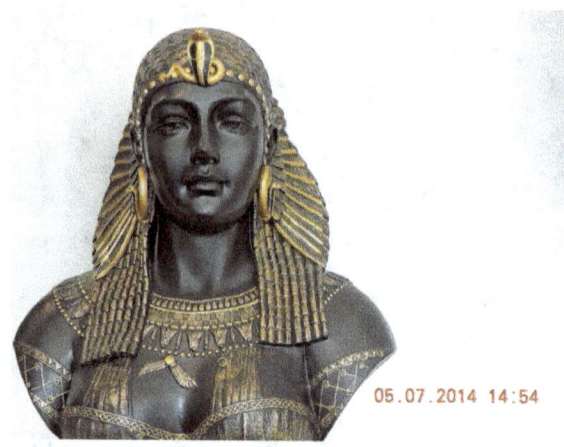

05.07.2014 14:54

Figure 7-14. Print Date Option in Use on Image

This option places this information permanently on the image, and the information cannot be deleted (unless you use Photoshop or similar software to edit it out). You might want to use this feature if you are taking images as part of a scientific experiment in which you need to record this information as part of your data, but you probably would not want to use it for general picture-taking, because the date (or date and time) information will mar the image. For ordinary images, you can always use editing software to retrieve the date and time information, which is recorded invisibly with the images (assuming the camera is set to the correct date and time). To use this feature, go to the Print Date option on the menu, then select either Date, Date and Time, or turn the option off altogether.

Vibration Reduction

This is one of the more important settings for the camera, particularly because of the extreme telephoto capability of the P600's lens. When you activate Vibration Reduction (VR), the camera uses its lens-shift system to stabilize the image. When you are handholding the camera, there is bound to be a slight amount of camera motion or shake. At slow shutter speeds, this motion can cause blurring of your images. Any such blurring is magnified at higher telephoto levels, as you can see if you look through the viewfinder or at the LCD screen at a zoomed-in level. The slightest motion can make the image appear to jiggle uncontrollably.

There are three available settings for the VR system: Off, Active, and Normal, as shown in Figure 7-15.

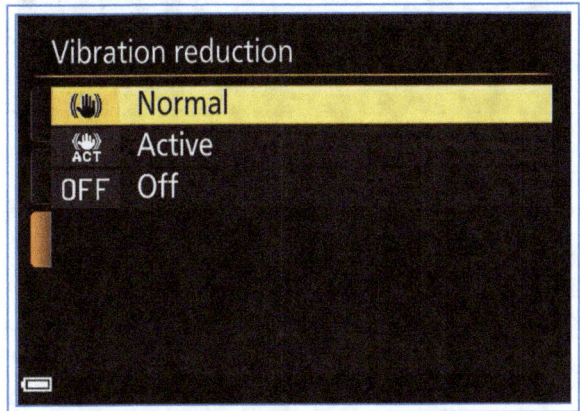

Figure 7-15. Vibration Reduction Options Screen

These settings are applicable when you are shooting either still pictures or movies. When you have the camera on a tripod, you should make sure the VR setting is turned off, because the camera's circuitry can get confused and attempt to correct for camera shake when there is none, thereby degrading the image.

The Normal setting is intended to correct relatively mild camera movement, such as when you are handholding the camera and panning it to record a movie (moving side to side smoothly). The camera can detect the smooth horizontal motion, and will correct only for vertical motion caused by the handholding. It also can detect smooth vertical motion, such as when you are tilting the camera vertically to take a movie of a tall building. When the Normal setting is turned on, the camera places a hand icon in the upper right corner of the screen, as shown in Figure 7-16.

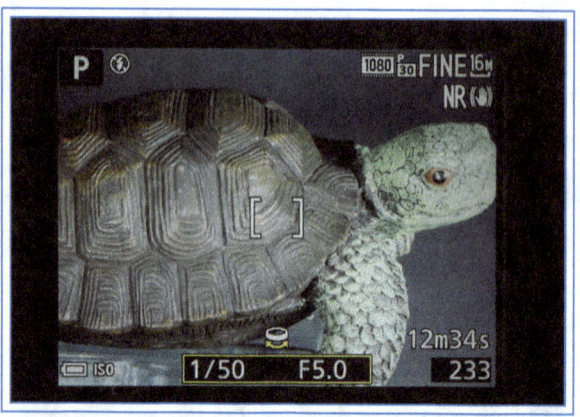

Figure 7-16. Hand Icon for Normal Vibration Reduction

The Active setting is intended for situations in which the camera motion is more erratic and dramatic, such as when you are shooting out of a car window, or from a boat or helicopter, and the camera may be jerked in various directions unpredictably. In this case, the camera does not allow for horizontal motion, but corrects for motion in any direction as well as it can. Of course, the camera cannot erase the effects of violent motion, but it can reduce the blurring effects of milder motion to a fair extent. When the Active setting is turned on, the camera displays the icon shown in Figure 7-17 instead of the plain hand icon.

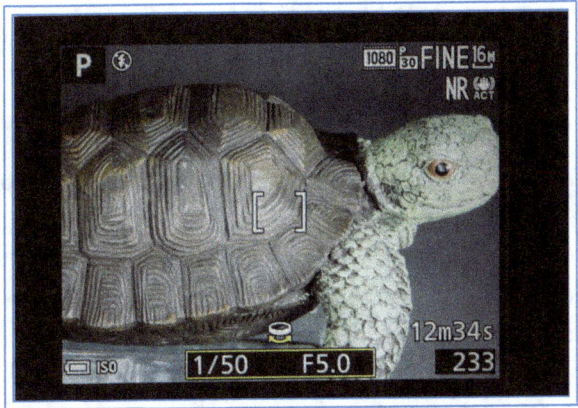

Figure 7-17. Icon for Active Vibration Reduction Setting

I recommend that you use the Normal setting when handholding the camera in most situations, if you are able to hold the camera quite steady. However, if you are a passenger in a vehicle on a bumpy road or otherwise encountering random motion, you may want to switch to the Active setting to see if it can help even out the jolts to the camera.

Motion Detection

The Motion Detection option on the Setup menu is related to Vibration Reduction (VR) but operates quite differently.

Just as with the VR system, the camera detects motion of the camera that could cause blur and takes action to counteract the possibility of image blur. However, instead of shifting the position of the lens, the camera adjusts its shooting settings. That is, when motion is detected, the camera automatically raises the ISO sensitivity level and sets a faster shutter speed in an attempt to use an exposure that is brief enough to avoid blur.

For example, if the camera would normally take a picture at 1/15 second at f/3.4, if the Coolpix P600 detects motion, the camera may increase the ISO level so the sensor's sensitivity to light is increased and less light is needed to expose the image. In that way, the camera may be able to take the picture at 1/50 second rather than 1/15 second, resulting in an exposure that is short enough in duration to prevent any camera motion from blurring the image.

There is one somewhat unusual aspect to this setting: It is not available in any of the more advanced shooting modes—Program, Aperture Priority, Shutter Priority, or Manual exposure. It is available only in Auto mode and with some (but not all) of the Scene mode and Special Effects mode settings. It is available with the Sunset, Dusk/Dawn, Close-up, Food, Museum, and Black-and-White Copy settings for Scene mode. It is available with all settings of Special Effects mode except High ISO Monochrome.

When this setting is in effect, an icon that looks like a ball with curves emanating from it displays in the upper right corner of the screen, as shown in Figure 7-18.

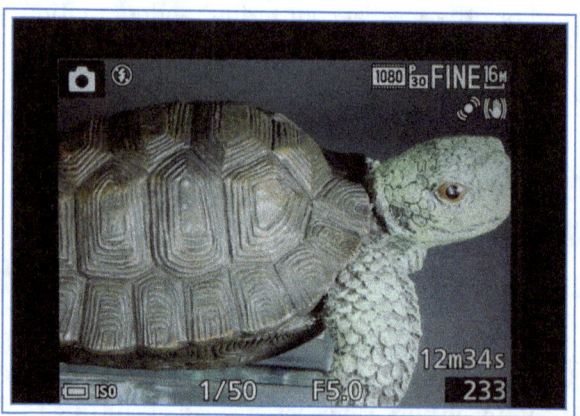

Figure 7-18. Motion Detection Icon

When the motion detection system actually causes the camera to change its settings, the icon turns green to let you know.

In my opinion, this is a useful setting, because it can possibly rescue a shot that would be unusable because of motion blur. Given that it is only available when you are using the more automatic shooting modes, I recommend turning it on by setting this menu option to Auto. If you want to exercise more control over the camera's settings, you can shoot in Program mode or one of the other advanced shooting modes and use the Vibration Reduction feature instead of Motion Detection. When you are using the Auto or Scene modes, the Motion Detection setting can be of considerable benefit if you are shooting in dim light where the use of a slow shutter speed may result in motion blur.

AF Assist

This next menu option lets you turn on or off the reddish light beam that shines from the autofocus assist lamp on the front of the camera. This beam illuminates when the camera is trying to focus in a dark area; the light helps the autofocus mechanism find the patterns and shapes it needs to evaluate in order to achieve proper focus. You should usually leave this setting turned on, but you may want to turn it off when you're taking pictures in a place where the beam could be distracting or annoying to others, or where it might alert the subjects of your candid photography. If the camera then has difficulty in focusing, you can switch to manual focus and adjust the focus yourself.

The choices for this setting are Auto or Off. With the Auto setting, the lamp will fire when needed, except with some focus settings and some scene settings in which it is disabled and cannot activate. The lamp will always light up when the self-timer is used; there is no way to disable the self-timer lamp, though you can cover it with black tape if you need to suppress it.

Now I will turn to the items found on the second screen of the Setup menu, shown in Figure 7-19.

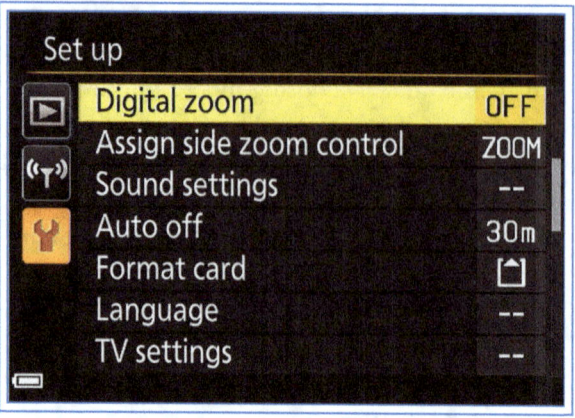

Figure 7-19. Second Screen of Setup Menu

Digital Zoom

This first item on screen 2 of the Setup menu lets you zoom in on a scene electronically, beyond the magnifying power of the camera's optical zoom. Because it is an electronic zoom and not an optical one, it does not increase the optical information received by the camera; instead, it enlarges the image digitally, which can result in a blocky, pixellated look. That's not to say that digital zoom is useless. It can help you to compose a scene the way you want to, or to measure the exposure on a small part of the scene before you zoom back out to take the picture without the digital zoom effect, for example. And, in some cases, the use of digital zoom does not actually degrade the quality of the image; it just uses a smaller portion of the image sensor's surface, resulting in a lower-resolution image, but without the pixellation of an artificially magnified image. In addition, Nikon uses a feature called Dynamic Fine Zoom that improves the quality of digitally zoomed images.

There are two settings available on the Setup menu for this feature: On and Off. If you choose Off, the camera will be limited to using its optical zoom, which is really not much of a limitation, since the P600's lens has the impressive range of 24mm to 1440mm.

If you choose On, the lens will "zoom" electronically beyond the optical limit of 1440mm, to a maximum of an amazing (though somewhat illusory) 5760mm. With digital zoom, beyond a certain level of magnification the camera will use its circuitry to "interpolate" pixels—that is, it will create new pixels in between the ones produced by the sensor, in order to expand the image to a greater magnification. When the camera is using interpolation, the image deteriorates to some extent because the camera is using pixels that are not part of the original image.

If you use an Image Size setting smaller than the maximum, then you can use digital zoom to a certain extent without image deterioration. This is because the camera needs a smaller number of pixels in order to create the desired image. Therefore, instead of interpolating new pixels among the existing ones, the camera crops out the actual pixels that appear on a portion of the image sensor, and enlarges that portion to fill the entire area of the sensor. In this way, the camera uses only the actual pixels captured through the lens to the image sensor; it does not have to interpolate any new pixels.

Whenever you move the zoom lever, a scale appears in the top center of the image to show how far the lens has been zoomed.

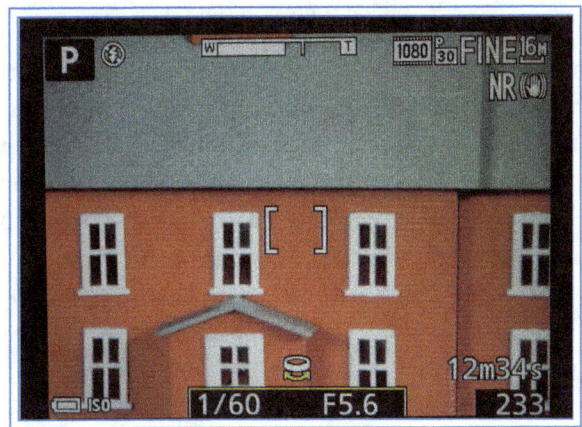

Figure 7-20. White Zoom Scale for Optical Zoom Only

The scale has a small vertical line past the halfway point; that line shows the point where the camera starts using digital zoom instead of optical zoom. As shown in Figure 7-20, when only optical zoom is in use, the zoom scale is white, and the bar stays to the left of that small line.

If you zoom the lens in so the zoom bar moves past the vertical line, the bar may turn blue, as shown in Figure 7-21, indicating that digital zoom is being used, but that the picture quality should not deteriorate too much.

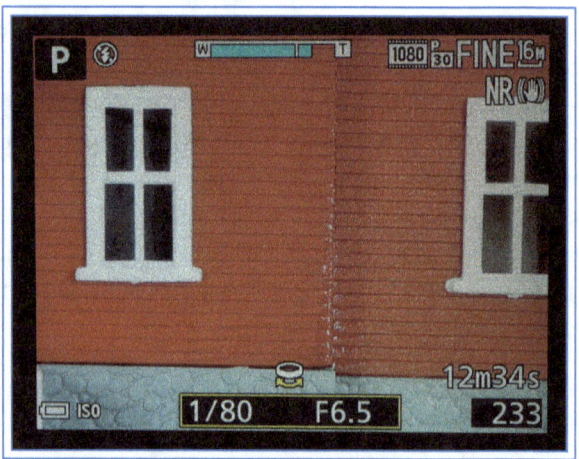

Figure 7-21. Blue Zoom Scale for Large Image

When the zoom bar turns blue, that can mean one of two things. Either the Image Size is set to a value smaller than the maximum of 3608 x 3456 pixels, so the camera can use the extra pixels to magnify the image without loss of quality, or the camera is using what Nikon calls Dynamic Fine Zoom, special processing that increases magnification without compromising image quality in the way that normal digital zoom does. According to Nikon, you can zoom the lens to a focal length of 2880mm, twice the optical zoom range, before image deterioration occurs, even when using the largest Image Size setting.

If you set Image Size to a value smaller than the maximum, the zoom bar will stay blue for longer ranges. If you use one of the smaller options, such as 2272 x 1704 (4M), the bar may stay blue for the entire digital zoom range, because the camera can use the pixels to increase magnification. An example of this effect is seen in Figure 7-22, where digital zoom was used with Image Size set to the 4M size and the zoom bar is blue to the end of its range.

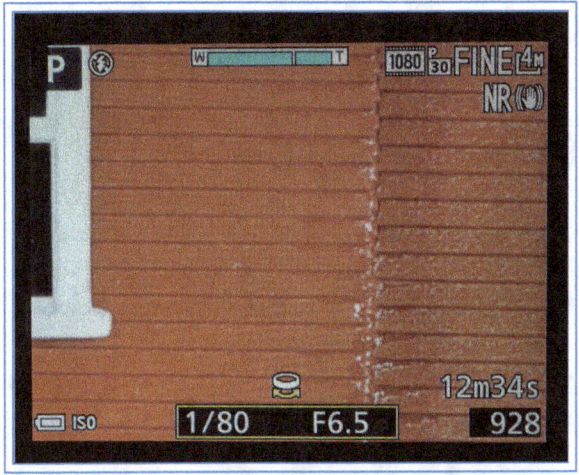

Figure 7-22. Blue Zoom Bar for Smaller Image

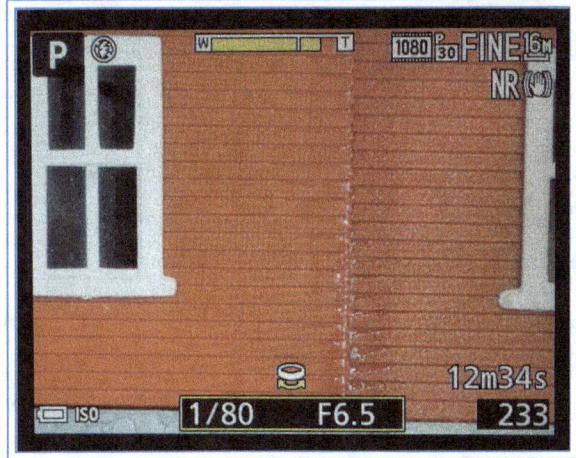

Figure 7-23. Yellow Zoom Bar for Large Image

If you continue to zoom the lens, the zoom bar may turn yellow, indicating that image deterioration will occur because the camera is adding extra pixels. For example, Figure 7-23 shows the zoom scale with Image Size set to its maximum value, and with the lens zoomed well beyond the optical zoom range.

How should you use the Digital Zoom setting? Well, the maximum optical zoom range of the P600's lens is so phenomenal (1440mm) that there should not be much need to zoom beyond that. It becomes difficult to maintain a completely steady image, even with a tripod, at magnifications greater than that. However, if you are trying to capture an elusive bird or other creature with your lens, or have some other special photographic need, I recommend you use the Digital Zoom menu option if it will help you, bearing in mind that you may want to use some of the smaller image sizes in order to preserve image quality. I suggest you keep the zoom scale in the white range if possible, and let it go into the blue range in some cases. I recommend that you avoid the full digital zoom, with its yellow zoom bar. There is usually no advantage to be gained from pushing the camera to this limit.

Digital zoom is not always available, depending on other settings in use. It cannot be used along with any of the following settings: manual focus, Smile Timer, Multi-shot 16, Zoom Memory, or AF Area Mode set to Subject Tracking. It also cannot be used with certain scene settings (Scene Auto Selector, Portrait, Night Portrait, Pet Portrait, and Easy Panorama). Focus will always be in the center of the frame when digital zoom is used.

Assign Side Zoom Control

I mentioned this menu option briefly in Chapter 5, in discussing the side zoom control. This switch, on the left side of the lens, ordinarily serves as an alternative zoom control. When you leave it set to that function, you may find you can hold the camera steadier by using the side control rather than the zoom lever on top of the camera. (Personally, I don't notice much difference;

when using the zoom lever I can hold the camera quite steady.) You also might want to use the side control for zoom when you have turned on the Zoom Memory menu option, because, with that option, the zoom lever can zoom only to specific focal lengths. You might want to use the side control to zoom continuously to all focal lengths when needed.

If you want to use the side zoom control for one of its two other possible purposes, use this menu option to choose either manual focus or snap-back zoom, as shown in Figure 7-24.

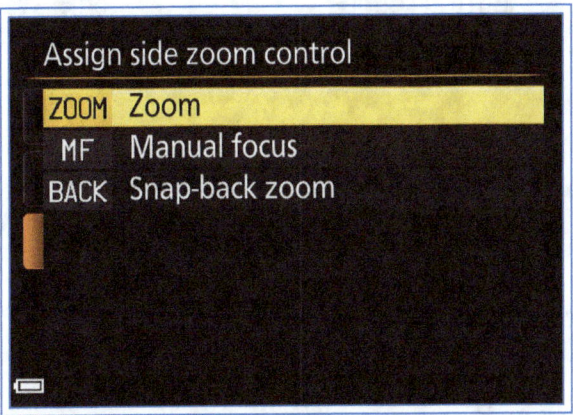

Figure 7-24. Assign Side Zoom Control Menu Option

If you choose manual focus, the side control can be used to adjust the focus point, but you can still use the multi selector dial to focus. If you choose snap-back zoom, the side zoom control can be pushed toward the W side to "snap" the zoom length back to about half of what it was each time, in several stages. Then, when you press the switch back in the T direction, the zoom reverts to its original length. In this way, you can experiment with various focal lengths, or get a broader perspective on your scene before returning the lens to the original focal length to take the shot. Of the three possibilities for this switch, I tend to prefer snap-back zoom, because it gives the camera a capability it does not otherwise have. Note, though, that snap-back zoom is not available for movie recording.

Sound Settings

This next option on the Setup menu, shown in Figure 7-25, gives you a quick way to silence all of the electronic beeps and chirps that sound off when the camera performs certain actions, such as turning on, achieving focus and exposure, or having the shutter pressed to take a picture.

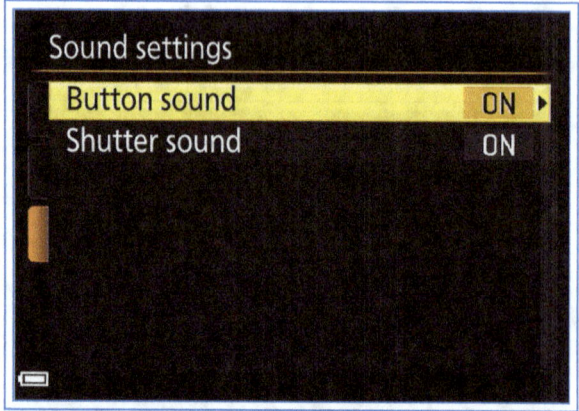

Figure 7-25. Sound Settings Menu Option

There are not many options here—first, you can turn the "Button sound" on or off. This option controls whether or not the camera beeps when it starts up, when settings are made, when it achieves focus, and when an error occurs. When the camera is set to the Bird-watching or Pet Portrait setting of Scene mode, sounds are automatically disabled, regardless of this setting.

The other option for this menu item is to turn on or off the shutter sound, which ordinarily is heard when you press the shutter release button all the way down to take a picture. Again, this sound is automatically disabled with the Bird-watching and Pet Portrait settings. It also is disabled during continuous shooting and during movie recording. (The camera makes a low clicking sound during continuous shooting, but not the distinctive sound of the shutter.)

Auto Off

This option controls the length of time before the camera enters standby mode to save power. By default, the camera will stay fully powered on for one minute when you are not touching the controls; after that time, it enters standby mode, in which the display goes blank and the green light around the power button blinks about twice per second. After about three minutes in that mode, the camera turns completely off. During standby mode, you can bring the camera back to full-power mode by pressing the power button, the shutter release button, the Playback button, or the Movie button, or by turning the mode dial.

If you want to set a different interval before the camera enters standby mode, you can choose 30 seconds, five minutes, or 30 minutes with this menu item, as shown in Figure 7-26.

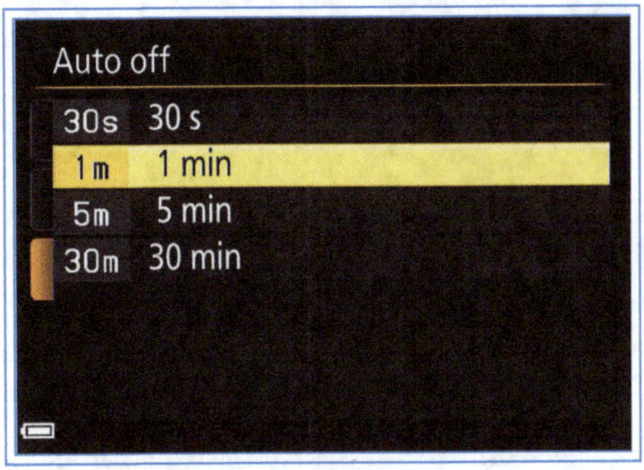

Figure 7-26. Auto Off Menu Option

Note, however, that those times apply only when the camera is in shooting mode, displaying the shooting screen. When menu screens are displayed, the camera will enter standby mode in three minutes, if a shorter setting than that is chosen for Auto Off. Also, during slide show playback, the camera will stay active for up to 30 minutes, and when the AC adapter is connected, the time before entering standby mode will always be 30 minutes.

Format Card/Format Memory

This is one of the most important menu options. Choose this process only when you want or need to completely wipe all of the data from a memory storage card or from the camera's internal memory.

When you select the Format Card option, as shown in Figure 7-27, the camera will warn you that all images currently on the card will be deleted if you proceed.

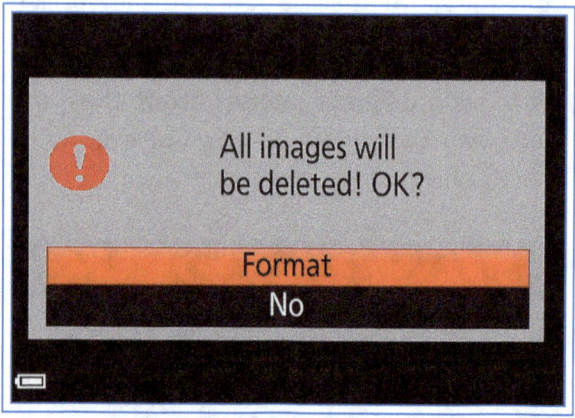

Figure 7-27. Format Card Confirmation Screen

Because of the seriousness of this step, the camera displays the selection bar in red if you highlight Format; the bar is yellow if you highlight No.

If you highlight Format with the red selection bar and press the OK button to confirm, the camera will format the card that is in the camera, and the result will be a card that is empty of images and properly formatted to store new images from the camera.

With this procedure, the camera will erase all images, including those that have been protected from accidental erasure with the Protect function on the Playback menu. It's a good idea to periodically save your good images and videos to your computer or other storage device and then re-format your memory card, to make sure it is properly set up to start recording new images and videos. It's also a good idea to use the Format Card command on any new memory card when you first insert it in the camera. Even though it likely will work without that procedure, it's best to make sure the card is set up with Nikon's method of formatting.

If you want to format the camera's internal memory instead of a memory card, just remove the card from the camera. The name of the menu option will then change to Format Memory, as shown in Figure 7-28.

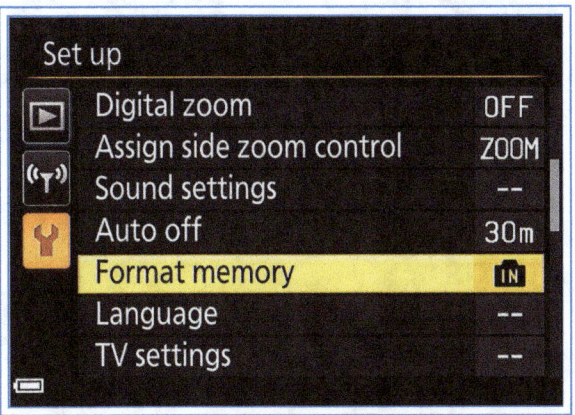

Figure 7-28. Format Memory Menu Item

With that command, the camera will format the internal memory. Before formatting the memory, you should copy any images that you want to preserve. You can copy them to a memory card by using the Copy command on the Playback menu, as discussed in Chapter 6, or copy them to a computer or other storage device.

Language

This option gives you a choice of 36 languages for the display of commands and information on the camera's display.

Once you have selected this menu item, scroll through the language choices using the multi selector dial or the direction buttons and press the OK button when your chosen language is highlighted, as seen in Figure 7-29.

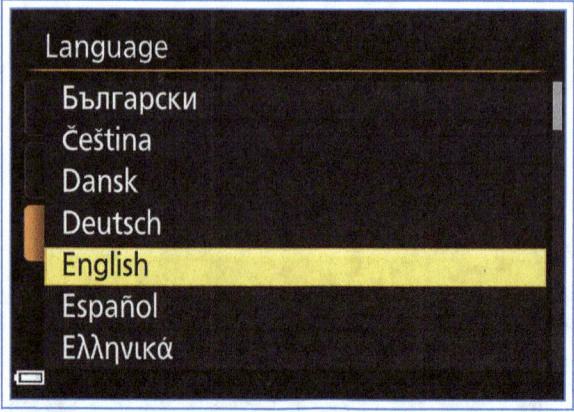

Figure 7-29. Language Selection Highlighted on Menu

TV Settings

This menu item lets you choose settings for two video-related items, as shown in Figure 7-30.

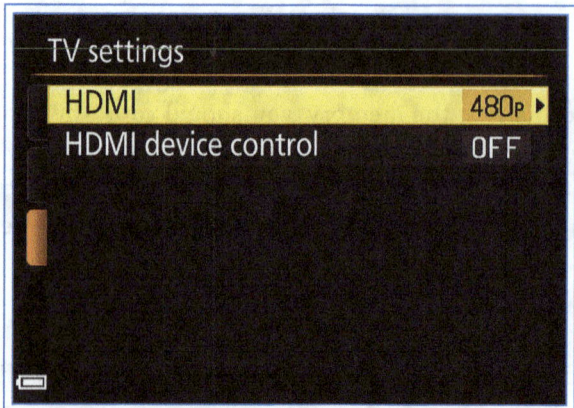

Figure 7-30. TV Settings Menu Item

The first sub-option for this menu item is HDMI, which can be set to Auto, 480p, 720p, or 1080i. Ordinarily, the Auto setting will work best; the camera will set itself for the optimum display according to the resolution of the high-definition (HD) TV set it is connected to. If you experience difficulties with that connection, you may be able to improve the image on the HDTV's screen by trying one of the numerical settings for this menu option.

The other setting under this menu item, HDMI Device Control, is of use only when you have connected the camera to an HDTV set and you want to control the camera with the TV's remote control, which is possible in some situations. If you want to do that, set this option to On, and follow the instructions for the TV and its remote control. You should be able to control playback of still images and movies using the remote control.

The next items to be discussed are found on screen 3 of the Setup menu, shown in Figure 7-31.

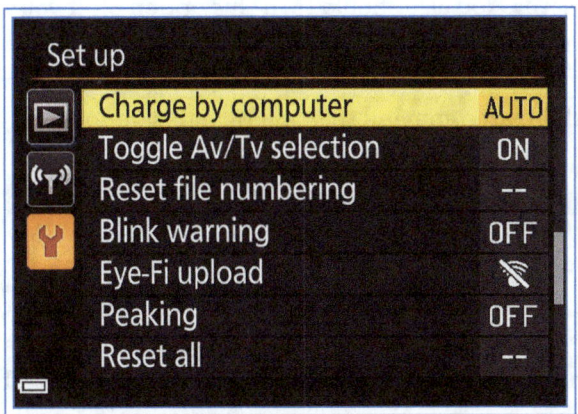

Figure 7-31. Third Screen of Setup Menu

Charge by Computer

By default, when you connect your Coolpix P600 to a computer using the USB cable, the battery is gradually charged by power from the computer through the cable. To disable this capability, choose Off from this menu item, shown in Figure 7-32, and the camera will not get power from the computer.

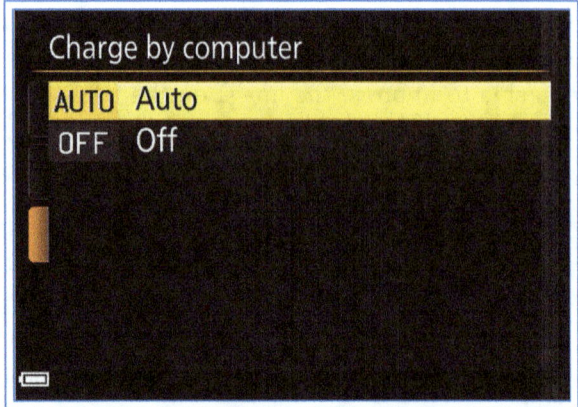

Figure 7-32. Charge by Computer Menu Option

You may want to turn this feature off when you are using a laptop computer and you don't want to run down the computer's battery unnecessarily. You also should turn this option off if you are going to connect the camera to a printer for direct printing of images. Unless you have some particular need to charge your battery by this method, I recommend that you turn this option off.

Toggle Av/Tv Selection

This menu option has just two possible settings: On or Off. The purpose of this setting is to determine whether the command dial is used to set shutter speed and the multi selector dial is used to set the aperture, as is normally the case, or not. On the menu screen, as shown in Figure 7-33, the On setting is described as Do Not Toggle Selection and Off corresponds to Toggle Selection.

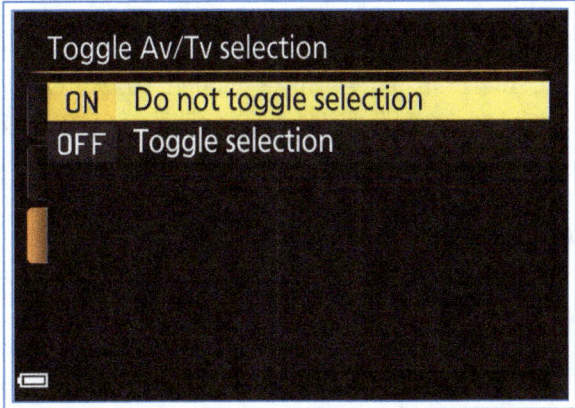

Figure 7-33. Toggle AV/Tv Selection Menu Option

I have to say that these assignments seem to me to be backward; I would think that, when you set a menu item called Toggle Av/Tv Selection to On, that would mean that you do toggle the selection, rather than the reverse. In any event, the descriptions on the long menu lines are accurate: When you select On (the default setting), the selection is not toggled, and the command dial is used to set shutter speed in the Shutter Priority and Manual exposure modes.

If you change the setting of this menu item to Off, then the camera switches the functions of the command dial and the multi selector dial for setting aperture and shutter speed in Aperture Priority, Shutter Priority, and Manual shooting modes. Ordinarily, the command dial sets shutter speed and the multi selector dial sets aperture. Using this option also affects the functions of those dials for controlling the Flexible Program option. Normally, the command dial has that function; you can re-assign that duty to the multi selector dial by setting this menu option to Off.

Reset File Numbering

This option resets the file numbering system back to 0001. Ordinarily, the camera assigns increasing file numbers to your images, even when they occupy many folders on the memory card.

For example, when you start out with a new camera and memory card, your first images will be stored in a folder named 100NIKON. The first image will be named 100NIKON-0001.jpg. (On your computer, there will be a prefix such as DSCN, so the name may be DSCN0001.jpg.) Once the 100NIKON folder has 200 files stored in it, the camera will automatically create a new folder called 101NIKON. If none of your files has been deleted, which would interrupt the numbering scheme, the first file in the new folder will be numbered 101NIKON-0201.jpg. That is, each folder can hold only 200 files before a new folder is created, but the individual files' numbers will keep increasing, even over multiple folders, until the individual file numbers reach 9999. Thus, after roughly 50 folders are filled with files, the individual numbers start over again at 0001.

If you don't like the idea of your folder and file numbers continuously increasing, you can use this menu option at any time to reset the file numbering back to the beginning. That is, if the file numbers have increased to a number such as 0476.jpg, and you don't want to wait until the numbers reach 9999 before they start over, you can invoke this procedure, select Yes when prompted by the menu, and the camera will start numbering your next image back at 0001.jpg. The folder numbers will continue to increase, however. Whenever the newest folder contains 200 files, a new folder will be created.

Blink Warning

This feature alerts you if the camera detects that a person blinked his or her eyes in a newly captured image. If you turn this option on, it will operate when you are using Face Priority for the AF Area Mode, including when you are shooting with the Night Portrait, Scene Auto selector, or Portrait mode.

If this option is turned on, the camera will display the message "Did someone blink?" on a special screen, as shown in Figure 7-34, if it detects what appear to be closed eyes in the image.

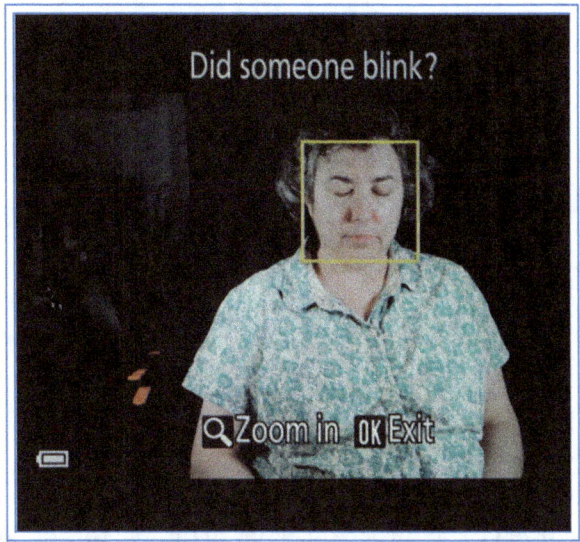

Figure 7-34. Blink Warning Screen

On this screen, the camera places a yellow frame around the culprit's face. You can then zoom in on that face using the zoom lever and take whatever other action you wish, including deleting the image or re-shooting the picture.

This option is not available when continuous shooting or exposure bracketing is in effect.

Eye-Fi Upload

As discussed in Chapter 1, an Eye-Fi card can be a useful storage option for your Coolpix P600 because it uploads your images to your computer (or other device) over a wireless network. In order for those uploads to work, this menu option, shown in Figure 7-35, must be turned on. (It is turned on by default.)

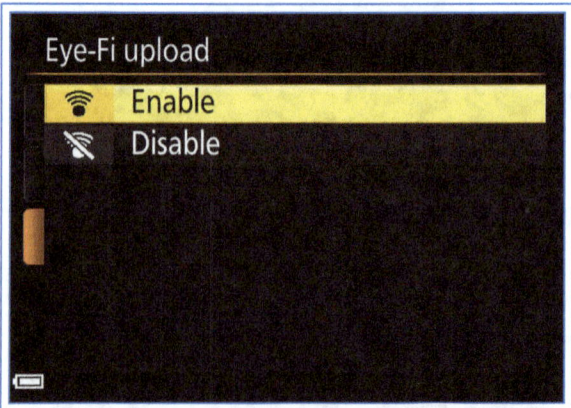

Figure 7-35. Eye-Fi Upload Options Screen

If you are on an airplane or in some other area where such devices are not allowed to be turned on, you can disable this option using this menu item.

You also may save some battery power by disabling it when it is not needed. Of course, if you are using an Eye-Fi card and the images are not uploading properly, you should check this menu option to make sure it is turned on.

Peaking

The Peaking feature, which is turned on by default, provides additional assistance for accurate manual focus. When Peaking is active and you are using manual focus, the camera displays white pixels in areas that are in sharp focus, as shown in Figure 7-36. As the focus gets sharper, you will see thicker areas of white. Try to adjust the focus to get the white areas to be as thick and obvious as possible.

You can adjust the intensity of the Peaking feature by using the Up and Down buttons to choose a value on the scale that appears at the left of the image. The higher the value, the greater the intensity of the feature. If your subject is one with naturally high contrast, such as straight lines and clear differences in color or brightness, you may see the Peaking pixels more clearly with a lower value. If the subject has low contrast, you may do better with a higher Peaking level. If you find the white pixels distracting, you can, of course, just turn the Peaking feature off using this menu item.

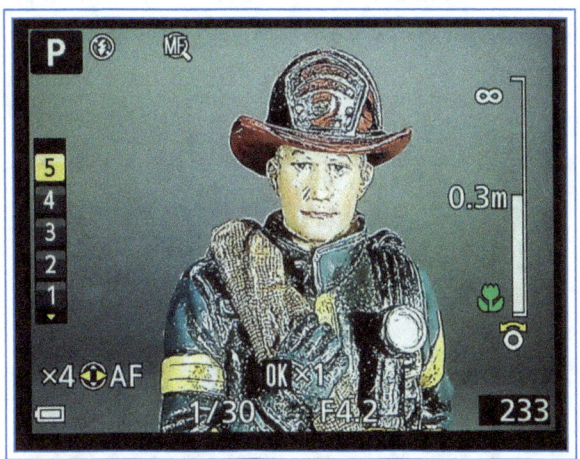

Figure 7-36. Peaking in Use

I have found Peaking to be of considerable help with some subjects, particularly those that are dark enough for the white Peaking pixels to show up clearly.

Reset All

Choose this menu option when you want to reset all of the camera's settings to their original (default) values. This action can be useful if you have been experimenting with different settings and you find that something is not working as expected. It will give you a fresh start with known values for all of the major settings on the menus and for shooting. There are a few settings that will not be reset, including items such as date and time, time zone, and language. In addition, user settings that you selected for the User Settings shooting mode are not reset by this menu item. To reset those settings, use the Reset User Settings option on screen 3 of the Shooting menu.

Firmware Version

The final entry on the Setup menu is the only item on screen 4 of the Setup menu, shown in Figure 7-37.

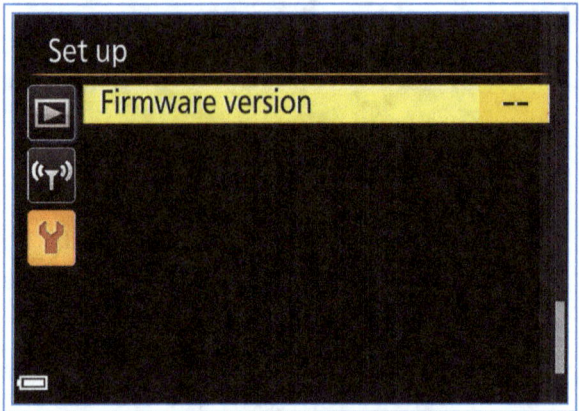

Figure 7-37. Firmware Version Menu Option

This option lets you see the current version of the firmware that is installed in your camera. The Coolpix P600, like other digital cameras, is programmed at the factory with firmware, which is a semi-permanent set of computer instructions that are electronically implanted in the camera. These instructions control all aspects of the camera's operation, including the menu system, functioning of the controls, and in-camera processing of your images. The reason you might want to check to see what version is installed is that, in many cases, the manufacturer will release an updated version of the firmware that may fix problems or bugs in the system, provide minor enhancements, or, in some cases, even provide major improvements, such as including new shooting modes or menu options.

To see what firmware version is currently installed in your camera, highlight this menu option, then press the OK button or the Right button, and the camera will display the version number, as shown in Figure 7-38.

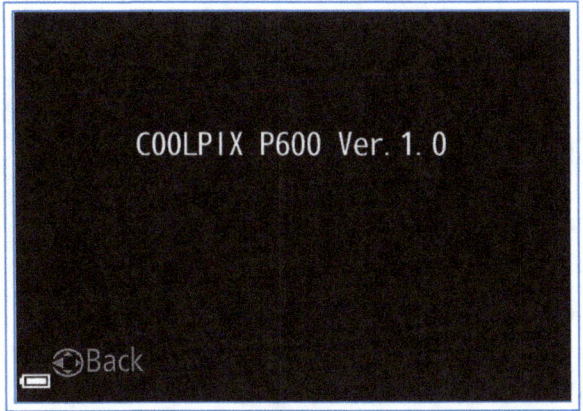

COOLPIX P600 Ver. 1. 0

Back

Figure 7-38. Firmware Version Displayed

To determine whether any firmware upgrades have been released, I recommend that you visit Nikon's support web site; for United States customers, the address is http://support.nikonusa.com; for Europe, the site can be found by starting at http://www. europe-nikon.com. Find the Download Center, and look for the link to current firmware versions. The site will provide detailed instructions for downloading and installing the new firmware.

Chapter 8: Motion Pictures

The Nikon Coolpix P600, like most advanced compact cameras, includes high-definition (HD) video recording among its capabilities. Along with HD video, the P600 offers extra benefits such as high-speed video recording, which results in slow-motion footage when you view it. I will explain the various options for movie-making in this chapter. Before I discuss the specific settings you can make for your movies, I'll begin with a brief overview of the process.

Movie-making Overview

In one sense, the fundamentals of making videos with the Coolpix P600 can be reduced to four words: "Push the red button." Having a dedicated motion picture recording button makes things easy for the user of the P600, because anytime you see a reason to take some video footage, you can just press the Movie button while aiming at your subject, and you will get results that are very likely to be usable. So, if you're more of a still photographer and not that interested in movie-making, you don't need to read any further. Be aware that the red button sits on the camera's back just under the mode dial, and if interesting action starts to happen before your eyes, you can press that button and record the events on video with a minimum of effort.

But for those P600 users who would like to delve further into their camera's motion picture capabilities, there is considerably more information to discuss. Even though you can just press the red button at any time to start recording a video sequence, there are several settings that can have a significant impact on your footage. The shooting mode the camera is set to for still images, and the menu and control-button settings you make, all have some effect on your movie recordings. So, it is helpful to be aware of the current settings, even if you just want to capture a brief clip of a scene during your vacation.

QUICK GUIDE TO RECORDING A MOVIE CLIP

I will discuss the details of movie-related settings later in this chapter. For now, here are suggested guidelines for quick settings when you want to record the action and you don't care about fine-tuning menu options and other settings. I'll discuss these steps with extra detail, in case you have turned to this section before reading about the camera's various controls and menus.

1. Turn the mode dial on top of the camera, to the right of the viewfinder, so the green camera icon is at the white indicator mark, putting the camera into the Auto shooting mode, as shown in Figure 8-1.

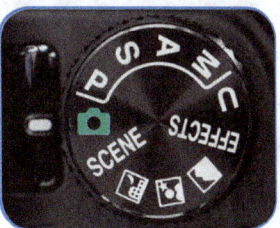

Figure 8-1. Auto Mode

2. Remove the lens cap and turn on the camera with the power button.

3. Press the Menu button at the bottom left of the control area on the right side of the camera's back, and then press the Left

button (left edge of the ridged dial that surrounds the OK button), which will move the yellow selection block to the far-left column of menu icons.

4. Press the Down button to move the yellow selection block down so it highlights the movie camera icon.

5. Press the Right button to move the yellow selection block into the list of menu options. Using the direction buttons or the multi selector dial (the ridged dial that surrounds the OK button), highlight the top line of the menu, Movie Options.

6. Press the Right button to get to the next menu screen, and make sure the top line is highlighted. It should say 1080/30p. (If it says 1080/25p, see the discussion of Frame Rate later in this chapter.) Press the OK button to select this option, as shown in Figure 8-2.

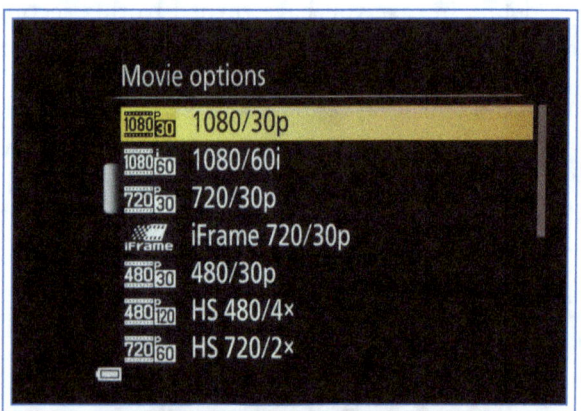

Figure 8-2. 1080/30p Option Highlighted

7. Press the Menu button to go back to shooting mode.

8. Aim at your subject and use the zoom lever on top of the camera to frame the scene as you want, zooming in or out as needed. Press the shutter button halfway down until you hear a beep, to have the camera evaluate the exposure and focus. When the action starts or you're ready to begin, press the red

Movie button to start the recording. Then take your finger off the button and hold the camera as steady as possible.

9. Continue to hold the camera steady, and pan (move the camera from side to side in one direction) slowly and smoothly if appropriate to take in the scene before you. When the scene has ended, press the red Movie button again to end the recording.

OTHER SETTINGS FOR MOVIES

The above steps will get you started recording video with the Coolpix P600 using the highest quality recording format and standard settings for white balance, autofocus, and other options. Once you are familiar with the basic steps for movie-making, though, you may want to experiment with some of the other available settings. There are quite a few items that can be adjusted for recording videos with this camera.

Still Photo Settings Available for Movies

When you record movies with the Coolpix P600, several settings you make for still photos, either through controls or through the Shooting menu, carry over to your movies, as long as the camera remains set to a shooting mode in which that setting remains in effect. For example, if, as discussed above, the camera is in the Auto shooting mode, the Auto mode settings will be in effect, including autofocus and Auto White Balance. If the camera is set to the Program mode, the settings for focus and white balance will be whatever you have set through the Shooting menu. In Program mode you can select manual focus, any white balance setting you want, and several other options, though not all items on the Shooting menu will carry over to affect your video recordings. You also can shoot movies in Special Effects mode, and the movie will take on the appearance of the setting you select, such as Painting, Nostalgic Sepia, or High ISO Monochrome. (Some Special Effects settings are not available with all movie formats.) I will discuss below other settings you can make that will work for movies.

Focus Mode

The first setting that carries over to video shooting is the focus mode, set by pressing the Down button, as shown in Figure 8-3.

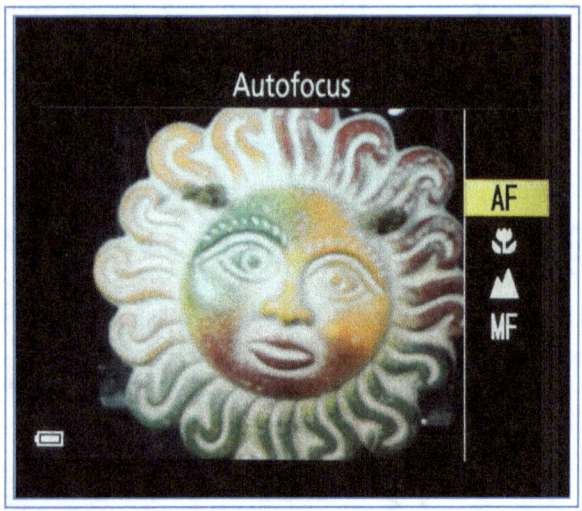

Figure 8-3. Focus Mode Menu

You can adjust this setting to some extent in Auto mode and some of the scene modes, and you can adjust it more fully in the advanced shooting modes (Program, Aperture Priority, Shutter Priority, and Manual exposure) as well as in the Special Effects mode.

Whatever setting you make will remain in effect for video shooting, as long as the camera stays set in the mode in which you made the setting. Note that you have to make the setting before you press the red Movie button to start the recording; you cannot change the focus mode once the recording has started.

For example, you can use macro focus if you are taking close-up footage. Also, in the P, A, S, M, or Special Effects shooting mode, and in the Sports setting of Scene mode, you can select manual focus. In that case, you can adjust the focus manually while recording the movie, by turning the multi selector dial or using the side zoom control, if you assigned it to adjust manual focus using the Setup menu. The Peaking feature does not work for movie recording, though. Later in this chapter I will discuss other focus settings you can make for movie recording.

Exposure Compensation and Exposure Lock

The next adjustment you can make that stays in effect during video recording is exposure compensation, available in all modes except Manual exposure and the Fireworks setting of Scene mode. Whatever adjustment you make before pressing the red Movie button, to either brighten or darken the image, will stay in effect during video recording, and you will see the effects on the screen in the brightness level of the image. You cannot make any changes to this setting during the video recording.

Apart from exposure compensation, there is another exposure adjustment you can make for movies, and this one can be made during video recording. You will see a prompt at the bottom of the display stating that you can press the Right button for AE-L, or autoexposure lock, as shown in Figure 8-4.

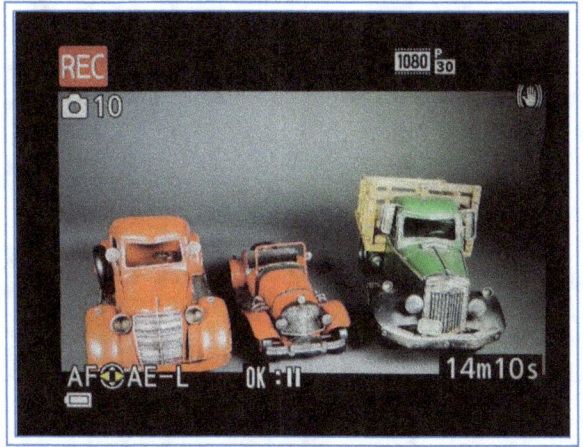

Figure 8-4. Icon Indicating Press Right Button for Exposure Lock

If you press the Right button to lock exposure, the message will change to indicate that you can turn AE-L off by pressing the same button again, and a message at the top of the display will state that AE-L is in effect. Although this button is the same one used to adjust exposure compensation, in this situation the button will not affect exposure compensation, only exposure lock. However, any exposure compensation that was in effect before the recording started will remain in effect, even if you use this button to lock the exposure. The exposure will be locked, taking into account any exposure compensation value that has been selected.

You cannot change the exposure mode used by the camera for recording movies; it will use automatic exposure adjustment, as if it were in Auto or Program mode, no matter what mode is set on the mode dial. For example, even if you select Manual exposure on the mode dial and make fairly extreme settings for shutter speed and aperture, such as 1/500 second and f/7.6, the P600 will use its autoexposure programming to expose the footage as normally as possible, subject only to whatever exposure compensation and exposure lock functions you employ.

Self-timer

The self-timer also will function for movie recording. Just set it as you normally do, by using the Left button and selecting either 2 seconds or 10 seconds for the delay. Then, when you press the red Movie button, the camera will delay the designated length of time before starting to record.

Picture Control

Turning to menu options, the first item on the Shooting menu that works for movie recording as well as stills is the Picture Control feature, as shown in Figure 8-5.

The availability of this selection for movies can be quite useful, because it lets you add a distinctive style to your video footage. You can shoot in black-and-white, for example, or you can use the Vivid setting to enhance colors. In most cases, though, you are likely to be satisfied with the Standard setting.

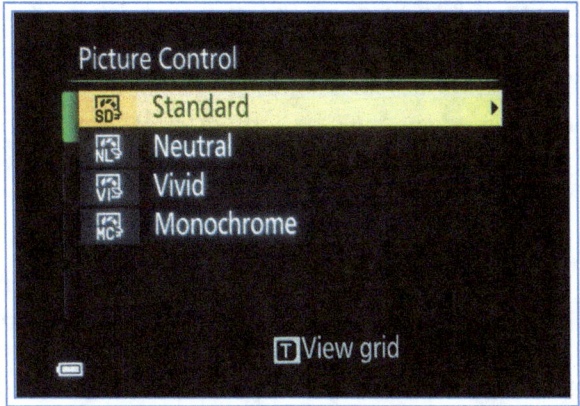

Figure 8-5. Picture Control Main Options Screen

Of course, you can only use this option for movie recording if you set it while the camera is in the P, A, S, or M mode, and if the camera remains in that mode during the video recording.

White Balance

The next Shooting menu option that carries over to video shooting is White Balance. Generally, Auto White Balance is adequate, so you can usually use the Auto shooting mode with no problem in this respect. However, if you are shooting your movie indoors, perhaps with non-standard artificial lighting, you may want to turn to the P, A, S, or M mode and use one of the specific white balance settings or even the Preset Manual option. Being able to set white balance however you want it gives you the option of purposely setting a "wrong" white balance to achieve an unusual color cast. For example, if you set manual white balance using a blue surface as the standard rather than a gray or white one, your footage will take on an eerie reddish appearance, suitable for some science fiction or horror scenes, perhaps.

Metering

You can set Metering however you want it for movies, if you set it while the camera is in one of the advanced shooting modes (P, A, S, or M). Of course, normal limitations apply, so you cannot change the metering setting if Active D-Lighting is turned on.

Here, as with White Balance, the standard setting (Matrix) is likely to be satisfactory for most of your shooting. However, having the option to use Center-weighted or Spot metering may be of use in some specific lighting situations. You need to be careful, though, because using Spot metering can result in a dramatic, and potentially unwelcome, shift in the lighting of a scene if the center spot is pointed at a particularly bright or dark object. Also, note that the camera does not display any circle or other indicator showing the area that Spot or Center-weighted metering uses, so you will not have any reminder that a different metering mode is in effect until you see a sudden change in the scene's exposure.

Vibration Reduction

The Vibration Reduction setting on the Setup menu carries over for your movie recording. I recommend that you usually leave this setting at Normal for movies unless you have the camera on a tripod. When you are hand-holding the camera, this setting can reduce the shakiness that may result from an unsteady hand. You don't need to worry when you are purposely moving the camera in a panning motion, because the camera will detect that motion and ignore it for purposes of vibration reduction; it will attempt to counteract only the vertical shakiness that may be caused by your hand motions. I don't recommend using the Active setting for movie recording unless you are in an unusual situation, such as handholding the camera in a moving car on a bumpy road.

Zoom

The optical and digital zoom both will function during video recording. However, to use digital zoom, you have to stop at the limit of optical zoom, release the zoom control, and then start zooming again to cause the digital zoom to start working. I have to say that I don't have much of a problem with this limitation of the P600. My own preference is to zoom in, if necessary, before starting the recording. I try to avoid zooming while shooting a video if at all possible, because I find that the zooming motion can be unsettling to the viewer. Also, as Nikon points out in its reference manual, the noise of the zoom mechanism is likely to be audible on your recording. So, unless you're following action that requires you to adjust your zoom range, you're probably better off adjusting it before you start recording. (Of course, if you don't mind using editing software, you can later edit out any parts of the movie where you adjust the zoom range.)

USING THE SHUTTER RELEASE BUTTON FOR TAKING STILL IMAGES

When you are shooting movies with the Coolpix P600, you can capture a few still images at a limited resolution. When a video sequence is being recorded, the camera will display a camera icon and a number in the upper left corner of the display, as seen in Figure 8-6, meaning that the indicated number of still images (in this case, 8), can be captured while the recording is in progress.

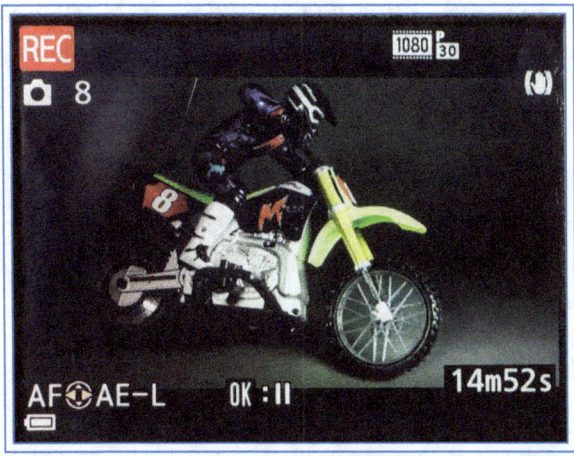

Figure 8-6. Icon For Number of Still Shots Available During Movie Recording

That number will reduce to zero as you take more still pictures.

All you have to do is press the shutter button while the movie is being recorded. This is a useful feature to have available for situations in which you want to record an entire event on video, such as a school graduation ceremony, but retain the ability to capture a few still images at critical moments (such as when the graduate you are most interested in receives his or her diploma). There are several limitations to this feature, as you might expect. First, the maximum number of still images for any given video sequence is ten. Second, the sound of the shutter being activated will be recorded, although the sound is not that loud, and does not interfere with the audio track of the video too severely.

A more significant limitation is that all of the images will be recorded at the relatively low resolution of 1920 x 1080 pixels, or about 2 megapixels. So, these images will not be useful for making large prints, but they will provide a record of the event, and you will have them immediately available for viewing, e-mailing, or other uses.

In addition, this feature is not available for all video recording formats; it is not available when the Movie Options setting on the Movie menu is set to 1080/60i, 480/30p, or HS (High Speed). If one of these formats is selected, the camera will display a camera icon with a diagonal line drawn through it during video recording, indicating that still pictures cannot be recorded for the current video format.

You also cannot capture a still image while a video recording is paused, or when there are fewer than 10 seconds of video recording time remaining.

Pausing Recording with the OK Button

When you are recording a video, you can pause the recording by pressing the OK button and resume it by pressing that button again. The camera indicates this capability by displaying two vertical lines for the pause function next to a symbol for the OK button, as shown in Figure 8-6. This function can be handy if, for example, you are filming action at a sporting event and you want to pause during a lull in the action, but you don't want to completely stop and re-start the video each time the action stops.

The pause cannot last more than 5 minutes; after that time, the recording will terminate. Also, this feature is not available with the iFrame or HS settings of Movie Options.

FN BUTTON: DOES NOT OPERATE DURING VIDEO RECORDING

Several of the settings that you can program for the Function button are not applicable for movie recording, such as Image Size, continuous shooting, ISO, and AF Area Mode. However, there are a few settings that you can assign to this button that do affect video recording: Picture Control, White Balance, and Metering. The Function button does not operate while a movie is being recorded. However, you can, of course, press this button before pressing the Movie button, to activate whatever setting is programmed into the Function button.

SETTINGS THAT ARE NOT ADJUSTABLE FOR VIDEO RECORDING

Although, as discussed above, several settings for still photography are available for use during video recording, several others are not. You cannot adjust the ISO, aperture, shutter speed, Autofocus Area Mode, or Active D-Lighting. Several other settings from the Shooting menu do not apply for shooting movies, either because there are specific settings for movies (Image Quality, Image Size, and Autofocus Mode) or because, by their very nature, they apply only to still photography (exposure bracketing, flash exposure compensation, and long exposure noise reduction).

The Movie Menu

When the camera is in shooting mode, you can get access to the Movie menu, represented by the movie camera icon, as shown in Figure 8-7.

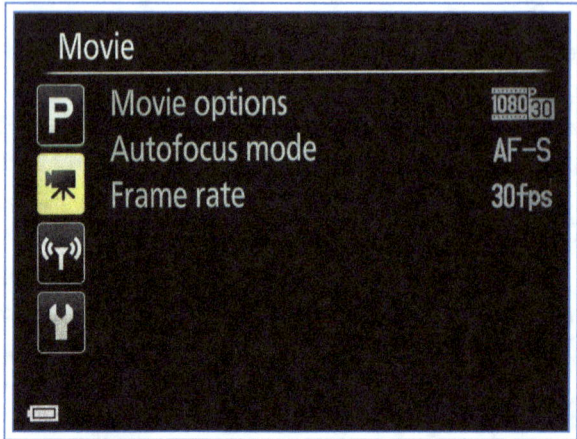

Figure 8-7. Movie Menu Icon Highlighted

To reach this menu, press the Menu button, then use the Left button to move the selection block to the left column and use the Up or Down button or the command dial to move to the movie camera icon.

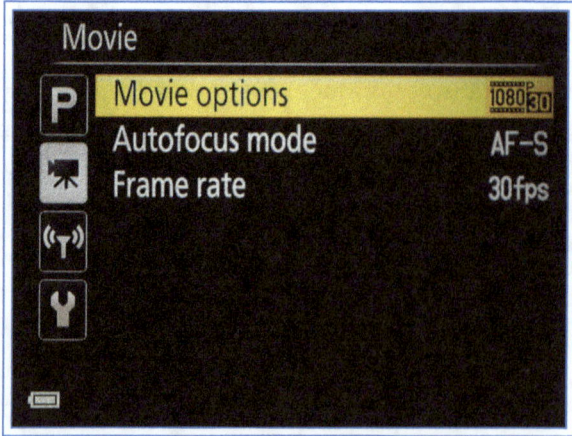

Figure 8-8. Main Screen of Movie Menu

Then use the Right button to move the yellow block back into the list of menu options on the main part of the screen, as shown in Figure 8-8. There are only three main options on this screen, though there are numerous sub-options.

Before I discuss the specifics of these options, I will point out a limitation of the Coolpix P600 with respect to the length of its video sequences. Like many modern digital cameras that are not primarily video cameras, the P600 is limited to recording only about 29 minutes or 4 GB of video, whichever comes first, in any single sequence. You can store considerably more than that amount of high-quality video on a large SD card, but you can only record 29 minutes at a time; you have to then stop and re-start your recording. And, as noted, any one sequence cannot exceed 4 GB in size. So, choosing a lower-quality video format that lets you store a great deal of video may not mean as much as it would if you could store a very long single sequence.

FRAME RATE

As you can see in Figure 8-8, the three Movie menu options are Movie Options, Autofocus Mode, and Frame Rate. Ordinarily, I would discuss these in that order. However, the selection you make for Frame Rate determines what choices you can make for the first item, Movie Options, so I will discuss Frame Rate first.

There are two major video standards used in various countries—NTSC and PAL. NTSC is used in the United States, Canada, much of South America, South Korea, and other areas; PAL is used in Europe and some other areas. With the NTSC system, the standard rate for video playback is 30 frames per second; with the PAL system, it is 25 frames per second. These differences are reflected in the Movie Options menu choices. If you are using your camera with the NTSC system, the selections for the HD formats will include the number 30 or 60, such as 1080/30p or 1080/60i. If you are using the P600 with the PAL system, the options will include the number 25 or 50, as in 1080/25p or 1080/50i.

Similarly, the primary choices for the HS (high-speed) options will include numbers that are multiples of 30 for NTSC and 25 for PAL. The final HS option, for recording video at half-speed, will include the number 15 for NTSC or 12.5 for PAL.

Some camera makers sell different versions of a camera for the North American (NTSC) and European (PAL) markets. With the Coolpix P600, though, Nikon provides the Frame Rate menu option to let you set your camera to whichever system you prefer to use. The choices for this menu option are shown in Figure 8-9.

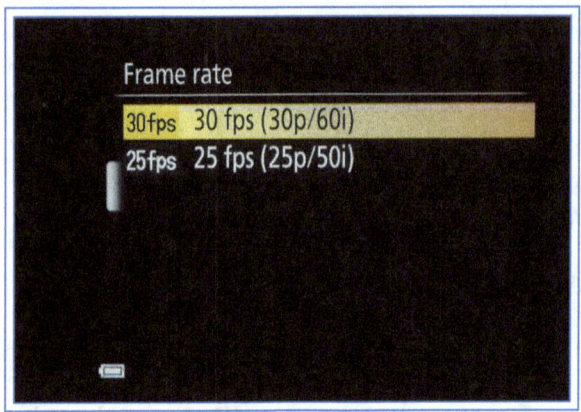

Figure 8-9. Frame Rate Options Screen

If you are using your camera in North America with the NTSC system, you should set Frame Rate to 30 fps; if you are in Europe or otherwise using the PAL system, you should set Frame Rate to 25 fps.

Now that I have discussed Frame Rate, I will discuss the first item on the Movie menu, Movie Options. I will assume in this discussion that the NTSC/30 fps system is being used, because that is what is used in the United States, where I am located. If you are using the PAL system, you should substitute 25 or 50 for the numbers 30 or 60 in this discussion.

MOVIE OPTIONS

The first choice on the Movie menu, whose main options screen is shown in Figure 8-10, lets you set the aspect ratio, quality, and speed of your video footage from 8 possibilities.

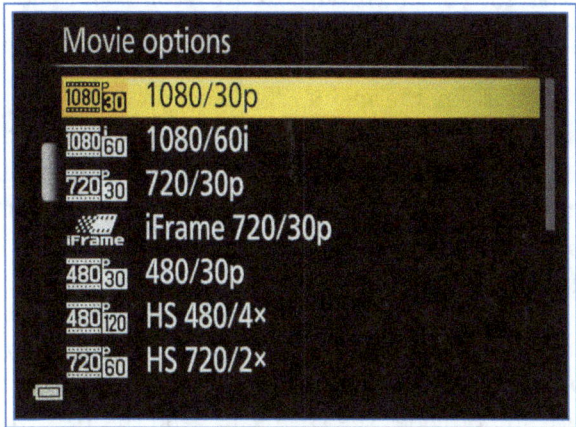

Figure 8-10. Movie Options Selection Screen

The top selection is designated as 1080/30p, which means it provides high-definition video with 1080 vertical pixels and 1920 horizontal pixels, the same amount on many HDTV sets. This standard is sometimes called "Full HD" to distinguish it from the lesser-quality HD that provides only 720 vertical pixels and 1280 horizontal pixels. The letter "p" following the number 1080 stands for "progressive," which provides higher quality than 1080i, where the "i" stands for "interlaced."

The second option on the Movie menu screen, 1080/60i, provides the same quality as the top choice on the menu, but, instead of a full 30 frames per second, it provides 60 "fields" per second, a field being one-half of a frame. Those fields are then combined, or interlaced, to make up the same 30 frames. You may find the 60i footage to be smoother for some scenes involving fast motion, and it may be useful for a technical reason, such as compatibility with a particular format for recording a DVD or Blu-ray disc. However, you cannot perform any in-camera editing with footage recorded in this format, you cannot take still pictures while recording, and you cannot save a frame from the footage, as discussed later in this chapter. You also cannot use the Painting setting of Special Effects mode. Unless you are aware of a reason why this format is preferable for your own purposes, I recommend choosing the 1080/30p option.

The next option on the menu, 720/30p, produces footage with 720 vertical and 1280 horizontal pixels, which still provides high-definition video in the 16:9 aspect ratio, but with fewer pixels and somewhat reduced quality. Choose this option if you want HD, but with less-taxing storage and speed requirements for your memory card and computer.

Next, you can choose the iFrame standard, which also records your footage with 720 vertical pixels and 1280 horizontal ones. This choice still provides the HD quality and the 16:9 widescreen aspect ratio of the standards discussed above. This format was developed by Apple Computer, Inc.; its purpose is to provide increased ease of editing your footage with Apple's iMovie software. So, if you plan to edit your video on a Macintosh using iMovie, you may want to try using the iFrame format. Otherwise, there probably is no advantage to using it. And, as with the 1080/60i format, you cannot use the camera to edit or extract a frame from a video made in this format.

The next option on the list, 480/30p, is the last option available for normal-speed movies, and it is the only non-HD format offered for non-high-speed video recording with the Coolpix P600. This format is also known as VGA, which is a term for the standard resolution of an old-fashioned (video graphics array) computer monitor, which has a display of 640 horizontal pixels and 480 vertical ones, resulting in an aspect ratio of 4:3, like that of the camera's LCD display. This format has the advantage of using virtually all of the area of the camera's display, but, of course, it does not provide the quality of high-definition video.

Its appearance will be coarse and rough in comparison to that of HD footage. You may want to choose this option if you don't need high quality and just need to record information, such as doing a video inventory of your household goods. Or, you may choose this option if your memory card is running out of space or does not provide the speed that is required for recording HD formats. Also, if you plan to send the footage by e-mail, this format will be easier to deal with than the HD ones.

HS (High Speed) Movie Options

The next choice on the Movie Options menu, HS 480/4x, is the first one for recording silent HS (high-speed) movies with the Coolpix P600. I have not discussed the HS capabilities of the camera before now, so I will take this opportunity to explain the use of this interesting feature.

First, the abbreviation HS, for high-speed, is really a misnomer, because the HS choices include both high-speed and low-speed options. It would be more accurate to use a term such as "non-standard-speed." HS is a convenient shorthand, but bear in mind that it is not precisely accurate.

Here is a brief explanation of how the HS feature works. The standard rate for recording and playing back video (in the United States) is 30 frames per second. That is, the camera takes 30 individual images each second and then plays them back at that same rate. When your eyes see those images, the pictures follow each other so rapidly that it seems as if the motion in the scene is continuous, rather than 30 separate still photos, which is the actual situation.

If you have seen old silent movies, they sometimes seem unnaturally fast and jerky. That happens because those movies were recorded at a slower speed than movies of today, but sometimes are played back on modern projectors at a faster rate. If a movie was recorded at, say, 15 frames per second, and then played back at 30 frames per second, the action in the movie would appear to be twice as fast as normal, resulting in a jumpy, jerky, speeded-up appearance. Similarly, if you set a camera to record at 60 frames per second and then play back the footage at 30 frames per second, the action will appear to be slowed down to one-half its normal rate.

The Coolpix P600 gives you the ability to either increase or decrease the frame rate at which it records video footage. It's important to note that the video will always play back in the camera at the standard 30 frames per second; the only factor you can change is the speed at which the video is recorded.

With that background, I will discuss each of the HS options on the Movie Options menu screen.

The first choice, HS 480/4x, sets the camera to record video at 120 frames per second, 4 times faster than the normal 30 fps. (If you have set Frame Rate to 25 fps, the recording speed will be 100 frames per second.) When this footage is played back in the camera, any movement will appear to be at one-fourth normal speed. This setting provides a capability for slow-motion video, which you can use to analyze a golf swing, slow down the beating of a hummingbird's wings, or for any of a myriad of sports and nature applications. Or, you might just like slow-motion video for its dreamlike, underwater-style appearance.

One major caveat with this setting is that, not surprisingly, the use of this setting requires a sharp trade-off of speed against quality. When you set the camera to record 120 frames per second, it automatically reduces the quality to VGA, which provides noticeably lower quality than HD. The aspect ratio is 4:3. There also is another limitation: The camera can only record for 7 minutes and 15 seconds at this rate, which results in a playback time of 29 minutes, the limit for video playback. However, for many applications, that amount of time should be sufficient.

Also, with this setting, you cannot use the Soft, Nostalgic Sepia, or Painting settings of Special Effects mode.

The next setting, HS 720/2x, gives you half as much slowing of motion as the first one, with higher image quality. In this case, your footage is recorded at 60 frames per second (50 frames per second if Frame Rate is set to 25 fps), so it will play back at one-half normal speed, and at 720p HD quality. You can record at this speed for 14 minutes and 30 seconds, again resulting in the full 29 minutes of playback time.

Finally, we come to the last option on the list, which turns the whole exercise in a different direction. This option, HS 1080/0.5x, is shown on the second screen of the Movie Options menu, as seen in Figure 8-11.

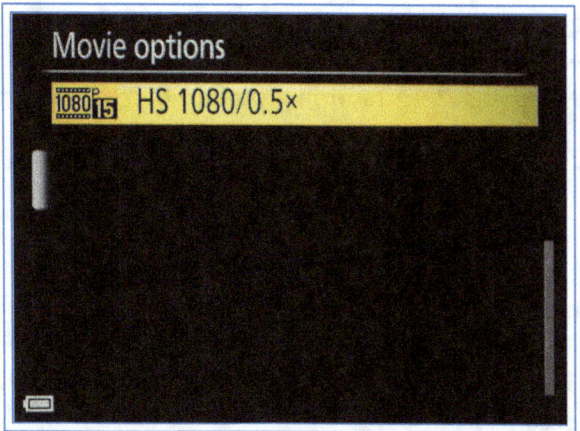

Figure 8-11. HS 1080/0.5x Option for High-speed Movies

This is the only setting with which the camera records video at a slower than normal speed. In this case, in which the footage is recorded at 15 frames per second (12.5 if Frame Rate is set to 25 fps) and played back at the normal speed (30 or 25 frames per second), the footage will appear to be speeded up to twice the normal speed. And, as a bonus, because the camera is actually doing less work in terms of speed, it can provide higher-quality video: full HD, at 1920 by 1080 pixels, recording for 29 minutes, with a playback time of 14 minutes and 30 seconds.

What would you use this option for? One possibility is to create a movie with the speeded-up look of old silent films, maybe to inject a light touch into a business presentation, or just for fun with footage of the family at the beach. You also could use this mode for some situations in which you need a video record, but you don't need (or want) to have a real-time recording. For example, if you would like to record the patterns of automobile traffic at an intersection near your home or office, you could set up the camera on a tripod, set it to HS 15 fps mode, and you would then have a video that would reveal the pattern at twice the normal speed, which actually might be easier to interpret than a real-time movie.

Of course, shooting half-speed movies (to show them at double speed) is a mild form of time-lapse photography. If you want to do time-lapse photography for applications such as showing a flower opening up or recording the progress of a construction project, you probably would be better off using the interval timer function of the Continuous shooting item on the Shooting menu, as discussed in Chapter 4.

With all of the HS options, the video is recorded with no sound. The zoom position of the lens, the focus, exposure, and white balance are all set when the Movie button is first pressed; no further adjustments to those settings can be made while the video is being recorded.

Autofocus Mode

This second choice on the Movie menu controls how the camera focuses when recording videos.

Your focus options for movie-making are a bit tricky, so I'll discuss them again here. First, it's important to remember that the shooting mode you select has an impact on focus options for video recording. That is, if you choose the Auto shooting mode, the camera will use autofocus for video shooting. However, if you choose the Program, Aperture Priority, Shutter Priority, or

Manual exposure mode, you have the option of choosing manual focus, and that choice will carry over to video shooting.

So, if you want to use the Autofocus Mode option while shooting a movie, make sure you have the camera set for autofocus, not manual focus. If the camera is set for manual focus, you will still be able to set the Autofocus Mode option on the Movie menu, but it will have no effect. When you press the red Movie button to start recording, you will see the MF indication on the screen, indicating that manual focus is in effect, as shown in Figure 8-12.

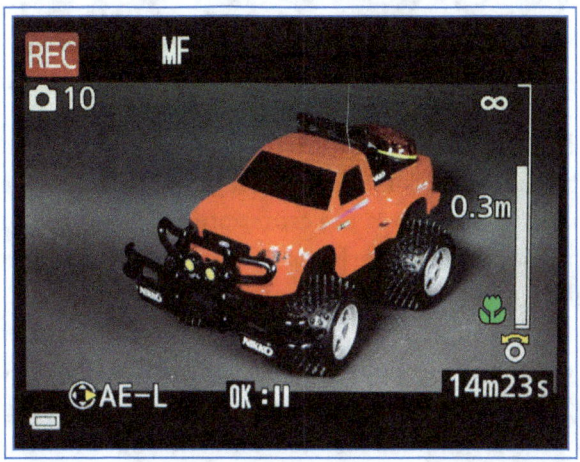

Figure 8-12. MF Icon for Manual Focus During Movie Recording

At that point, you cannot switch the camera into autofocus mode; you will have to focus manually using the multi selector dial or the side zoom control, if you have programmed that control to handle manual focus.

Assuming you have activated autofocus, you have the choice of two options for Autofocus Mode on the Movie menu, as shown in Figure 8-13: AF-S for Single AF, or AF-F for Full-time AF.

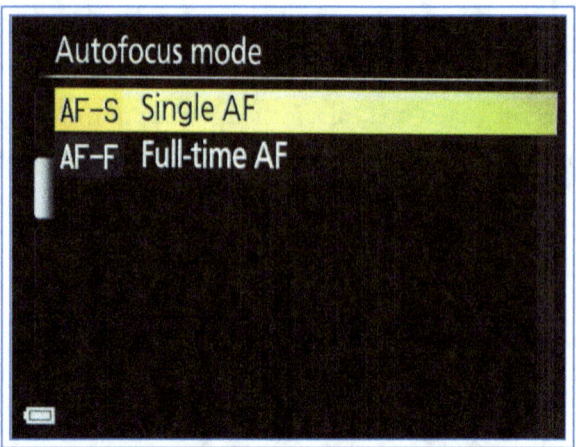

Figure 8-13. Autofocus Mode Option on Movie Menu

These labels are self-explanatory. If you select AF-F, the camera will continually adjust its focus as the scene changes. The camera will focus on any object in the center of the frame. The advantage of this mode is that the focus will remain sharp (with some blurring during focus adjustments) throughout the scene; the disadvantage is that the battery will be drained more quickly because of the demands on the focus mechanism. The Nikon user's guide says that, with this setting, the camera is likely to record the sounds of the continuous focus adjustments, but I have not found any such sounds to cause problems. The zoom mechanism makes sounds that can be distracting, but the continuous autofocus adjustments have been quiet, in my experience. Therefore, if you are in a situation in which the distance to the subject may change during the recording, I recommend that you use the AF-F setting.

If you select the AF-S setting, the camera will initially focus just once, when you start recording. However, while the recording is in progress, you can force the camera to re-focus at any time by pressing the Left button. You will see a prompt at the bottom the screen, with an icon that highlights that button in yellow, as shown in Figure 8-14.

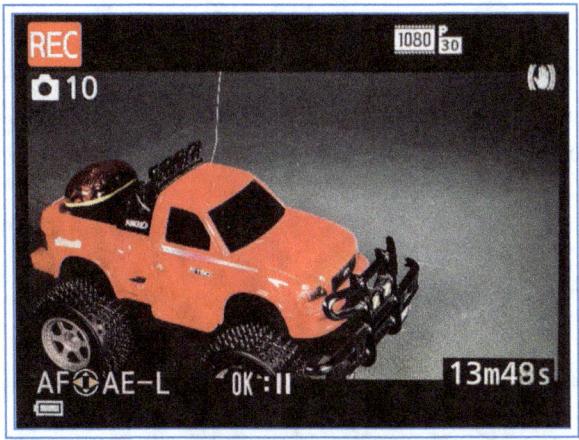

REC 1080 30
☐10 (•)
AF⊙AE-L ʻOK˸ll 13m48s

Figure 8-14. Prompt to Press Left Button for AF During Movie Recording

So, you don't need to worry that the scene will get out of focus if the distance to the subject changes; just press the Left button and the lens will focus again.

I recommend that you choose your autofocus setting according to the situation. For example, if you are filming in an environment where the focus distance is likely to keep changing and you have sufficient battery power to last for the entire recording session, I recommend using the AF-F setting so the camera continues to adjust its focus as needed. However, if you are recording a school play or concert, where the focus distance should not change that dramatically and the battery needs to last for a long time, you may be better off using the AF-S setting, with the knowledge that you can adjust the focus at any time by pressing the Left button if necessary.

Movie Playback and Editing

In Chapter 2, I discussed the fundamentals of movie playback. Now it's time to go into more detail about that topic and to discuss how to edit your video footage in the camera.

PLAYBACK

When the camera is in full-screen playback mode, you can recognize a movie by the movie format icon in the lower right corner of the display, as shown in Figure 8-15.

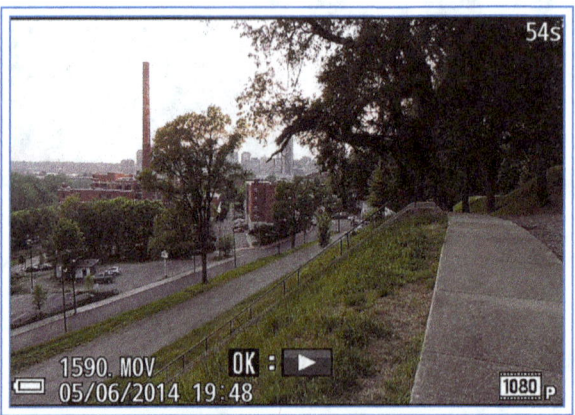

Figure 8-15. Movie Format Icon on Movie Ready to Play

(You may have to press the Display button to show the screen that includes that information.)

On index screens of 4, 9, or 16 images, you can recognize a movie by the sets of small gray blocks that look like movie film sprocket holes on the sides of the images, as in Figure 8-16.

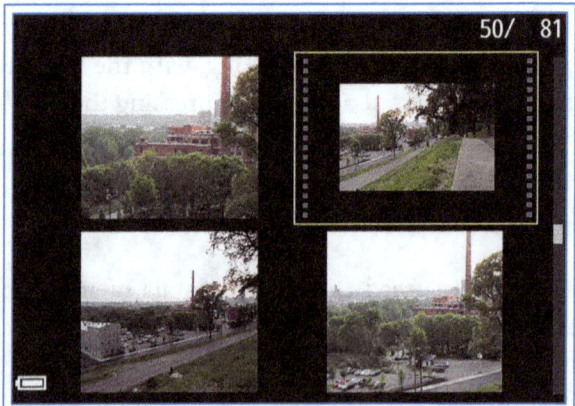

Figure 8-16. Sprocket Holes Indicating Movie on Index Screen

(With screens of 72 thumbnails, the sprocket holes do not appear, but, when a movie is highlighted, a small movie camera icon appears at the top left of the display.)

With a movie's frame on the display, press the OK button to start it playing. You will see a line of VCR-like icons at the bottom left, as seen in Figure 8-17.

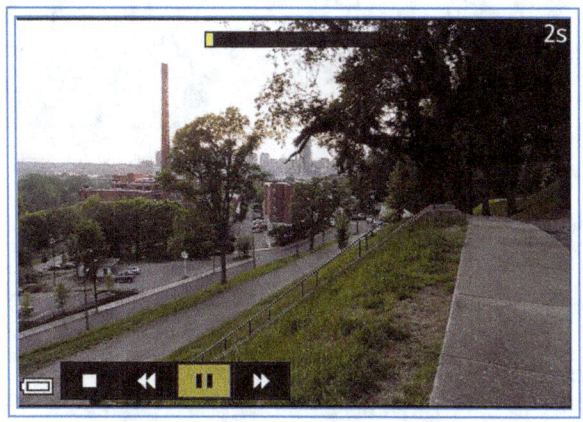

Figure 8-17. Initial Set of Movie Playback Controls

Use the Left and Right buttons to move to any of those icons, then press OK to choose that function. The controls are, from left, stop, rewind, pause, and fast-forward. You can also turn the command dial or multi selector dial to the left or right to rewind or fast-forward the movie. You can press the zoom lever to the right or left at any time to raise or lower the audio volume.

Shortly after the movie starts playing, the playback icons will disappear. You can then press the OK button to pause the playback and bring the icons back on the display. At that point, while the movie is paused, there will be a somewhat different group of icons, as shown in Figure 8-18.

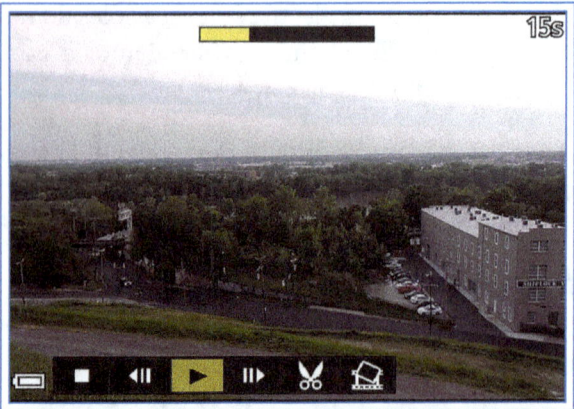

Figure 8-18. More Detailed Set of Movie Playback Controls

From the left, those icons represent stop, single-frame back, play, single-frame forward, edit, and extract and save a single frame. If you hold down the OK button while highlighting the single-frame forward or back icon, the frames will advance continuously, one at a time, at a slow rate. You can also use the command dial or the multi selector dial to advance and rewind the frames at that rate.

In some circumstances, when you pause a movie you will not see all of the icons shown in Figure 8-18, because the functions for those icons are not available. This happens when the movie was recorded using the 1080/60i or iFrame 720 format, neither of which permits in-camera editing. Also, if the battery status icon shows only one segment remaining, movie editing functions are not available.

EDITING

Of course, you cannot do anything like full-blown video editing in the camera; if you want to get really involved in editing, you need to import your video footage into a computer program that has serious editing capabilities, like Adobe's Premiere Pro or Premiere Elements, or Apple's Final Cut or Final Cut Express. If you don't want to purchase a dedicated editing program, if you're a PC user you may already have Windows Movie Maker; Mac users often have iMovie available. Finally, you can use Nikon's software suite, which includes Nikon Movie Editor software.

However, if you're on a camping trip away from your computer or you need to put together a quick video to play on a hotel's TV screen, you can do some basic trimming of your P600 video files in the camera. (As noted earlier, you cannot perform in-camera editing with videos recorded in the iFrame format or the 1080/60i format, or when the battery is low.) Here is what you can do.

First, you can save a portion of an original video to a new file by trimming away footage at the beginning and/or end of a clip. To do this, start by playing the video to the approximate location where you want the new, shorter clip to start. Then pause the clip by pressing the OK button, and quickly (while the icons stay on the screen), use the Right button to highlight the scissors icon and press OK to select that icon.

You will now see a vertical menu of icons, representing, from top to bottom: Choose Start Point; Choose End Point; Preview; Save; and Back, as shown in Figure 8-19.

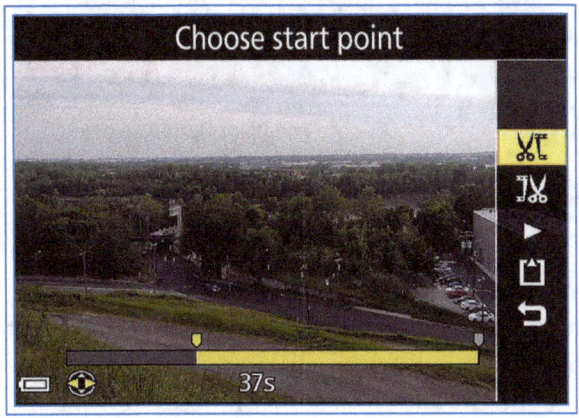

Figure 8-19. Menu of Movie Editing Controls

There will be a yellow bar at the bottom of the screen, with a yellow pointer at the left end and a gray pointer at the right end.

The top icon, Choose Start Point, will be highlighted. You can now use the Left and Right direction buttons to adjust the position of the yellow pointer, indicating the starting point for the new clip. If you prefer, you can use the command dial or the multi selector dial to move the pointer. If you have to move the start point more than a few seconds, it may take you quite a while to do so, because each press of the direction buttons or turn of the dial moves the pointer only a small fraction of a second in the clip.

When you have finished moving the left (start) point, press the Down button to highlight the second icon down in the menu, for Choose End Point, as shown in Figure 8-20.

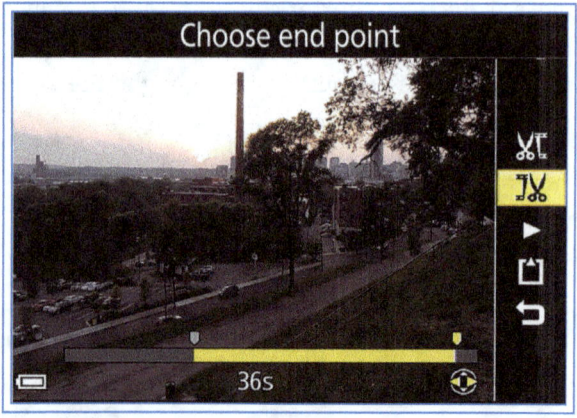

Figure 8-20. Choose End Point Option Selected

Repeat the previous procedure, but move the right (end) point in toward the center of the yellow bar.

When both the start and end points are set as you want them, highlight the third icon, which looks like a Play button; this control lets you preview the adjusted clip. If the preview looks okay, press the OK button to stop it if necessary, and move down to the next icon, a rectangle with a small triangle at its top. When that icon is highlighted, as shown in Figure 8-21, press the OK button, and the camera will display a message saying Save OK?

asking if you want to save the clip in its new length. The camera will place Yes and No bars at the bottom of this screen.

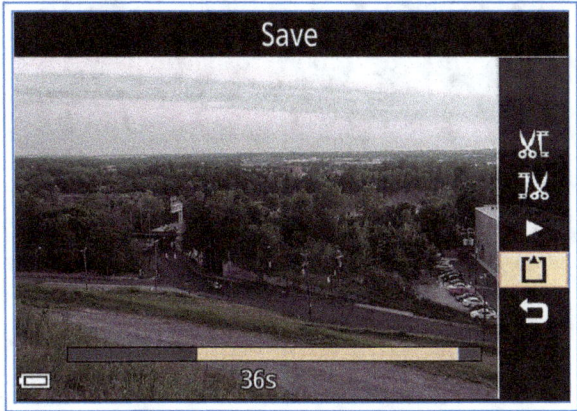

Figure 8-21. Save Icon Highlighted

If you want to save the clip, highlight the Yes bar and press the OK button. The camera may take quite a while to save the new, shorter version of the clip; the original will remain untouched.

Finally, you can save a single frame from any video clip taken with the P600, except for clips made in the iFrame or 1080/60i format. To do this, start playing the movie to the approximate point where you want to extract a frame, then press the OK button to pause the movie. You will then (briefly) see the icons for playing, advancing or reversing by single frames, as well as editing and saving a single frame. (If the icons disappear before you can use them, press the OK button to bring them back on the screen.)

Use the advance and reverse controls to move to the exact frame that you want to save. Then, if necessary, press the OK button to bring the icons back onto the screen, highlight the one at the far right that looks like a frame next to some movie footage, and press the OK button. When the camera displays a message asking if you want to copy that frame as a still image, as shown in Figure 8-22, highlight the Yes bar and press the OK button to confirm.

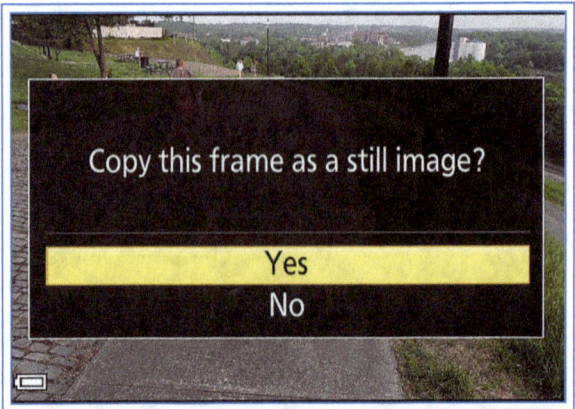

Figure 8-22. Confirmation Screen for Copy Single Frame

The camera will display the new still image with a .jpg file name. The still picture is saved in the Normal quality, with the same image size as that of the format of the movie it was extracted from.

Chapter 9: Wi-Fi, Superzoom Lens, and Other Topics

Wi-Fi Features

The Coolpix P600 has built-in Wi-Fi features, meaning that it can communicate with a smartphone or tablet computer over a Wi-Fi (wireless) network. Using these features, you can transfer still images and control the camera remotely from the other device. I will describe the use of these features here, and then I will discuss the items on the camera's Wi-Fi Options Menu.

TRANSFERRING IMAGES TO SMARTPHONE OR TABLET

Using the built-in Wi-Fi features of the Coolpix P600, you can transfer still images (not movies) from the camera to a smartphone or tablet that uses the iOS (Apple) or Android operating system. I will outline the steps here, using an iPhone for the example.

1. Download the Nikon Wireless Mobile Utility app for your Apple iPhone or iPad from the Apple App Store or from the Google Play Store for an Android phone or tablet. If you search for "Nikon Wireless," the name of the app should appear in the search results. The icon for the app is seen in Figure 9-1.

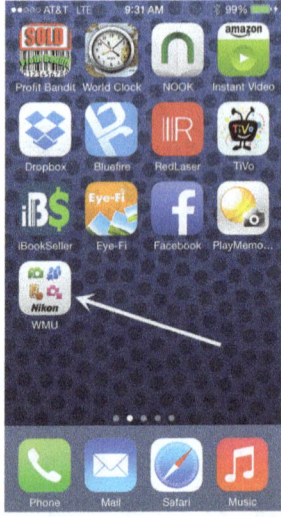

Figure 9-1. Nikon Wireless Mobile Utility Icon

2. On the Coolpix P600, go to the Wi-Fi menu by pressing the Menu button and go to the Wi-Fi Options menu by pressing the Left button and then moving to the Wi-Fi tab, as shown in Figure 9-2.

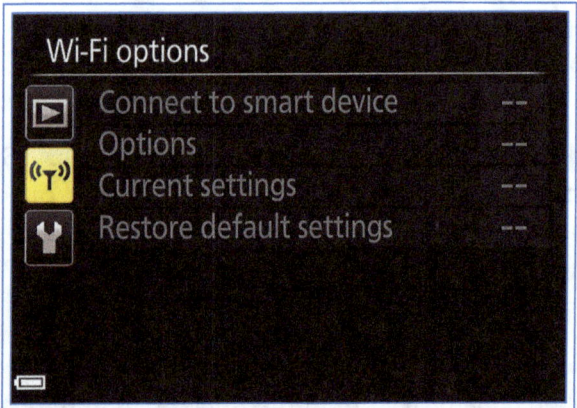

Figure 9-2. Icon for Wi-Fi Options Menu Highlighted

3. Press the Right button to highlight Connect to Smart Device, and press the OK button or the Right button to select that option. The camera will show a screen like that in Figure 9-3.

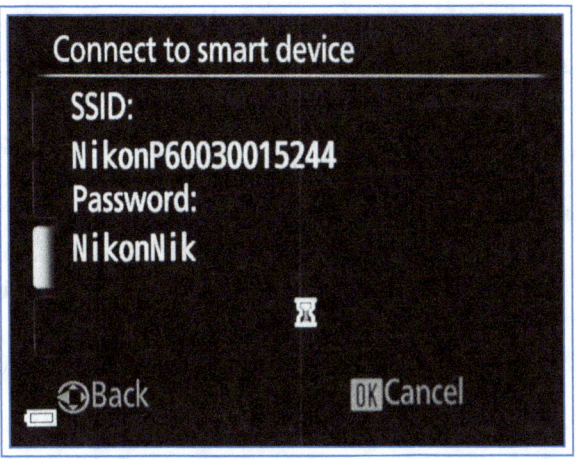

Figure 9-3. Connect to Smart Device Screen

4. On the phone or tablet, go to the Settings or Wi-Fi area, and select the SSID (network name) shown on the camera's screen, as shown in Figure 9-4.

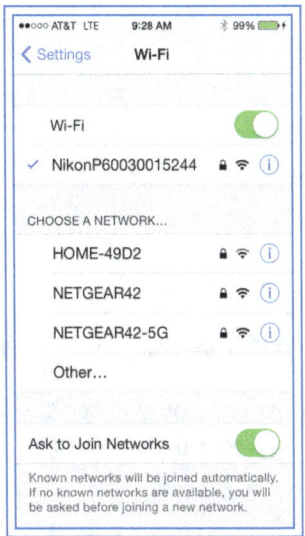

Figure 9-4. Camera's SSID Selected on iPhone

5. As soon as a check mark or other indicator appears to show that that network has been connected to the phone or tablet,

go to the Nikon Wireless Mobile Utility app on the phone or tablet and start it by selecting it. You should now see a screen on the phone or tablet like that shown in Figure 9-5, giving you the options to Take Photos or View Photos. To control the size of images downloaded from the camera to the phone, tap the gear icon at the top of the screen to go to Settings, then select Image Size. On an iPhone, you can choose Recommended Size, which resizes photos for your display, or VGA, which sets them at an even smaller size. On an Android device, you also may be able to select Original for the size, to keep images at full size.

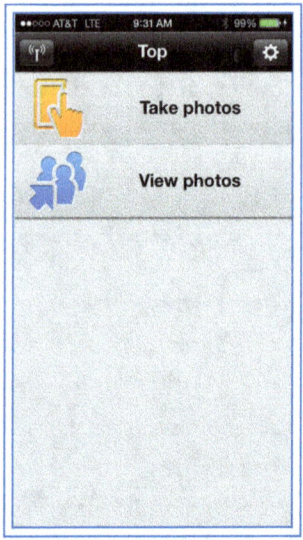

Figure 9-5. WMU Main Screen on iPhone

6. Select View Photos, and you will see the screen in Figure 9-6, with options to view Pictures on P600, Camera Roll, or Latest Downloads.

7. Select Pictures on P600, and you should see a screen like Figure 9-7, with thumbnails of the still images on the camera's memory card. If there are movies, they will be represented by red Xs, meaning they cannot be viewed or transferred.

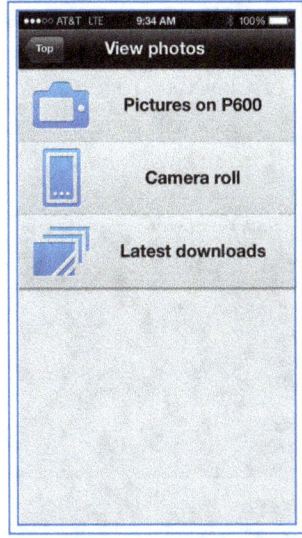

Figure 9-6. WMU View Pictures Options on iPhone

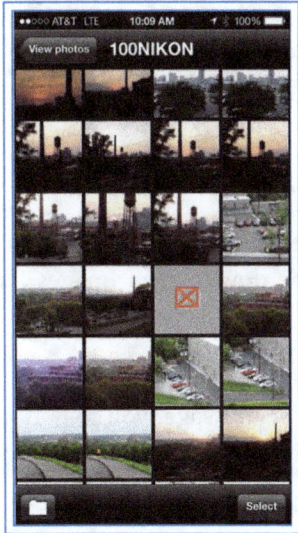

Figure 9-7. Thumbnails of P600 Images Viewed on iPhone

8. Press the Select icon at the lower right of the display, and then tap each picture you want to download to the phone or tablet. A green check mark will appear on each selected image, as shown in Figure 9-8. Then press the Download icon

at the bottom of the display. The app will display a message asking you to confirm. If you say yes, the download will start and the app will display its progress. When all selected files are downloaded, the app will announce that the download is complete. Press OK, then the Done icon.

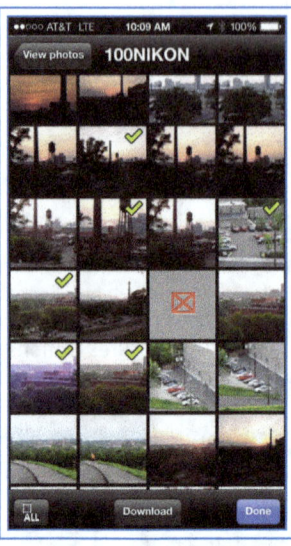

Figure 9-8. Check Marks on Images Selected for Transfer to iPhone

9. You can now select Latest Downloads from the View Photos option to see the downloaded images. You also can see the images in the Camera Roll area of the iPhone, or in the Gallery area of an Android device.

If you receive an error message, you may have to go to Settings-Privacy-Photos on the iPhone and turn on permission for the Wireless Mobility Utility app to get access to photos on the phone.

CONTROLLING THE CAMERA USING A SMARTPHONE OR TABLET

Using the Nikon Wireless Mobile Utility app, you can control the P600 camera remotely to take still images (not movies) from a distance of about 50 feet (15 meters) in a limited way. You might want to use this option for taking pictures of wildlife with no humans nearby, for example. Here are the steps to set up the remote control option, again using an iPhone as an example.

1. Set up the camera so it is pointing toward the subject you want to photograph. For example, you might set it up on a tripod aiming at a bird feeder so you can get images of birds without standing near the camera. Remove the lens cap and set up the shot as you want it.

2. Follow steps 1-5 as outlined above for transferring photos.

3. Select Take Photos from the options on the screen of the phone or tablet. The phone or tablet will display a screen like that shown in Figure 9-9, showing what the camera sees through its lens and with icons at the bottom for taking a picture or adjusting the zoom lens.

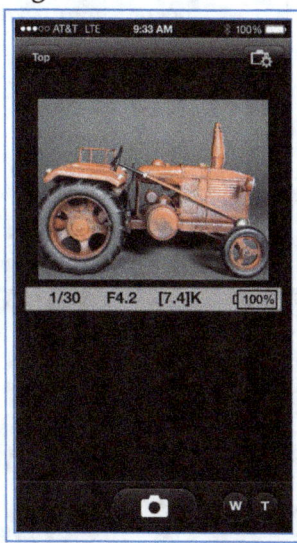

Figure 9-9. View Through Camera Seen on iPhone

4. Zoom the lens out by pressing the W icon at the bottom right of the app's display or zoom it in by pressing the T icon. When the image is composed as you want, press the camera icon at the bottom center of the display to take the picture.

The camera's shutter will operate and the image will be downloaded to the phone or tablet. A thumbnail will appear in the app below the view of the scene through the lens.

5. You can adjust settings for downloading the image and the use of the self-timer by clicking the settings icon, with a gear and camera, in the upper right corner of the app's screen.

When the camera takes images using this remote control function, it acts as if it were set to Auto mode with autofocus in the center of the frame. You cannot adjust any settings on the camera from the remote control app, but you can set Image Quality and Image Size to any values on the P600 before you connect the camera to the phone or tablet.

WI-FI OPTIONS MENU

The Coolpix P600 has a special menu with several options for controlling the camera's Wi-Fi functions. That menu is represented by the wireless network icon, which is highlighted in Figure 9-10.

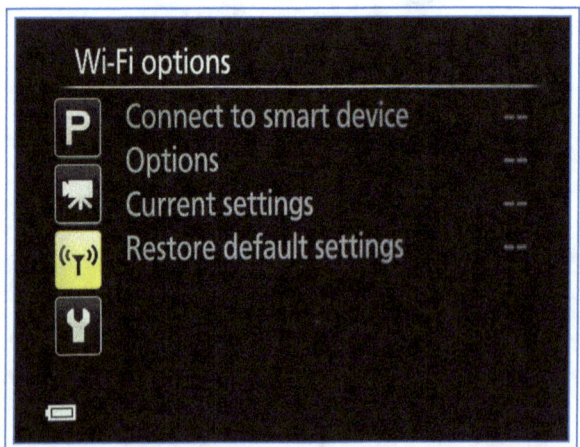

Figure 9-10. Wi-Fi Options Menu Icon Highlighted

Once you have highlighted that tab, press the Right button to move the highlight into the list on the single screen of the menu, as shown in figure 9-11. I will discuss these items in order.

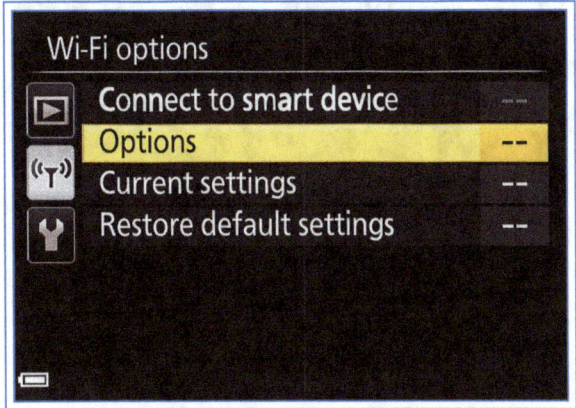

Figure 9-11. Options Screen for Wi-Fi Options Menu Item

Connect to Smart Device

I discussed this option earlier, in connection with the steps for transferring images or controlling the camera remotely. For either of those operations, you start by selecting this menu option, which causes the camera to generate its own wireless network. The camera will display the SSID (identifying name) of the network on its screen. By default that name starts with NikonP600, though you can change it, as discussed below. Then, go to the Wi-Fi area of your smartphone or tablet and select the camera's Wi-Fi network. When that selection is made, the two devices will be connected.

Options

This second item on the menu has several sub-options, as shown in Figure 9-12. The first selection, SSID, lets you change the SSID, or identifying name, of the wireless network generated by the camera. By default, it is given a name such as NikonP600 followed by several numbers.

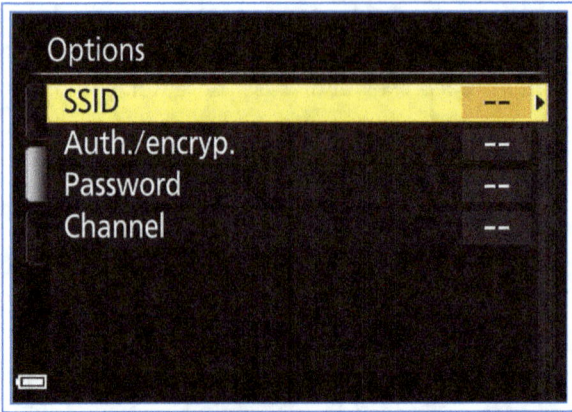

Figure 9-12. Options Screen for Wi-Fi Options Menu Item

You can change this to any combination of characters using the on-screen keyboard that the camera displays when you choose this option, as shown in Figure 9-13.

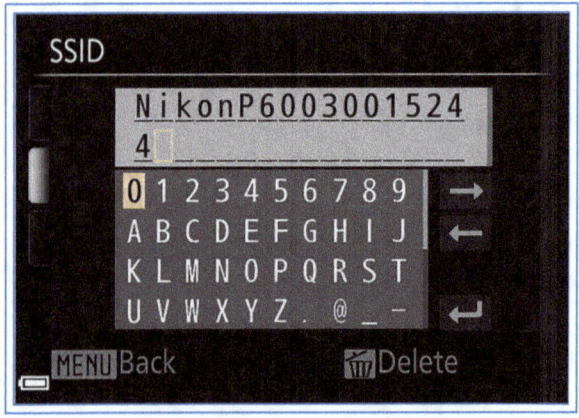

Figure 9-13. On-screen Keyboard for Entering Wi-Fi Information

Scroll through the characters using the right and left arrows at the far right of the keyboard and select the bottom arrow when you have finished entering characters.

There is not much reason to change the SSID, because it will appear on the screen of the phone or tablet you are connecting to, and you can select it there; you don't have to remember it.

You might want to change the SSID if you are in an area where other people have Nikon cameras with similar SSIDs, to avoid confusion.

If you select the second option, Auth./Encrypt, the camera displays the screen shown in Figure 9-14, where you can choose whether or not to have the camera's Wi-Fi network secured with a password.

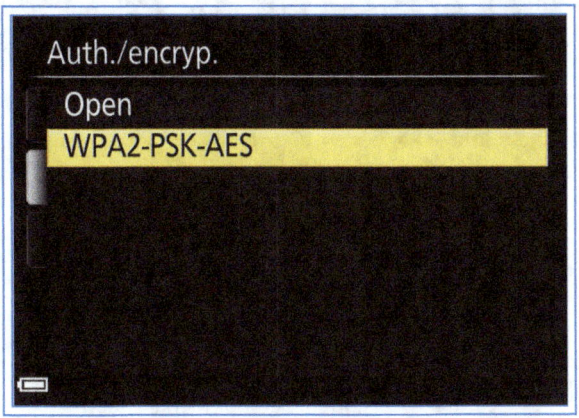

Figure 9-14. Authentication/Encryption Menu Option

To avoid the risk of having nearby smart devices connect to your camera without authorization, select the WPA option so the connection will be secured. Otherwise, choose Open.

The third sub-option, Password, lets you change the password for the camera's network if you choose to require a password. The password must be at least 8 characters in length and no more than 16. You enter it using the same on-screen keyboard described earlier. The camera comes with a default password, so you can just leave it in place if you want to.

The final sub-option for the SSID menu item, Channel, lets you specify a channel, from 1 to 11, for the camera to communicate on over the Wi-Fi network. I have left the default option of Channel

6 in place with no problems, but you can change the channel if you experience difficulties in communicating over the network.

Current Settings

If you select this option, the camera displays the current settings for its Wi-Fi network, as shown in Figure 9-15. This option may help if you need to troubleshoot a problem with the connection.

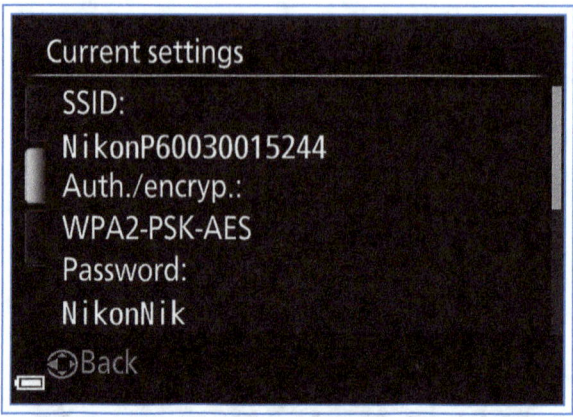

Figure 9-15. Current Settings Menu Option

Restore Default Settings

This final option let you reset all Wi-Fi settings to their original, factory values. This can be useful if you are having problems getting the camera to connect to a smartphone or tablet and you want to get a fresh start with the original settings.

ADDING LOCATION DATA TO IMAGES

The Wireless Mobile Utility app provides a limited way to add location data to images taken with the P600. The P600 does not have GPS capability built in, so it cannot record locations itself. However, the WMU app has an option in its settings for embedding location data when you transfer images. If you turn on that option, the app will add location data from the phone or tablet as it saves the images. This data will reflect the location of the phone at the time an image is transferred, which is not necessarily the location where the image was taken. But, if you use this option right after taking pictures, it will record location data with your images. When I used this option with my iPhone, the app added latitude, but not longitude data. The location data was added properly when I tried this using an Android tablet.

Using the Superzoom Lens

Probably the outstanding feature of the Coolpix P600 is its lens, which has an amazing range of focal lengths, at both the wide-angle and telephoto ends of its zoom. The focal length of a lens is a measure of how wide is its view of a scene and how powerfully it enlarges the view.

A "normal" lens—used for everyday shooting of family scenes, portraits, and the like—is often considered to be a 50mm lens. A "wide-angle" lens is in the range of 35mm or lower, and a "telephoto" lens is one with a focal length of 100mm or greater. The P600, of course, has a zoom lens, which means it can change its focal length. The focal lengths of this lens range from a very wide 24mm to an astounding 1440mm at the telephoto end, for an overall range of 60 times optical zoom. (None of this discussion will involve digital zoom, which is not a "real" zoom capability, as discussed in Chapter 7.)

Of course, there are trade-offs for having this great zoom range. It is not possible to provide the same quality in a zoom lens of this type as in lenses used by professional photographers at major sporting events, for example. A good Nikon zoom lens for a DSLR can easily cost more than $1,000, and a top-quality Nikon telephoto (non-zoom) lens can cost more than $10,000. However, for everyday photography, the P600 provides you with the ability to capture scenes with an array of focal lengths that is practically unmatched in the world of consumer cameras.

At the wide-angle end, the P600's lens gives you several millimeters more than most cameras in its class. A wide-angle range starting at 28mm is often considered quite adequate, and relatively few compact digital cameras offer a zoom range starting as low as 24mm. The 24mm focal length of the P600 is very useful when you need to photograph a large group of people without standing back a great distance. Also, if you need to photograph the interiors of rooms, this focal length is a great bonus, because you will likely be able to capture an excellent view of the entire room by standing in one corner.

But the telephoto range of the P600's lens is the most dramatic feature of the camera, so I will concentrate on its use.

First, the telephoto range of the P600's zoom lens is so powerful it can capture details you cannot begin to see with the naked eye. For example, the image in Figure 9-16 was taken at an arts festival with the lens zoomed out to its 24mm wide-angle setting. In this view, you cannot see any details in the top of the bell tower at the right of the image.

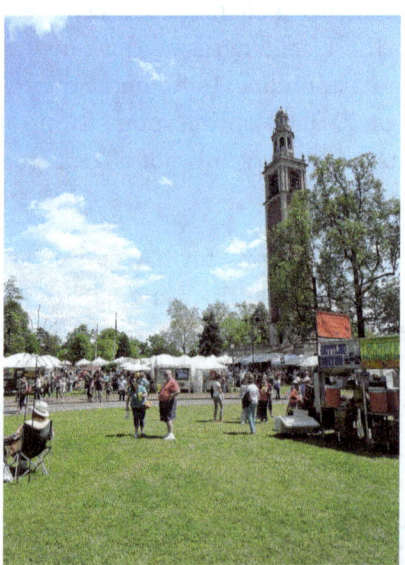

Figure 9-16. Wide-Angle View of Scene with Bell Tower

Now, look at Figure 9-17. This shot was taken at the same time and place as the wide-angle shot. This time, though, the lens was zoomed in to the full 1440mm extent of the optical zoom.

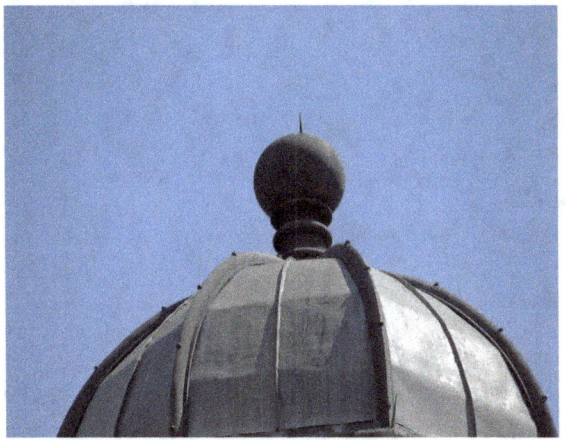

Figure 9-17. Shot of Bell Tower with Full Optical Zoom

This image shows a detailed view of the top of the bell tower that appears in the distance in the first image. This shot includes a level of detail that is not even hinted at in the first image.

When you use the Coolpix P600's powerful zoom lens at its highest power, you will encounter some issues that you should take into account when deciding whether to rely on the long reach of the lens rather than trying to get closer to your subject.

For one thing, as you may be able to tell from Figure 9-18 (a telephoto view of a motorcycle policeman approaching in the distance), images shot at this power can suffer from the compression of the atmosphere. In other words, you're shooting through a lot of air, which can add a foggy aura to the image, especially on a hot or hazy day. In this view, the subject appears somewhat faded because of the great distance from the lens and the heat of the day.

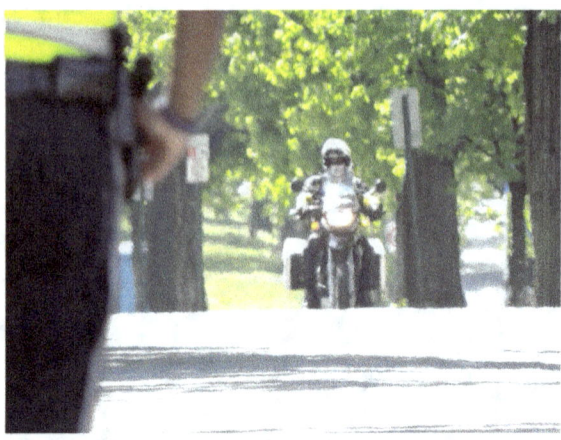

Figure 9-18. Haze and Compression Effects of Long Telephoto Image

Figure 9-19, also taken at the full optical zoom range of 1440mm, illustrates another phenomenon—flattening or foreshortening of the objects you are photographing.

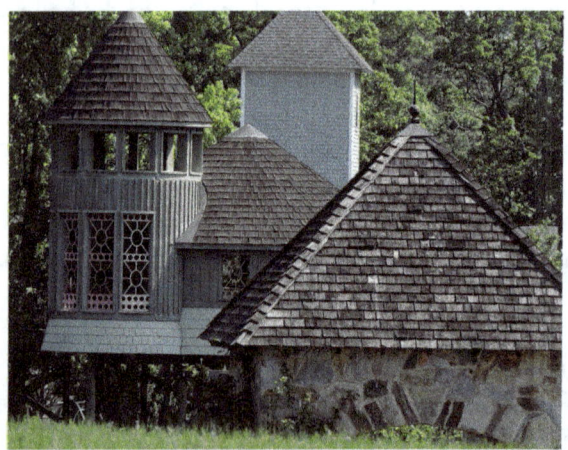

Figure 9-19. Compression and Flattening Effects of Long Telephoto Shot

In this case, I used the long zoom range to photograph a couple of buildings, one in the far distance and one much closer. The result of using such a powerful zoom in this case is that everything appears flattened up into a single plane, so that it looks as if the two buildings are right next to each other, even though they are widely separated in reality. So, if you take photographs that show people or objects at various distances from the camera, don't be surprised if they are flattened out with a two-dimensional effect.

However, you very well may find creative uses for this flattening effect, which can give a distinctive look to your photos.

Another positive side of the super-long zoom range is its ability to isolate a single subject. If you use the zoom to focus on a particular person in a crowd or on a particular animal in a pack, you can fill the frame with that single subject, thereby limiting extraneous objects and emphasizing the subject you want to concentrate on. Another advantage can be the ability to take a photo of a subject from a distance without disturbing him, as was the case with Figure 9-20.

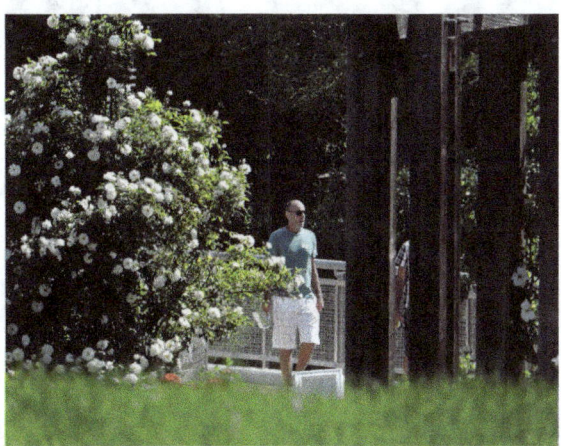

Figure 9-20. Isolation Effect of Long Telephoto Shot

When I spotted this man walking through the park, I wanted to get a picture of him but did not want to get close enough to disturb him. Using the long zoom range of the P600, I took this shot from a considerable distance, which isolated him from other objects, and resulted in an image with the scenery flattened into a somewhat indistinct background.

Another benefit from using the P600's zoom lens in its telephoto range is that, when the lens is zoomed in, it has a very shallow depth of field. As a result, when you take a picture at the long end of the zoom range, particularly when the lens is fairly close to the subject, the background will be blurred to the point of becoming indistinct. This effect, often called "bokeh," as discussed in Chapter 3, can reduce distractions from the background and emphasize your primary subject in the foreground. This was the case with Figure 9-21, in which I took a shot of a bird with the lens zoomed in to its full optical zoom range, thereby blurring the background with indistinct circles of light.

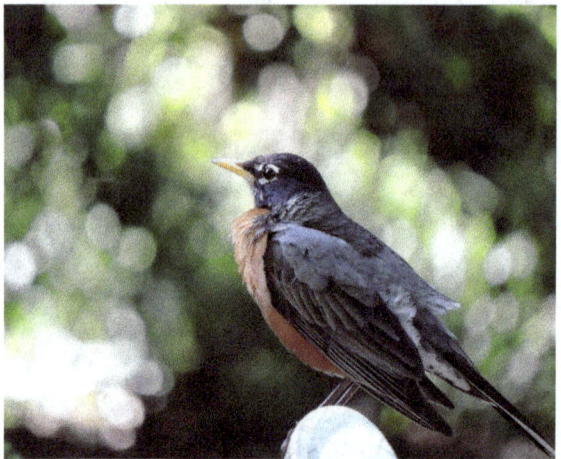

Figure 9-21. Bokeh Effect of Long Telephoto Shot

Beyond the specific advantages from the long reach of the zoom lens, perhaps the greatest overall benefit of the superzoom lens on the Coolpix P600 is that it gives you the equivalent of a whole range of focal lengths without the need to carry around a bag crammed full of lenses. In practical terms, with the P600 you have at your fingertips every focal length that a photographer could reasonably want or need for everyday photography, ranging from the wide-angle 24mm with a strong macro capability to the super 1440mm telephoto.

If you were to work for National Geographic or a professional photography firm, you would not use a P600 to capture your images. But, if you have a chance to go on a safari or a cruise around the world and you want to be able to bring back a complete photographic record of your trip using one lightweight, easy-to-use camera, the P600 fills the bill very nicely.

Now, I will discuss how to avoid a major problem that comes along with a superzoom capability—image blur caused by camera movement. When the lens is zoomed in to its full 1440mm focal length or anywhere close to that range, any motion of the camera is multiplied because of the magnification of the image. You will notice how jittery the image looks on the display, and it is hard to keep the picture steady.

There are several steps you can take to reduce the effects of camera movement. First, if possible, use a tripod. It can be inconvenient to do, but using a solid tripod is one of the best ways to ensure high-quality images. If you can't manage a full-blown tripod, use a monopod, a lightweight travel tripod, or any support available, such as a fence post, or just sit on a bench and hold the camera steady on your lap, folding the LCD display up toward your face to view your image.

Suppose, though, that you are walking through a field in search of wildlife shots and there is no physical support available. There are several things you can do to minimize the effects of camera shake. First, you should make sure that the Vibration Reduction feature is turned on through the Setup menu. This system counteracts camera movement quite effectively, up to a point. As is discussed in Chapter 4, I recommend you use the Normal setting for most situations, but consider using the Active setting if you are shooting in a turbulent environment. Also, you may find you can hold the camera steadier if you activate the electronic viewfinder (by folding the LCD screen in with its display against the camera), so you can hold the camera against your forehead and look into the viewfinder, rather than using the LCD display at some distance from your face.

Next, use the fastest shutter speed you can. If the shutter is open for only a very brief instant, there will not be time for camera motion to register on the image. According to one rule of thumb, when hand-holding a zoom lens you should use a shutter speed no slower than the fraction of a second with the focal length of the lens as the denominator. So, if the lens of the P600 is zoomed all the way in to 1440mm, you would use a shutter speed of 1/1500 second or faster. In the case of the P600, the choices would be 1/1600 or 1/2500, because the speeds faster than that are not available when the lens is zoomed all the way in.

If you want to control the shutter speed, you should use Shutter Priority as your shooting mode, as discussed in Chapter 3. You also could use Manual mode, if you are willing to accept the added task of setting the aperture correctly. Or, if you would like to use Program mode, you can let the camera set the shutter speed and aperture initially, and then use the Flexible Program feature, which lets you turn the command dial to select new combinations of shutter speed and aperture that are equivalent to what the camera selected.

However, you are likely to run into a problem if you use the camera's standard settings and try to set a fast shutter speed. One of the limiting characteristics of the superzoom lens on the P600 is that, as was discussed in Chapter 3, its maximum aperture when zoomed in is quite narrow. When the lens is zoomed all the way out to wide-angle, the maximum (widest open) aperture is f/3.3, which is not exceptionally wide to start with, though it is wide enough for most purposes. But, when the lens is zoomed in, it rapidly loses the ability to use a wide aperture.

When the lens is zoomed all the way in, the maximum aperture is f/6.5. In order to use a shutter speed of 1/1500 second or faster at that rather narrow aperture, there will have to be a good deal of light, unless you change some other settings.

Your best option probably is to increase the ISO sensitivity of the camera, which will mean that the camera's image sensor will require less light to expose the picture, at the risk of increased visual noise in the image. Using the ISO Sensitivity setting in the Shooting menu, you may want to try setting ISO to Auto, in which case the camera will set the value as high as 1600 if conditions warrant. If you want to be sure a high ISO is set, you should use a specific level, such as ISO 800, ISO 1600, or even ISO 3200.

If you prefer not to boost the ISO, which likely will introduce grainy noise into the image, one strategy you can employ is to zoom back out somewhat until the camera can use a wider aperture, such as, say, f/5.0 or f/4.5. Later on, when editing your photos with software, you can crop them to achieve the same field of view you originally saw with the zoomed-in lens, though with some loss of quality because of the cropping.

Another possible strategy for getting good, clear images with the superzoom lens is to take advantage of the P600's excellent array of continuous-shooting options. With several of these options, the camera will take multiple shots in rapid succession, increasing the likelihood that one or more shots will be usable. You also will experience a decline in image size and quality with some of these settings, though, so you need to consider the balancing factors.

One more excellent feature of the Coolpix P600, also found on the list of continuous-shooting options, is Best Shot Selector (BSS), the 7th choice down on the menu of those choices. When you select BSS, the camera takes a series of 10 shots and preserves only the single shot that includes the sharpest detail. The downside to this feature is that you can't second-guess the camera; you will never see the nine shots it discarded. However, using BSS is a great way to increase your chances at getting a good, clear shot. Also, it is available in the more advanced shooting modes, so you can, for example, use Shutter Priority mode and select a fast shutter speed while using BSS to cast a wide net for a super-sharp shot.

If you are not comfortable making so many settings through the menu system and otherwise, all is not lost. You can set the camera to the Auto shooting mode by turning the mode dial to the icon of the green camera, and then make just one setting: Go into the Setup menu and set the Motion Detection item to Auto. Then, if the camera senses motion, it will automatically raise the ISO level and use a faster shutter speed in order to counteract the effects of camera motion.

One more note: Don't forget that the Coolpix P600 offers the very useful U slot on the mode dial, for User Settings. If you use the lens zoomed in frequently, you may want to save your preferred settings for those occasions, so you can quickly call them up just by turning the mode dial to the U setting. For example, you may want to set up the camera in Shutter Priority mode, with the lens zoomed all the way in, with a shutter speed of 1/1600 second, with an ISO setting of 1600 and with BSS enabled.

Finally, I recommend that you take advantage of the side zoom control on the P600—the switch on the left side of the camera, below the flash pop-up button. As discussed in Chapter 5, this switch can be of use in two ways in connection with your use of the zoom lens. First, with its default function as an alternative to the zoom lever around the shutter button, this switch can let you hold the camera more firmly in both hands. If you zoom with the left-side switch, you can use your right hand to keep a tight grip on the right side of the camera without having to reach up to use the zoom lever.

Second, if you use the Setup menu to assign the snap-back zoom function to this control, you gain a different benefit. In that case, you can use this switch to quickly pull back from a zoomed-in view, so you can get your bearings and see exactly where your subject is in relation to its surroundings, before quickly zooming back in to take the picture. It can be very difficult to locate your subject when the lens is zoomed all the way in to its 1440mm maximum; use the snap-back zoom to get the wider view quickly when you need it for orientation.

Macro (Close-up) Photography

Macro photography is the art or science of taking photographs when the subject is shown at actual size (1:1 ratio between size of subject and size of image) or magnified (greater than 1:1 ratio). So if you photograph a flower using macro techniques, the image of the flower on the image sensor will be about the same size as the actual flower. You can get wonderful detail in your images using macro photography, and you may discover things about the subject that you had not noticed before taking the photograph.

The Coolpix P600 is quite capable of shooting macro photographs, like the one in Figure 9-22 providing an extreme close-up of a flower in an indoor exhibition at the botanical garden.

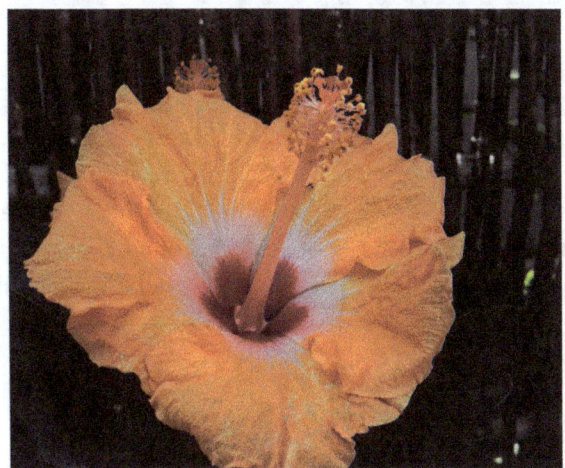

Figure 9-22. Macro Image, Program Mode, Macro Focus Mode

This image was shot at the full wide-angle setting of 24mm, using the macro autofocus setting.

As discussed in Chapter 5, to activate macro focus, press the Down button to bring up the focus menu, then use the Up and Down buttons, the command dial, or the multi selector dial to select the flower icon, indicating macro autofocus mode, as shown in Figure 9-23.

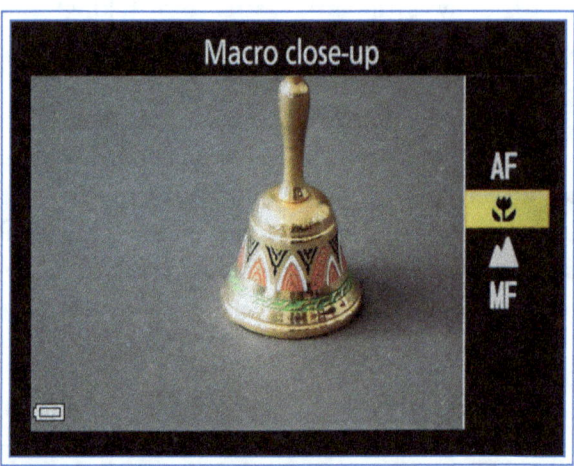

Figure 9-23. Macro Focus Mode Selected

You can choose macro autofocus in Auto mode or in the Program, Aperture Priority, Shutter Priority, or Manual exposure mode, as well as the following Scene mode settings: Beach, Snow, Museum, Black and White Copy, and Pet Portrait. In the Close-up and Food modes, macro focus is selected automatically. Macro focus is available for selection with all settings of the Special Effects shooting mode.

With the autofocus mode set to macro, the Coolpix P600 is able to focus as close as 0.4 inch (1 centimeter) when the lens is zoomed out to the wide-angle position or close to that position. The range for which the closest focus is available is indicated on the zoom scale by a small triangle icon, as shown in Figure 9-24.

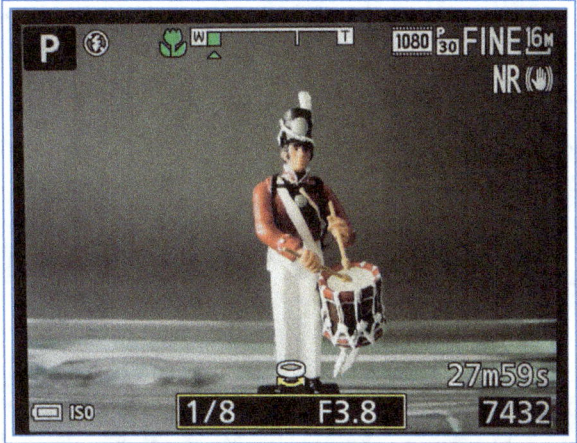

Figure 9-24. Zoom Scale at Macro Mark

When the bar of the zoom scale does not extend past the center of that triangle, the lens can focus down to this minimum distance.

Once the zoom bar goes past the triangle, the lens can focus as close as 4 inches (10 centimeters), as long as the zoom bar stays green. In Figure 9-25, the zoom bar extends as far to the right as possible before it turns white, indicating the end of the macro focus range.

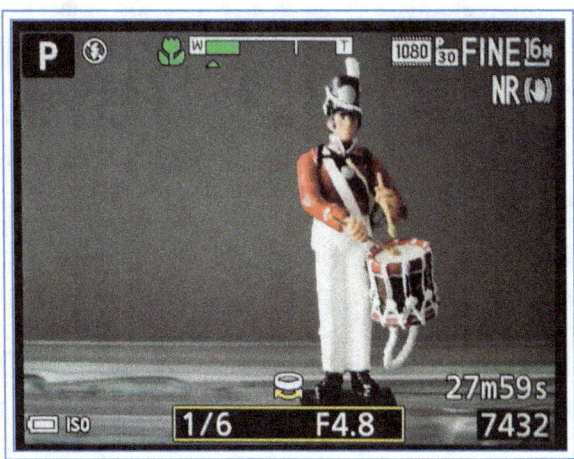

Figure 9-25. Zoom Scale at Far End of Macro Range

With normal autofocus, the camera can focus as close as about 1 foot 8 inches (50 cm) at the wide-angle position, and only as close as about 6 feet 7 inches (2 meters) at the full telephoto position.

If you don't want to have to fine-tune the zoom position to set macro focusing as close as possible, there are two easier methods. First, you can use the Close-up setting in Scene mode (with the Single Shot option). The camera will adjust for the closest possible macro shooting, setting the focus and the zoom position. It also will turn on continuous autofocus and set the AF Area Mode to Manual, so you can adjust the position of the focus frame on the screen. To move the frame, press the OK button and then use the direction buttons or turn the multi selector dial to adjust the frame's position. Press OK to anchor it in place.

Another possibility for close-up focusing is to select the Food setting within Scene mode. This setting is similar to Close-up, except that it adds an adjustment slider so you can fine-tune the hues of the foods (or other items) you are photographing.

You don't have to use the macro autofocus setting or one of the Scene mode settings to take macro shots; if you set the camera to manual focus by pressing the Down button and then selecting MF from the on-screen menu, you can also focus on objects very close to the lens. You do, however, lose the benefit of automatic focus, and it can be tricky finding the correct focus manually. However, the camera enlarges the view on the screen when manual focus is in use, and I have had good success using manual focus for macro shots.

When shooting extreme close-ups, you should use a tripod or other solid stand whenever possible, because the depth of field is very shallow and you need to keep the camera steady to take a usable photograph. It's also a good idea to take advantage of the self-timer. If you take the picture using the self-timer, you will not be touching the camera when the shutter is activated, so the chance of camera shake is minimized. Another option is to use the camera's Wi-Fi capability to trigger the shutter from a distance using a smartphone or tablet, as discussed earlier in this chapter. You should also leave the built-in flash retracted so it can't fire, unless you have a system for diffusing the flash to avoid harsh shadows and glare.

Using Flash

As I discussed earlier, pressing the Up button on the multi selector, the one marked with a lightning bolt, gives you access to the various settings for the built-in flash unit on the Coolpix P600, as shown in Figure 9-26.

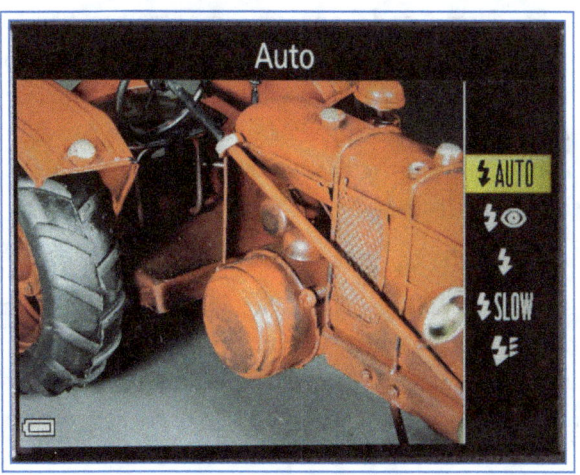

Figure 9-26. Flash Mode Menu

Before I discuss the details of those settings, it's important to recall one basic fact about this camera: The flash cannot fire unless you first pop it up by pressing the flash pop-up button marked by a lightning bolt on the left side of the flash housing, near the top of the camera. If you think there's any chance the flash may be needed, go ahead and press that button to have the flash ready. (If you're shooting movies, though, you should make sure the flash is down out of the way, because it can't be used and might interfere with your shooting.)

The next point to note about the built-in flash on the P600 is that a lot depends on the shooting mode you have set on the mode dial. If that dial is set to Auto, you will generally have access to all five possible settings for the flash. However, other shooting modes place limits on your flash choices. For example, with the Program and Aperture Priority modes, Auto Flash is not available. With Shutter Priority and Manual exposure, Auto Flash and Slow Sync are not available. With the Night Portrait mode, the flash is set to Auto with Red-eye Reduction—in other words, the flash will fire if necessary, and the camera will use its built-in processing to counteract the red tinge that may result from the red-eye effect of shooting straight into human eyes.

In Night Landscape and Landscape modes, the flash is forced off and cannot fire. With various settings available in Scene mode, the behavior of the flash varies according to the particular characteristics of the setting. For example, the Museum setting forces the flash off, on the theory that museums generally do not permit the use of flash.

Apart from the shooting mode, there are other factors that affect how the P600 uses flash. So, if you have the camera set to Program mode, in which you normally would have four flash modes available, there are some conditions that will disable the flash. For example, you cannot use the flash if you have set the focus to infinity, turned on exposure bracketing, or activated any of the continuous-shooting options other than interval shooting. If you believe the flash should fire but you are unable to turn it on using the flash mode button, check to see if one of the settings mentioned above has been set.

Once you have set the camera to a mode that allows choice of any of the five possible flash settings, such as Auto mode or the Portrait setting of Scene mode, you have to decide whether to choose Auto Flash, Auto with Red-eye Reduction, Fill Flash/ Standard Flash, Slow Sync, or Rear-curtain sync.

Auto Flash is a setting you are already familiar with—the camera's automatic exposure system will fire the flash if it's needed to achieve a good exposure. This setting is available only when the mode dial is set to Auto, certain Scene mode settings, or Special Effects mode.

Auto with Red-eye Reduction is a special flash mode that adds a technique to prevent or minimize the effects of "red-eye," the unpleasant reddish glow that can appear in people's eyes when the light from the on-camera flash bounces off their retinas and picks up the red from blood vessels. In order to correct for this effect, the P600 performs in-camera processing to remove the red tint from eyes as the image is being saved. In some cases, this processing could affect other areas of the image in unexpected ways, so you should use this setting with care. I personally prefer not to use it; if red-eye appears in an image, it can be corrected with Photoshop or similar software.

However, the red-eye reduction processing of the P600 does work quite well. Figure 9-27 includes a pair of shots I took of a mannequin. I pasted small red circles on her eyes and took two shots—one with Standard Flash and one with Red-eye Reduction turned on. The camera removed the red from her eyes quite effectively.

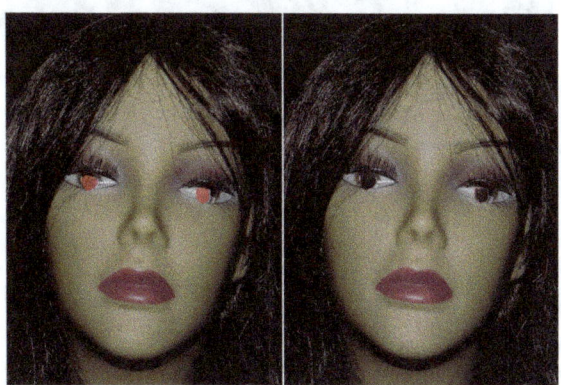

Figure 9-27. Left: Standard Flash, Right: Flash with Red-eye Reduction

The next option, the Fill Flash/Standard setting, forces the flash to fire, whether or not the conditions are dark enough for the camera to fire the flash on its own. This setting is useful when there is enough backlighting that the camera's exposure controls could be fooled into thinking the flash isn't needed. If, in your judgment, the subject will be too dark for that reason, you may want to force the flash to fire. Another such situation could be an outdoor portrait for which you need fill-in flash to highlight your subject's face adequately.

This setting, as indicated above, has different names with different shooting modes. If the camera is set to Auto, Scene, or Special Effects mode, this flash mode is called Fill Flash. With the Program, Aperture Priority, Shutter Priority, and Manual exposure shooting modes, this flash mode is called Standard Flash. There does not appear to be a significant difference between Fill Flash and Standard Flash. With either setting, the flash fires whenever the shutter button is pressed, and the exposure metering system takes it into account. If you want to vary the intensity of the flash yourself, you can use the Flash Exposure Compensation item on screen 2 of the Shooting menu.

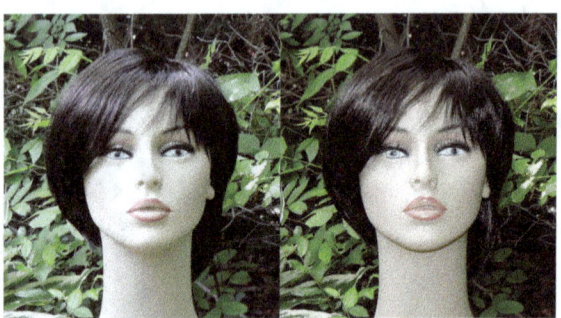

Figure 9-28. Left: No Flash, Right: Fill Flash

For Figure 9-28, I took two shots of a mannequin's head in an outdoor setting with good natural lighting to illustrate the effect of Fill Flash. I placed both shots into this composite image for comparison. In the shot at the left, with no flash, the image was exposed normally, with no problems from excessive shadows or glare. For the shot on the right, I used the Fill Flash setting. As you can see, there is a definite difference, although it is fairly subtle. With the shot on the right, the shadows are evened out and the mannequin's eyes, lips, and hair are given added definition and sparkle by the flash, leading to a more pleasing overall appearance, at least in my opinion.

The Slow Sync setting is useful when you are taking a portrait in a dark environment. If you use a normal flash setting such as Auto Flash or Fill Flash, the camera will use a fairly fast shutter speed and let the flash illuminate only the portrait subject. If you use the Slow Sync setting, the camera will attempt to take the picture with a considerably slower shutter speed so that the ambient (natural) lighting will have time to register on the image and illuminate the background also. In other words, if you're in a fairly dark environment and fire the flash normally, it will likely light up the subject (say, a person), but, because the exposure time is short, the surrounding scene and background may be black.

If you use the Slow Sync setting, the slower shutter speed allows the surrounding scene to be visible also. For example, the two images shown in Figure 9-29 were taken at the same time and in the same conditions.

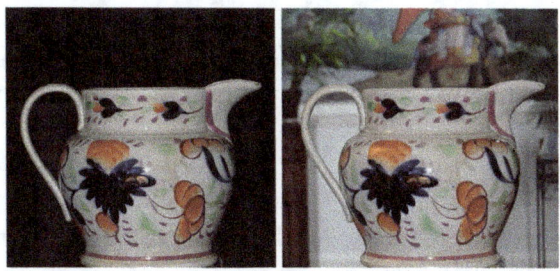

Figure 9-29. Left: Standard Flash, 1/60 Second, Right: Slow Sync, 1/8 Second

The only difference is that the photo on the left was taken with the shutter speed set at 1/60 second in Standard Flash mode, while the one on the right was taken in Slow Sync mode with a shutter speed of 1/8 second, which allowed the ambient lighting to light up the surroundings, including a colorful mural on the wall behind the pitcher.

The last setting on the flash mode menu is Rear-curtain Sync. This option is one you may not have a lot of use for unless you encounter the particular situation it is designed for. If you don't activate this setting, the camera uses the unnamed default setting, which could be called Front-curtain sync. In that mode, the flash fires very soon after the shutter opens to expose the image. If you choose the Rear-curtain setting instead, the flash fires later, just before the shutter closes.

The reason for using Rear-curtain sync is to help you avoid a strange-looking result in some situations. This issue arises, for example, with a relatively long exposure, say one-half second, of a subject with lights, such as a car or motorcycle at night, moving across your field of view. With normal (Front-curtain) sync, the flash will fire early in the process, freezing the vehicle in a clear image. However, as the shutter remains open while the vehicle keeps going, the camera will capture the moving lights in a stream extending in front of, or superimposed over, the vehicle. If, instead, you use Rear-curtain sync, the initial part of the exposure will capture the lights in a trail that appears behind the vehicle, while the vehicle itself is not frozen by the flash until later in the exposure. With Rear-curtain sync in this particular situation, if the lights in question are taillights that look more natural behind the vehicle, the final image is likely to look more natural than with the Front-curtain (default) setting.

Figure 9-30 is a composite image that illustrates this concept using a remote-controlled model truck with a red taillight. Both pictures were shot using an exposure of 1/4 second in Shutter Priority mode. In the top image, using the normal Front-curtain setting, the flash fired early in the exposure, and the truck continued on during the long exposure to make the trails of light in front of and over the truck. In the bottom image, using Rear-curtain Sync, the flash did not fire until the truck had traveled to the right, overtaking the place where the lights had traced their trails.

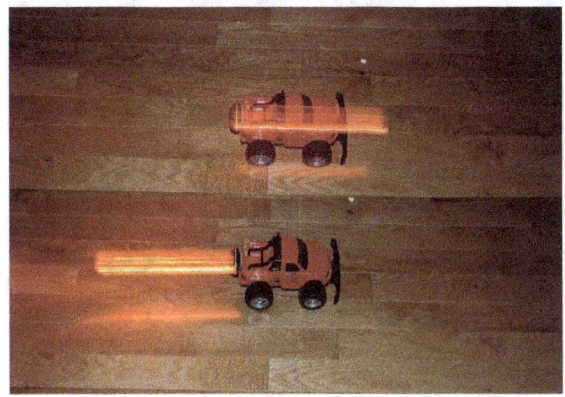

Figure 9-30. Top: Normal Sync, Bottom: Rear-curtain Sync

A good general rule is not to use Rear-curtain sync unless you have a definite need for it. Using the Rear-curtain setting makes it harder to compose and set up the shot, because you have to anticipate where the main subject will be when the flash finally fires late in the exposure process.

One other setting you should keep in mind is flash exposure compensation, which is available through the Shooting menu when the camera is set to the more advanced shooting modes. This setting reduces the intensity of the flash, even when the camera is automatically setting the exposure. Just as with normal exposure compensation, when using flash you can adjust this setting if your test shots appear too bright or too dark. Just go into this menu item and set the value to a positive number to brighten the image or to a negative number to darken it, as shown in Figure 9-31.

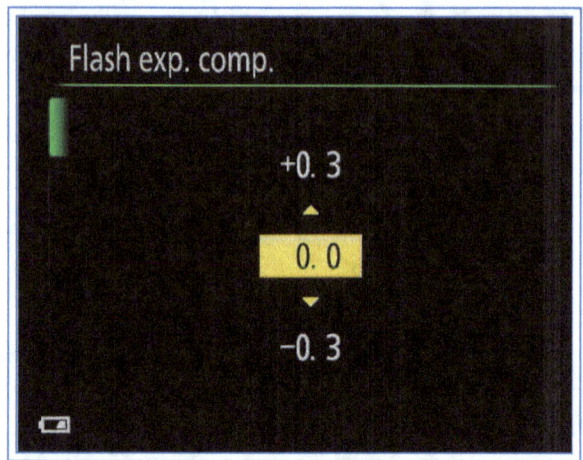

Figure 9-31. Flash Exposure Compensation Adjustment Screen

Be sure to set it to zero when you no longer need the adjustment so it does not affect other shots when you don't need it.

Infrared Photography

Infrared photography involves recording images that are illuminated by infrared light, which is invisible to the human eye because it occupies a place on the spectrum of light waves that is beyond our ability to see. In some circumstances, cameras, unlike our eyes, can record images using this type of light. The resulting photographs can be quite spectacular, producing scenes in which green foliage appears white and blue skies appear eerily dark.

Shooting infrared in the times before digital photography involved selecting a particular infrared film and the appropriate filter to place on the lens. With the rise of digital imaging, you need to find a camera that is capable of "seeing" infrared light. Many cameras nowadays include internal filters that block infrared light. However, some cameras do not, or block it only to a relatively small extent. (You can do a quick test of any digital camera by aiming it at the light-emitting end of an infrared remote control while pressing a button on the remote; if the remote's light shows up in the camera as bright white, the camera can "see" infrared light at least to some extent.)

The Coolpix P600 can take good infrared photographs. In order to unleash this capability, you need to take a few steps. The most important is to get a filter that blocks most visible light, but lets infrared light reach the camera's light sensor. (If you don't, the infrared light will be overwhelmed by the visible light, and you'll get an ordinary, non-infrared picture.)

A good way to make infrared photographs with the P600 is to get an infrared filter along with an adapter that lets you attach the filter to the camera. There is an adapter available from a company called Kiwi Fotos, which I found on eBay. This adapter is not ideal, because it extends fairly far out from the lens to avoid letting the filter hit the lens as the lens is zoomed in. Because of its length, the adapter causes considerable vignetting—that is, when the camera's lens is at the wide-angle end of its zoom range, your pictures will be shown in a circle, with much of the surrounding image cut off. However, you can work around this problem by zooming the lens in partway or by cropping away the darkened corners of the image. (I discuss this adapter in more detail in Appendix A.)

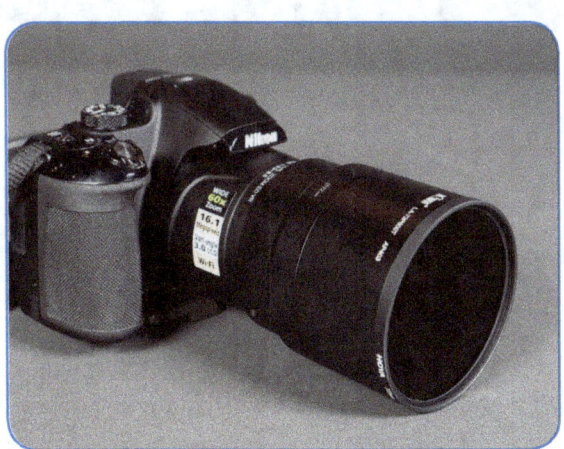

Figure 9-32. Infrared Filter Attached to Camera with Kiwi Fotos Lens Adapter

The infrared filter I use most often is the Hoya R72, which is a very dark red and blocks most visible light, letting in mainly infrared light rays in the part of the spectrum that produces interesting images. In Figure 9-32, it is shown attached to the lens of the P600 using the filter adapter discussed above.

The next question is to figure out the settings. For the image shown in Figure 9-33, I set a custom white balance, using brightly sunlit green foliage as the base. That is, I used the camera's White Balance menu option on the Shooting menu, and, in the screen for setting a Preset Manual white balance, I aimed the camera at the bright green foliage and pressed the OK button. The results were essentially what I expected from infrared photography—scenes with grass, leaves, and bushes that look white, and other unusual but pleasing effects.

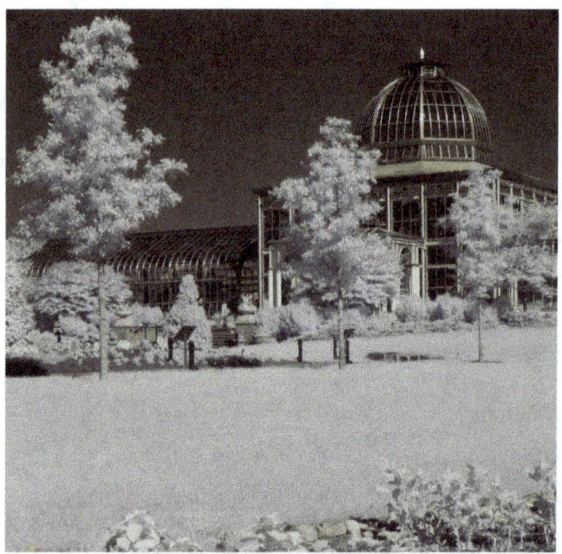

Figure 9-33. Infrared Example Image

For exposure, I set the camera to shoot in Manual exposure mode and experimented with shutter speeds and aperture until I found good settings at f/6.3 and one second, with ISO set to 100. I set the camera on a tripod and used the two-second self-timer to minimize vibration during the long exposure. You can often get interesting results if you include a good amount of green grass and trees in the image, as well as blue sky and white clouds.

Street Photography

The Coolpix P600 is not the first camera that would come to mind for what I think of as street photography—that is, shooting candid pictures in public settings, often without the subject's knowledge. In my opinion, cameras that are well-suited for this type of work are small, lightweight, and unobtrusive in appearance, so they can easily be held casually or hidden in the photographer's hand. The P600 is somewhat bulky and not that easily concealed from view. However, it has its good points for this type of photography.

Its 24mm equivalent wide-angle lens is excellent for taking in a broad field of view, for times when you shoot from the hip without framing the image carefully on the screen. In addition, I have come to appreciate the P600's movable LCD screen for street photography, because, if you fold it out so it is parallel to the ground, you can look down at the screen to frame your shots without drawing attention to yourself. With this system, I have found that I can zoom in on a subject a considerable distance away and keep the framing accurate while looking down at the screen. Also, the camera shoots quickly and performs well at high ISO settings, so you can use a relatively fast shutter speed to avoid motion blur. The numerous options for continuous shooting, including the Best Shot Selector setting, give you a good chance to get a sharp image under difficult circumstances. And, you can silence the camera by turning off the beeps and shutter sounds through the Setup menu.

What are the best settings for street shooting with the Coolpix P600? I will mention some guidelines as a starting point. The answer depends in part on your own personal style of shooting, such as whether you will talk to your subjects and get their agreement to being photographed before you start shooting, or whether you will fire away from across the street with a zoomed-in lens and accept the risk of blurry photos from camera shake at such a long focal length.

Here are a couple of approaches you can start with and modify as you see fit. Some photographers like to shoot in color at the highest quality and image size and then use post-processing software such as Photoshop or Lightroom to convert their images to black-and-white, along with any other effects they are looking for, such as extra grain to achieve a gritty look. (Of course, you don't have to produce your street photography in black-and-white, but that is a common practice.) I recommend you shoot in Shutter Priority mode at a fairly fast shutter speed, say, 1/100 second or faster, to stop action on the street and to avoid blur from camera movement. You can set ISO to Auto, or possibly use a high ISO setting, in the range of 800 or so, if you don't mind some visual noise. You may want to set the aspect ratio to 16:9 (by selecting an image size of 4608 x 2592 pixels) in order to take in a wide field of view for street scenes. (You could shoot at the maximum image size and then crop down to this size, but then you would not have the benefit of seeing the 16:9 aspect ratio on the screen as you composed your shots.)

Another option is to set image quality and size to their highest settings and set the Picture Control feature on the Shooting menu to the Monochrome option. You can use the standard settings for Monochrome, or you can go beyond the standard screen by pressing the Right button, and tweak the settings a bit. For example, you may want to try boosting contrast by one notch and reducing sharpening the same amount. To get the gritty "street" look, you also could try setting the camera's ISO to 1600 to include some visual grain in the image while boosting sensitivity enough to stop action with a fast shutter speed.

If you don't mind ignoring labels and trying something unconventional, you might consider turning the mode dial to the Scene setting and choosing the Black and White Copy option. Of course, that mode is designed for taking pictures of pages from a book and similar items, but it gives you another avenue for taking black-and-white photos without having to fiddle with menu settings. I suggest you at least try this option if you have an interest in street photography.

Also, consider using continuous shooting so you'll get several images to choose from for each shutter press. For the best combination of quality and speed, choose Continuous H, though that setting limits you to seven shots at a time.

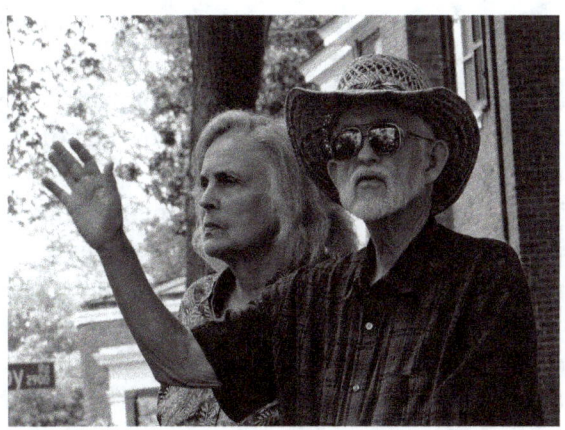

Figure 9-34. Street Photography Example Image 1

For Figure 9-34, I shot in Program mode with Picture Control set to Monochrome at f/5.3 with a shutter speed of 1/100 second, zoomed in to 220mm, at ISO 100. I used high-speed continuous shooting to increase my chances of getting a good, clear shot.

If you don't mind letting the camera choose which shot to keep out of the 10 it takes, try the Best Shot Selector feature. For any of these options, though, you have to use one of the advanced shooting modes (P, A, S, or M)—you can't shoot in the Auto or Scene modes. Also, one drawback to using continuous shooting is that you'll have to wait for the camera to finish recording its sequence of rapid shots before you can start shooting again, so you could miss a photo opportunity while waiting.

I generally use normal autofocus for this type of shooting, though some photographers like to use manual focus with the range set for the approximate distance where you expect your subjects to be. If I am shooting at street level, fairly close to my subjects, I often leave the lens zoomed back to its full wide-angle position to maintain a broad depth of field and keep most of the image in focus.

With the P600, though, you may want to at least experiment with long-range street photography, taking advantage of the superzoom lens. This approach has the advantage of letting you stay at a comfortable distance from your subjects. It has the disadvantage of producing a shallow depth of field, so it is harder to keep the entire scene in focus. Also, you may find that the foreshortening effect of a powerful zoom lens is not the look you are seeking for street photographs. And, you may find it difficult to get really sharp images at a long focal length unless you use a tripod, which limits your options for candid shots. On a bright day, though, or at high ISO settings, you may be able to use a fast enough shutter speed to avoid blur from a shaky camera, even without a tripod.

Although I use the term "street photography" to discuss candid photography in public places, I have found myself drifting away from city streets and taking more pictures in parks and other public areas where I find more people and where there is usually more time to find a good setting. For Figure 9-35, I used this approach at a crafts festival. I set the camera to shoot in color at the full optical zoom range of 1440mm, so I could isolate the subject from her surroundings. For this image, using Program mode, the camera took the photo using f/6.5 at 1/250 second, at ISO 140.

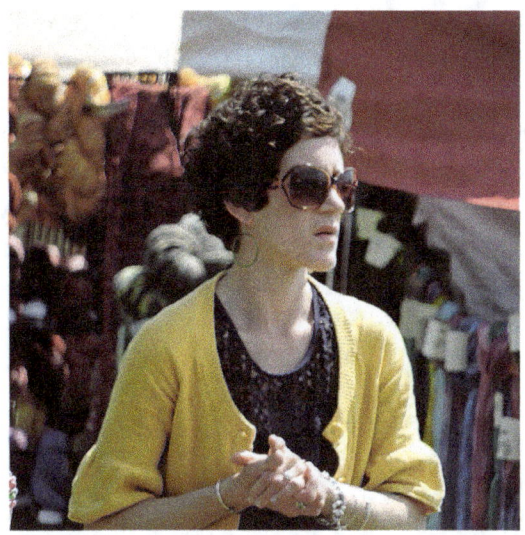

Figure 9-35. Street Photography Example Image 2

Connecting to a Television Set

To connect the Coolpix P600 to a television set, you need to purchase an optional HDMI cable and connect the camera to a high-definition set. Nikon does not offer such a cable, but you can use any generic HDMI cable, as long as one end has a micro-HDMI (type D) male connector, and the other end has a standard HDMI male connector, as shown in Figure 9-36.

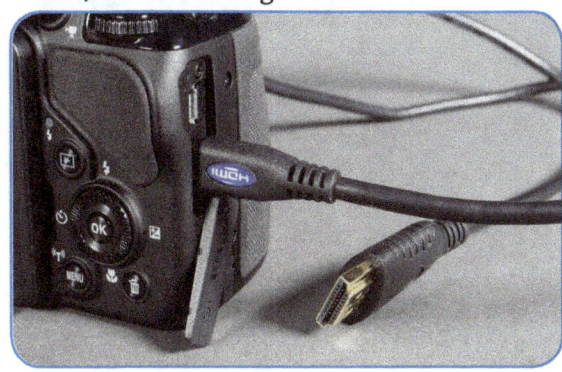

Figure 9-36. HDMI Cable Connected to Camera

Once you have connected the Coolpix P600 to a TV set, the camera operates much the same way it does on its own. Of course, depending on the size and quality of the TV set, you will get a much larger image, possibly better quality (on an HD set), and certainly better sound for your movies. When the camera is connected to an HDTV using an HDMI cable, it will only play back images and videos; it will not go into Shooting mode and cannot record.

APPENDIX A:
ACCESSORIES

When people buy a camera, especially a fairly expensive model like the Nikon Coolpix P600, they often ask what accessories they should buy to go with it. I will hit the highlights, sticking mostly with items I have experience with.

Cases

There are endless types of camera cases on the market. At least for me, there is no "perfect" case for the P600. The type of case I use with this camera depends on what my purpose is for carrying the camera at a given time. One case that fits the camera well, the Lowepro Rezo 110 AW, is shown in Figure A-1.

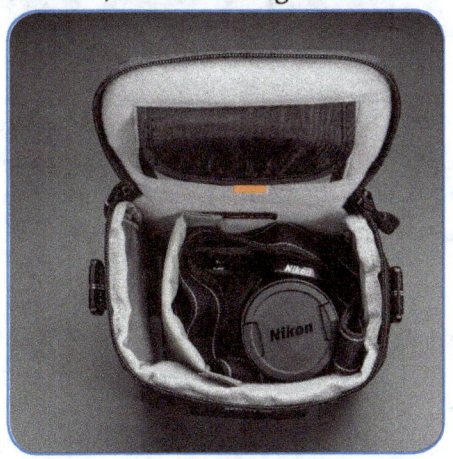

Figure A-1. Lowepro Rezo 110 AW Case

This case is an excellent all-around choice. It accommodates the camera easily with room to spare for extra batteries, filters, and other small items. It has a divider in its main compartment, and also has a built-in microfiber cloth, which is very handy for keeping the LCD screen clean and free of smudges. It has a loop for attaching to a belt and a handle on top for easy carrying.

When I'm going on a day trip that's specifically oriented to photography, I often put the camera into a case that can hold the camera along with some accessories and a few items such as a water bottle and note pad. One case I have used a good deal is the Lowepro Inverse 100 AW beltpack, shown in Figure A-2 with the P600 in the middle compartment.

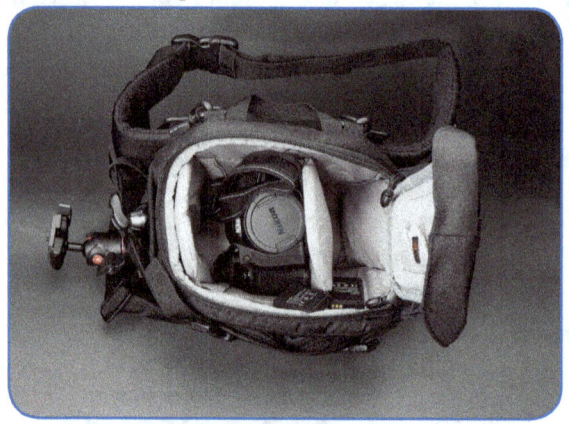

Figure A-2. Lowepro Inverse 100 AW Beltpack

This case can easily hold extra batteries as well as one or two small water bottles and other odds and ends. One feature I especially like about this pack is that it has straps for attaching a tripod to the bottom, as shown here.

Another carrier that has worked well when I am traveling light is not especially designed for photography. That is the Eagle Creek Tailfeather waistpack, shown in Figure A-3. This light pack can hold the camera along with extra batteries, and it has two pockets for small water bottles. There are many other options, though, including good cases from Kata, Tamrac, and other companies.

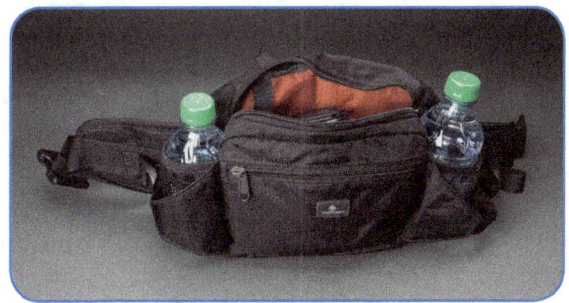

Figure A-3. Eagle Creek Tailfeather Waistpack

Batteries and Chargers

Here's one area where you should go shopping either when you get the camera or right afterwards. I use the camera pretty heavily, and I find it runs through batteries quickly, especially when Wi-Fi functions are activated. You can't use disposable batteries, so if you're out taking pictures and the battery dies, you're out of luck unless you have a spare battery (or an AC adapter and a place to plug it in; see discussion below). The model number of the official Nikon battery is EN-EL23. You can get a spare Nikon battery for about $45.00 as I write this. It won't do you a great deal of good by itself, because the battery is designed to be charged in the camera, and you can't use the camera while the battery is charging.

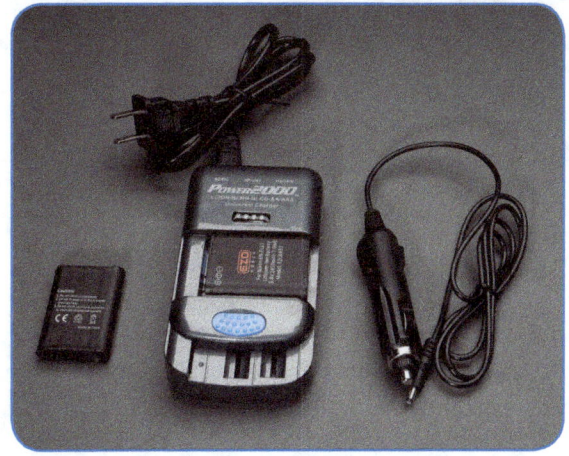

Figure A-4. Generic Charger and EN-EL23 Replacement Batteries

There is an easy solution to this problem. You can find generic replacement batteries, as well as chargers to charge the batteries outside the camera, inexpensively on Amazon.com and elsewhere. I purchased a package including two generic replacement batteries and a charger for $30.00 on eBay and the batteries and the charger, shown in Figure A-4, work fine. With this setup, I can have one battery charging while another is in the camera.

If you like charging the battery while it's in the camera, you don't necessarily have to use the charger that comes with the camera. You can use a charger with a standard USB port, as long as it meets the needs of the P600's battery, which requires 5 volts and 1 ampere of power. Figure A-5 shows the Anker 40-watt desktop USB charger, which has 5 slots for charging devices such as smartphones or tablets.

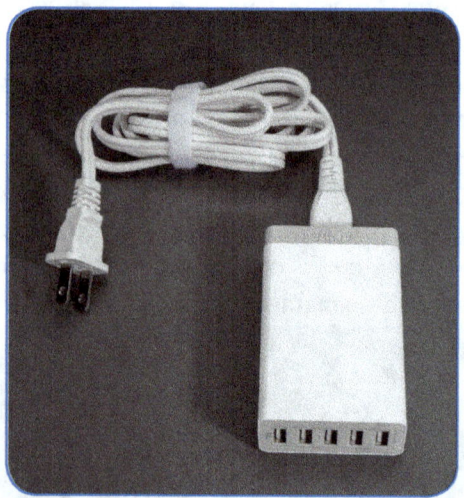

Figure A-5. Anker 40W 5-Port Desktop USB Charger

I have used it to charge my iPhone and iPad, and it also does a good job of charging the EN-EL23 battery inside the P600 camera at the same time. There undoubtedly are other USB chargers that can handle this process; just make sure the charger meets the necessary specifications.

AC Adapter

The other alternative for supplying power to the P600 is the AC adapter kit, Nikon model number EH-67A, shown in Figure A-6.

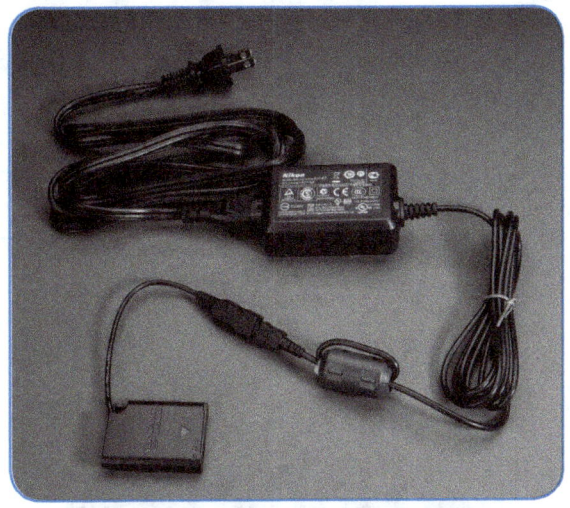

Figure A-6. Nikon EH-67A AC Adapter

This accessory works well for providing a constant source of power to the camera. It includes a standard-sized AC cord that you plug into a power brick and into an AC outlet. The power brick is attached to a long cable that is then connected to a plastic piece the same size and shape as the camera's battery. You insert that plastic piece into the battery compartment. Before you close the battery compartment door, you have to pull down a small rubber flap that covers an opening where the camera's side meets the battery compartment door. You then place the cable from the AC adapter into that opening, so you can close the battery compartment door fully, as shown in Figure A-7.

Providing power to the camera is all this adapter does. It is not a charger, either for batteries outside of the camera or for batteries while they are installed in the camera. It is strictly a power source for the camera. It is useful if you are using the interval timer or doing extensive work in a studio or laboratory setting, to eliminate the trouble of constantly charging and replacing batteries. It also could be useful if you are recording many images or movie scenes in a setting where you have access to AC power. However, the AC adapter's cables and power brick are bulky, so using the adapter can be inconvenient. If you don't have a real need for this setup, I recommend you invest in one or more extra batteries, and perhaps even an extra battery charger, so you can always have a couple of batteries ready for action. In short, the AC adapter should not be considered a high-priority purchase for most photographers.

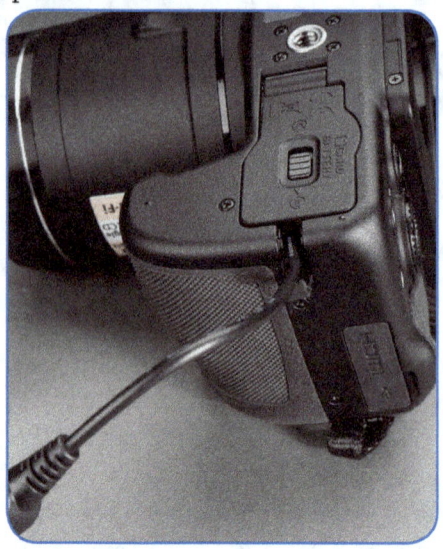

Figure A-7. Cord of AC Adapter Going into Camera

Add-on Filters and Lenses

There is no way to attach a filter or other add-on item, such as a close-up lens, directly to the lens of the Coolpix P600, as you can with DSLRs and other larger cameras, whose lenses are threaded to accept filters and auxiliary lenses. The lens of the P600 is not set up to accept such attachments, and Nikon does not offer any adapter that accepts them.

There is at least one solution available, though it is not ideal. To add filters or other lens accessories to the P600, you need to get a third-party adapter. Figures A-8 and A-9 show one such adapter, which I found on eBay, made by a company called Kiwi Fotos.

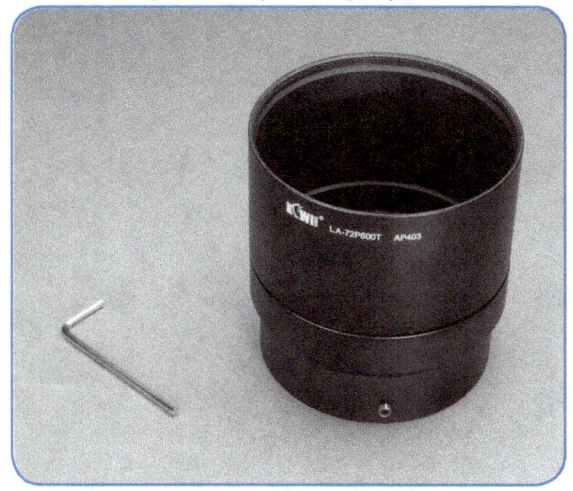

Figure A-8. Kiwi Fotos Filter Adapter for P600

The adapter consists of a sturdy metal tube that fits snugly over the end of the P600's lens housing and is secured by tightening two screws with the included Allen wrench. With this adapter tube in place, you can screw onto its end any filter or other accessory that has a 72mm diameter. For example, as discussed in Chapter 9, I attached an infrared filter using this system.

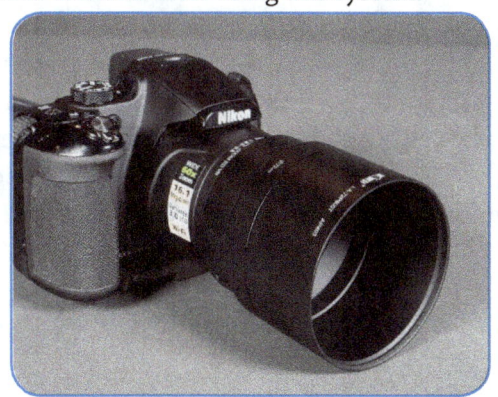

Figure A-9. Kiwi Fotos Filter Adapter on Camera

As you can see from Figure A-10, one major flaw of this adapter is that it causes serious vignetting because of the distance between the camera's lens and the tube's end, when the lens is at a wide-angle setting.

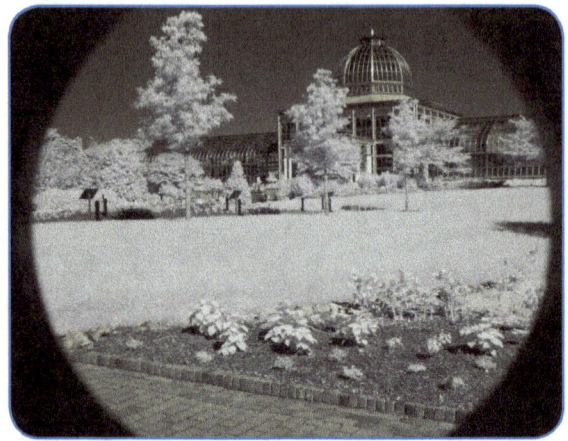

Figure A-10. Image Illustrating Vignetting from Use of Filter Adapter

You can cure the vignetting by zooming in somewhat, or by cropping your photos in your editing software to remove the dark corners and edges.

In addition, the adapter is quite bulky, and you need to use the included Allen wrench to attach it securely to the lens.

Despite the drawbacks of this adapter system, just having the ability to attach filters enhances the usefulness of the camera considerably. You can use a neutral density filter when you want to force the camera to use a wide aperture to blur a background, or to use a slow shutter speed to smooth out a waterfall with a long exposure. You can use infrared filters, UV (ultraviolet) filters, polarizers, or any of a wide assortment of close-up lenses, as well.

External Flash

Clearly, Nikon did not consider the use of external flash units to be a high priority for users of the Coolpix P600, because the camera does not have an accessory flash shoe on top, as many other advanced compact cameras do. You might conclude that this camera does not need a very powerful flash, for a couple of reasons. First, it has a sensor that is capable of taking good pictures in low light, with ISO settings reaching up to 6400 (and higher, with the High ISO Monochrome setting) and features like the Best Shot Selector setting that help you avoid photos that are blurred from camera shake in low light.

Second, even apart from the P600's dim-light shooting abilities, for everyday shots not taken at long distances, the built-in flash should suffice. It works automatically with the camera's light-metering system to expose the images well. It is limited by its low power, though. According to Nikon, at the wide-angle focal length, the range of the built-in flash is about 24 feet (7.5 m), and, at the telephoto setting, about 13 feet (4 m), when ISO is set to Auto. This range is not very strong. Also, because the flash is built into the camera, you cannot move it to one side to get the softer look of less direct lighting.

So, if you will often use the camera to take photos of groups of people in large spaces, or otherwise need additional power or versatility from your flash, you may want to supplement the built-in unit with an external flash unit.

Because of the lack of a hot shoe or any other interface for a flash unit on the P600, your options are limited. However, the camera's built-in flash unit can trigger an external flash unit if the external unit includes, or is connected to, an optical slave trigger. The optical slave is a device that can "see" the flash burst from the P600 and trigger the external flash instantaneously, adding to the flash output for the exposure that is taking place.

This type of system can be straightforward with some cameras; the built-in flash fires, and the external flash also fires. With the P600, though, there is a complication because the built-in flash fires a "pre-flash" burst. It does this so the camera's metering system can evaluate the light from the flash before the flash fires again for the actual exposure. The problem with this system is that the pre-flash "fools" the optical slave into thinking the flash has fired, and so the external flash is triggered too early, and the additional flash burst is wasted; it fires along with the pre-flash, before the exposure is taken.

The solution to this problem is to use an optical slave that is designed to account for, and ignore, the pre-flash. I have found three units that work in this way with the Coolpix P600. The first of these is the Yongnuo YN560 III.

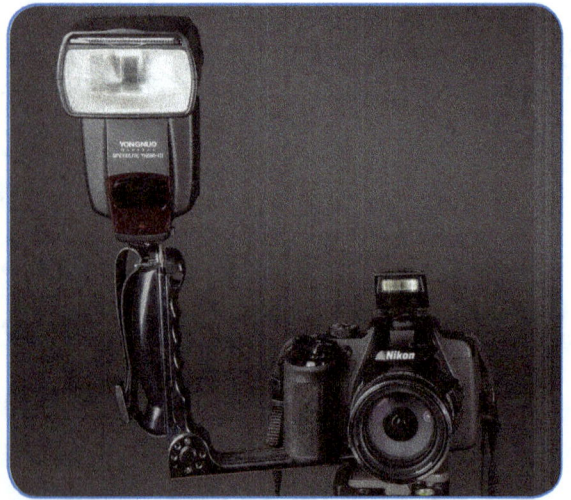

Figure A-11. Yongnuo Flash Attached to Camera

This flash has a built-in optical slave with several different modes. When I set it to its optical slave mode, using either slave setting S1 or S2, the external flash fired at the right instant, in synchronization with the flash from the P600. Figure A-11 shows the Yongnuo unit attached to the P600 with a standard flash bracket. This flash is somewhat large and bulky, but it works very well with the Coolpix P600 and appears to be a reliable, solid unit.

Another unit that works in a similar way is the very inexpensive Zeikos Digital Slave Flash, pictured in Figure A-12.

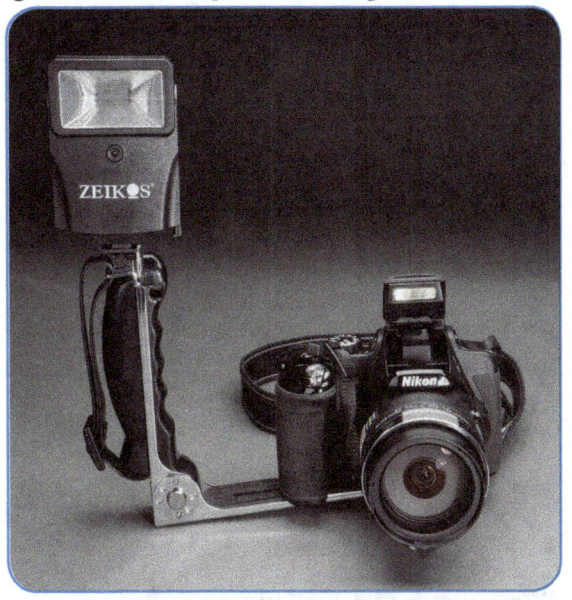

Figure A-12. Zeikos Flash Attached to Camera

This unit can be set to the Slave On setting with setting S2, and it does a good job of ignoring the pre-flash and firing at the proper instant when triggered by the flash from the P600. When I attached this flash to the standard bracket shown here, I found that I had to put a piece of electrical tape on the bracket's flash shoe to avoid having the flash's contact point touch the metal of the bracket; without the tape, the flash would not fire.

A third unit that synchronizes with the P600 is the Canon HF-DC2, not pictured here. Although it works as the other units do, it is quite small and does not add much flash power. But, if you happen to already have one of those units, it could be worth trying as a supplementary flash for the P600. I had to use the

Auto setting on the Canon unit to get it to sync with the flash on the P600.

With all of these units, I use the P600 in Manual exposure mode, activate Standard Flash or Fill Flash mode, and set the shutter speed and aperture using trial and error to determine the best settings.

There is one other approach to using external lighting that does not involve flash, but is worth considering.

Figure A13 shows the Coolpix P600 with a portable LED (light emitting diode) fixture attached to it by means of a standard flash bracket.

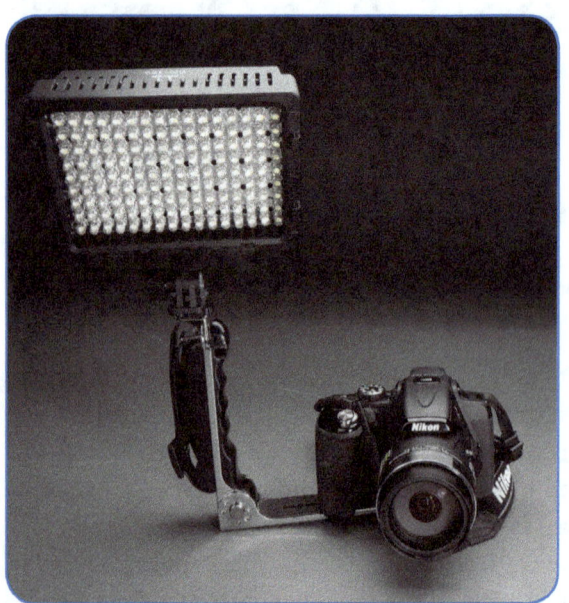

Figure A-13. CN-160 LED Light Attached to Camera

This battery-powered unit has 160 LED lights, and it is continuously dimmable, so you can vary the light from very faint to quite bright. The advantage with this system is that the light stays on, so you don't have to worry about synchronization, as you do with flash, and you can see the effects of the light on your subject before you shoot. The light shown here is a model called CN-160, which at this writing is available on Amazon.com for about $30.00. I have found it to be a reliable and useful light. You do have to purchase a compatible battery, which adds to the cost; several types of batteries can be used, including some rechargeable models for Sony cameras. There also are larger models available, including one with 216 LEDs.

Tripods

If you want to get the best possible results from the Coolpix P600, especially when using its superzoom lens at its longer focal lengths, you should use a tripod whenever possible. Unless I am shooting candid shots when walking around or otherwise am unable to use a tripod, I always attach the camera firmly to a tripod and use the 2-second self-timer to trigger my shots.

There are many tripods available at all price ranges. I will not make any attempt to discuss the choices in any detail. I will just mention one tripod that I have found to be solid and reliable, and sufficiently compact and light to take along on hiking trips without causing a burden. This is the Manfrotto BeFree model, shown in Figure A-14.

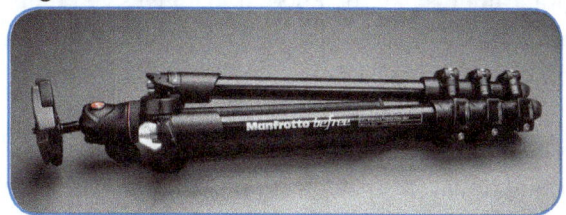

Figure A-14. Manfrotto BeFree Tripod

The tripod, which includes a versatile head, reduces to about 20 inches (50 cm) long just by collapsing the legs, and to about 16 inches (40 cm) if you take the trouble to fold the legs backwards. It weighs about 3 pounds 5 ounces (1.5 kg).

APPENDIX B: Quick Tips

This section includes tips and facts that might be useful as reminders, especially to those who are new to digital cameras like the Coolpix P600. I have tried to include bits of helpful information that you might not remember from day to day, especially if you don't use the P600 constantly.

Use continuous shooting. The P600 has great burst-shooting capabilities, which can help you capture images that other cameras might not manage. I recommend that you consider using continuous shooting as a matter of routine in some situations, unless you are running out of memory storage or battery power, or have a particular reason not to use it. When you are using film, burst shooting is expensive and inconvenient because you have to keep changing film and you have to pay for film and processing. With digital cameras like the P600, it just gives you more options. Even with stationary portraits, you may get the perfect fleeting expression on your subject's face with the fourth or fifth shot. So, go to the Continuous item on the Shooting menu (or press the Function button if it is assigned to this menu item), scroll down the list of options, and turn one of them on. Remember that continuous shooting is not available in the Auto or Special Effects shooting modes, in most of the Scene modes, or in some other situations, such as when the flash is used.

Take advantage of the User Settings mode. Use this feature to store your most important group of settings. For example, right now I have the U slot set up for my latest settings for street photography: Shooting mode = Program; Image Quality =

Fine; Image Size = 4608 x 2592; Picture Control = Monochrome; Metering = Matrix; Continuous shooting = Continuous H; ISO = 800; Sound Settings = Button Sound and Shutter Sound off.

Play your movies in iTunes, and on iPods, iPhones, and iPads. Because the P600 records movies in the .mov format, which uses Apple's QuickTime software, it's easy to play these movies on your computer if you have downloaded Apple's free iTunes software. Open a window on your computer to display the icon for a movie file (Windows Explorer or Macintosh Finder), open iTunes on the same computer, and drag the .mov file from the Explorer or Finder window to the Movies area of the Library in iTunes. You can then play the movie from iTunes. If you want to play it on an iPod, iPhone, ipad, or Apple TV, you will need to take one more step: Select the video in iTunes, then, from the iTunes menu, select File—Create New Version—Create iPod or iPhone version, or Create iPad or Apple TV version, as appropriate. Then you can sync iTunes with your device, and the movie will play on that device.

Explore the P600's creative potential. The Coolpix P600 has several advanced features that let you explore experimental photographic techniques. Some suggestions: Use Manual exposure mode with its shutter speeds as long as 15 seconds to take night-time shots with trails of lights from automobiles, storefronts, and other sources. Use shutter speeds as fast as 1/4000 second to freeze moving motorcycles, track and field runners, skateboarders, and other speedy subjects in mid-motion. Try zooming in or out during a multi-second exposure. Use long exposures (on a tripod) to turn night into day.

Adjust the camera's color settings. The Coolpix P600 has several settings that let you make color-related adjustments: Picture Control, White Balance, the Special Effects shooting mode, and the Food and Moon settings in Scene mode, which let you adjust a hue slider. Try different values for these settings until you find color and monochrome adjustments that convey what you would like to express with your images. With white balance settings, you can achieve unusual effects by purposely setting a custom white balance while aiming at a colored surface, rather than a white or gray one.

Use a neutral density (ND) filter for some shots. There are some times when you want a slow shutter speed, but, in bright light, you can't achieve it, because the aperture can only go as narrow as f/8.2. One solution is to get an adapter (discussed in Appendix A) that permits the use of filters, and use an ND filter to cut down on the light reaching the sensor, resulting in slower shutter speeds. You might want to do this to slow down the rush of a waterfall to a smooth, blended look, or to achieve a motion blur in a shot of a passing runner or walker. Note that you will have to zoom in the lens somewhat or crop the image to avoid vignetting.

Diffuse your flash or reduce its intensity. If you find the built-in flash produces light that's too harsh for close subjects or other shots, try using translucent plastic pieces from milk jugs, other food containers, or broken ping-pong balls as homemade flash diffusers. Just hold the plastic up between the flash and the subject. Another approach when using flash outdoors is to use flash exposure compensation to reduce the intensity of the flash by about -2/3 EV.

Use Special Effects mode for recording movies. Don't overlook the fact that you can shoot movies in this mode, with its image-altering settings, such as Painting, High ISO Monochrome, Nostalgic Sepia, and others. All of the effects are available with Movie Options set to 1080/30p and a few other settings; some of the effects are not available with certain settings. See Chapter 8 for details.

Use the self-timer to avoid camera shake. The Coolpix P600 has an excellent self-timer capability that is easy to use; just press the Left button and choose your setting. This feature is not just for group portraits; you can use it whenever you'll be using a slow shutter speed and you need to avoid camera shake. It can be useful when you're doing macro photography or using the superzoom lens, also, because those are both sensitive to camera motion.

Set zone focusing. If you're doing street photography or are in any other situation in which you want to set the camera on manual focus for a specific zone or general distance, here is a quick way to do so. Set the focus mode to autofocus, then aim the camera at a subject at approximately the distance you want to be able to focus on quickly. Once focus is set, press the Down button, select MF from the focus mode menu to select manual focus, and press the OK button to lock the focus. Now you have locked in the manual focus at your chosen distance, and you're ready to shoot any subject at that distance without the need to re-focus.

Speed up your use of the menu system. There are a couple of shortcuts that will let you zip through the menus to change your settings. First, remember that the menu screens wrap around, so it sometimes is faster to scroll down past the last item on the menu to get to the items at the top. Also, when you are setting items with changing values, such as ISO Sensitivity, Continuous shooting, White Balance, Picture Control, Metering, and others, you can use the command dial to change the settings without having to go to the secondary screen. Just scroll to the line for that item and turn the command dial to make the setting. You don't even have to press the OK button to confirm.

Leave good settings when you end a shooting session. There are several settings on the Coolpix P600 that are "sticky"—they will remain set on their current value when the camera is powered off and then on again. These include items such as exposure compensation, ISO, and continuous shooting. It is a good idea to check the camera when you stop shooting to make sure you have not left some settings in place that could cause problems if you have to start shooting again in a hurry. For another example, you might want to leave the Special Effects mode set to the Selective Color option, with no color selected, which results in normal shots. Then, if you pick up the camera in a hurry and turn the mode dial to the EFFECTS position, you will get normal-looking shots, rather than shots with High Contrast Monochrome, Nostalgic Sepia, or some other unwanted look.

Be aware of Movie Options settings when recording movies. When you press the red Movie button to record a movie, the camera will use whatever setting is currently selected for Movie Options on the Movie menu. If you have this menu item set to one of the HS (High Speed) settings, the resulting movie will be either in slow motion or speeded up, and will have no sound. If you want to be ready to record a good-quality, normal movie, leave Movie Options set to the first setting at the top of the menu screen, which is 1080/30p unless you are in an area that uses the 1080/25p option.

Shoot larger panoramas. When you are shooting a horizontal panorama using the Easy Panorama setting as discussed in Chapter 3, you can increase its height using a simple technique. Select your setting, such as Normal, and then hold the camera vertically, as if you were shooting a tall building, but pan it horizontally. With this approach, the dimensions of the panorama will be 1536 pixels tall by 4800 pixels wide, instead of the normal dimensions of 920 by 4800.

Use the Filter Effects setting on the Playback menu. With this setting, you can add some interesting and attractive processing to your recorded images, including Cross Screen, Fisheye, Miniature Effect, Photo Illustration, and several others. One nice bonus is that you can add these effects even to images that were taken with the Special Effects mode. In that way, you can use two effects with the same image, such as Painting with Photo Illustration, or High Contrast Monochrome with Fisheye.

APPENDIX C: RESOURCES FOR FURTHER INFORMATION

Photography Books

A visit to any large bookstore or a search on Amazon.com will reveal the vast assortment of books about digital photography that is currently available. Rather than trying to compile a long bibliography, I will list a few books that I consulted while writing this guide, which are useful resources for further exploration.

C. George, *Mastering Digital Flash Photography* (Lark Books, 2008)

J. Gulbins & R. Gulbins, *Photographic Multishot Techniques* (Rocky Nook, 2009)

C. Harnischmacher, *Closeup Shooting* (Rocky Nook, 2007)

C. Harnischmacher, *The Wild Side of Photography* (Rocky Nook, 2010)

H. Horenstein, *Digital Photography: A Basic Manual* (Little, Brown 2011)

J. Paduano, *The Art of Infrared Photography* (4th ed., Amherst Media, 1998)

D. Sandidge, *Digital Infrared Photography Photo Workshop* (Wiley, 2009)

Web Sites

Since web sites come and go and change their addresses, it's impossible to compile a list of sites that discuss the Coolpix P600 that will be accurate far into the future. One way to find the latest sites is to use a good search engine such as Google or Bing and type in "Nikon Coolpix P600." I recently did so in Google and got more than 5 million results.

Another approach can be to go to Amazon.com, search for the P600, and read the users' reviews, though you have to be careful to weed out reviews that don't have anything to do with the camera itself. You can also visit a reputable dealer's site, such as that of B&H Photo Video, and read the users' reviews of the camera there. I will list below some sites I have found useful, though some may not be accessible by the time you read this.

DIGITAL PHOTOGRAPHY REVIEW

http://www.dpreview.com/forums/1007

This is the current web address for the "Nikon Coolpix Talk" forum within the dpreview.com site. Dpreview.com is one of the most established and authoritative sites for reviews, discussion forums, technical information, and other resources concerning digital cameras.

REVIEWS OF THE COOLPIX P600

The links below lead to reviews of the Coolpix P600 by several sites.

http://www.photographyblog.com/reviews/nikon_coolpix_p600_review/

http://www.cameralabs.com/reviews/Nikon_COOLPIX_P600/

http://www.ephotozine.com/article/nikon-coolpix-p600-review-24417

http://www.cnet.com/products/nikon-coolpix-p600-black/

http://www.dpreview.com/products/nikon/compacts/nikon_cpp600

http://www.digitalcamerareview.com/default.asp?newsID=5561

http://www.imaging-resource.com/PRODS/nikon-p600/nikon-p600A.HTM

http://www.techradar.com/us/reviews/cameras-and-camcorders/cameras/compact-cameras/nikon-coolpix-p600-1246494/review

THE OFFICIAL NIKON SITE

The United States arm of the Nikon company provides resources on its web site, including the downloadable version of the user's manual for the Coolpix P600 and other technical information.

http://www.nikonusa.com/en/Nikon-Products/Product/Compact-Digital-Cameras/COOLPIX-P600.html

http://nikonimglib.com/manual/coolpix-p/p600/index_en.html

http://nikonimglib.com/ManDL/WMAU/index.html.en

http://nikonimglib.com/ManDL/WMAU-ios/index.html.en

INFRARED PHOTOGRAPHY

This site provides some helpful information about infrared photography with digital cameras.

http://www.wrotniak.net/photo/infrared/

CAMBRIDGE IN COLOUR

This is an excellent site with general information and tutorials about many aspects of photography.

http://www.cambridgeincolour.com/

Index

D

www.ingramcontent.com/pod-product-compliance
Lightning Source LLC
Chambersburg PA
CBHW071247220526
45468CB00001B/25